The Love Spell

AN

EROTIC MEMOIR

OF

SPIRITUAL AWAKENING

Phyllis Curott

GOTHAM BOOKS

GOTHAM BOOKS
Published by Penguin Group (USA) Inc.
375 Hudson Street, New York, New York 10014, U.S.A.

Penguin Group (Canada), 90 Eglinton Avenue East, Suite 700, Toronto, Ontario, Canada M4P
2Y3 (a division of Pearson Penguin Canada Inc.); Penguin Books Ltd, 80 Strand, London
WC2R 0RL, England; Penguin Ireland, 25 St Stephen's Green, Dublin 2, Ireland (a division of
Penguin Books Ltd); Penguin Group (Australia), 250 Camberwell Road, Camberwell, Victoria
3124, Australia (a division of Pearson Australia Group Pty Ltd); Penguin Books India Pvt Ltd,
11 Community Centre, Panchsheel Park, New Delhi - 110 017, India; Penguin Group (NZ),
Cnr Airborne and Rosedale Roads, Albany, Auckland, New Zealand (a division of Pearson
New Zealand Ltd); Penguin Books (South Africa) (Pty) Ltd, 24 Sturdee Avenue, Rosebank,
Johannesburg 2196, South Africa

Penguin Books Ltd, Registered Offices: 80 Strand, London WC2R 0RL, England

Published by Gotham Books, a division of Penguin Group (USA) Inc.
Previously published as a Gotham Books hardcover edition.

First trade paperback printing, January 2006

10 9 8 7 6 5 4 3 2 1

Gotham Books and the skyscraper logo are trademarks of Penguin Group (USA) Inc.

ISBN: 1-592-40165-1

Printed in the United States of America
Set in Fournier
Designed by Jennifer Ann Daddio

For You

*and for all those who believe
in the magic of love . . .*

Ever since I heard my first love story I began looking for you,

not realizing how futile that is. Lovers don't finally just meet

somewhere; they are in each other all along.

—RAINER MARIA RILKE

Acknowledgments

My heartfelt thanks to the remarkable Lauren Marino and Bill Shinker of Gotham Books for their continuing support—I am blessed by a long-standing and creative relationship with editor and publisher. I am eternally grateful to my agent, Cullen Stanley, who is just simply the best. Allyson Peltier was my gift from the Goddess who generously gave her time, invaluable advice and loving encouragement. Nancy Peske provided insightful assistance. My thanks also to Hilary Terrell and all the folks at Gotham Books and to my many foreign publishers and all those who so kindly gave quotes for the book's jacket. The Elders of the Tradition and Temple of Ara, Charles Boyce, Linda Maglionico, Kirsten Rostedt and Allyson Peltier; the Temple's initiates and members; my beloved Thirteen Circles of Aradia in Italy; and countless readers around the world remind me why I write, and have sustained me with love and filled me with gratitude. I am blessed with the love and encouragement of many dear friends, some of whom were particularly generous readers—I single them out for embarrassing thanks: Janice Garrimoni, Giampaolo Gianese, Maurizia Merati, Barbara Bacelli, Davide Marrel, Fiona Horne, Janet Farrar, Gavin Bone, Ray Buckland and Angie Buchanan. Henry Jaglom appeared as if by magic and changed my life—something he has done for countless other women who struggle to be heard and seen—I will always treasure our friendship. I send my heart to the sisters of my first circle who may recognize certain elements of themselves honored within these pages. I am deeply grateful to the men I have loved and who have loved me. Both the good and the difficult were gifts that I will always treasure, as I will always cherish you. I hope you will see and feel that in these pages. And finally, of course, my sweet and steady heartbeat—Webster.

Contents

The Final Spell

The First Spell

.1.

Longing

One sees clearly only with the heart.

Anything essential is invisible to the eyes.

—ANTOINE DE SAINT-EXUPÉRY

How do you know when it's real? I glanced over to find him smiling at me. I smiled back.

He pulled his old Scout off the worn gravel road, bumping along the tractor path at the edge of the field. I laughed as I bounced in my seat, and then he stopped the car and turned the engine off. We sat in the startlingly silent, sudden darkness. His arm reached around my shoulders, heavy, warm and undeniable.

"Oh, look!" I whispered. Thousands of fireflies, each a quick flare of hope searching for its perfect other, hovered in the air. He got out and opened my door. I took his hand and he eased me around so that my back was pressed against the warm hood of the car.

"Beautiful," he said softly.

The air was a potion of plowed earth and wildflowers. "Yes, it's a gorgeous night." I leaned back, looking from the shimmering field to the star-sprinkled sky.

"That too," he said with a soft, half laugh. He was handsome in a rugged, old world sort of way, weathered as much by wisdom as work done out-of-doors, with a square jaw and firm mouth; his nose was aquiline and he needed a shave. His hair was dark and curly, ruffled by the wind; he reached a hand up and dragged quickly through it. It was a large hand, and callused. His eyes were as dark as his hair, with deep lines running from their corners, a furrow between his brow. But it was the steadiness of their gaze, the way they held me fast that made my heart stumble.

I blushed in the dark. He moved closer, laying his palms on either side of me on the car's hood. I felt the blaze of heat rising as he edged closer—explicit, unadulterated, animal attraction. It was more.

He pressed against me, his lips brushing the side of my neck, whispering softly in my ear. The shell that held me together shattered. His hand curved around the small of my back, slipping beneath my blouse, fingers rough like flint against my skin, leaving trails of fire. His lips came to mine, with heat and greed as if he couldn't get enough, and all I could do was believe, and feel. It was the first time he'd kissed me like that.

More. I wanted more of his recklessness, his fever. I wrapped my arms around his neck, kissing him back as I drew him into me. I softened and let go, falling backward into a whirlpool of wanting. Dizzy, overwhelmed and overloaded with sensation, I tried to pull away, but he followed, pressing forward, pursuing and holding me close.

"Oh!" I gasped as he suddenly gripped my waist, lifting me off my feet and seating me on the car's hood. He leaned into me, spreading my legs as he stood between them. Heat radiated from his body; I rested my hands on his chest, feeling its hardness, his strength. His hands cradled my face and this time the kiss was soft and slow, ruthless and persuasive.

His hands ran up and down my bare arms, and I shivered as I began to burn. He pulled me tight to him, bit my neck softly, kissed, lingering, nuzzling, his breath hot; my defenses crumbled and I let myself be swept away. He cupped my breasts, groaning as I tugged his shirt from his jeans and my hands slid along his waist.

We kissed and clutched wildly, as if gasping for air, starving for the fire that rushed through us, that fueled a deeper hunger. He tugged the bra from my breasts. Need plunged through me as he rubbed and stroked and squeezed. My hands fisted in his hair, my head fell back and I trembled, breathing quick and shallow, as his tongue and teeth and lips found my nipples.

He slid his hand along the edge of my hoisted skirt, dipping down to the inside of my thigh. "Let me . . ."

"Hi roomie!" Gail singsonged cheerily, banging open the door to our apartment with her usual enthusiasm. "Eric called earlier—sorry I forgot to leave you a note."

My daydream evaporated. *If only Eric made me feel that way!* I sighed and grudgingly returned to reality.

"No problem!" I called back. I stepped around the pile of lawbooks, closed my bedroom door and stared at the phone. My first date with Eric had been two years ago. I could taste the whiskey and cigarettes when he kissed me—sharp and smoky. Smart and rebellious, roguishly good-looking with long dark hair, dark eyes and darker moods, I didn't want him to stop. But that was our first date, and now it seemed our kisses never felt the way they used to—they were no longer intoxicating.

For months, I'd wanted things to be as they once were, to be swept away by desire and the certainty that we were meant to be, that everything would be all right. I stared at the photograph of the two of us I kept on my dresser, his arm draped over my shoulders, both of us smiling. A rush of longing seized me, but it wasn't for him. I could feel it pressing urgently in around me, rising up inside like a strand of panic, like an animal catching a scent of something unseen but present.

I couldn't think about it now. My final year of law school had begun, I had my goals and my strategy for reaching them, and I was focused. I was looking forward to my advanced labor law classes and excited about my volunteer work at a foundation that provided assistance to union members fighting organized crime and corruption within their unions. While most students were scrambling to find well-paying jobs with corporate law firms, I was hoping to make a difference in the world. I'd already been offered the very low-paying position I wanted—working with a rank-and-file organization fighting the Mob within the Teamsters, and after the bar exam, I'd be heading to their main office in Washington, D.C., with a chance to do just that.

I pushed away the restlessness, pushed away the tug of Eric's phone call and went back to my books.

"*Starlight, starbright,* first star I see tonight, I wish I may, I wish I might, have the wish I wish tonight," I murmured with a longing I could no longer deny. I stood at my bedroom window looking up at a tiny glimmer in a sky surfeited with urban light, asking for a sign that love *was* possible.

If only wishes came true, or prayers could be answered . . . I was tired of waiting for life to begin and I felt suffocated, by the case law I had trudged through, by Eric waiting for my nightly call, by a yearning that clenched my heart to the point of bursting. A police car ripped through the streets, siren screaming as if responding to my edginess. *I have to get out.*

I washed my face, brushed my hair and put on some lipstick. Staring at the young woman in the mirror, I saw a very visible mix of my parents— tall and slim like my father, with his fine, sandy hair but with my mother's dark eyes, full lips and the slight overbite that all the women on her side of the family shared, and that always made me doubt my attractiveness. I shoved my wallet into the rear pocket of my jeans, pulled on my beat-up leather jacket and headed out the door and down the five flights of worn tile stairs.

It could have been noon instead of midnight—Greenwich Village was filled with people, so many that I had to step off the curb in order to pass the knots of tourists. Even at midnight, I could shop for almost anything I wanted—I could eat a bag of Italian pastries on my way to pick up tomorrow's newspaper and then buy an impossible-to-find 45 pressed by some Jersey garage band. But, striding along Bleecker Street, I was in pursuit of something I couldn't buy—or name.

It was late September but felt like summer, the air sultry and peppered with exhaust and garlic, bags of restaurant garbage and the immoderate perfume of women who'd been frightened away from what sex smells like. I dashed across the street, hunching my shoulders and digging my hands into my pockets.

I loved the West Village with its labyrinth of zigzagging streets. It was a place of undercurrents and eruptions—the Village had been America's center of innovative and radical thinking for a long time. Reformers and rebellious intellectuals, writers and artists, bohemians and beatniks, hippies and homosexuals, and anyone else who might be thought avant-garde or unacceptable came from all over the world to make this village within a city their home.

I don't want to be a detached observer, I thought with a sudden flare of impatience. *I want to feel alive. I want to feel excitement and passion.* A couple was walking toward me, their arms wrapped around each other, her head resting on his shoulder, his lips against her forehead. I stared past them, all the while noticing each small gesture—her fingers curled through a belt loop of his jeans, his arm wrapped protectively around her, and his breath softly sending a wisp of her hair up and down against her cheek. She smiled as she leaned into him. Every nuance of contact between them seemed to expand outward into the night, like ripples suddenly visible in a pond. As they passed me, I was hit by a wave of sensation. *I want to feel love.*

The Village was romantic, not just because of its quaint cafés and brownstones but because of the infamous and passionate couples who had resided here: John Reed and Louise Bryant, Dashiell Hammett and Lillian Hellman, Bob Dylan and Joan Baez. My parents had romanced each other here in the late forties, and as I walked past the tiny Cherry Lane Theatre I thought of them, young and in love as they were in the old photographs on my dresser. He was her working class hero, and she was his princess. Romantic and passionate, it was also tinged with the tragedy of the McCarthy era's brutal persecution that wounded my father's spirit and my mother's hopes.

My father was a tall, handsome Norwegian-American who'd gone to sea at the age of twelve after his mother had died, and while his father, a sea captain, was at sea. He was brilliant and self-educated, had served in the Navy and the Merchant Marine during World War II. But his true heroism was as one of the founders of the National Maritime Union. After the McCarthy witch-hunts, the NMU expelled him and the government revoked his passport. He found work in a New York brewery, a job he hated, and often drank too much to ease his pain.

My mother was a petite, raven-haired beauty from a prosperous Jewish-American family. She'd gone to Barnard College, interrupting her master's at Columbia to work as a community and civil rights activist with the NAACP. She'd worked with Nelson Rockefeller in the State Department and was later part of the Venezuelan delegation to the United Nations. She was elegant and gregarious, with a musical laugh, but she worried too much—about her job, my father's drinking, our future, the country's future. After McCarthy, she had to leave the U.N., becoming a businesswoman in an era when women rarely worked.

And then, after their lives had been thwarted, I was born, the child of promise. Because his work shifts rotated, my father spent hours with me all through my childhood, taking me to used bookstores in the city, or to the chess store on Thompson Street, in the Village, where I would sit on phone books while he played for hours. Or we would sit together on the front porch that he had converted to a studio where he would paint in vivid colors, revealing a depth of emotions otherwise hidden. And I would try, with rare success, to get him to tell me the stories of his adventurous past—but it was my mother who shared them with me. She devoted herself to me when she'd return home from work at the end of the day, reading to me every night before bedtime and spending weekends taking me to museums and galleries, concerts and theater. I was raised on Steinbeck and Shakespeare, Woody Guthrie and Chopin, Pollock and Monet.

This is where I belong, I thought as I headed to the triangular corner of the Riviera Café. The outside tables were full. I pushed open the heavy glass door and was hit by a wave of loud, cool air. Immersed in cigarette smoke, laughter and rock and roll, I slid into a seat at a window table.

"You're out late," Cutter said, reaching to empty the overflowing ashtray. That was his nickname from summer jobs working in a stone quarry. It was also his stage name. He flashed his Hollywood smile at me. With green eyes and thick black hair that hung to his shoulders, he was the reincarnation of Errol Flynn in an apron. Built like an athlete, he moved like a dancer. Women always flirted with him, and he flirted back. But he drew as much attention from some of the male customers, and flirted with them just as easily. He'd gone to Yale Drama School, and now, like most actors, he was waiting on tables while he waited for his break. He wiped the wet table with a white terry towel.

"I'm . . . restless."

"Where's that fine-looking boyfriend of yours?" He winked.

"Ha." I frowned.

"It's like that, is it? Well, anytime you need your best friend, you just tell me and I'll make sure you get a good night's sleep." Cutter grinned. "The usual?"

I'd been trying to develop a taste for Scotch, figuring it would be a necessary skill once I graduated. An impulse seized me. "No. A cognac—that's what I want."

He gave a little snort of a laugh. "Good night for a Dionysian offering. I'm gonna get you something special."

I stared out the window, watching the yellow cabs stream downtown, the gay boys dressed in drag and leather and cowboy hats. Cutter returned and with a flourish put a well-filled brandy snifter in front of me.

"Delamain—it's called Vesper."

"Vesper's an evening prayer, isn't it?"

"Actually, the prayer's named for what a vesper really is—an evening star. First one, the one you wish upon."

"You're kidding, right?"

"Not tonight. Those Renaissance bad boys, the alchemists, invented distillation and created *eau de vie*—waters of life. Add the magic ingredient of time and presto: cognac."

"I thought they were trying to turn lead into gold."

"Some, but the guys who really knew what it was about were after the gold of the enlightened spirit."

"Well, here's to wishes that come true!" I took a swallow and coughed.

Cutter laughed. "Take your time with that. I gotta get back to my drudgery." He went to take an order.

I rolled the cool glass between my palms, buried my nose in it and then sipped, slowly. A trickle of burning, flashing gold slid over my tongue—and lasted long after the glow of burnt wine had heated my throat and spread through my body. I felt the burn become heat and the heat become warmth and the warmth become pleasure. I lost track of time as my restlessness turned to reverie and the bar slowly emptied.

Cutter slid into the seat across from mine.

"Time for a break." He smiled and tapped my glass with a snifter of his own. Music suddenly filled the empty bar. "The bartender loves that album." It was Springsteen's *Darkness on the Edge of Town*. The music rushed along, driven by the drums, cresting and breaking, then rising again to another hungry, whispered climax.

"I've been playing it all summer."

"Yeah. It's kinda dark, isn't it?" He grinned.

"Very sexy."

"So let's open the doors to heaven, shall we? Here's to Mr. James Byron Dean." We tapped and drank. "May the little bastard rest in peace," Cutter said.

"The actor?"

He nodded, lit a cigarette, took a long drag and exhaled heavenward. "My guiding star. Died twenty-three years ago today—in a car crash. He liked to race, bought himself a Porsche Spyder and got nailed on his way to a race in Salinas—you know, where *East of Eden* is set."

"That's one of my favorite books," I said, surprised. Written by Steinbeck, it was an American Cain and Abel story, with a Cain both tragic and sympathetic.

"Kazan made it into a film," Cutter replied. "It was Dean's first picture, he played Cal Trask. Anyway, so what are the odds? Big empty road, no one around, and at the exact moment this guy turns left, Jimmy's there. Weird." He sighed. "Ah, what the hell, he wanted to be immortal, and he managed it."

"Listen to those lyrics."

He listened to a song about racing in the street and smiled. "Synchronicity. Everybody experiences it, but very few pay attention."

A shiver shot through me.

"What's the matter?"

"Don't know. What's that expression? Feels like somebody just walked on my grave."

"Well, don't you go riding around in any old Porsches, honeychild. You're just starting your trip." Cutter was staring past me into some romantic vision. "I grew up in a small town not so far from where he did, and I always thought it was so strange how most of the kids knew who he was, but they didn't really give a damn—I mean, a lot of them had never even seen his movies. They just wanted to play basketball and get married. But me, I was haunted from the minute I saw him. I had to do what he was doing. He showed us what we all want—and what we're all afraid of. Hell, he wasn't acting, he was *being*. He was completely present, and most of us are barely here. He was so present, even though he's dead he's sure not gone." Cutter gazed out the window. "I'd trade my life for his in a New York minute, even if it meant I'd already be dead. I gotta help close up." He knocked back the last of his brandy and headed to the bar.

The restlessness I'd been feeling earlier seemed to pour out of the speakers, and back into me. *Well, Jimmy, wherever you are, here's to fire in the darkness and here's to you.* I toasted him silently, inhaled the last of my elixir and finished it off. I felt the final shimmer of warmth and waved to Cutter for a check.

He mouthed back: "On the house."

I left him a big tip, stretched and pulled on my jacket. A gust of wind yanked the front door from my hand, slamming it wide and rushing past me into the smoky bar. The sky was an unearthly pale gray, mottled with garish colors from the shop lights and streetlamps below. I stood in the doorway as the rain began, a few heavy drops followed swiftly by sheets of water. It was glorious—wild and reckless and then as quickly as it hit, it was over. I headed out into the night.

The streets had been emptied by the storm. The air was cool and clean against my skin, and I breathed deeply, something I rarely did in the city. It smelled like rain and felt like a fine stream of clarity coursing through me. And then I heard it—a guy giggling, as if he were being tickled, as if he were standing right behind me. I turned quickly—but there was no one there.

I crossed Seventh, headed down Bleecker and found myself walking a few yards behind a young couple. His arm was around her, and their laughter drifted back to me as I heard him trying to impress her:

"Really, it's one of the prophecies that before the end of the earth people will see a star getting brighter and closer every night. And as it gets closer, the weather's gonna change, the north and south poles'll reverse, and the ice caps are gonna melt, the seas'll get warmer, and all the coasts are gonna be flooded. You don't want to be in New York when that happens."

"Well, a meteor changed the earth's climate and that wiped out the dinosaurs. I guess anything's possible," she said sweetly to his prophecies of doom. And then he leaned down and kissed her. She seemed to melt into his embrace and the waters began to rise.

I walked quietly past, and as I did sweetness seemed to flow from them, hitting me. I had the strangest sensations of déja vu and premonition—as if someone, as if true love, was waiting for me just around the corner. *Yeah, well, that's the second time tonight that couples have got you going.* I laughed to myself, shaking off the strange feelings.

Yeah, well, if a certain star approached you, your ice caps would sure melt.

I stopped dead in my tracks. I knew no one was behind me, or anywhere near me. And the couple was still kissing. I shook my head. *No more cognac for you, missy. Home!*

My pace quickened as I headed past the stuccoed old southern Italian church on the corner, and down sleeping Carmine Street. I took the stairs two at a time, racing as if I were going to be late. Out of breath, I opened the door quietly. Gail wasn't home. *Hooray, the place is mine, for all the good it'll do me tonight.*

More than you can guess.

There it was again. *That's not me. I know what my own thoughts feel like.* I sure ought to, since I'd pretty much lived in my head my whole life. And that "voice" came from somewhere else. I shook off the uneasiness, stripped off my clothes and showered the cigarette smoke off my body. I lost track of time, letting the hot water lull me into sleepiness. But as I wrapped my robe around me, I began to feel fidgety again.

Turn on the television.

What the hell? Okay, well, if I'm going to hear voices I guess we might as well have a conversation. So since when do disembodied voices watch television?

Turn it on. Now. Hurry.

What's the rush anyway? But okay, TV ought to narcotize me. I turned on the small black-and-white set, and the sound of an elderly man's voice shouted at me. Quickly turning down the volume, I heard his words clearly:

"For many days before the end of our earth, people will look into the night sky and notice a star, increasingly bright and increasingly near."

I stared in disbelief as James Dean walked into a planetarium.

He whispered to the teacher checking names at the door: "Stark, Jim Stark."

The class turned to see him; the lecturer looked at him, hesitated and then continued: "As this star approaches us, the weather will change. The great polar fields of the north and south will rot and divide, and the seas will turn warmer."

I was paralyzed, holding my breath and trying to understand what was happening. But as I wrestled the circumstances to earth looking for a logical explanation, the night's relentless tensions finally exploded—like a flare of light followed swiftly by a swelling tide of heat. A whirlwind rushed into the sudden vacuum created by the implosion, enfolding me in an invisible swaddling, and the relentless sounds of the street below disappeared. I found myself sitting at one end of a long tunnel, surrounded by darkness, the tiny set with its incandescent blue light far in the distance.

Am I dead? Isn't this what they talk about—a tunnel with light? Instantly, a beam of blinding illumination and a strange sound—like a cow mooing, or a bull bellowing—shot toward me, hitting me in the chest. I felt as if something, or someone, had just slammed into me. And then everything was normal again—or rather, I found myself sitting on the bedroom floor with the little television set glowing and James Dean mooing like a cow.

My heart was pounding in my ears, I was light-headed and there was intense pressure in my temples. My breathing was quick and shallow. All of my senses seemed suddenly heightened as I watched, transfixed, *feeling* what Cutter had talked about: James Dean was wounded and wild, sexy and sensitive, passionate, courageous, honorable, daring and romantic. He was unlike so many men I'd known who had been taught to hide or suppress their feelings; every emotion was visible. His vitality poured out from a realm of captured time, radiant tubes, and electrons, his living presence filling the room. It filled me. I was electrified by a pulse-racing desire, as if I was falling in love.

I could feel my own numbness being stripped away by his intensity, and like Sleeping Beauty awakened with a kiss, my slumbering heart awakened as he wore his on his sleeve. Somehow, as the images and the energy aroused my heart, the fairy tale on the screen became increasingly real. I was between the worlds, or in a waking dream, and yet it was all so alive, more real than reality. The film ended as Jim became a man and a new day dawned over the planetarium.

Unwillingly, I turned off the technology that had become a portal between realities, resting my hand on its hot surface. I was afraid the connection had ended with the film and that it might never happen again. All I wanted was to continue the night's journey—with him. I listened for the voice, *his* voice. But he did not exist outside that brief and strange medium of light and energy. He was dead.

It was dawn as I stood at the window, watching the garbage trucks bellow and gobble. Wondering what had happened, realizing that somehow, something extraordinary and erotic and very alive had surged into my life, I climbed into bed and disappeared into dreamless sleep. When I awoke, I had less than an hour before my afternoon class. I rushed into my clothes, grabbed my books and raced to class; I took notes, asked questions, did my reading and research at the library, all the while wrapped in an enchantment that made the invisible visible and the dead live.

When class ended, I left the building. Somehow, I expected to turn a corner and see him standing in front of me. I found a table at Café Reggio, across from the law school, and sat, resting in a luminous space of interconnections and messages and longing. I knew I had experienced something far more than a simple coincidence. The explanation I'd been searching for came to me—Cutter had said it last night: *synchronicity*. It was Carl Jung's term for the coincidences that go so far beyond the ordinary flow of events that both instinct *and* common sense demand we pay attention to them. They are circumstances that reveal the deepest, and often most hidden, truths about ourselves and, perhaps, reality. The reasons for certain kinds of coincidences are not found in normal notions of cause and effect, but in an entirely different realm of being where other laws of nature rule. And in that realm, according to Jung, *we* are the causes of these amazing events, the source of the mysteries is deep within our psyches, our souls. *But,* I wondered, *could that be true even for someone as skeptical as I am?*

I'd been raised to believe that the irrational was illusory, even dangerous. But Jung's was another educated and respected point of view that, though meaningless to me when learned in college, now explained the inexplicable. The events of last night had tapped against the iridescent screen that separated and united two worlds—the over-rational in which I was a particularly gifted resident, and another of passionate mystery. In fact, last night had shattered the boundary between those realms. A portal had swung open and an evanescent visitor had climbed through. *Why was James Dean calling to me, pulling me in?*

Or had I somehow called *him*?

Well, he's not my dream come true. I mean if Billy Joel walked in here and proposed, I'd say yes before the last word was out of his mouth. God, I used to have such fantasies about him." Gail pulled another dress from the closet, held it in front of herself and looked in the mirror, then tossed it on her bed. "I still do. But Billy's not calling and David's fun. Besides, I don't want to get serious with anybody." She was getting ready for a date with a guy she'd met at the post office.

"That's an understatement." I sat with my legs propped against her bedroom windowsill.

"I don't know how you can stand being so serious with Eric—all the time. I mean, dark and moody may've been sexy at first, but it's boring already. You need to get out and have a good time." She held up another dress, studying herself. She picked the shortest one.

I shrugged. "Sometimes love is serious." I walked out of the bedroom as she began spraying Halston perfume with her usual abandon. She followed me into the tiny living room and plopped onto the couch. I tapped a little food into my fish tank and put the tip of my finger into the water waiting for my favorite, a large black and silver angel fish I'd named Joe, to swim up and nibble on me. Watching the fish was my highly effective, low-budget therapy when I came home stressed out from class. Gail started filing her nails and I tucked myself into my study chair, the black leather Eames chair my mother had bought for me during college.

"So who's your dream guy?" Gail asked without looking up.

James Dean. My bedroom wasn't filled with posters, I didn't have a picture of him taped inside my notebook cover, and I hadn't joined a fan club. I was too old to have a crush on a dead movie star. But we all have our idols—what is it that they provoke in us? Are they just some ideal that we try to find in mortal form? Or is it something more? Certainly ever since that night I couldn't shake the unwavering desire he'd aroused. My longing now had a face, a name, but no body. "Passionate . . ."

"You mean moody."

I shot her a look. "Someone independent, who doesn't toe the line . . ."

"Moody."

"Jeez, if you're going to keep interrupting . . ."

It was her turn to shrug.

"Someone who wants his life to mean something, who wants to make a difference in the world. I want a guy with principles, with integrity. Maybe a union organizer or an activist. Eric shares those values with me."

"Moo—"

I cut her off. "Don't even go there. What's wrong with wanting a guy who actually has some ideals and some feelings? And can express them? I mean, all these guys you go out with just want one thing, they get it, they're gone."

"We want the same thing and they're not gone . . . This is the third time I've gone out with David."

"As long as you're happy." I shrugged again.

She blew the powdery filing dust from her nails and held up her hand, studying it. "I am. Can you say the same?" She began filing the other hand. "When was the last time you had sex that really did it for you?"

"A one-night stand doesn't do it for me. I need more. I don't want to have sex. I want to make love. I want to feel it in my heart, not just my body. Maybe I just need . . . the One."

Gail stopped filing. "You really believe in that, don't you?"

I nodded. "I do. As sure as I know I'm alive, I know there's a man out there meant for me."

She shook her head. "Well, I hope you find him. Personally, I like having a long line of men that are meant for me." She finished with a flourish and blew another cloud of dust into the air, picked up a bottle of red polish, gave it a hard shake and started painting. The smell of better living through chemistry filled the small space and I could feel the start of a headache snaking in through my nose.

"I'm not criticizing." I softened my tone. "More power to you if it's what you want. But I want a man to build a life with, who has the courage to fight for what he believes in, who'll lay it on the line. Someone who shares my dreams and who'll stand by me."

"Yeah, you want a hero. They're a dime a dozen on every street corner. But what about the important stuff—what does this rebel with a cause look like?"

I laughed at her choice of words. She was more right than she knew. I did have an ideal in terms of values and principles. But James Dean had somehow triggered a very physical, erotic image. He'd aroused an undeniable hunger to be kissed by a man with that kind of fire, loved with that kind of sensuality. "Sometimes he looks a lot like James Dean, but with dark hair and dark eyes. Sometimes he's a little more like . . . Gary Cooper. And the way he moves—earthy, you know, really in his body." I tried to bring the blurry vision into focus. "And there's something about his hands . . . He knows what it's like to work with his hands, to struggle and to win. Not spoiled and soft like all those silver spoon babies at school. A man who knows who Tom Joad is."

"What's that—some kind of code?"

I laughed. "I guess you could say so. Doesn't ring a bell?" She shook her head. "Well, then I guess it's not you."

"I'm so relieved." Gail looked up at me and grinned. "Anyway, what's wrong with a silver spoon? How much fun is no money?" We were increasingly on different tracks—all she wanted was the in-house legal job waiting for her at the paint company where her father worked, and a mink coat. And I wanted a world where everyone could afford a mink coat, or at least a decent life. Recently, she'd started what she referred to as "big game hunting," pursuing boys with trust funds and Roman numerals at the end of their names. I'd dated that crowd in college and was bored to tears.

"It's not about money. It's about his . . . energy. I mean, these lists that women make about what they want in a man—it sounds like the same guy: handsome, smart, funny, considerate, successful. Likes long walks on the beach and dinners by candlelight." I wrinkled my nose.

"What's wrong with perfect?"

"I don't want a guy who's perfect. I just want the guy who's perfect for me. I think it's just something you feel—that electricity. The way he'd look at me, you know, *really* look, deep, without flinching or hiding or pulling back. Like he wants to be right where he is because he knows we're meant for each other. And I want him to kiss me like he means it, like he wants to *possess* me, not just . . . fuck me. Like he knows that it's more than just sex—that it's love. *That's* hot." I sighed and Gail blew on her blood-red fingertips. "Present and sincere and passionate—those are the most important things."

She nodded. "Yeah." She sounded sad, and then the iron breastplate clamped back into place over her heart. "David'll be here any minute. Would you mind if he and I hung out here for a while—alone?"

"No problem. I'll go to the library."

It was cold and clear and the streets were filled with students instead of tourists. I found myself looking at them, searching their faces, even though I knew he wasn't going to appear. *Was it possible to find a man like that? Did he even exist?*

Other things were beginning to happen that I couldn't explain. I was in the middle of my New York Practice and Procedure class, shifting uncomfortably in my seat, feeling my heart beat a little quicker. It wasn't because of the cute professor; it was because suddenly I knew the answer to the question he was asking. I didn't raise my hand. He would have asked me to explain my reasoning and I couldn't give an explanation. I hadn't reviewed the case he was discussing, and I hadn't reasoned my way to the answer—it had simply come to me. And then I thought, *Carol Stewart is going to answer it.* Her hand shot up.

"Yes, Ms. Stewart." The professor nodded at Carol.

"The court would grant the plaintiff's motion for summary judgment."

"Can you tell me why?"

And she did.

After class, I walked over to Café Reggio for a quick cappuccino to jump-start my statute-saturated brain. And to get a few minutes alone. Instead of reviewing my notes for the next class, I pulled my journal from the knapsack and started jotting down what had happened. And then I found myself rereading other quickly scribbled accounts: *"Mom called again today, and I knew the phone was going to ring before it did, and that it would be her."* She never called at a fixed time. And yet as I read my notes, I found a dozen different examples over the last few weeks of having known she was about to call.

"I ran into Mrs. Cardozzi today and before she opened her mouth, I knew what she was going to say. It was as if I was reading the words across her forehead right before she said them. She wanted to tell me a story about the Strega who had lived and died in my building. I asked her what a Strega is, and she said it meant Witch. A good Witch, she said. And I thought of Glinda the

Good Witch except with black hair like Anna Magnani. And then she gave me this old Italian amulet that she said belonged to the Strega, she called it a cimaruta."

I ran my fingers over the ornament hanging from a silver chain around my neck. It was made of silver, shaped like the branches of a plant with little objects at the end of each branch—a key, a heart, a moon.

There were also dreams that had come true—one about an accident, another about the death of a relative. And there was the mysterious dream I'd had just a few days ago, a dream that I'd had before, of a woman sitting serenely, holding a book in her lap. Her breasts were bare and she wore a necklace with a six-pointed star and an unusual crown. She would appear briefly, sit silently, and then disappear in a flare of light from which I would awaken, wondering.

At first, I thought my odd experiences were happening because I was under too much stress, but I didn't feel stressed. I was enjoying my last year, my job. Since the intuitions, insights and premonitions were frequently right, I knew that I wasn't having a paper chase nervous breakdown. Instead, I was beginning to realize there was more to reality than met the eye.

And I sensed it was all linked to Jimmy, for it had all begun with his arrival. A raw sexual current had coursed into my life, but its power had opened more than my heart. It seemed to have opened something in my mind. It was as if I'd been watching the world on a little black-and-white television, and suddenly I was walking around in a vivid, multidimensional, full-color reality. It was . . . magical.

Why were these things happening? It wasn't enough to say I'd had some kind of visitation and it had triggered latent psychic talents. I was a rational person. I wanted, I needed, rational explanations. I wanted a scientific answer. I went to the university library with its tiled floor that looked like an M. C. Escher drawing of infinitely shifting perspectives, and I searched out books on physics—the science that explained the physical laws of the universe. It was in quantum physics that I began to find an understanding of what had been happening and why.

I didn't understand most of the pages I struggled to read, and the mathematical formulas were an alien tongue. But I did understand what was most important: *everything is energy; everything is interconnected in that energy field, and the human mind, in various ecstatic states, has the capacity to interact with and affect the outcome of events in that field.* It sounded like magic, just like my experiences, but it was real. Just as I answered one question, however, another appeared. I'd moved from physics to metaphysics and I was now confounded, for there were those like Stephen Hawking who claimed that were we to delve deeply enough into the laws of nature, one day we would know the mind of God. The answers lay within, it was argued. There at the deepest levels of the quantum domain, Paradise would be restored once we recognized ourselves as a mirror of God.

But I wasn't looking for God. I was looking for James Dean. In the midst of all these odd experiences, and school, and work, I longed for him to reappear—on film or in the flesh as my living, romantic hero. And even though I'd read it scientifically explained in black and white, I didn't realize the power of that longing, nor the full measure of what it had unleashed. But somehow, I sensed it.

I stared down at the image on the cover of *The Mutant King*. The book was a birthday present from Carla, an old friend from high school.

"I saw you two had the same birthday, so I figured you might enjoy it."

She hadn't known anything about my . . . what? My crush? My fascination? I still didn't know what to call it.

"We have the same birthday?" I said quietly, stunned, holding the biography of James Dean gingerly, as if it might crumble to dust in my hands. Synchronicity—it felt like a magic word, as if each time one happened, the two spheres—of my mundane life and one of enchantment—merged.

I was up most of the night reading. A few days later, when I got to the final chapters, I began to understand that there was indeed something more happening to me than just a belated schoolgirl crush. I hadn't taken drugs during the sixties—I lived in New York, not California; I came from an intellectual home. Other than the few concepts from physics that I thought I understood, I had no framework for my strange new experiences, or the intense passionate longing Dean's appearance had aroused. But the author had a theory.

He described Jim and movies as a combined force that could enter our unconscious and unleash the hidden powers waiting there. I used my carefully honed analytical skills, taking notes as if I were studying case law, calmly considering until I came across words that made me shiver: "He is I and I am he . . . The god is buried in us; he knows the future and waits for us there . . . Movies are a form of magic with their projection of a 'thin insubstantial human image, its nature a sort of vapour, film or shadow.' Its animated current can penetrate and divert our energy. We become what we behold and what we choose to behold. It is through our eyes that we have taken Jimmy into ourselves, and he remains there magically present like Osiris, god of regeneration."

I didn't understand it all, but at some deep gut level, I knew I'd found a very important clue to the mystery I'd been living in, and it was stranger than physics. The biography was littered with tiny hieroglyphs and references to the Greek god Dionysus and the Egyptian God Osiris. They were odd and unfamiliar, but reminded me of the myths my mother would read to me before bedtime when I was a child. The next day, between classes, I returned to the undergraduate library to crack the code.

I found the ancient *Egyptian Book of the Dead* referred to in the biography, and, immersing myself in it, I discovered the unexpected—a love story. I read of how Isis—Goddess, wife, sister, and Witch—journeyed to the Underworld and by her magic restored life to her beloved husband, the murdered and dismembered Osiris, God of fertility and the Underworld. They were strange, remote and archaic ideas that seemed more appropriate in a college course on ancient religion than my modern search for . . . what?

What was I looking for? What words had Isis uttered as she restored Osiris to life? Were there words that I could speak that would bring my longings to life?

By the time I finished the biography of Dean, I had begun to understand how he had crossed the boundary between story and truth, film and reality. He had also crossed a boundary between my world and one of utter mystery. The dream of the enigmatic woman recurred, and with it came dreams of women singing and dancing, the name Isis floating from their lips. In waking time, I found myself drifting through the Metropolitan Museum of Art's Egyptian collection, entranced by paintings of women with dark, almond-shaped, kohl-lined eyes, great white ibis hunting for fish in reed-filled waters, and men plowing fields with oxen. There were statues, and jewels and stones carved with indecipherable hieroglyphs; and the ancient world of these remnants often seemed more sensuously alive than the daily, dry and dusty world of cases and statutes.

And I continued to watch for the slightest sign of James Dean. Then, a week before the bar exam, an ad appeared in the paper—a double bill of *East of Eden* and *Rebel Without a Cause*, playing at a small movie theater on the Upper West Side. I tore the ad from the paper.

Two days before the exam that would determine the rest of my life, I put away my notes. Filled with nervous anticipation, not for the exam but for the encounter waiting for me at the theater, I entered the icy dark cave to once again watch time captured and life immortalized.

Our first encounter had been through a small screen with life shrunk to diminutive proportions. And yet the scale made the emotions no less human and real. I sat back against the worn red velvet seat in a theater designed like an ancient Greek temple and raised my eyes to a screen filled with an enormous image. Now the scale made the image, the emotions, the energy not only deeply human but also something grander, something profound. *Everything is energy and everything is interconnected—past, present, future, man, film, image, viewer.*

I left the theater in love, and sensing that it was more than Dean whom I loved. I was captivated by something he embodied, something mysterious, erotic and necessary.

I took the bar exam, broke up with Eric, packed up my apartment and left for my job with the rank-and-file reform organization. Immediately, my intuitions and premonitions ended. To my great disappointment, James Dean didn't seem to live in Washington. But I continued searching for him—in real men, in the faces of the truck drivers I represented, in bookstores, at the rock-and-roll clubs in Georgetown. Although I met a lot of unsung heroes, the man I was looking for was nowhere to be seen. Within a year of graduating, my job ended; I returned to New York and to the foundation that I'd worked for while in law school. I hoped that the magic would return.

I tore a piece of tissue and shoved it in my ears. It wasn't enough but it helped muffle the deafening sound. CBGB's was a tiny club on the Bowery and the band's amps were cranked loud enough to fill Madison Square Garden. I was happy to be back home and determined to recapture the enchantment I'd lost. After work at the foundation, I'd begun hanging out on the downtown rock-and-roll scene, where countless boys dressed like James Dean, posturing for a role they didn't know how to play and a life they didn't know how to lead. But somewhere in the midst of that crowd of wannabes I was hoping to find the real thing—my working class hero with the heart full of poetry. He had become the magic I longed for.

I pushed my way through the sweaty crowd to the back room behind the stage where the band I'd started managing, Blind Alley, was waiting to go on. The tiny room was entirely covered with the scrawled names, comments and stickers of every band that had ever played the infamous club. The drummer, who was no James Dean but was every bit the sexy bad boy I'd been doing, was standing on a chair adding his two cents to the ceiling.

The door opened. It was Sophia, a friend who was also managing a band, which was how we'd met months earlier. She was smart, hip and funny. She just had one idiosyncrasy—she called herself a Witch. I thought it was strange, though not particularly scary—I didn't believe that anyone had the power to put a hex on me, least of all sweet and sunny Sophia. As I got to know her, I saw she wasn't weird or flaky, in fact she was sharp, successful and incredibly kind. And one afternoon, sitting in her band's rehearsal studio, I had finally gotten up the nerve to ask her what this Witch stuff was all about. Her answers surprised me because they actually made sense.

Sophia had plopped onto a sagging coach, sending a cloud of dust into the air. "First of all," she said, "before I can tell you what it is, I have to explain what it isn't. It has nothing to do with Satanism. That was a completely false accusation made by the Church in an effort to suppress the Old Religion. They called it Satanism and that justified their use of torture and violence to do away with the competition."

I nodded. I was all too familiar with the practice and consequences of witch hunts. "Go on."

"The word *Witch* actually came from an old Anglo-Saxon word: *wicce*." She pronounced it just like Witch, adding a soft a to the end of it. "It meant a wise one, a seer, a shaman. We call it the Old Religion, because it is. It predates the biblical faiths by thousands of years. It's got a lot in common with Native American spirituality—everything that exists in nature is experienced as sacred; it's the modern revival of the indigenous earth religion of Europe and the Fertile Crescent, what we now call the Middle East. There's a Goddess as well as a God. Their worship was called the Mystery Schools—the primary mythos was the story of the Goddess's descent into the Underworld to find the God and restore life to the world. Like Isis and Osiris, Persephone and Hades, even Dionysus and Ariadne—although there he saves her."

Isis and Osiris! A thrill shot through me. Feeling too awkward to ask more questions in front of her band, I let the subject drop, but wondered about casting spells, and riding on broomsticks, and magical potions. I didn't care what she called herself, I cared about who she was, and we became good friends—one reason she was here tonight was to support my band the way I supported hers.

"So," Sophia asked me, dropping her bags and getting right to the point as usual, "are you going to take up Maia on her invitation?"

Her friend, Maia, who was also a Witch, had read my tarot cards a few weeks ago and I'd been amazed by her insights, her "second sight." Maia had known things that no one else knew about—the experiences I'd been having, the woman in my dream, and the love I'd been longing for. When we finished, she'd asked me if I'd like to join her women's spirituality group.

"Ummm, it was nice of her but, you know, between work and managing the band . . ." I trailed off. The real reason I hadn't followed through was because it just felt too strange.

Sophia shrugged. "Up to you, but it's only once a week. You have to have some time where you're not at the beck and call of everyone else's needs." She glanced over at the drummer, who was too engaged in playing air drums to listen in to our "girltalk." "And a chance like this doesn't come along every day."

"I'll see," I said noncommittally. Maia's reading was the closest I'd come to experiencing the early magic, but it was still Witchcraft after all, and despite Sophia's explanations, my uneasiness lingered.

The door opened and the band that had just finished playing burst into the already-crowded room. It was time for my guys to go on.

A month later I was curled up on the couch of my cramped studio apartment, trying not to be depressed because my grant money had run out and my job with the foundation was over. I'd been struggling to find another job in the labor movement. The bitter irony was that none of the labor law firms would hire me because I'd been involved with the union reform movement. I was discouraged, worried and almost broke, and increasingly restless.

I dug out my old leather jacket and headed for the Metropolitan Museum. It had been more than a year since I'd visited and the cool marble and granite hallways were soothing and familiar. I strolled aimlessly until I found myself standing in front of a delicate statue of Isis. *Whatever became of you? Did you live happily ever after with your love? And why were you in my dreams? What happened to all the magic? Why haven't I experienced a synchronicity or a visitation from Jimmy in over a year? Why has he abandoned me?*

I had thought my drummer captured that James Dean passion, but I'd ended up disillusioned. I was beginning to feel a little silly. Perhaps it was nothing after all but a schoolgirl crush on a long-dead icon. But still, something kept tugging at my heart. I drifted through the museum, pushing open a high glass door and stepping into a newly constructed wing. It was a light-filled atrium several stories high with glass walls enclosing an area that had once been outside the museum. The space was filled with marble statues surrounding small pools of water amid banks of ivy.

I strolled from one great marble statue to another, enjoying the tranquillity, not thinking about my dilemmas. Turning a corner, I stopped as if I'd struck a wall. Sitting directly in front of me was the woman in my dream— carved from luminescent white marble, with the crown upon her head, a six-pointed star at her throat, and a sheaf of papers in her hand! Her head cupped in her palm, she was staring into a realm of mystery and into me.

The room bleached white. I sank into a chair and waited for the room to stop spinning. I was afraid to look at her, but when I finally raised my eyes I saw a little plaque: "The Libyan Sibyl." I spent the rest of the day in the presence of a revelation, and when the museum closed I raced back to my little studio at 86th Street and Riverside.

I pulled the *Oxford English Dictionary* from the shelf and found her name: "Sibyl . . . 1. One of various women of antiquity who were reputed to possess powers of prophecy and divination . . . 2. A prophetess, a fortune-teller, witch."

My recurring dream was of something *real* and I'd had no idea—until today. And of all things—it was about a Witch! *Was that what all of this was about?* I silently asked Jimmy. *Have you been leading me to this moment? To this encounter and this decision?*

It was more than a synchronicity. It was magic. I accepted Maia's invitation and began to attend her weekly gathering. This large group of very diverse and fascinating women—with not a single wart or green face among them—had found the Goddess, the Divine Feminine. And, apparently, so had I. But my search for love was far from over.

.2.

Mysteries

Appear, appear, what so thy shape or name, O Mountain Bull,

Snake of the Hundred Heads, Lion of the Burning Flame!

O God, Beast, Mystery, come!

—EURIPIDES

I climbed out of the subway into my old neighborhood, and darted across Seventh Avenue to the Riviera. It was still cold enough for a coat, but I could smell spring in the air.

"Well, don't you look good enough to eat!" Cutter came up behind me. We exchanged a quick kiss. "I hope he's worth it."

"So do I," I laughed. I was meeting Mark, who'd arrived from Los Angeles today, and I was flushed with new relationship hopefulness. It had been almost two weeks since his last visit; it felt like forever. We'd been dating for almost two months, but were rarely together for more than a few days every few weeks. He was based in L.A. working on his new television show, intended to compete with MTV, airing music videos. A band didn't stand a chance if they didn't have a great piece of film to go with their music. But network television hadn't quite caught the wave and so Mark was constantly hustling. Whenever he was in New York we got together, and the last few visits he'd stayed with me.

"So, what does he look like in case he wanders in?"

"My height with heels."

"He wears heels?" Cutter's black eyebrows rose an inch and he leered lopsidedly.

I poked him. "Short brown hair receding a little bit, wire-rimmed glasses, nice looking but not handsome, slight build, wearing a suit."

"With that description, even with the heels, there'll be a line of men at your table in five minutes."

"His name's Mark."

"Like I said. So whatdaya want while you're waiting?"

"How 'bout an Oloroso sherry?"

He nodded and disappeared. I stared out the window. There was something about the energy of this tiny corner with the taxis racing past that added to my anticipation. As I watched the time slipping away, that relentless speed also began to add to my tension.

Mark was over an hour late when he finally arrived. "I'm sorry, babe, I got hung up with that last meeting." He leaned down and gave me a quick kiss, then dropped into the chair across from me and surveyed the scene. "New York, man, it's good to be back. Whadaya drinkin'?" He grabbed my glass, and drank. And made a face. "What is that?"

"*That* is a very good sherry."

"Old ladies drink sherry." He ordered a beer and the details of his day rushed out of him. "So, we might have a deal. It's syndicated, not network, but it's a start. I got two days here to hammer details then I gotta get back. Oh yeah, this guy gave me tickets to a Yankee game tomorrow night—ya wanna go?"

Tomorrow night was my women's circle, my "coven," to use the old vernacular. It was still a word that could conjure a well-entrenched image of hags tossing weird critters into a bubbling cauldron. Like all the other stereotypes about Witches, I'd discovered that the truth was utterly different from the image. Relentlessly investigating, I'd found out that the word *coven* came from the old Scottish word *covent*, which simply meant gathering, and that was, amusingly, also the origin of the word *convent*. And the cauldron, like the original Holy Grail, was a symbol of the Goddess's womb.

It was time to tell Mark. After a year of study and an initiation by which I became a Wiccan priestess, it was too important a part of who I

was to remain silent. Looking at him with his loosened tie and his distracted gaze, the nervousness that had kept me quiet until now once again
stopped me dead in my tracks. What was I supposed to say? *Mark, there's
something I need to tell you. I'm a Witch.* But the moment of truth had come.
After all, how could we have a real relationship if I wasn't honest? I took a
deep breath.

"I'd love to, although I'm a Mets fan. But I'm busy tomorrow night."

"What's more important than me, and the Yankees?" he asked after
ordering another beer.

"It's just that I have a standing commitment on Thursday evenings and
it's very important to me. It's my . . . women's group."

"What? Like some consciousness-raising group?"

"Well, in a way. We . . . just raise consciousness a little bit higher. A
friend introduced me to it." I plunged ahead, explaining just as Sophia had
explained to me. "So I'm not mad about the word mostly because it makes
people think of green-faced hags and all that nonsense. But I am a . . ." I
took another deep breath and exhaled hoping for the best. "I'm a Witch."

He laughed. "You're kidding, right?"

I shook my head. "Just think of yourself as Darrin Stephens, except I
don't wiggle my nose to get the housework done. But I do look great in a
little black dress."

"All women are Witches," he shot back, shaking his head. "At least
you're honest."

I paused, uncertain what to say, then cheerfully pressed on. "I was
really skeptical at first too. It just seemed like a lot of, well, mumbo jumbo
and superstition. But it's fascinating, really. It's mostly very easy practices,
a lot like yoga in some ways. In fact, there's some overlap. And they work.
They help you take the blindfold off and experience the Divine. Inside
yourself and in the world."

"Yeah, well, those guys I'm dealing with have got somethin' inside
them, but I wouldn't call it 'the Divine.'"

I laughed. "They just haven't found it yet. Without a crisis or a calling,
most people don't even bother to look. It certainly wasn't on my radar,
until I found this group to work with. I mean, my college yearbook certainly didn't say: 'Aspiration—Witch.'" We laughed together and that
eased my nervousness. "But seriously, it's opened a whole amazing world

for me and now I'm just exploring with an open mind. And frankly, it makes a lot of sense. I never believed in any of this stuff, but once you feel it, *experience* it, well, you *know* divinity's present in everyone, and in the world. We're all connected, sort of one big soul." As the phrase emerged, I suddenly thought of Tom Joad. "And that's where magic comes from."

"Magic, huh? Like what you do to me in bed?" He grinned. "I can connect with that."

I smiled back. *So far, so good.* "The world's full of magic. Other religions call it a miracle, some people call it positive visualization, scientists call it quantum reality. But it can slip right past you if you're not paying attention. Really, that's what a Witch is—someone who's paying attention to those manifestations. And someone who's learned how to work with the energy, for good."

"You're seriously telling me you're a Witch?" Mark put down his beer and stared at me.

I nodded, holding my breath.

"Do you cast spells?" He squinted at me.

I nodded. "We do, just not the way people think we do."

"You gonna turn me into a frog if you get mad at me?"

"You'd have to be a prince first."

He laughed, and I sighed with relief.

"Actually, a spell's a lot like a prayer. Except instead of asking a male divinity to do something for you that you can't do for yourself, a spell draws upon your own inner, Divine gifts. It's a way of giving that gift shape or form in the world."

"Can you cast me a spell to nail this deal?" he asked slowly, looking at me intently as if considering the possibilities of what I'd explained.

I smiled. "If you want it to work, you really need to do it yourself. But I could help you. Believe it or not, a lot of spells work, so you need to be very careful what you ask for."

"You gonna cast a love spell on me?" He cocked an eyebrow and leaned across the table, taking my hand and rubbing the inside of my palm with his finger. "Maybe you already have." He grinned.

Had I? I smiled and continued. "The only person you can control with a spell is yourself. You never cast a spell on someone else. You can do a healing spell, or something helpful, but only if someone asks you to."

"Well, babe, you got my permission to put a love spell on me anytime you want. In fact, why don't we start right now? Let's get outta here." He headed to the bar to pay the bill.

"Not really your type," Cutter muttered in my ear as I rose from the table.

It struck a note. "I'm trying not to have a type. Just a good time with a good guy," I said with a small smile.

He shrugged. "As long as you're happy, doll."

Am I happy? I wondered as I got into the cab with Mark. *Really happy?* I'd given up the idea of finding my working class hero. It was hard enough to find a guy I had real chemistry with who was looking for more than a one-night stand. Mark put his arm around me and pulled me into a beer-flavored kiss. If my being a Witch didn't matter to him, the beer wasn't going to matter to me.

He pulled back and stared past me out the window as Eighth Avenue flew past. "So what about tomorrow night? You gonna go do your witchy thing with your little Witch pals and your brooms, or you gonna come with me? I mean, it's a Yankee game. Nothing's holier than that."

I took a final deep breath, exhaled and opened my eyes. Mark had returned to L.A. and my life had returned to its routine. I'd resumed practicing yoga, finding that many of my old skills were part of the practices I was using with Wicca, like breath, meditation, experiencing the body as a vessel of Divine energy and moving that energy through the body. I stretched slowly and stood up.

Feeling relaxed, clear and energized, I looked around my small studio. It was filled with warm spring sunshine, and piles of clothes, books, mail, newspapers and work. Being a solo practitioner who worked at home was not what I'd intended so early in my legal career, but it was where I found myself as the economy struggled through another recession. Though I was barely getting by financially, I was developing a nice area of expertise representing comic book writers and artists. I picked up the pile of clothes on the couch and dumped it on the chair, opened a folder filled with drafts of a contract from Marvel Comics and settled on the couch to work.

I had clicked my pen and started to scribble some notes when the sound of a small avalanche started in a corner of the room. A mountain of stuff slid into a strewn mess at my feet. It was time for spring cleaning. I put away the contract and started to work. I organized and dumped, swept, scrubbed and even cleaned out my closets. I took a small bowl and filled it with water into which I stirred some salt, then carried it around the room's perimeter, sprinkling as I moved counterclockwise, or *widdershins,* the direction of banishing and cleansing. I opened the windows, lit a bundle of sage, and as the cool, clean air rushed in, I wafted the smoke around the edges of the small apartment. I opened the door, poked my head out to be sure there were no neighbors about, took my broom and swept out the last of the musty energy of winter.

Finally, I stood in a neat, clean apartment that looked as good as I felt. *How do you really feel?* I asked myself as a small bubble of sadness surfaced. I wasn't really sure. I was glad I had work that paid the bills, but I missed my union work. I was glad to have Mark in my life, but deep down I knew I was settling for less than what I wanted. I was glad to have my circle, and the friends it had brought me, but what good was "magic" if I didn't have what I most desired in my life?

I stared out at the rooftops and the George Washington Bridge in the distance as a pigeon landed on my windowsill, puffing and cooing, spinning and flapping its wings.

"You're right. I need to get outside." I needed to clean out the internal clutter. I picked up the phone and called Gillian, one of my closest friends from my circle. She was busy, but yes, I could borrow her car. An hour later I was speeding along Route 80 heading to the Delaware Water Gap in her snappy '66 Mustang convertible, thinking about the unusual turn my life had taken.

When I began studying with the women who called themselves Witches, I had been very uncomfortable. It seemed odd to be participating in rituals when I hadn't been a part of any formal church or temple as a child. At six years old, when my friends were either being confirmed by their churches or starting Hebrew school, I went to my mother and asked her what religion we were. She sat me down and explained that she and my father did not believe in a God who punished you if you were bad, and rewarded you with heaven if you were good. What they did believe in was the goodness of the human heart, that we are each responsible for the life we lead, that it is up to us to create and share a promised land with every-one, and to experience heaven here on earth. She said most people need religion in order to know how to treat one another, but that really all you need is the Golden Rule: *Do unto others as you would have them do unto you.*

And when I grew up, she continued, I could decide for myself whether God existed or not. My father told me that if anyone asked, I could tell them I was half-Viking and half-Maccabee which, he said, made me all warrior. At the holidays we continued our family practice of having a Christmas tree, with presents, and a menorah that my grandmother and I would light, with more presents. From where I stood, it was a very good arrangement.

I never intended to go looking for God. I was more than content living in a world where people were good because it was our nature to be good. And even when that certainty was violated by murder during the civil rights movement, and the corruption behind the Vietnam War, and count-less other examples, the fire of conviction still burned in my heart because there was always someone who stood up for justice, and compassion, and the promised land. I didn't know that the fire my parents had lit within me was a sacred flame, because they never used a religious vocabulary.

After the synchronicity with my Sibyl, who had appeared in my dreams and then in the museum, and after my introduction to this group of women, I concluded that perhaps the Goddess had come looking for me. But at first, without a religious background, what these women were doing felt foreign to me—the language, the symbols, the gestures, the references to Goddesses and elements of Nature. What they did was also undeniably beautiful—the artistry of their circles and their rituals; the perfume of incense and oils; the altars filled with fruits and flowers and representations of Divine shapes and sizes, and gender, I'd never considered; the music and dancing; the poetry and sincerity with which they expressed them-selves; and most of all the light in their eyes and their laughter.

Of course, it also helped that they were a group of women like Sophia—smart, interesting, accomplished. And so I kept myself open to it all, and I kept exploring. As the weeks and months passed, I learned the vocabulary, the symbols and gestures and everything that had once seemed so mysterious became utterly natural. That was exactly how it felt, how *I* felt—natural. Perhaps, in pursuing James Dean, I had fallen sufficiently far down Stephen Hawking's quantum rabbit hole to find what I didn't know I'd been looking for.

As I swung the car into the forest of the state park, I was reminded that Nature makes the Divine tangible. Like a smile expressing your inner joy, the natural world is the outer expression of an inner grace. Living in the city it was easy to forget that simple and profound truth. And though we began every circle by honoring the four directions and all the blessings of the earth that sustained our lives, we were usually indoors, or at best in a city park, when we did so. And so much of what we did involved meditating, or visualizing—imagining—being in a forest, feeling a breeze or the sun's heat, floating in the ocean or standing on a mountaintop. Today, all my instincts were telling me I needed to be *in* Nature to really feel the Sacred in the world. And in myself.

I drove deeper into the Gap, along a road that ran past abandoned farms and parallel to a high ridge from which the melted winter's snow ran in loud, rushing currents. Finally, I parked the car, pulled on my hiking boots and another layer of warmth, took a small knapsack with the things I was going to need and headed into a barren field. The air was cool but the sun was warm, and striding along, I felt as if I'd been sprung from a dark, musty cave. I felt like jumping, singing, laughing, and so I ran until I reached the center of the field.

Dropping my bag and catching my breath, I looked up at the bright blue sky, felt the sun, smelled the damp, awakening earth stretching all around me, and I spun around with my arms extended, just as I had as a child. And then I cast a circle around myself. It was a simple way of shifting my point of view from the mundane to the Divine, a way of taking off that blindfold the culture had tied on. I wanted to see the Sacred. And as I felt the circle of energy building around me, I created a container for my energy, like a pot holding water to be boiled.

With my arms outstretched I turned to the east. Silently, I called to the powers of the air, powers of the mind, and I remembered its gifts of wonder and imagination, laughter and music. I reached out to the powers of the breezes that blow, the air that was my breath, the creatures of the wing, birds and butterflies in flight. I felt the cool breeze brush against my cheeks, slowly and deeply inhaled its freshness, listened to the songbirds that had returned, and felt my mind grow still and clear.

And then I turned to the south, calling the powers of fire, powers of passion, courage and determination, powers of the sun in the sky that makes all things grow and that burns within us. I felt the power of fire that was my will, and I reached out to creatures of the claw, to desert lions, mythical dragons and the magical phoenix. I felt the life-stirring heat of the sun bringing me back to life, and as I looked around me, I could see the green emerging from the earth, drawn forth by the life-sustaining star.

I turned to the west, lifted my arms and called to the powers of water, the powers of love and emotion, compassion and dreaming, to waters that fall from the sky and flow through the earth, water that was my blood, and to the powers of the creatures of the sea—dolphins, whales and otters who play among the waves. I felt the moisture of my lips, felt the waters of life running red through my veins, saw the snows of winter transformed into the waters of spring to soften the earth and make her fertile.

And then I turned to the north, calling to the power of the earth, the power of life, fertility and creativity, powers of abundance and generosity. I recognized the gifts of field and forest, fruit and grain, and the earth that was my body. And I honored the creatures of the paw and hoof, bear, wolf, stag. I felt my own strength, my ability to create and nourish the life I longed for, and I gave thanks for all the blessings I'd been given.

And then I turned to the east, ending where I had begun and completing the circle and my connections to all the blessings of Nature, and life, and I gave thanks. Every element corresponded to a part of myself—my mind, will, emotions and body. As I cast my circle, I journeyed around the four points of myself. And standing in the center, I was the point where heaven and earth, spirit and matter were conjoined. Casting a circle was what the Buddhists would call an active meditation. I'd come to learn that because Nature is the embodiment of divinity, it is also our greatest spiritual teacher, showing us how we are all interconnected and how accessible deity is—in the world around us and within us.

I took another deep breath and let out a happy shout. I lifted my knapsack, took my circle with me like Glinda's magical bubble and headed for an enormous willow tree at the edge of the field. I asked if I could learn from it and smiled as I spotted my first robin, big, fat and red breasted, fly into the branches above me. I spread out my rain poncho beneath the tree, sat and leaned back against its wide trunk.

I closed my eyes, quieting my mind by breathing slowly and deeply, and then, like the tree supporting me, I grounded and centered myself, a powerful technique for working with the earth's energy. I sent roots down from the base of my spine into the ground beneath me. I could feel them slowly penetrating the awakening earth, felt the moisture, the coolness, the force of new life beginning to course through the rich soil. I inhaled and drew the energy in through those roots and up my spine, into my heart and then, carried by blood and nerves, through my entire body.

It was like electricity running through me; it was the power of the earth, of life and rebirth, the energy that makes all things grow, that nourishes all of us every day in the foods that we eat. It coursed through me, filling me with exuberance and well-being. I sat, nourished myself, and then placed the palms of my hand on the ground and let the excess energy drain back into the earth from which it had come. Gently, I pulled up my roots, opened my eyes and saw a world that was radiant and beautiful. I thanked the tree, thanked the earth, the sun and the robin, and scattered some birdseed on the ground, for I'd been taught that whenever you do magic—and receive a blessing—you should make an offering back to the Divine.

I rolled up my poncho and continued into the woods, letting the sound guide me to just what I wanted—a cascading, winter run-off waterfall. I shed my jacket, pulled off my sweatshirt and sweater and stuffed them in my knapsack. Shivering, I scrambled over the slippery rocks, picking my way closer. I braced myself carefully and leaned forward, quickly ducking my head under the tumbling water.

Freezing water slammed into me. In an instant the pounding wrenched away all thought, anxiousness or delicate intention to clean away cobwebs. Gasping for breath, I yanked my head back. Water slid down my back and into my sleeves like melting ice cubes. I scrambled back to my knapsack, grabbed my towel and wrapped it around my dripping hair. I grabbed my sweatshirt to dry myself, pulled on my sweater and fell on the ground, laughing. Sitting, emptied of thought and filled with joy, I was completely in my body. I leaned back on my elbows, listening to the water, the birds, my heart pounding, my breathing.

This was *real* magic. I knew that I could make the best magic in Nature because Nature makes the best magic. Nature *is* magic, because it *is* the body of the Divine. All I had to do was experience and honor its lessons. This was the "right relationship" Native Americans and Buddhists referred to, that Taoists and Witches recognized. And it filled me with gratitude.

Spring had begun; it was time to let go of the old and outworn and open myself to the changes that I could feel coming.

The moon had passed through a full cycle since I'd visited the Gap—four weeks as it waxed from new to radiantly full, then waned to darkness again. I stared into the black and empty sky. *You know you won't see any stars*, I reminded myself. *It's the city, filled with man-made light, that wipes out the lights of heaven.* But a moonless night was a night of revelations, whether by divination, sign or synchronicity. The old restlessness was back and I needed to know why.

I missed Mark; the distance was taking its toll on our relationship. I wanted it to work. I tried to appreciate what we had, accept him the way he was, but deep down inside I was struggling with the knowledge that he wasn't the One. I was still yearning for a man I hadn't met, except within my heart. I was longing for *him*, for *his* arms to hold me, *his* eyes to look into mine. And part of me worried that my longing was preventing me from making a relationship with Mark work.

I tugged my leather jacket on and headed out into the New York night. I turned up my collar and hunched my shoulders against the damp April chill. The wind was whipping down the street, overturning empty garbage pails and blowing dry leaves and loose bits of paper along the street. *Where are you? Why can't I find you?* A thousand bugs buzzed over my head and I looked up as the streetlight went out. It was an old sign that had begun in law school, a warning that startled me out of my dolefulness.

I jumped on the subway and headed downtown to CBGB's; maybe I'd find Sophia and some of my old friends. Striding purposefully down Third Avenue, I was quickly trapped in the smoky quicksand of the crowd outside Joseph Papp's experimental theater.

"Interesting, huh, the way they look alike, and he moves like him, but he's not imitating him, you know, he's definitely being himself. I mean, you know it's not James Dean."

I slowed my pace, startled to hear his name. It was a *cledon*, the ancient

Greek term for a voice in the crowd that brings you a message from the gods. I strained to see who was talking. He was standing on the stairs, a few feet away, in his thirties, heavyset, with a scruffy beard and a T-shirt that said "Fight the Machine." "It's like you're watching something that's living through these guys."

"Like they're possessed." His companion was a skinny girl with a Mohawk, heavy black motorcycle boots and a dog collar. She pulled a pack of Luckys from her purse, and as she leaned into the flame in her cupped hands, I saw the poster for the film my two messengers had been discussing—*Badlands* was showing in one of the theater's screening rooms.

I bought a ticket and found myself following the two into the small screening room. I leaned against the back wall waiting for my eyes to adjust. The landscape of Terrence Malick's cinematic conjuring was stark, ironic and dreamlike—and there he was, but it wasn't James Dean, it was another actor, named Martin Sheen.

I was fascinated by his performance, which captured Dean's mannerisms and his visceral intensity, and riveted by a moment where he stands in the Christ-like pose assumed by Dean in *Giant*, arms hanging loosely over each end of a rifle swung carelessly over his shoulders. Though the character was thrilled to be compared to James Dean, the actor didn't seem like he was trying to imitate Dean. Instead, it felt as if he was in touch with the same numinous source that had filled his predecessor, expressing it in his own unique but immediately recognizable way.

I watched an antihero adrift in the barren West of 1950s America, a bloodthirsty young man longing for life, trapped in a dead world, so alienated that the only part of him that was still alive was the part that loved his girlfriend Holly. For a time they returned to Paradise, living like Peter and Wendy in tree houses and leaf shelters. The character was another Cain, cast out into the wilderness by the old, punishing fathers. But he was a Cain without redemption because, unlike Cal in *East of Eden*, or the biblical Cain whose wife awaits him, love was not enough to heal him, and he finally became one with the wasteland he sought to escape.

After so much time, I felt spellbound to experience that compelling male energy again. I was exhilarated and simultaneously confused. I had thought through the intensity of Dean's impact on me and decided that for all the otherworldliness and the synchronicities, he was really just a role model, a template for the kind of man I wanted. But emerging from the theater, I realized there was something far more extraordinary and erotic about this whole fascination than my rational mind had accepted. *Is love enough to heal?* I wondered as the credits rolled and I rose slowly from my seat. Could it bring a man's soul back to life? Could love bring the world back to life? Could it bring me what I longed for?

I hated leaving the temple where my being of light has manifested. Being of light? I startled myself with those words. I descended the stairs back to the other, real world. My work as a priestess had shown me that there was indeed far more to reality than what we usually believed. But I wanted more than an image on a screen, more than synchronicities or a rush of energy that made me question the nature of reality. I wanted a real flesh and blood man.

Was it wrong to long for more than these genuinely magical manifestations? But how could I not want more when they stirred such powerful desires? *Would he ever come to me in the flesh?* Music began playing in my head and an answer emerged from the ether, a melancholic telling of the movie's tale in Springsteen's latest album, *Nebraska*. I felt the emptiness of that night as I rode home in an empty subway car rattling unseen beneath the badlands. I felt the hollowness in my heart that came from being cut off from the work I loved, without hope of meeting the man I already loved, in a world disconnected from divinity, where we'd all been expelled from Paradise.

When I got to my apartment, I unlocked the door, tossed off my jacket and pulled off my boots. I went to my stereo and put on Springsteen's answer to my despair, the answer my heart wanted to hear: *I believe in the faith that could save me . . . Badlands . . .*

I stood naked in front of the closet trying to decide what to wear. Mark would be here tonight. The question I rarely asked myself came squarely into my mind: *What are you feeling?* I always knew what I was thinking, but what I was feeling—that was a mystery. I didn't feel excited about seeing him—that I knew.

I had skipped circle to spend the evening with him, but I'd done that before. It was probably just nerves, I reassured myself. Or the memory of our last visit. He'd been stressed, short-tempered and self-involved. And the way he approached sex had been just as tense and selfish. But he'd also begun making fun of me in front of his friends, then dismissing my hurt feelings by saying he was just kidding.

At first, he hadn't seemed to care that I practiced Wicca. But during his last visit he'd introduced me in patronizing tones to some of his friends as a "real Witch," and had acted like he was trying to wipe off makeup to reveal my green skin. I'd survived their jokes about putting hexes on their exes and why kissing Mark still hadn't cured him of being a frog. I'd even made a few jokes myself about how the lawyer was my dark side, hoping to show that I was relaxed and had a sense of humor. I didn't expect Mark to practice Wicca, or even understand what I was doing—after all, it had been a *very* long time since Western culture had experienced the world as sacred, or magical. But I did want him to accept and respect me, and occasionally make love with me.

I wanted tonight to be different from his last visit. I'd created a beautiful setting, transforming the room with red candles, flowers and Mark's favorite music. I'd shopped and bought foods reputed for their aphrodisiacal (a word derived from Aphrodite, the Greek Goddess of love) qualities—chocolates and champagne, almonds and fresh figs.

For the evening to be truly divine, however, I had to feel divine. I stared into my closet. Clothed in suits, or jeans and a leather jacket, my severe exterior reflected my rational, tough interior. For me, the Goddess was empowerment, success, intelligence, strength. She was a warrior, a creatrix of culture, not a Barbie doll. But tonight I wanted clothing for seduction, not battle. The Goddess of love and beauty was still elusive.

I pulled out a scarlet shawl, letting the silk glide between my fingers. I slid the scarf back and forth across my bare back, letting it drop and cradle the curves of my backside, moving it slowly, stroking my skin. I pulled the silk across my breasts, my belly, between my thighs. And I stared at myself, catching a fleeting glimpse of a soft and lovely woman. Smiling, I padded into the bathroom, rolling the passionate attraction potion I'd made between my palms. I inhaled deeply—ground rose petals, patchouli, cinnamon and damiana mixed with musk and almond oils, bundled in a lace handkerchief that had belonged to my grandmother. The tub was almost full. I lit a red candle, dropped the herbal pouch into the water, and looking into the mirror, I quietly recited my charm:

Aphrodite from the sea
Hear my call and come to me
Bless me with your radiant power
And open me as passion's flower

Although such a simple spell had once seemed foolish, I'd learned that spells did work, and they worked best when set to easy rhyme and rhythm. In this way they were like mantras, simple to memorize and capable, through repetition, of quickly shifting one's consciousness from mundane to magical.

I repeated the lines as I lowered myself into the warm water and as I soaked. I lost track of time, the words dissolving and reconnecting, then receding like the tide pulling my worries away in their undertow. I thought of Mark—his lean body, his energetic determination and how I felt when he focused it on me. I remembered how we had met, and flirted, and how the chemistry had flowed between us. I remembered the heat of our first kiss, his hands on my breasts, the way he felt inside me. I began looking forward to being with him.

I rose from the water, saw it cascading from my body. I stretched and watched my wet skin glow in the candlelight, a million rainbows shattered across my body. I could *feel* Aphrodite radiating from within.

I put a drop of her oil—almond, musk, cinnamon, vanilla, patchouli, orange—on each of my pulse points, at my ankles, behind my knees, in the crevice where my thighs cradled my womb, at the base of my spine, under my breasts and over my heart, at my wrists, the crook of my elbows, my throat, behind my ears and at my third eye. I dried and brushed my hair, and applied some makeup—a base to cover the darkness beneath my eyes, a smudged stroke of eyeliner, some mascara, and lipstick.

It was almost eight o'clock. I dressed quickly—new lace lingerie, a black dress that had a great neckline and showed my figure, but no shoes. I lit the rest of the candles, put the champagne in its bucket, and the feast on my grandmother's beautiful plates. I turned the music on, and I waited.

At eleven o'clock, I turned the music off, blew out the candles and returned the champagne to the refrigerator. I ate some figs, undressed, put on my robe and turned on the television. It was after midnight when Mark finally arrived. He dumped his bags and grabbed me, pulling me into a boozy kiss and squeezing my breasts.

"I shared a cab from the airport with Pete and we stopped for a quick drink with the syndication guy. What an asshole." Mark pulled off his tie, tossed his jacket on the chair and collapsed on the couch. "You know how it is, we gotta work him."

"I wish you'd called" was all I said. I was angry but I held my tongue. I knew what it meant to be climbing the ladder of success. It was late, but he was here—I tried to push my bad mood aside. I went for the champagne and returned to find him passed out on the couch. I covered him with a blanket, and climbed into bed.

I cried, hating how vulnerable I felt. Opening myself only to be neglected was more pain than I had the strength to deal with. I wanted to love him, but I couldn't. And he didn't love me. But even knowing it wasn't the dream I'd longed for, I still had feelings for him. In the morning he wanted to make love and I wanted him to leave. We fought.

"I can't make love with my eyes closed anymore," I said desperately.

"And I can't deal with this Witch stuff," he shot back. "My friends give me so much crap. And what about my business? What am I supposed to say about you?"

"Why do you have to say anything? Do you introduce your friends by telling people what their religion is?" I could feel my temper rising.

"I can't deal with this now," he snapped, yanking on his clothes.

I didn't reply. He was forcing me to make a choice. "This isn't what I want to do," I said quietly, resting my hand on his arm.

Mark stared at me. He put his arms around me and we kissed. I allowed my feelings for him to surface, letting myself believe that everything was going to be all right. We made love . . . we had sex. I could feel my feelings, I couldn't feel his, and I began to cry. His eyes were closed and he didn't know.

"I guess we shouldn't've done that," he said afterward, feeling my tears run onto his shoulder.

"No."

We got up and he showered while I made the bed.

"I don't think this shirt goes with these pants," he said walking back into the room.

"What?" I stared at him. He was preoccupied with clothes at a time like this? "Put the sweater on and it'll look fine."

It was over.

After he'd left, I stared around the room at all the melted candles. It was the right decision—I couldn't be with a man who didn't respect me or what was important to me. *Then why do I feel so awful and empty?* Automatically, I reached for my briefcase, pulling out a file. I stared blindly at the papers, unable to concentrate. I could still smell the perfumed water and the oil on my skin. I knew that magic didn't always work, but I couldn't help wonder whether it would *ever* work when it came to love.

Had I fallen in love with Mark? My heart felt as empty and broken as if I had. But maybe it was just the emptiness that had been there from the very beginning, a void that Mark had never filled. In the end, I hadn't expected much, and I hadn't gotten much. I went to the mirror that had offered such promise last night. Aphrodite was nowhere to be seen. All I saw was the dullness in my eyes, and my flaws—the dark circles beneath my eyes, my overbite, the little mound of my stomach. I wasn't beautiful, I wasn't sexy. I didn't know who I was.

What a gorgeous day! This weekend's going to be such fun." Nonna stretched her arm out the car's open window and let the air push against her cupped palm. "It's good to get away, do something different." She looked like Anna Magnani in round, black Jackie O sunglasses and a Hermès scarf. Nonna was the very first person I'd met when I walked into the women's gathering two years ago. She'd seemed to know who I was before we were even introduced, and I felt as if I'd known her all my life. Nonna also had the disarming ability to know what I was going to say, or what was going to happen, before I did. She had tucked me securely under her wing, and then, taking me with her, she took flight. My feet still hadn't touched the ground, and as my studies moved increasingly from group to personal work, she had become my mentor. Tired of looking at my long face, she'd suggested we spend a weekend out of town.

"My grandparents took my parents to Atlantic City, and when I was little my parents brought me," I said. "I still have the pictures."

Nonna reached into her bag and pulled out a peach and a paper towel. "The big old hotels, the bicycle carriages on the boardwalk, everyone dressed for dinner at night." She sighed. "And there were bands and dancing. It's nothing like what I remember from my childhood. But it'll be fun."

"And we have other places to go along the shore," I answered.

Everyone referred to Nonna, the eldest of the group, as our "Crone," a title of honor meaning she was the wise one, the matriarch, though she couldn't have been much older than sixty. Her dark eyes were full of light and she had embraced me with a warmth I'd never received from anyone, not even my own mother, who adored me but who was an elegantly formal woman. With her full figure, her mane of black hair, her laugh and her wisdom, Nonna epitomized abundance.

I hit my turn signal and moved into the passing lane. It wasn't even noon and the road was already crowded with escapees from the city. But that was to be expected on a hot summer weekend. Nonna pulled the map out of my hands and tossed it in the backseat.

"Hey! How'm I supposed to get us to Atlantic City without that map?"

"Life's a labyrinth, full of twists and turns. You can't see the pattern when you're in the middle of it. Can't see where you've been, where you're going, but if you'll let go of the need for a map, and just trust, you'll find you're way to the center." Only Nonna could talk like that and make sense, because she talked to the wisdom of my heart and not just my head. "And you'll have much more fun getting there."

"Yes, but isn't there a monster waiting at the center?" I asked.

"The Minotaur." She laughed. "He's only a monster to those who deny him."

"Deny what?"

"The Minotaur is Dionysus, the Greek God of ecstasy. If you deny yourself joy, eroticism, love, all his delicious intoxicating gifts that make life worth living, he'll drive you mad. But if you embrace him," she inhaled and let out a happy little *ummmph*, "you get a life filled with pleasure and grace. The greatest tragedy of this culture is that we've lost our ability to honor what he offers."

"Well, I can't deny the madness." I had just turned the radio off, unable to listen to the grisly account of yet another murder. *Badlands*.

Nonna nodded. "All our sad substitutes for real joy—all the addictions to alcohol and drugs, the materialism, those inside traders in the stock market, the bed-hopping for that initial rush of conquest or romantic love—none of it fills the hole."

"Sometimes I wonder if all this stuff I'm doing with Wicca is just another one of those substitutes," I said quietly.

From the corner of my eye I could see Nonna studying me. She smiled. "Yes, for some people religion is a crutch, even this spirituality can be nothing but the consolation of easy answers so they don't have to think. It depends on how you use it. But for you, I think this path offers a set of tools to find your own way. Through the labyrinth."

We drove the next slow, few miles in comfortable silence.

"I didn't realize the Minotaur and Dionysus were the same," I finally said, images of a man with the head of a bull in my mind's eye. "I only know the myth because my mother used to read it to me as a child."

Nonna shook her head. "The story is meaningless to most people, but the Gods don't cease to exist just because we've forgotten them or reduced them to characters in stories. They're everywhere, it's just that people don't recognize them. At best, nowadays they're understood as psychological forces. Jung's archetypes—the 'first patterns.'" She stopped to finish her peach and I wove through maddening traffic.

"Okay, but what does that mean? To me, or to that guy driving the truck." I nodded at the semi I was passing.

"Him? He's Arjuna, the charioteer." She laughed, and waved to the driver, who smiled at her as we passed. "Archetypes are like blueprints of basic human modes of behavior. And they're constant, regardless of culture or historical period. We use them to explain people all the time, we just don't realize what we're doing. Think about it, I bet you can give me an example." The truck pulled parallel to us and the driver winked at Nonna.

"Well, there's an easy one—like when we refer to movie stars as sex goddesses, like Marilyn Monroe."

Nonna nodded as she reapplied her crimson lipstick. "Exactly, movie stars are perfect examples—Monroe was the Goddess of love; Paul Newman is such an Apollo, the golden boy."

"Now it's Harrison Ford. Arnold Schwarzenegger is Hercules, or he could be Aries or Mars, the God of War. So could Stallone's Rambo."

Nonna nodded. "For my generation, it was John Wayne. Actors are particularly powerful magnets for archetypal forces. They enact our stories, our modern myths, and myths are populated by archetypes. Just the way a dream is a message from your unconscious, a myth is a culture's dream. Decipher the symbols and the meaning of a dream and we understand ourselves better. It's the same with a myth—understanding it gives us insight into a deeper level of our humanity that we all share. And movies are very powerful modern myths. It's common for certain people—particularly actors or musicians—to embody archetypal energies. In the past it was also the poets and writers."

There was something vaguely familiar about Nonna's observations, an auditory déjà vu.

"And that energy is a part of us, so they . . . act it out for us," I said slowly.

Nonna nodded. "People recognize that energy; they also project it onto actors. As if they were not just people, but a mirror for us to see our own archetypal natures, to see ourselves."

And suddenly it struck me like a bolt of Zeus's lightning. I pressed down on the accelerator in my excitement and we shot up to eighty-five as I shot through the traffic like in a movie car chase.

Nonna looked over at the speedometer and then at me. "What just happened?"

"James Dean. Nonna, who's James Dean?" I cut through three lanes and flew down the next exit ramp.

"He's Dionysus, of course." Nonna eyed the speedometer, exhaling in relief as I slowed for the stop sign. "Very erotic, ecstatic, a little androgynous with all that emotion. And dying young the way he did. Or he could be Osiris, but then the two were often virtually the same; and sometimes he's also identified with Hades. Do we need gas?" Nonna asked as I pulled into the service station. I turned off the engine and put my dizzy head down on the wheel. "What's the matter, dear? Is it the heat? Do you need water?" I felt Nonna's hand on my back. "Just breathe slowly, dear. That's it, slow, deep breaths."

I looked up and out the window, trying to ground myself in the mundane details of New Jersey while my mind raced between centuries and cultures and realms of reality. "Let's find a diner. I have a lot to tell you."

The moon was rising, huge, golden and full from the ocean and a high wind was blowing off the water, as it did at night. We strolled arm in arm along the boardwalk, bundled in sweaters, her hair pulled back, mine whipping wildly about my face. I had told Nonna my stories, my worry that I had fallen in love with a dead movie star, and the dawning realization that it was not him, but the energy, the *archetypal* energy, that I was responding to.

"Do you know what a daemon is?" Nonna asked as a small pack of boys flew past on their bicycles leaving the wooden walkway humming beneath our feet.

I recognized the term from my philosophy classes. "Well, I know Socrates said he had one and he's supposedly the smartest man who ever lived. As I recall it was his spiritual guide, his inspiration. And he chose to die rather than deny the reality of its existence."

Nonna smiled, nodding. "It's an ancient Greek term for a divine being. Your daemon guides you into the realm of the numinous, to the sacred part of yourself."

"Is he . . . an archetype?"

"Jungian psychologists would say so, probably call him your *animus,* a masculine mode that resides deep within your unconscious. For men it's a female figure, the *anima,* which means soul. The Goddess. One of the steps to wholeness and maturity is to wed the two aspects of yourself together."

"So he's a part of me."

"He resides within, but he's more. As I said, he's a spiritual being. A God, or an aspect of God. Do you remember when you asked me whether the Gods and Goddesses are real, objective, whether they existed independently of us, outside of us, or are just inner, psychological forces? Archetypes?"

"Yes," I replied and laughed, remembering her reply. "It's not either/or; it's *and.*"

Nonna nodded. "The ancients, and plenty of modern religions, thought the Divine was outside them, on Mount Olympus, in heaven. Nowadays, the old Gods are confined within, restricted to being nothing more than psychological forces. But the Divine is all around us *and* dwells within us."

I stared out at the moon and the path of light it made in the dark ocean. "I did feel as if he led me to this path. I was pursuing him, but I found the Goddess instead."

"Pan piped and you followed. He led you to the Goddess *and* the God."

"I've always had a problem relating to God, to Jehovah—angry, jealous, vengeful, punishing." I sighed and shook my head. "It just doesn't make sense."

Nonna pinched my nose. "You can't let yourself, or your experience of the Sacred, be confined to such a narrow interpretation. God is infinitely richer. To encounter a daemon is to encounter the God—in the world *and* in yourself." She smiled as the door to a bar swung open and the sound of a live band poured into the cool night air along with a group of laughing couples. We stopped to listen to the electric guitars, the horns and driving drums. The door swung closed and we walked on. "It can take a little longer to recognize the opposite gender deity and its role. A daemon is also a source of creative inspiration. If you're open to him, he'll unlock the door to your hidden potential, the reasons why you're here. Male or lesbian artists generally have a muse—a manifestation of the Goddess who's their source of inspiration, like Dante's Beatrice. That's what a daemon is, but it's a manifestation of the God. Goethe believed Byron was his daemon." I stopped walking. She nodded at the thoughts displayed on my face. "Yes, there's an old notion that a daemon can be the spirit of someone who's crossed over."

"James Dean's middle name was Byron, for the poet."

Nonna nodded. "A very fitting synchronicity for the passing of the torch."

"But what's a daemon got to do with love?" I asked the question I most wanted Nonna to answer. I watched the laughing couples, embracing, kissing, strolling along in front of us.

"Everything, *mia figlia*," Nonna said quietly. "He's a messenger of love, an initiator into its deepest mysteries. So, it appears your daemon is Dionysus, he's Eros, the God of love. That's where the word *eroticism* comes from. In a sense, your daemon is your mystical lover who prepares you for love with a real man."

I shook my head. "Prepares? I've been wondering if he isn't making it impossible for me to love a real man. I mean, no one lives up to . . . what I long for."

Nonna squeezed my arm. "In the Italian, the old term was a *folletto*. In mystical Judaism he's a *basheirt,* a kind of predestined partner."

"Socrates said we were once one being, and were split into two when we came to the earthly plain. And now our search for love is the search for our other half."

"One of the mysteries of life."

"So, you're saying the daemon, or the muse, guides you on that search?"

Nonna nodded.

"But what about sex?" I watched a couple kissing as if alone in the world.

"Remember how you described the way you felt the first time you saw James Dean? How erotic it was? The desire it aroused in you?"

I nodded. "It's still there, like some kind of dream . . . but I still feel it. I'm still longing to experience it—with a man, not a . . . spirit."

"Ah, but it's a daemon that awakens a woman to her sexuality. He's the power that connects eroticism and spirituality. He may come to you in dreams, in synchronicities, and use whatever's appropriate, whatever will reach your heart, your soul—myths and stories, poetry, symbols, music, movies, real men. He's not a mortal male, but it's common to project his image onto a real man."

"James Dean."

She nodded. "And he'll shape-shift—move from one figure to another, change as you change. You may find that it's as if he's always one step ahead, leading you in the dance. And it's a dance of love, because it's love that makes sex truly sacred and truly erotic."

"So all this time, what I've felt, what I sensed, it *was* real. It was . . . my daemon." A ripple of excitement rolled through me.

"It's a lot to take in. Try not to think too much. Let's go back to that club." She turned around and tugged me back toward the bar. "I want to go dancing. Tomorrow, I'll teach you a way to call your daemon."

We danced until they shut the place down and then we sat on a bench with coffees, watching the sunrise, crimson and blindingly bright. Nonna had helped me to understand, and so I could finally, unreservedly, believe in the daemon and in the mystery—a chance encounter when I least expected it, a captivating glance that penetrated, a feeling that was completely, electrically connected.

Believe and your love will find you.

The Second Spell

.3.

Casting

Love will find a way through paths where wolves fear to prey.

—LORD BYRON

Nonna sat in a low, red and white nylon beach chair, her feet buried in the sand, a yellow *pareo* wrapped around her hips and a huge straw hat shading her face as she did the Sunday *Times* crossword puzzle, in ink. I swam out beyond the pounding breakers and turned onto my back, spreading my arms, letting the salt water buoy me, watching clouds float above me as I floated on the blue below.

After riding weightless on the water, walking out of the ocean was like being on Jupiter. I plopped down on the towel beside Nonna, panting, dripping, tying back my wet hair. She tossed me the sunscreen.

"Put on plenty of that. You're very pale and you don't want to burn." Nonna inspected me over the top of her sunglasses. "And then, I'm in the mood for something naughty. Would you mind walking back to the board-walk to buy me an ice cream?"

I nodded contentedly. "What flavor?"

"Chocolate."

Happy to execute Nonna's indulgence, I made my way back to the boardwalk. I returned with two rapidly melting dishes of ice cream and found Nonna reading a romance novel.

"The erotic secret of the American woman." She smiled as she tucked it next to the crossword puzzle.

"So," I said between spoonfuls, "you were going to teach me how to call my daemon."

Nonna nodded as she licked her spoon. "You know the best way already."

"I do?" Somehow, with Nonna, it felt utterly normal to eat ice cream while talking about spirits and divine messengers.

"Well, where do you think he came from?"

"I don't know," I admitted.

She chuckled. "There're all sorts of ways to make magic, and all sorts of ways to cast a love spell. But none of it works unless it comes from here." She tapped her heart. "You opened your heart to the Universe, and it heard you."

"But people do that all the time and they don't materialize a . . . divine being."

"Oh, you'd be surprised. There are angels everywhere, especially at the beach at dawn and twilight." She smiled, staring down the long stretch of sand.

"But you said a daemon is . . . well, sexy."

Nonna smiled. "He is that. He's a very special guide—to the sacred *and* the sexual. In this culture, those two things seem incompatible. But at the origin of Western civilization, and in other religions, the two are inseparable. Most creation stories are about how a Goddess and God fell in love, made love and created the Universe out of their union. Everything that exists comes from that original act of love."

"Ha, the real big bang." I snickered and Nonna playfully kicked sand at me.

"It was called the Sacred Marriage, the *hieros gamos* in Greek. And it was the centerpiece of some of the oldest and largest religious traditions— the Mystery Traditions. Isis and Osiris, Persephone and Hades, Shakti and Shiva, Dionysus and Ariadne."

Nonna had my complete attention.

"What you're learning now is the modern rebirth of those ancient spiritualities. At the core of the Mystery Traditions and their rituals is the personal experience of union with Divinity. No matter our religious background, there's a yearning in all of us to be connected to the Sacred, call it Goddess, God, the Tao, the collective consciousness, the quantum field, whatever you choose. And I believe that the yearning for a soul mate is also a yearning for that reconnection with the Divine."

"Oh, Nonna, I feel like I've spent my whole life longing for him."

"When you're ready. The Supremes were right—you can't hurry love." Nonna smiled and kept eating.

"So my soul mate is my connection to God?" Nonna's point penetrated my momentary daydream.

She nodded. "Ideally, a soul mate; but it's possible to have the experience in any loving relationship. One of the most powerful ways to experience that union is sex. You make love in a state of greatly heightened sensitivity and awareness, and each partner literally embodies the Goddess and God. You share in the mystery of the creation of the Universe, and the sex is sacred. It's true ecstasy."

"Sacred sex? I'd be thrilled just to have *good* sex."

Nonna smiled. "It can be very difficult in a world that's so distrustful and exploitive of sex."

"But what does any of that have to do with calling my daemon?"

"I'm going to teach you a very basic, very powerful practice to experience and heighten your connection with your daemon. *And* it's the foundation for sacred sex, and most sex magic, which can also be practiced on your own."

"Sounds like a lot more fun that chanting." I cocked an eyebrow. "Or dancing."

"Well, just like with chanting or dancing, you raise energy. Sex magic is basically the use of sexual arousal to raise energy that, at the moment of orgasm, is directed to the achievement of a goal. Because it can be difficult to visualize an objective during orgasm, it's a common practice to send the energy into a symbol of your intention."

"That sounds so much simpler than what I've read. Or what people talk about."

"It's always been disguised in arcane, symbolic language—not surprising given the Victorian nature of this culture. But it's not nearly as obtuse or inaccessible as some would have you think. It's hiding in plain sight, as it were. And of course there are both Eastern and Western traditions. The Eastern tends to focus more upon sustained sexual arousal as a means of achieving enlightenment; the Western tends to use the release of orgasm to achieve a goal. But there's a lot of overlap as well."

I grinned. "So you're going to teach me sex magic?"

Nonna stared at me over the top of her sunglasses. "I'm going to teach you the most fundamental technique for raising and moving and directing sexual energy. You may use it for sex magic, or you may use it to experience divine love. The choice is always up to you."

"Can't I do both?"

Nonna laughed. "Why don't we just start by teaching you the techniques."

"Now?"

"When we get back to New York. When the time is right. In the meantime, you might want to learn a little more about Dionysus."

I was ready to leave for New York immediately, but Nonna wanted a last swim. I watched as she stroked strongly and confidently through the ocean. And I wondered, *Which would I choose? Magic or divine love? But why couldn't I use sex magic to experience divine love?*

"*Listen, sweetheart,* I don't care what Jack promised you, he didn't have the authority to make those promises. You're dealing with me now and I'm telling you we don't care if he's got a clause in his contract." Todd Regan sat back in his seat and folded his hands across his stomach. He was communicating his disdain, but what I really noticed was the small stain on his blue silk shirt. He was Hollywood—no tie, no jacket and more money in his production budget than a Third World nation's GNP—in town on behalf of his very powerful L.A. production company. "He doesn't have a clause with us. I'm just taking this meeting as a courtesy to Bill."

I kept my poker face firmly in place, refusing to rise to the bait, particularly his term of ersatz endearment. His production company had purchased the rights to make a film based on a comic book character written by one of my clients. My client didn't own the character, the publisher did, but I'd negotiated a clause with the publisher that gave him the opportunity to write the screenplay if movie rights were sold. Now I had to persuade Mr. Hollywood to honor that clause.

I had to keep my cool, be twice as tough and twice as good without acting like the bully across the table from me. My appearance was part of my strategy. Red was the big "power" color, but I also knew it was a color that, like waving a flag in front of a bull, would antagonize my opponent. So instead I had worn a navy blue pinstripe suit, with a square cut that concealed my figure, and shoulder pads, in vogue at the moment, that added bulk to my slim frame. My hair was pulled back and my sole gesture toward my gender was a pair of pearl earrings that said, *Yes, I'm a woman, but let's not make a big deal of it.* The rest of my appearance said, *Let's not even notice I'm female, I'm just one of you. Now let's talk business.*

The rest of my strategy required that I keep my voice low and even and my arguments reasonable and strong. "Bill's a great guy. Very smart." Bill was the vice president of the publishing company. "That's why he agreed to that clause in Steve's contract. He knows how good he is and how valuable he is to the property." I paused and then carefully added some pressure. "Listen, the clause is very clear. Rights were sold, he travels with the rights. You violate the terms, it's actionable—"

"My deal's with the publisher. Not some writer." He cut me off, his voice loud and condescending. "You want to sue, go ahead. It's going to cost your client a lot more than it's going to cost us."

"A summary judgment is not going to cost my client. But it will cost you, because you'll cover my fees." I eased back on the pressure and smiled. "Look, nobody wants to lose time litigating. You want to make a movie, he wants to help you make a movie. A great movie. And he's not 'some writer.' He's the guy who made this book the best-selling comic book in America. He's an asset to you—he gives your movie credibility with the fans; hell, he'll *bring* fans to the film."

"He's never written a screenplay." The tone was still tough, but it was a step in the right direction.

I pressed my small advantage. "Comic books are the closest thing out there to movies. They're stories told in dialogue with illustrations— storyboards. He knows these characters, he created them. And besides, you know these things end up with dozens of rewrites. Nothing says you can't bring in a co-writer. But his name on this project is valuable to you."

"Like I said, it's a movie, not a comic book." He'd lowered his voice to a normal range.

And mine was now friendlier. "The contract calls for him to do a treatment. That's all. A story. And no one's got a better insight into what would make a great story—he's been writing them for ten years. Just give him a shot. Anyway, it's a lot cheaper to pay him to do a treatment than to litigate."

"I'll have to talk to Tom. And he'd have to fly out to L.A."

"That's not a problem." I was starting to feel good.

"Scale, that's all he gets." He almost sounded friendly.

"Scale plus his expenses. You fly him out, put him up."

"Okay, I'll get back to you." He stood up and stuck out his hand. I took it, firmly, and we shook.

"Great. I'll look forward to hearing from you." It was too soon to say the deal was sealed, but we were almost there. I wanted to dance on the overpolished conference table in my high heels. It hadn't taken the superpowers of Steven's characters, but sometimes it felt like I was turning into a full-fledged Amazon. I picked up the phone to call my client.

I wrapped the sheet around myself and watched as he pulled on his blue T-shirt. *Why did I do it?* I wondered with numb disbelief. I knew why—because I wanted to be swept away. I wanted to believe the lyrics, the movies, the fairy tales that you could fall in love across a crowded room. I wanted to believe that with one look you could know you were meant for each other. I would've settled for a night of satisfying sex with a good-looking stranger.

Mr. Across-the-crowded-room leaned down and gave me a quick peck. "It was great. I'll call ya."

And he was gone.

I climbed out of bed and headed straight for the shower. It was several years before AIDS would rear its terrifying head, and condoms were not the rule. None of the women I knew even thought about using them. Birth control was entirely a woman's responsibility. And I took it seriously. I wanted to have a baby someday, but when I did, it would be at the right time with the right man.

I stared into the mirror. The person looking back seemed completely mysterious to me. I felt like I knew myself less than I knew the man who'd just walked out my door. I needed a reality check. I picked up the phone and starting calling some of the women from my circle. Naomi and Gillian suggested that I meet them downtown. I was dressed and in a cab in a flash.

"You just need a better dating pool, that's all. With the work you do, you're always meeting guys. You got plentya bait, don't tell me you can't hook a good one." Naomi took a swig of her beer and grinned. She rose from the table and looked around. "I gotta get some cigarettes."

I pointed toward the stairs that led to the lower level of the Riviera. "Or you can probably bum one off Cutter. Not that I'm condoning your suicide."

She grimaced and trotted off down the stairs. In her late twenties, Naomi was stunning, with long brown hair, high cheekbones and blue eyes, but she never wore makeup, and downplayed her figure in baggy jeans or overalls. She was a sculptor by day, and by night a bartender at Violet's, the most popular lesbian bar in the city.

The smell of Chanel Number 5, one of my mother's favorite perfumes, displaced the cigarette smoke. I turned to see Gillian picking her way through the tables, turning several heads on the way in her tight Claude Montana suit and spike heels. She waved a manicured hand, and a brilliant smile lit up her face. Gillian, whose socially prominent last name was immediately recognizable even to those who didn't read Page Six, was a fashion magazine editor with a master's degree in Middle English Literature, which is how she'd found the Goddess and our little circle of incipient priestesses.

She leaned over and I was kissed on both cheeks, in the French style, a charming remnant of her boarding school days.

"I love the new haircut."

Gillian's hair had been highlighted and cut in a short, twenties-style bob. She reached up with a distinctively feminine pat. "I'm not used to feeling the air on the back of my neck! But I needed a change after breaking up with Chris." She sighed, then instantly brightened as Cutter appeared at the table.

"To what do I owe this rare inundation of beauty? And what'll ya drink?" Cutter grinned at us.

"A Manhattan." Gillian launched a dazzling smile at him.

"I'm fine." I put my hand over my Chardonnay as Naomi slid back into her seat.

"One more, Mr. Cutter." Naomi handed him her bottle, leaned across the table and gave Gillian a hug. "Nice hair. Little shorter and I'd take you to Violet's."

Gillian stuck her tongue out.

"Very good." Naomi grinned.

We all laughed.

"So—dish." Gillian pulled off her jacket and turned to me.

I shrugged again.

"Her love life sucks," Naomi offered for me.

"Doesn't everybody's?" We laughed. "Why don't you date lawyers? You're surrounded by them."

"I don't know, I haven't met one yet that I'm attracted to. They're just all so . . . buttoned down. There's no fire, no passion. It's like they're stamped out of a boring mold in law school."

"You just need to jump back in the water," Gillian urged.

"I think someone's drained it all. I am stuck in the mud with nothing but frogs and I don't think I can stand to kiss one more."

"Okay, you guys need the dope on the *real* story of the princess and the frog." Naomi tapped the tabletop for attention. "So once upon a time, a beautiful, independent, confident princess came upon a frog sitting by a pond. The frog said to the princess, 'I was once a handsome prince until an evil Witch put a spell on me.' "

We all made faces and Naomi pressed on. "So the smart-assed frog said, 'If you will just kiss me, I will turn back into a prince. And then you'll marry me, move into the castle with my mother, and you can cook for me and clean my clothes, have my children and live happy ever after while I go rescue a damsel in distress.' "

Gillian and I groaned but Naomi ignored us.

"Later that night, the princess laughed as she sat down to dinner. 'I don't *think* so,' she said, and dug hungrily into her plate of frog's legs. And she lived happily ever after."

I realized I was feeling better as we all laughed. "I'm just not good at frogs and one-night stands."

Gillian shook her head. "Personally, I think we got a raw deal—all that free love that we're supposed to be enjoying comes with a price tag—and it's a broken heart. I mean, we're expected to 'put out' on the first date, and we even expect it of ourselves, but how fulfilling is the sex?"

"Yeah, there's a rush of someone new, but how often can you do that? I can't. I mean, without emotion it's just not . . . erotic." I thought of all the times like last night when, instead of enjoying myself, I found my head was working overtime, wondering why I wasn't feeling anything. "It's not all their fault. I mean, it's definitely me too. I start out all hot, but then I can't shut off the voice that's wondering what they're feeling, whether I'm turning them on, doing it right. Why they're *not* doing it right. And why they're doing it so fast. I lose track of what I'm feeling. I just sort of get turned off. Sex with the body and not the heart just isn't . . . hot. Am I making sense?"

Naomi nodded. "Doesn't matter if it's with a woman or a man, a diet of one-night stands doesn't cut it."

"Do you tell them what you want?" asked Gillian.

"It's so hard, I mean I feel so self-conscious. Besides, you have to cut a guy some slack. I can't say 'a little to the left, not so fast, how about parking your tongue someplace different for a change.' I sound like I'm directing traffic. And when I try to be a little more in control—at least of myself—they're more and more passive. And I want them to be *more* active, not less."

"Mind if I join you? I'm on break." Cutter dropped into a chair. "And I want to make my boss jealous."

"Please do, and while you're at it, maybe you can explain the male psyche to us." I batted my eyelashes at him.

Cutter held Naomi's cigarette to the end of his until it took light, then exhaled a relieved cloud of smoke over our heads. "Okay, I'm supposed to speak for all men everywhere?"

We all nodded, laughing.

"Don't get me wrong. I do *not* think men are the enemy. I *love* men." Gillian turned to Cutter. "But I don't get them. The guys I've actually done it with, they all do virtually the exact same thing—they make out with you the first time or two, but once you fuck, forget foreplay. And even when you start to have a relationship, there's chemistry at first, but then they fall into this passionless pattern." Gillian's Manhattan had clearly kicked in and she was on a roll. "It's like they all went to the same school for sex. I mean, it's so *predictable*. And I don't know any woman who can get aroused and come as fast as they think we can, given what little foreplay there's been. And then they just pump away. They might as well be wind-up toys. And I might as well be a blow-up doll for all the connection."

"Way too fast, and mechanical. What *is* that?" I asked as we all turned to Cutter.

"Well, not to oversimplify, but we *are* wired differently. I mean, a guy gets turned on right away and it takes a woman longer. So there's part of it. And guys are very focused on their dicks, that's where the pleasure is. Except it's more like this buildup of pressure that you just can't wait to release. I mean, you can kiss a woman behind her knee and she'll get turned on. But you do that to a guy and he's just like, could you come around front and do it where it counts?"

The three of us, even Naomi, sat silent and fascinated. The door to an alien world was being opened to us.

"We all learned about sex when we were teenagers. We'd take a picture into the bathroom and wank off. No emotions, lots of variety. Just raw, animal lust. It's great. But for you women, sex and love are all tangled up with each other. It takes a while for a guy to get his heart and his dick connected."

Gilly nodded. "Women have sex to get love, men give love to have sex."

Cutter shrugged. "It's been said. But men do love; it's just that it's easy for us to have sex without it. If it's any reassurance, I can tell you, on behalf of the all the men in the world, having done it both ways, sex *with* love is definitely hotter. It's just not easy. And for us, easy is good."

"I always thought men and women were the same. But we're definitely not." I sighed.

Gilly poked me. "Don't give up hope—opposites attract. We were designed to fit together, even if it's difficult getting the parts to match."

"Some puzzle," Naomi said, chuckling. "I think with women lovers, maybe they're more sensitive, 'cause they're female. They know what's going on from the inside out, and they're just more emotional. Even when men get inside, they're still on the outside, ya know? Maybe you're fishing for the wrong thing?"

I shook my head, smiling at her suggestion. "Hah, how many times have we said, 'If you were a man I'd marry you'? But women just don't do it for me sexually." I sighed. "Maybe I want someone who just doesn't exist."

As Cutter went back to work and our talk turned to jobs, I found myself wondering if a man could express his feelings, and most of all, could really love, the way I longed to be loved and to give love. Of course he could. But would I ever find a man like that?

The Magickal Cauldron, the only Wiccan/Pagan bookstore in New York City, where my circle met every Thursday evening, was about to close for the night. The long, narrow shop was also stocked with giant jars of herbs and oils, candles and statues and items so dusty and bizarre it looked like a movie set. In fact, a few horror films had been shot in the shop, much to the dismay of the rest of us—for we knew that its weird appearance was just a legerdemain, an illusion to scare away those who didn't have the wisdom, or the courage, or the common sense, to see beyond the gargoyle at the gate.

I had spent the evening perched on a stool in the Oil Office, the small area at the back of the shop where all the essential oils were kept, and where potions were prepared. I sat slowly turning page after oil-stained page of the old formularies, leather-bound books filled with spells and potions. I was also searching through the less romantic but very practical index cards with their modern recipes.

"What mischief are you up to do?" I heard Nonna's quiet voice behind me.

"I want to cast a love spell." I turned and put down my pen.

"Everyone wants a love spell!" She studied my face carefully. "Why do you?"

Her question surprised me. Nonna didn't understand this simple thing? "I hate the endless, empty dating, all these superficial guys. I want to fall in love."

"Isn't there another reason?"

"Yeah, I'm tired of all the lousy sex."

She arched an eyebrow. An unexpected rush of sadness seized me. I didn't realize how close to the surface my longing was. "I'm lonely," I said quietly, as if admitting some terrible weakness. The tears I always hid from everyone, including myself, escaped me. I began to cry, feeling like a lost child—alone, scared, desperately wanting someone to find me and take me home where I'd be safe. And loved. Nonna reached out and I stepped into the hug she offered. She patted my back, quietly offering reassurances.

A wave of self-consciousness hit me as quickly as the sorrow had, and I went flat. The tears stopped and I pulled back.

"It's all right to cry. You don't have to be strong all the time," Nonna said gently.

I dug in my purse for a tissue, wiped my face and blew my nose. "I hate being weepy."

"You know," she said gently, "you have to be careful when you cast a spell . . ."

"Because I might get what I ask for. But what would be wrong with that?" I felt the tears returning.

"You have to be even more careful when you cast a love spell—you have to be ready. And you have to know who's right for you, who's meant for you." She shook her head and studied me intently. "Love can be dangerous. It can break your heart."

"There isn't a particular guy that I want to make fall in love with me, if that's what you mean. I know you never use a spell to control or manipulate someone else." I looked over at the pile of index cards and the pages of meticulous notes I had made. "Can't you help me?"

"Love's a mystery. Most people—even Witches—think of spells as if they were recipes. All they need is the right list of ingredients and the magic words and *presto*—instant gratification!" She picked up the stack of index cards, tapped them briskly together and returned them to their metal box. "You know it's not that simple. A spell has to come from your heart, from your soul, and it has to be uniquely your own, especially a love spell. The only thing that really makes a spell work is your connection to the Divine—that's where the power and the magic come from. And the love."

"But divinity isn't going to wrap its arms around me and hold me, or make love to me, or—" The words tumbled out.

Nonna raised a hand. "You asked me how to cast a love spell, but you're not listening to my answer. Sit down. Now listen with your heart, not with your anxious head. You must begin by finding the quiet place inside; then you must journey to the temple. Where is that?"

I pointed to my heart and Nonna nodded.

"In the temple you must make an offering, and you must call to the God—with all your heart—to come to you. That's where your love spell must begin."

"The God?"

She nodded. "Most people, certainly most women, call the Goddess, usually Aphrodite or Venus, to help them find love. But you need to call your daemon. I promised I'd teach you a way to call him. I'll show you the basic technique—and you'll practice and then I'll leave you to work on your own. When you've reached the center and the energy is flowing through you, I want you to call him from your heart, not your head. When you're done, ground and close the circle."

"I don't have an offering." I said.

"You're the offering. Let's get you started." I followed Nonna to the modest room at the back of the bookstore that we used as a temple. And that is what it became as we used it. The moon shone through the skylight above, the candles added a soft, golden glow, the old Persian rugs resumed their original luster, and the space became beautiful, as did those who worked within it. Nonna lit a stick of sandalwood incense and four white candles, one in each of the four directions. I put two exercise mats on top of the rugs and Nonna placed a red candle at either end of my mat.

"Cast your circle, but do it simply, not a lot of words, and focus on connecting to each of the elements physically. Don't imagine—*feel*. Air is your breath, fire your will, water your blood, earth your body," she instructed me. When I was done, I sat beside her in the center of the circle. We used breathing to quiet our minds; then we grounded and centered, bringing the energy up from the earth and running it through our bodies and out the fontanel at the crown of the head, to fall like a fountain of light back to the earth. When I opened my eyes, Nonna was smiling at me.

"Your head, body and heart must be connected for the energy to flow properly. And especially *you* need to move from your head into your body, and your heart. That's where your true self lives, and that's where your daemon lives. That's where true love is to be found. You can't love until you can give love. You can't give love to another until you can give it to yourself." She handed me the matches and I lit each of the red candles and put them back at the head and foot of my mat.

"You use your head to protect yourself, to maintain control. But to love fully and deeply you have to give up control—and that can be very frightening. You can't experience love until you surrender yourself to it completely. And to do that you have to trust yourself, and your partner. There are no other road maps, no rules."

"But then how do I start?"

"You start by entering openness and space where the energy flows blissfully, naturally and intuitively, *without* thinking. Let's begin."

I rolled my neck and shoulders, stretched my lower back and legs and then sat, comfortably, facing the red candle at the base of the mat.

"Relax the muscles of your entire body, squeezing and releasing each muscle group one at a time, starting with your toes and moving up to the top of your head," Nonna guided me. "Inhale slowly and completely, hold the breath for a count of three. Now exhale."

I felt myself growing still and quiet, coming to center with the basic relaxation technique.

Nonna continued. "You've learned to move energy through your body with grounding and centering, but now you're going to raise, and direct, erotic energies. We're going to arouse the Kundalini."

I recognized the term from yoga. "The sacred fire that rests at the base of the spine."

Nonna nodded. "It's symbolized by twin, spiraling snakes that are actually the two major nerves running up the spine. The energy travels up those nerves, through the body and connects you to the Sacred—in oneself, a lover and the Universe. That energy is shared, exchanged and ultimately directed. We'll begin with the Kegel contractions of the *pubococcygeus* muscle, or PC muscle. It's part of the pelvic floor and stretches between your legs, from your genitals to your anus. It's the muscle you use to stop when you urinate. Now squeeze as if you were stopping yourself from peeing and hold it for a moment."

I squeezed and my eyes flew open. I was startled to immediately feel the rush of energy that shot through my vagina into my stomach.

"You feel the energy moving already? Good! I want you to squeeze and release—not your stomach muscles—just the PC. Squeeze and hold. Do five."

Each time I squeezed I could feel the energy shooting through my vagina and into my stomach. I was starting to feel very warm and a little squirmy.

"Now rest. Good work." I opened my eyes to see her smiling at me. "You're already starting to glow. You'll practice these in groups of five, resting in between, inhaling with each contraction, and then relaxing."

I squeezed and released, rested, squeezed and released. The energy was flowing more easily.

"Do guys do this too?" I asked her jokingly, but her reply was serious. Nonna nodded. "The relaxation part is especially important for a man because he can last much longer if he learns to control and relax the PC. Now I want you to squeeze and hold it for a count of three. Inhale, slowly and deeply, and contract, hold for a count of three, exhale and relax for a count of three."

My muscles felt as if they were releasing a burst of energy that my breath pulled upward through my vagina. I felt aroused and energized as it moved into my stomach where a ball of fire seemed to burn, filling me with an unfamiliar sense of power.

"Can you feel the muscles moving from front to back as you squeeze?" I nodded. "Good. Concentrate on the physical sensations. Use your breathing to move the energy and feel it moving through you."

I inhaled and squeezed, feeling the power spin up my spine and into my heart where it exploded like a flower bursting open with the light of an inner sun. "My heart's pounding and I feel as if all this light is coursing through me," I said softly.

Nonna's voice replied gently. "The most important thing is the rhythm and the energy flow. With practice you'll become skilled at moving it up through your spine, through the chakras, through your organs, and throughout your entire body."

I was familiar with chakras—the seven points of spiritual energy within the body. I opened my eyes and the room seemed filled with light, and Nonna was bathed in a lavender glow. I smiled, a little stunned and flushed.

"Are you all right?"

I nodded happily.

"You'll learn to exchange this energy with a partner—through eyes, breath, touch, intention and intercourse, sacred sex. And to direct it, if you choose, towards the manifestation of a goal—sex magic. You can also love each other as deity, sharing the energy of divine love."

Nonna smiled as I felt another ripple of excitement roll through me.

"So let's practice raising and directing the energy. Close your eyes. With each Kegel contraction I want you to concentrate on the feeling of light and love that is pouring through you. And with each exhalation call the God, say the sacred name of your daemon. You may say 'daemon,' or 'Dionysus,' or whatever comes to you. Say it aloud and clearly. As you do, visualize, *feel* your heart open to receive his love."

"What should I expect?"

"You may feel waves of bliss, a sense of opening, rushes of energy. A pervasive sense of pleasure. Sexuality is the life force, the holy manifestation of Spirit, the power of attraction that holds the web together. This is the force you're unleashing, and harnessing, and it's part of the Mysteries you long for. The rest is up to you to discover. Stay as long as you want, but when you feel the energy beginning to wane, ground, rest, close the circle. I'll be outside." She rose, patted me on the head and left.

I sat, breathing and quieting my racing heart. And then I began. I could feel the luminous energy shooting through me as I squeezed and inhaled. I held the breath for a count of three, feeling the soft, warm light flow through me, dissolving the boundaries of my mind and body, of inner and outer.

"Daemon," I called softly.

Again I squeezed, inhaled, rode the wave of joy and, without thinking, exhaled "Jimmy!" It was louder than my last call and seemed to ripple outward into an ocean of energy that surrounded me, that I was a part of. I squeezed and inhaled and the energy flowed through me in waves of expanding ecstasy. "Dionysus!" And then "Osiris!" And finally "My love!"

I felt my heart open, and a moment later rushes of desire began coursing not just through but *into* my womb, and from there through the rest of me. I sat in a radiant pool of love and contentment. The candles had burned to little castles of dribbled wax as I grounded the last of the energy. I said thanks and closed the circle. I felt like every molecule in my body was dancing.

Nonna was waiting for me, reading. "You need to ground. Eat." She folded her glasses and waved toward the fruit and juice. "You're radiant, *mia figlia*. You know, there's an old Tantric expression that love is the way light feels."

I couldn't believe how good everything tasted. "It was so powerful— at first I was raising the energy, but after I began to call, it was as if . . . my heart, my body opened and energy entered me."

"You were both active and receptive," Nonna nodded. "Good."

"I called Dionysus, and I don't know where it came from but I called Osiris." I suddenly realized what I had done. "Oh no, am I going to have to play the cosmic dating game?"

She laughed. "Plutarch and Herodotus both wrote that Osiris and Dionysus were the same. Each has unique qualities, but their essence is one."

I felt very self-conscious as I remembered whom else I had called to. "I called James Dean."

Nonna chuckled. "Did you really?"

"No, I called my daemon," I said quietly, drawing all the pieces together into one. "Shape-shifting you called it—Jimmy, Dionysus, Osiris, the daemon—they're all one?"

Nonna nodded. "Tonight, you experienced some of the magic of the great love stories of creation. You've got quite a journey ahead. But I will tell you one secret," she continued. "The feelings of bliss you experienced are coming from within you, not just the God you called. You're awaken- ing your natural gifts of love and pleasure."

" 'All acts of love and pleasure are my rituals,' " I quoted softly from the *Charge of the Goddess*, the only piece of contemporary liturgy that Witches have.

Nonna smiled. "Until you feel it in your body, the Divine isn't real; it's just an idea." She cupped my chin in her hand. "If you wish, the path can lead to the union of male and female, God and Goddess, within yourself. The Sacred Marriage. The rest is up to you and your heart. And destiny."

I sat cross-legged on the floor, a small purple candle burning on my simple altar. There was also a sprig of ivy I'd cut from my parents' garden, a small statue of the head of the famous Minoan bull, and a glass of Mavrodaphne of Patros, a sweet Greek desert wine, that I sipped slowly. In my lap was the heavy, old copy of *Bullfinch's Mythology* my mother had read to me when I was a little girl. It lay open to the story of Dionysus and I took careful notes, as if I was preparing a case or contract.

The only God who is also part mortal, Dionysus was born to the God Zeus and a mortal woman, Semele, with whom Zeus was deeply in love. While Semele was pregnant with Dionysus, she begged Zeus to reveal himself in his true form. He had sworn to grant her wish and so, heartbroken, he appeared to her; the fiery radiance of his true being was so great that Semele was instantly reduced to ashes. But Zeus was able to save the baby, whom he placed within an opening in his thigh.

Upon his rebirth, Zeus gave Dionysus to the Nymphs of Nysa to raise and protect him from the jealous wrath of Hera, Zeus's wife. The Nymphs hid him in a remote mountain cave and fed him on honey and milk. They dressed him as a girl and at one point transformed him into a goat to hide him. But Hera sent the Titans, who found him and tore him into seven pieces, which they ate, but for his heart.

Learning what they had done, Zeus was enraged and he destroyed the Titans; they were left as nothing but ashes. It is said that humans arose from their ashes, and thus have within them a divine spark which is Dionysus, for his essence was indestructible. Thus human nature is part mortal, part divine, and blessed with eternal life.

Dionysus was reborn from his heart, and thus he was thrice born. But Hera afflicted him with madness. He roamed the world until cured by his grandmother, Rhea, who also initiated him into the mysteries of women. During his travels, which stretched as far as India to the east and Rome to the west, the God blessed humanity with the gift of winemaking, the love of life, and the ecstasy of the Spirit, and his retinue of followers grew, most of them women known as Maenads or Bacchantes. They formed thyasi (holy bands) dancing wildly to the rhythm of flute and drum, inspired by the God, and were believed to possess great visionary and other powers, including the ability to charm snakes and suckle animals, as well as extraordinary strength. Dionysus accompanied them, often shape-shifting from his form as a beautiful young man into a goat, panther, lion, fawn, or most famous of all, the bull, and he was often called Dionysus, the "bull horned." He was also the vine and the grape itself.

I wanted to know my daemon. Somewhere beneath the seemingly odd and ancient details lay clues to who he was. And, perhaps, how I might find him.

The match splintered in two as I struck it against the narrow flint strip. "Shit." I threw it in the garbage pail. *Okay, take a deep breath. Just relax.* I felt the stiffness in my fingers, my arms, my heart. *Slow down. Now, strike cleanly, just focus on the flame.* A flare of yellow exploded. I exhaled. *Here we go.*

I lit the first candle. It was a large red pillar carved with my name and the word *love.* I lit the charcoal with the candle flame and quickly placed it in a bowl of sand, watched the sparks travel across the disc, smelled the release of sulfurous smoke. I sprinkled the burning charcoal with a spoonful of the incense I'd made—ground sandalwood, patchouli, dried red roses and dried orange peel; a pinch of red pepper to speed up its manifestation; and drops of orris, ambergris and musk oils. It rose in a smoky, fragrant spiral.

I stared at the centerpiece of my spell, the amber-colored contents of a large Pyrex measuring cup. I'd started it hours ago, following the simple but important directions with apprehensive precision. I'd used my lawyer's thoroughness in doing research and I'd read the warnings, but I was aware that I did not, and could not, know all the risks I was taking. Yohimbe bark, when properly prepared, was reputed to effect a profound shift in consciousness and to be highly arousing. And certain indigenous African cultures gave the potion to couples on their wedding night to heighten desire to ecstatic levels.

Although it was legal, it was potentially dangerous. The bark had to be soaked in the right amount of water for precisely the correct amount of time, and its toxins offset by various essential ingredients, without which it could be lethal. I didn't know anyone who had used it. I stirred cautiously, watching the enigmatic clouds swirl and dissolve. *Am I really going to drink it?*

One last thing and I could begin. I opened my journal and pulled out the piece of blue card stock. I stared down at the image—a young woman sat nestled in the arms of a king as they rode a beautiful, long-maned, great-hooved horse through a magical wood. The king's face was gaunt yet handsome, with high cheekbones, and framed by long hair that fell to his shoulders. He wore a simple crown, carried a long sword and a spirit shield with a magical countenance.

I held the drawing to my heart. Somewhere, east of the sun and west of the moon, there was a king searching for me, and all I wanted was to ride securely within his strong arms as we journeyed through the enchanted forest of life. Tonight, I would call to him, and knowing that we were connected by love, somehow he would hear and he would find me.

I placed the picture beside the candle. It was almost time. I undressed and quickly cast my circle. "I call to my love with the powers of eloquent air," I said, creating a circle with the musky incense. "I call to my love with the powers of passionate fire." I encircled the altar with the burning red candle. "I call to my love with the powers of loving water," I called out, sprinkling herbed droplets in an infinite circle of love. "I call to my love with the powers of fertile earth." I cast a final circle sprinkling seeds, corn and salt.

I sat before my altar, grounded, centered, and began to feel my heart and mind open as I breathed deeply. I called to Goddesses of love and fertility, to Freya, Goddess of my Nordic ancestors, and to Hathor, Isis and Yemaya—Goddesses of the land from where my herb of transformation had come. I called to Aphrodite and to Venus. I lifted the potion, holding it before the candle, watching the flame glowing within the enchantment-infused waters. I poured the first portion into my chalice, lifted it to my lips and drank. It was bitter, but I drank it all.

I lay down on the couch. I breathed slowly and deeply, and then began to squeeze and release groups of muscles, moving slowly through my body from my toes to my head, relaxing. I continued to breathe deeply, moving into a light meditational state. *What's going to happen?* I waited anxiously. I relaxed. I worried. I focused on my breathing. And then an insinuating lethargy began to creep along my limbs. Time seemed to distend, slowing to an infinitesimal pace. But my mind began to race. *Maybe I didn't drink enough.* My limbs were leaden as I rose to pour and drink another dose.

I dropped back onto the bed. The room filled with glowing amber light, clouds swirling and dissolving within themselves, within me. Waves of agitated need began to surge through me; I stirred listlessly, but lassitude pinned me to the couch. I closed my eyes against the room's growing brightness, felt my heart pounding as if it would explode.

You overshot yourself this time, kid. Simple sex magic was just not enough, no, first time out you had to add aphrodisiacal hallucinogens.

A tidal surge of desire swept over me but I could barely move, barely breathe. And then, from far beneath any expectation, something rose from unconscious depths, breaking through the membrane of my inhibitions. I felt as if some ancient sea dragon was squeezing me in its tightening coils. My simple intent of casting a love spell disappeared, dragged beneath the dark surface of longing. I gasped for breath, afraid of drowning. My chest compressed and I struggled, as Nonna's warning came back to me, *Love is dangerous. It can break your heart.*

The pressure tightened and I gasped raggedly, feeling my heart skip beats. I tried not to panic. *Don't struggle to escape.* The strain released slightly and I exhaled. *Don't be afraid, stop trying to control it. Just let go and feel.* I stopped resisting, focused on my breathing and tried to relax each breath. Gradually the compression in my chest eased and slowly I gave myself to the pulsing. *Work with the energy.* I inhaled slowly, focusing my attention on the restless blaze that rippled through me like twisting snakes, like fire-breathing dragons.

I squeezed the muscles I had been training, and released them, squeezed and released, each pulsation deepening and moving the Neptunian arousal from between my legs into my belly. My hands moved slowly along phosphorescent skin, dragon and princess now one. Coils unfurled around my bound body; I moved as if underwater, feeling the soft curve of my breast against the palm of my hand, and the palm of my hand against the smooth skin of my breast. *I am the source.*

My fingertip made small, swirling circles around one nipple and I felt it rise, reaching out for a longer caress by another's hand as my hand slid down my stomach and into the moist triangle between my parted thighs. I breathed slowly and easily now, felt the sinuous oscillations as my fingers swam to the sea change. In my other hand, I held the little drawing to my heart.

Come to me, please come to me, I whispered.

The hand between my legs was no longer mine. It was his fingertips that moved with perfect certainty, slowly stroking me to quickened throbbing. I ached, longing to feel his invisible mouth materialize against mine, to have his body submerge in mine. My longing ignited and each breath pulled the fire from between my legs. My heartbeat pushed the heat through my body.

I stared at the picture, whispering over and over until the luster of starry arousal blazed uncontrollably and I abandoned myself to the imploding nova and the spinning of sensation and the words that whirled around me. *Come to me!*

The spell was cast.

I floated in the tremoring reverberation. The light faded, the stars receded and I saw him, seated quietly upon his horse, emerging from the dark forest below me. The gentle sound of hooves upon the earth echoed my slowing heartbeat. I rode my breath back into my body, into my apartment, into the world that I had, for a time, left.

The candle was flickering in a small red pool of wax. "Thank you," I whispered as I blew it out. I wrapped myself in a blanket and fell into dreamless sleep, oblivious to the golden thread that was spinning from the center of my heart, unaware of the Cimmerian fiber winding out of a dark well of longing. Entwined and inevitable, it slid into an ancient labyrinth.

.4.

Desire

We trifle when we assign limits to our desires,
since Nature hath set none.

—CHISTIAN NESTELL BOVEE

I awoke dazed, in a blur of exhaustion and exhilaration, and immediately looked for evidence of last night's visions. There was no tangible proof that anything had changed—no hoofprints in the rug, no token or talisman left behind by a suitor from between the worlds. The only signs of the night's magic were the empty measuring cup and a hardened puddle of red wax on the old Chinese rug. But something had disappeared. A desperate search finally produced the drawing from beneath the couch. I snatched it up and stared at it, the forest, horse and romantic riders exactly as they had been the night before. Carefully, I placed it on my altar.

Could I conjure him into my life? Even though Nonna's warning was still ringing in my ears—that love was dangerous—a thrill rushed through me. *Why couldn't I?*

But what do I do now? I wondered, and then realized that I hadn't opened the circle, but instead had slept within it. Perhaps that accounted for my lingering disorientation. I quickly thanked each of the four directions and the Goddesses I had invoked.

I tried not to think about the spell as I washed the measuring cup and chalice and put them away; I cleaned the melted wax with a paper bag and a hot iron, and returned the blanket to my bed. I showered and dressed with a sudden rush of anticipation. I checked my date book—I'd completely forgotten the meeting I was supposed to attend. I grabbed my jacket and purse and emerged from my building into the sharply angled autumn sunlight. We were entering the dream-time, the season of death and desire.

All new life starts with a dream, a seed planted deep within the womb of darkness, an invisible blueprint distilled from the past that determines the future. Last night I planted a seed; would my dream come true? What if it didn't? *Don't think about it,* I reminded myself sternly. *Doubt kills a spell. Doubt kills love.*

I walked to the corner trying not to stare at every man who passed. *It can't be the blond with the blue blazer who looks like he's on his way to Wall Street.* He didn't notice me. *It's certainly not Mr. Kim watering his vegetable stand, and it can't be that overweight guy with the bulldog pulling him across Broadway. But what about that cute rock-and-roll-looking guy?* He got on the bus and disappeared. *I'm going to drive myself crazy if I keep doing this. Try not to think about it. Just let the spell work—these things take time.* I hailed a cab.

I stared out the window at the rainy, cold day. Everything was dying and my hopeful certainty was disappearing along with the leaves on the trees. It had been more than a month since I'd cast my love spell and I couldn't help wondering whether it had all been just a folly.

I needed perspective, a mirror, a way of seeing within and into the future. I needed guidance. I needed to do some divination. Before I'd begun practicing Wicca, I'd had no interest in any type of fortune-telling. While I was in law school, a "gypsy" had taken up residence in a shoe box–sized storefront in the building next to mine and for ten dollars she would read my palm, or my tarot cards, and for a hundred dollars she'd take the curse off my unlucky money. She confirmed my notion that fortune-telling was the kind of thing superstitious, uneducated people engage in because they are fearful and don't feel they have control over their lives. Or, at best, it was a parlor game, an amusement on a Saturday night date, after a movie and dinner at a good restaurant.

But, like my misperception of Witches, my misunderstanding was based on negative stereotypes. Working with my circle, I'd learned that divination was an ancient and sacred art, practiced by virtually every culture in every age: the Italian *tarrochi* or tarot; Scandinavian runes; Chinese *I-Ching;* African "bones"; the ancient Greek *cledon;* astrology; interpretation of signs, dreams; the altered state of a shaman, Witch or priest/ess; or my favorite, the library angel—simply letting a book fall open to a passage of meaning. Even fundamentalist preachers let the Bible fall randomly open to the "words of God."

And that's what divination is. I had swiftly discovered that these tools did more than just allow a glimpse into the morrow. The word *divination* comes from the Latin *divi,* which means deity. It is an oracle—literally the mouth of the Divine, the voice of the Sacred. Divination is a means by which anyone can engage in dialogue with divinity, to ask for and receive divine guidance. It was also a mirror in which I could see myself more clearly, and better understand my hopes and fears, conflicts and motivations. It was the means by which the powerful forces and patterns at play in my unconscious, both utterly human and profoundly holy, that might otherwise remain hidden or misunderstood, could be brought to the surface of my awareness.

How does it work? I wasn't sure, but it seemed to me that the event, my emotional response and the various divinatory symbols were all connected in the quantum dimension. And if the Divine is the creative force animating the Universe—the innate energy of that field—it can certainly be the force animating the movement of symbols to send sacred messages. Though I didn't know all the hidden mechanics, I knew that the answers were invariably wise and helpful. Whatever method I chose, I was consulting an oracle, the voice by which deity makes known its will and its wisdom. And I was experiencing a Universe that was alive, interactive and aware of my presence, my deepest soul and truest self.

When you consult an oracle, you must ask the right question to get the right answer. I took out my tarot deck, held it to my heart and silently honored it as an oracle. I asked if it would guide me to insight and to the greatest good for all. And then I asked my question: *Will my spell bring me love?*

I began shuffling the oversized cards slowly, clearing my mind and open-ing my heart. *Now!*

I stopped shuffling. The card practically jumped into my hands—two of cups. Marriage. A surge of excitement hit me.

Can you give me a sign of who he is? I drew another card, turned it over slowly and marveled at the image—the king of swords, a mature man, with long hair, his arms folded in front of his chest, a cape blowing in a strong wind, a long sword and shield by his side, that reminded me of my spell. It meant he would be an air sign—Libra, Gemini or Aquarius, a man older than I, who made his living with words, communication, ideas or music.

Again I closed my eyes, held the cards to my heart and, silently, said thank you. As I started to put the deck away, three cards fell to the floor. I picked them up, one dropping again as if it had burned my fingers. It fell, picture side up. A shrouded figure held a banner with a white rose. The word *Death* unnerved while the image reassured me. I knew that it was to be taken symbolically, not literally, that it meant a transformation from old to new. But it was still a haunting image.

Cautiously, I turned the first of the other cards over—the eight of cups. A figure stood beneath a waning moon and a sky filled with dark clouds and flying geese. He, or she, had turned her back on eight cups, walking away from the forms of love that had been experienced. Before her was the sea, symbol of infinite love that cannot be contained in the few small cups. The final card was the king of cups—a handsome, mature man, happy and content, sitting on a throne made of a huge scallop shell, hold-ing a cup in his hands. It foretold a man with a deeply loving nature whose feelings were also important to his work; and he was a water sign—a Can-cer, Scorpio or Pisces.

I had an answer, but I also had more questions. I sighed, returning the cards to the deck and the deck to its gold silk bag. I needed to get my mind on something else. Saturday was the busiest day at the Magickal Cauldron and there was bound to be someone from circle helping out. When I arrived, I found a line of people waiting at the Oil Office for spells and potions. A young gay man wanted a potion to heal a broken heart; a middle-aged woman wanted one to help her conceive a child; and a stun-ning redhead who could have stopped traffic with a glance wanted a spell to rekindle her husband's lagging passion.

Hundreds of people came into the store every week looking for love spells. Because it was a system of practice so ancient, instinctual and sensible, I was sure there was a Witch in everyone. And at some intuitive level, deep down inside, people wished or prayed, visualized or sought out a spell because everyone knows that when you fall in love, the world is full of magic. From the *Song of Solomon* to Shakespeare's sonnets, *Cosmo* magazine to psychological studies, love casts an eternal spell—nothing is more magical than love. Regardless of one's religion or the lack of it, magic and love have always been intertwined, and whether it's the love potion of Tristan and Isolde or the pop tune "Love Potion #9," like Nonna said, everyone wants a love spell that works.

I was listening with one ear while I methodically thumbed through the formularies and index cards, carefully writing down love potions. If something didn't happen soon, I was going to try again. Naomi was assisting Nonna—she was quickly becoming our coven's Green Witch, skilled in herbs and plants and the potions that could be created from them. She was particularly interested in their healing gifts.

"Can you cast a love spell?" a small voice asked. I looked up to see a mouse of a girl with a pleasant face and bluntly cut brown hair. "I was told to come here, that you could help me, I mean, I think I need help . . ." She wore her confusion like a cloak of invisibility, and a large woman standing behind the young woman started talking over her as if she weren't there.

Nonna firmly addressed the line cutter: "Please be patient, we'll get to everyone in their turn." She smiled and stepped out from behind the counter, steering the mouse a few feet away to the little table where tarot readings were done. "Tell me your name."

"Stephanie."

"Yes, Stephanie, I can cast a love spell. But if the love spell is for you, you have to cast it yourself."

"But I don't know how," Stephanie said, a gray wisp of powerless despair floating up toward the ceiling. "It's just that I don't know what else to do. I'm so in love with him, and he doesn't know I'm alive. I don't think I can live another day without him. Please, can't you help me make him fall in love with me?" The words rushed out with sudden fervor and she straightened from her defeated slouch. I watched intently, startled to find myself thinking how much she looked like me.

"No, I can't, and neither can you. A spell can't manipulate or control another person. It can only affect you. But you can cast a love spell that will help you find the love that's right for you."

"But *he's* right for me. I know it. I just need him to know it." Stephanie began to evaporate into a cloud of smoky sorrow.

"Has it occurred to you that if he doesn't know, it's because he's not the right one for you?" Nonna spoke gently but firmly. Stephanie was not hearing what she wanted.

"He's so good-looking, and he's talented, and successful—he guest conducts for the American Philharmonic." She shrank into her uncertainty. "I'm nobody."

Nonna tried again: "You have to love yourself before someone else can love you." Taking Stephanie's left hand, she looked into the young woman's misty eyes. I knew the power flowing from Nonna; I'd felt that love before and knew that it could make magic.

"You have too much passion to be nobody. You must begin your love spell"—with Nonna's words Stephanie the mouse looked suddenly hopeful—"by feeling good about yourself. It's not about what you look like on the outside. Believe me, I've seen plenty of beautiful women whose husbands were drawn to them only for their looks—and love can't grow from such shallow soil." Nonna turned her head slightly to the beautiful redhead whose eyes had lost their light. "The greatest aphrodisiac in the world is a woman's self-esteem. When you have confidence in yourself, you'll shine and the man who is meant for you will be drawn to you like a moth to a flame. You'll probably have more men than you'll know what to do with. Now, tell me something you like about yourself."

Stephanie struggled to answer. "I do well in school. I'm going to Juilliard, for the violin." She sighed. "That's where he teaches."

"Is there anything more beautiful than music?" Nonna asked.

I could see a small light starting to shine in the young woman's eyes as she nodded. "I'm happiest when I'm playing. I love what I do." She'd said the magic word.

"All right, now I can give you a spell for love," Nonna said. "But it is not a spell to make this man fall in love with you, do you understand? If you try to use it that way, it won't work. But if you do what I tell you, love will find you."

Stephanie's smile was luminous. "Thank you so much."

"But you must follow my instructions very carefully." I watched as Nonna began to open one herb jar, then another. "First, when the moon is waning—you know what that means? After the moon is full and before it's dark."

Stephanie nodded.

"You must banish your negative thoughts about yourself. You're going to wash them away—every day for two weeks I want you to take a purification bath in sea salt and this mixture of lavender, sage and peppermint. Then when the moon is waxing—do you know what that is?"

"Is it between the new moon and the full moon?" Stephanie offered cautiously.

"Yes, very good. You *are* smart. So when the moon is waxing, every day until the moon is full you stand in front of a mirror, look at yourself, really look into your eyes, and I want you to smile at yourself. And then I want you to repeat this spell; if you prefer you can think of it the way psychologists do, as an affirmation, or a visualization, or if you practice another religion, it's a prayer. All the same thing—just do it. You smile at yourself, see that light in your eyes and you repeat three times:

In my eyes I see the fire
That will light true love's desire
As I shine you'll come to me
And as I will, so mote it be.

"So mote it be, that's our way of saying amen. So this is your mantra of true love. Write it down, so you don't forget it." Nonna handed Stephanie a pink index card and a pen. "It would be good for you to repeat it to yourself—do it as often as you like, during the day, on your way to school, after you're done practicing—that's the best time, before you go to bed. But once a day at least, and always when you look at yourself in the mirror. Also, once a day, after you recite your spell, you will light a red candle on which you carve your name and the words 'true love.' Once the candle's lit, while it burns, I want you to play your favorite piece of violin music. Play in front of the mirror. Something that makes you feel good, not sad. And I want you to look at yourself and smile. You can blow the candle out when you're done playing. When you do, make a wish for your true love to find you."

Stephanie nodded and suddenly hugged Nonna, who patted her gently on the back. "One last thing—we call it acting in accord. A spell won't work unless you act in a way that enables it to manifest. So you, young lady, every day you are to tell yourself that you are worthy of love, and you must remind yourself that you love to play the violin, and you play beautifully. Only a beautiful soul can play beautiful music. All right? Do you promise me?"

"Yes, oh yes!"

"Good. Remember, if a Witch gives her word, she must keep it."

"Oh, I'm not a Witch . . ."

"There's a Witch in every woman." I smiled as Nonna replied, looking at Stephanie over the top of her glasses. "And if you give your word to a Witch, it must be kept."

"Thank you so much."

"I was just your mirror, I showed you what was already there. Now, let's get you a big fat candle." Nonna took Stephanie by the hand and walked her down the aisle.

Naomi looked over at me. "Strangest thing, I thought she looked so much like I did a few years ago."

"I thought she looked like me, like a younger sister," I said, surprised.

We shook our heads and laughed. I went back to my research.

"What are you up to?" An hour later, Nonna stood over me. I rose and she held me at arm's length, staring into my eyes. Everything in me wanted to tell her, but I remained silent. "You cast a love spell didn't you, *mia figlia?*"

Of course she knew, she always did. "I didn't want to worry you. I just couldn't stand it anymore. I was tired of waiting for love to find me." I looked at the line that had gotten even longer. "Why shouldn't I turn to magic? Who wouldn't if they could?"

"So, you decided to take matters into your own hands." She sighed and shook her head. "Well, he'll find you now."

"I feel like a piece of my soul is missing." Sadness tugged at me. "I just couldn't bear the loneliness any longer."

"It will be as it's meant to be." She patted my cheek and turned away. A pang of confusion hit me, but I brushed it away as I heard Maia calling me. A dark haired, Sicilian firecracker with the bustling warmth of a mother hen, Maia was the cofounder of my women's circle and one of the High Priestesses who had initiated me. She and her partner Bellona were also my teachers in the early phase of my studies.

She was staring up the book aisle. "There's someone I want you to meet." She nodded toward a man who was standing with his back to me. He was tall, with long, blond hair that fell to his shoulders. "That's him," she said.

He turned and I saw his profile—the image from my spell had come to life.

Astonishment exploded inside my chest. I blinked, felt my heart jump, my breathing get shallow as he turned. I was staring into the clear, blue eyes of the most handsome man I had ever seen. A Roman candle flew between us, a swiftly arcing double-pointed arrow that punctured all the invisible barriers keeping the world at bay. I wasn't strong enough to resist. I didn't want to. He smiled—*had he felt it also?*

He was tall and broad-chested, with the kind of face you would vote for—senatorial and chiseled, with high cheekbones, narrow nose and strong jawline. But his long hair and offhanded flannel shirt spoke of other politics and values more seductive than his patrician features. Maia was already smiling and calling him over as I struggled to recover my sovereignty. The modest confidence with which he moved pressed against my opened psyche. He bent to hug Maia, pulled back and smiled at me. My pulse was racing, but calm strength radiated from him. I felt an instinctual conviction that he would fulfill all the ancient and unspoken promises that a woman longs for from a man. I was tumbling head over heels as the earth opened beneath my feet.

"I'm so glad you came! I've been wanting you two to meet," Maia purred happily. "Derek this is Aradia . . . er, Phyllis. Phyllis, Derek."

"Nice to meet you. Maia's told me quite a bit about you." His eyes were smiling as his hand wrapped warmly around mine. "Cold hands, warm heart," he remarked, rubbing my chilled hand between his for just a moment more.

A ripple of pleasure swept through me and I blushed. Maia was beaming. "I'll just leave you two to get to know each other. I think the temple's empty," she hinted broadly.

I saw Nonna observing it all, quietly, from afar. I felt awkward and shy as he held the door open for me, but my senses were also sharpening. The candlelit room seemed brighter, the smell of lingering incense pungent, the laughter and chatter from the store more euphoric. And I was keenly aware of exactly how close he was to me. We settled into the old velvet theatrical seats that ringed the temple.

"Aradia's an interesting name. So who are you, Aradia or Phyllis?" He smiled and my eyes went to the dimples I'd somehow missed.

"Aradia's my Craft name—it's rather like the name that Native Americans receive from their vision quest. It describes who you are and it's also like a spiritual role model, a guide you follow. Some people use them because they don't want to be known publicly, but actually I prefer using my given name. I am who I am."

"Well, nice to meet both of you." His smile broadened as he put out his left hand to shake again. He took my hand in his and I was swept away in rushing rapids. But despite the turmoil, our conversation felt easy.

"So who's Aradia?"

"She was an Italian, female version of Robin Hood. There's a whole mythology around her, but she may have been a real person. Apparently, she lived in the early 1300s and practiced and taught the Old Religion. And she was a leader in the rebellion by the serfs against the nobility who were converting to Catholicism. Supposedly she was captured, escaped and disappeared."

"Is that what you do? Lead the serfs in rebellion?"

I laughed at his teasing, a thrill shooting through me as his eyes dropped to my lips. "Well, I come from a family of union organizers and activists. And I started my career fighting organized crime in trade unions. Now I'm just struggling to make a living, but I try to keep my hand in. I'm on the board of the foundation I used to work for."

He nodded. "Interesting."

"What about you?"

"I'm working as a surveyor these days. It pays the bills. Gave up trying to support myself with music."

"Really, music? What instrument?"

"Sax. I had a nice little quintet. Hard to make a living, did time in one of those wedding–bar mitzvah–anniversary bands. Wasn't for me."

"What kind of music with your quintet?"

He looked pleased by the question and intrigued by me. "Do you know a lot about jazz?"

"Not a whole lot. I've always liked Bird and John Coltrane. I'm a little less familiar with Lester Young."

He looked surprised with my answer and launched into an explanation of his style and his influences, rebellions and innovations. The more he talked, the deeper down the rabbit hole I fell. Were women who dated doctors turned on when they talked about surgery? Or women who married stockbrokers—did the discussion of the day's trading make them want to jump into bed?

"I'd love to hear you play sometime." I slid a sidelong glance at him.

"I don't play much anymore. It's sort of behind me." A quick cloud covered his eyes. "But you never know."

We were inches from one another, so close I could see the fine hairs on his arm, the small razor nick above his lip, the pulse at the base of his throat.

"Want something to drink?" he asked suddenly.

I nodded. I wanted to kiss him. I looked at his hands and wondered what they would feel like against my skin. I felt him get up, watched him walk away, and wondered how he would move against me, inside of me. From the moment we had seen each other, we had entered a liminal space, and as he returned, the heartbeats of a thousand upsurging doves exploded in place of mine.

He handed me two cans of soda and reached behind the row of seats; pillows began flying out at me. We spread them out on the floor and he took my hand, pulling me down beside him.

Close the door, lock it, kiss me, touch me, prove to me that you're real, that magic is real. "How do you know Maia?" I tried to wrestle my eagerness under control.

"I've got a couple of close friends who are Wiccan; they introduced us. I'm still very into the Episcopal Church I was raised in, but I guess I've always been curious about alternative spiritualities. Jesus is very important in my spirituality, I consider him an avatar, but there are things missing from the Christian notion of God—like a sense of humor, sexuality, partnership with the feminine. There's no Goddess, no sense of the sacredness of the land. One of the things I like about Wicca is that the Divine is in all of us, not just Jesus. Actually, Jesus said it in the Gnostic Gospels: 'All that I am you can be too, and more.' "

A man who shared my perspective, even though he wasn't Wiccan! The incandescent bubble forming around us glistened as I studied his face. He spoke without pretense or affectation. His voice was rich and warm, with an almost musical intonation and a clarity and inflection that was reassuring, and almost hypnotic. I could see him nobly arguing on the floor of Congress like Jimmy Stewart in *Mr. Smith Goes to Washington*. I felt myself falling further into the mythic crevice that had opened when I first saw him.

"So where are you from originally?" I asked, wanting to know everything about him. And wanting him to know everything about me. I tried to slow my breathing, to calm the little rushes of excitement that kept firing through me. Especially when he looked at me. Especially when he smiled at me. I wanted to pinch myself to be sure that he was real, that my spell had manifested. I squeezed the skin of my wrist sharply between my thumb and forefinger. *Ouch!* He was still sitting beside me. It was real.

"Weston, Connecticut. My parents are still there; we're somewhat estranged. I studied music at Oberlin, did some traveling. If I settled down, I'd like to do it somewhere near the Delaware Water Gap."

"The Gap! That's one of my favorite places. I've had a few epiphanies out there." I could feel myself blush as he studied me.

"Have you camped?"

I nodded, remembering the first night I'd camped by myself. I'd gone down to watch the full moon in the black, snaking river. On the way back, disoriented in the dark, I'd stumbled into a gully filled with thousands of dancing fireflies. I felt like I was standing in a star-filled heaven as they flashed in endless unique rhythms, each seeking the one in all the world who pulsed to the same cadence. "There's an energy you can feel as soon as you enter the area."

He nodded. "It's the only place I know on the eastern seaboard where the population is dwindling. The land's coming back to itself, regaining its wilderness powers. You can feel it, you can smell it—the air's so clean. And you can see it, taste it in the food that's grown there. When the land's healthy, people are healthy."

"When the body's healthy, the spirit's healthy. The body knows—we just don't listen to it, just like we don't listen to the earth when she's teaching us." I knew what my body was telling me now. There was a quiet tap on the temple door and Naomi stuck her head in.

"Hate to disturb you two, but there's a yoga class that needs the space in a few." She winked at me.

We rose and put the pillows away. The busy shop was a shock and I realized how far into our own world we had traveled. I watched the easy way Derek joked with Maia, and noticed Nonna introduce herself to him. I wanted her to approve. I went to gather up my things from the office.

"He seems very nice, very genuine," Nonna said quietly. "All right, *mia figlia*, the journey begins." She looked into some unspoken future as she sighed and squeezed my hand. "You must go where your heart leads." An in-rushing impression of Nonna standing with me at a crossroads of uncertainty and sorrow flashed through me. I swiftly pushed the feeling down and away, gave her a quick hug and emerged from the office. A glance up the empty book aisle and my heart dropped. And then I heard his voice from the other side. *Calm down*, I told myself firmly. I tried to look casual as I walked up the aisle.

"Which way are you going?" Derek asked.

"Uptown," I replied as we walked toward the door.

"Ah, I'm on the Lower East Side."

Derek held the front door open. I smiled and slid past, brushing against him just slightly. The door banged shut behind us and we stood in a pool of golden light on the windy sidewalk.

He looked down at me and his energy followed his gaze. "It was really great meeting you. I hope I'll see you again." He took my hand as he spoke, rubbing it quickly between his. "Cold hands."

I smiled up at him. "Warm heart." A cab pulled up beside us and Derek opened the door for me.

"See you soon," he said as he closed the door.

"Eighty-sixth and Riverside." I settled back into the overheated cab, believing utterly in magic.

I sat up, tangled in the bedcovers. *My spell had worked!* I scrambled out of bed; the cold floor under my bare feet, the chill as I ran for my robe, the splash of water on my face insisted on alertness, but I moved as if still in a dream, a dream that had come true. I pulled open the blinds—but the light didn't dispel the sense of magic. *He's real, he's found me!* His smile, his steady gaze, his warm hands returned. And his magic words: *I'll see you soon.*

I threw open the window and a cool breeze flew in over the rising radiator heat. I leaned out, feeling the strange extremes of heat and cold simultaneously. I wanted to shout to the rooftops and the pigeons and the indifferent urban dwellers below me. *My spell worked!*

I danced around the room percolating with some unfamiliar internal potion. The world was completely different—it was a world where magic *was* real and anything could happen. I'd worked magic before—and whenever a spell had manifested I'd felt amazed and exultant. I never took the working of magic, or a prayer, or visualization for granted. It always seemed like a miracle. But this magic was the most extraordinary I'd ever experienced and I was intoxicated.

I didn't know what to do with myself. I wanted to see him, wanted to talk to him, to hear his voice, to walk around the city with him and discover how perfect buying the newspaper or sitting with coffee could be just because we were alive—together. I wanted so much more. I wanted to kiss him, to feel his arms around me, his body against mine, *in* mine. *Slow down. Take a deep breath.* I picked up the phone and dialed Gillian—she was in a meeting. I tried Naomi—no answer. Maia was busy with a reading. The rest of the world went on as if nothing had happened, as if magic wasn't afoot and the Universe wasn't alive and conspiring in the conjuration of love. People were sleepwalking while the magic of love unfolded all around us. *If it can happen to me, it can happen to anyone!* Open your heart to the Universe and magic happens, miracles manifest, prayers are answered, dreams really do come true.

The phone rang—the concierge had a FedEx package for me. I floated downstairs and opened it, all the while thinking about Derek. I felt the thrill of the nightingale that sang in the parking lot outside my window in the middle of the night—heart-stoppingly perfect because the impossible was happening. But it was daylight and I needed to work. The music played inside me as I picked up a file and tried to settle myself into the responsibilities of daily life.

"*Sorry I'm late.* What's the matter with you, girl? You look like someone shot your dog," Naomi slapped me on the back and slid into the other side of the booth.

"It's been two weeks and he hasn't called."

"Just coffee. I'm not hungry." Naomi looked up at the waitress and smiled. "Wait. I'll have a hamburger, rare but dead. And some onion rings. Instead of coffee, make it a chocolate shake, will ya? Thanks." Naomi gave her another smile and handed the plastic-covered menu into the waitress's well-manicured hands, then leaned around to check out her butt as she walked away.

"I thought you weren't hungry."

"I'm always hungry. So what's the deal? I thought you said he got your number from Maia."

"She told me he asked for it. So why doesn't he call?"

Naomi shrugged. "He seemed like a pretty decent guy. I don't know, you want me to explain men to you? Call Gillian."

"Gilly said to be patient. But I feel like I'm going to jump out of my skin. I cast a spell, it comes true—I mean that's amazing! And then he just disappears?"

"I cast a spell and it blew my mind when Marcia appeared, and in circle too."

"I didn't know that! I can't think of anything else—did that happen to you?"

Naomi nodded. "And it was like we'd known each other forever."

"Do you think that's how you know? That feeling that you've been together before?"

"Well, it's sure one way. You could always call him."

I shook my head. "If he wanted to talk to me, he'd call. I'm not going to chase after him. It was almost easier before I knew he existed—now I have to come to terms with a spell that came true and then evaporated." I sighed and pushed my coffee cup away. "I feel like I'm eating ashes."

"Well, you know magic doesn't always work. And love spells can be tricky. Work. It'll take your mind off him."

"I am. It isn't helping, but not working's worse."

Naomi tried to distract me, but after a while I had to go. "I've gotta run. Got an appointment with a potential client, guy's been offered a deal for a graphic novel. Thanks for meeting me." I slapped some money on the table and headed out. *Why doesn't he call?* The crashing sound of the door slamming behind me echoed in my emptiness.

Four weeks had passed since we'd met and still he hadn't called. After the first week, I was filled with anxiousness. After the second week, I was distracted and afflicted with flashes of despair. After the third week, I was consumed with doubt about the attraction I thought we'd both felt. And now I doubted the spell, and whether magic existed or was just a childish yearning for the impossible. I was beginning to doubt what was real and what wasn't, and my ability to judge.

Nonna had agreed to spend the afternoon with me at the Metropolitan Museum of Art and I was hoping she'd help me. The day was so beautiful we decided to sit in Central Park, which surrounds most of the museum.

"Nonna, he still hasn't called. I don't know what's going on." I didn't have to tell her how I felt; she knew.

"Well, I don't think you'll listen if I tell you to be patient. How old are you now?" she asked me.

"Almost twenty-eight."

She nodded. "Saturn return."

"What's that?"

"When women your age suddenly feel as if they will die if they don't fall in love. There's another Saturn return in your early fifties, but love is different then because you're different—wiser. Now you'll be reckless, even if I tell you to be careful—the influence of your childhood, your father, is very powerful at this age."

I sighed and squirmed like a kid being lectured.

"True love can take a lifetime to materialize. So, are you ready to show me your statue?" She rose from the park bench, and I knew she had nothing else to say on the subject, which was worse than feeling lectured to. She wrapped her arm through mine and we headed up the grand staircase and into the museum.

We paid our admission, folded the little purple metal buttons onto our clothes and entered the Egyptian section, the fastest route to *The Libyan Sibyl.* I forgot my worries as we strolled slowly, my attention caught by an ancient statue of the Goddess Cybele, reinterpreted as the Goddess Isis. I wanted to feel the cool weight of the curving alabaster, to place her on my altar and ring her with lotuses, dates and pomegranates.

"Nonna, what do you think desire is?"

She chuckled, once again sliding her arm through mine as we walked slowly around the Temple of Dendur, miraculously transported from Egypt to a vast atrium at the museum. This was how I walked with my mother, a sacrifice of speed that always rewarded me with indelible love. She nodded in the direction of the young couple seated beside the marble moat a few yards away. "Desire? It's the way they feel when they touch each other. It's *why* they touch each other. Let's sit, my feet are starting to hurt."

We settled on a marble bench by the leaning glass wall, an imposing row of leonine Sekhmet statues to our left.

"You mean you know it when you feel it."

"Yes, although people often confuse need for desire. It's sexual attraction, and it's so much more. It's the force that holds the Universe together, that makes it all dance. Desire is the life force. It's our creativity."

"But we live in a world that tells us desire is sinful," I offered, "that the body is our downfall. Either the earthly plane is an illusion, or it's fallen from grace, or it's just matter devoid of divinity."

"Most religions teach that we have to deny our desires in order to lead a spiritual life. It's puritanical, barren and deadly. And it's upside down. Suppress Eros, the life force, you end up *separated* from the Sacred. And deeply wounded. Desire is indispensable to life, to reality," Nonna continued. "When religions seek to repress it—that's also a desire, isn't it? It's a desire not to feel desire. And they desire to go to heaven, to please their God, to live without giving in to the body. It's the human condition to experience desire. It's impossible to truly follow a spiritual path *without* desire. And at the mystical core of most religious traditions you'll find that the language is almost always a language of love and passion."

"But history's never a love story."

Nonna laughed. "Well, it should be." She stood up and we walked around the ancient temple, studying the carved depictions of Hathor, Goddess of fertility.

"I guess the modern version is Freud—he said we have to sublimate our passions to create civilization," I recalled from a college Psych course.

"Brilliant man, except for that penis envy nonsense."

"Aside from when you're waiting on some endless line for the bathroom," I grinned.

Nonna shook her head and chuckled. "But no one's got all the answers. There'd be no civilization without passion." We stood beneath the carefully carved stone entrance to the temple. "Look where we are, surrounded by the greatest art of every civilization. Art can't be created without passion. Civilization comes from the harnessing and directing of passion. Suppress it and you end up with violence. Now, you have something to show me, don't you?"

I nodded and pushed open the heavy glass doors and we left the Egyptian collection behind, walking quickly through a hall filled with early American art and furniture. I pushed open another set of doors and we stepped out into a second atrium, home of *The Libyan Sibyl.* Nonna was the first person I'd brought here and a shiver of excitement shot through me as we approached her. She was waiting for us, serenely facing the autumnal park beyond the glass wall. I watched my two teachers as Nonna walked up to study her, goose bumps shooting across my skin.

"So," said Nonna, turning to me, "what *is* desire?"

My mind was empty.

"Well, tell me about what arouses your desire."

I stared at the Sibyl and a blush of self-consciousness rose and then passed. "Bruce Springsteen singing 'Fire.' Or better still, 'Thunder Road.'"

"You'll have to play those for me sometime. What else?"

"Well, I still get a rush whenever I see James Dean."

Nonna laughed. "So my darling, Mr. Dean, Mr. Springsteen, and what about Jim Morrison? Very potent archetypal Dionysian energy. You know his wife was a very brilliant Witch. And what else?"

The memory of Derek immediately released a rolling wave of heat in the center of my stomach. "That moment when you look at someone you're attracted to and your heart races and your breath catches and all you want to do is kiss. When he looks at you, *really* looks into your eyes, into *you*. And then when you finally touch—that fire that flares and burns and makes you dizzy."

"Yes, and what else?"

What else is there? I paused, uncertain about how to answer.

"Come, I'm hungry."

With a last look at my Sibyl, we headed to the museum's café. Nonna surveyed the filled tables, then stared at a well-dressed middle-aged couple who sat quarreling and ignoring the check. She lifted her right hand and gave a short wave, as if whisking away a pesky insect; within seconds the husband paid the bill and they left. We were immediately seated at the small table.

"How do you do that?" I asked, having seen her use the trick before.

"I just focus and send a very firm suggestion. Sometimes I make the seat a little too hard." We laughed, ordered sandwiches and two glasses of Burgundy. Nonna studied our neighbors, a diverse mixture that was both tired and animated, then returned to her question. "So what is desire? Desire is the sound of people laughing in a café, a rose opening to the sun, the moon rising over Firenze."

"Yes, of course. Whiskers on kittens and warm woolen mittens."

Nonna gave a short snort of a laugh. "The desires of children are very wise, but now you're a woman."

A baby began to cry and I watched his chic young mother lift him from the stroller and cradle him against her. She brushed his cheek and spoke to him softly. His crying stopped and she smiled at the baby and then at the young man sitting with her.

"There's desire and sorrow when I get my period." I sighed, then stared at another couple who looked to be in their eighties. "Desire when I see an elderly couple together holding hands." The waiter brought them a pot of tea and a plate of pastries and they laughed as she poured and he served. "Wearing this ring that I love so much, wanting a sip of that great wine you ordered, or when I lie in a summer field. Derek." I sighed again.

"Desire is the need of that silver ring to wrap itself around your finger and feel the warmth of your skin, it's the red wine longing for your lips, the field wanting to feel your body pressed against it."

"But they're objects. How can they desire me?"

"Change your perspective and you'll understand what desire *really* is. Remember, everything that exists is an expression of the Divine, an embodiment of Divine energy. You've already experienced this magic with your statue, the Sibyl. The statue first came to you in a dream, yes?"

I nodded, sensing a door begin to open.

"It came to you because *it desired you*. Desire is a message from the Sacred that leads you to the Divine. That's why our senses are so important. They're the means by which we experience our desires; they show us the presence of divinity."

The waiter placed two round glasses of dark red wine before us.

"Perfect—wine is the sacrament of your daemon." Nonna smiled as she lifted her glass. "In a sense it *is* your daemon."

I placed my two fingers around the base and swirled the wine in the bowl, watching it slide back into itself, leaving transparent trails that slowly followed.

"Here, it's so simple," she continued. "You don't taste a wine that desires you in the same way. Close your eyes."

It was always so easy to follow her advice; even in this public place I was able to lose any self-consciousness and simply listen to her voice guide me.

"Now breathe, slowly, deeply, and as you breathe feel the desire of the air to enter you, to fill you with life. That is what air does—it gives you life. Feel its desire to fill you with life."

I was used to the calming effect of our breath meditation, and had finally learned to release the distracting images that had made it so difficult at the beginning. I had also learned how to feel the energy of the air, the Taoist *chi* and yogic *prana*, the life force as Nonna called it. But I had never felt the air entering me because it desired me, because it was *meant* to fill me with life. The sensation was extraordinary, as if the air were soaked with champagne and filled with bubbles of light. The evanescence percolated through me and my eyes flew open. I began to laugh, consumed by a sudden trembling as if all the molecules in my body were vibrating.

Nonna laughed. "You should see how bright your eyes are! So, how do you feel?"

"Like I'm . . . vibrating all over."

"Now another simple practice for you. When you drink the wine, say to yourself: *The wine desires me*. Inhale the fragrance of the wine."

I raised the glass and breathed in deeply.

"Smell its perfume, taste it on your tongue, feel its warmth flowing into you."

I drank slowly, savoring the complex taste on my tongue, the sensation of liquid traveling down my throat, a stream of subtle heat entering me. And I remembered the night I met my daemon.

"As you experience each of these sensations, remind yourself that the wine *desires* you. Experience the wine by being the object of *its* desire and you will have an experience of the true nature of the world. You will *feel* the wine penetrate you. Sip slowly, and sense the wine longing for your lips, your tongue, your body."

I focused my attention on each sensation, and all were so acute I felt as if I were drinking wine for the first time.

"How do you feel?" Nonna's question brought me back.

"Like I've fallen in love—but I don't know who with. I thought I'd fallen in love with Derek," I admitted quietly.

She nodded. "This is what it feels like to be in love with the world, *mia figlia*. The world. To experience the object of your desire as desirous of you removes the distance between it and you. You don't look at your statue as if it were some dumb, inanimate, meaningless object. It's charged with meaning and life. Everything—the bird that sings in the tree, the moon in the night sky, the food you eat, that wine—desires *you*. All of your interactions with life change—they become expressions of desire. What's desire? The *world* is desire."

As best I could, I had let go of my desire for Derek. I worked, and went to circle, I spent as much time as I could with friends. I even dated. It was the beginning of another week, a Monday evening, and I was washing my hair when I heard the phone ringing. I raced down the hall for it.

"Hello." I was breathless as I tucked a dripping strand of hair into the towel.

"Hey, it's Derek. Maia's friend. We met at the Magickal Cauldron?"

"Oh yes, I remember you." I struggled to control the excitement in my voice.

"Sorry it took so long to call you. But I had something I needed to do first. So how've ya been?"

I sank into the couch, holding the receiver in both hands, a great wave of relieved joy washing away weeks of worry. *Be cool.* "Good. Busy, really busy." *Okay, not too cool.* "I'm really glad you called. So what have you been up to?"

"Well, I'd been seeing someone when we met, and, well," he paused and I stopped breathing, "I needed to end it before I called you."

"Oh, I'm glad, I mean I'm sorry." *I sound like an idiot.* Another wave of relief and happiness flooded me, along with a sense of responsibility to the woman he'd been seeing.

"It wasn't because of you. Well, you were the catalyst. It wasn't working, at least not for me, and it wasn't fair to her. Anyway, so how are you?"

The energy flowed through the receiver like honey in the sun, sweet, nourishing, intoxicating with a soft burn—it was mead slowly sipped as it saturated every cell of my body. We talked for a long time and I began to learn about this stranger with whom I'd fallen in love. We made a date for Saturday night and I carefully wrote "Derek" and his phone number on the beautifully blank page of my date book. Peace had returned, and with it the world fell back into its mysterious, magical order.

5

Enchantment

Love in its essence is spiritual fire.

—EMANUEL SWEDENBORG

Blow the dancing seeds of a billowy dandelion to your lover and he will hear your thoughts of love. Powdered root of an orchid burned with musk oil will increase your lover's passion and your own, but beware the poppy in any form for it makes your beloved forgetful of your love. Tie nine knots in your stocking, tie the stocking to your bedpost nine times around and that night you will dream of your true love.

Like making a wish, there is an old magical rule that you should not discuss your spell with anyone or it won't come true. Except for Gillian and Naomi, I hadn't said a word to anyone about my love spell, and yet to-night, just two nights before I was to have my first date with Derek, all the circle could talk about was love spells. Since my phone conversation and making the date with Derek, I knew that my spell had indeed come true and so, finally, I decided to share the story with them.

Gillian began sprinkling me with gold glitter and Naomi was shaking her beer bottle to bless me with a spritz à la some sports victory. I was plied with questions, only some of which I could answer, but we all knew that my magic had worked. And I had learned an important lesson: magic works on its own timetable; because it's organic energy, like a plant, you're not going to make it grow, or manifest, faster by tugging on it.

Onatah, at twenty the youngest in our group, told us that at the Summer Solstice, she had invoked the African/Brazilian Goddess Yemaya by dancing in the foamy edge of the ocean. Just as the sun set, she launched a toy boat carrying a burning candle and a prayer that she would find her love. Mindy, a chiropractor in her forties who was married with two children, kept a bouquet of yarrow, said to be an herb of enduring love, in her bedroom. Even Jeanette, who had for a time sworn off men, told us, with her West Indian accent as round and lilting as her style, that she was ready for love. She had just returned from a trip to Hawaii, where she'd visited the ancient volcano Pele, her patron Goddess, making offerings and letting the molten power flow through her, filling her heart and her body with desire.

And when the moon was waning and almost dark, Annabelle, our Southern steel magnolia whose flirtatious beauty charmed every man within ten feet of her, had created a ritual to end her old marriage. She burned rue, which banishes regrets, guilt and anger, with vetiver, which would break a run of bad luck in love, and witch hazel, which can mend a broken heart, and tightly tied a ribbon saved from a wedding gift around both of her ankles. As she bound herself, she thought of how confined and unfulfilled she had felt in her marriage. As the sorrow of being trapped rose within her, she took a knife and swiftly cut her bonds, calling out to Diana to help her regain her independence, and to Kwan Yin, the ancient Chinese Goddess of love and compassion, to help her heart mend. And then she summoned Aphrodite to revive her power to enchant.

Maia handed Gillian an old, leather-bound book. "Read this one."

"Oh, its wonderful!" Gillian read to us as we waited for our circle to begin. "Carefully chant the spell: 'Acorn cup and ashen key, bring my true love back to me' with an acorn and a sprig from an ash tree placed beneath your pillow for three nights and it will bring a faithless or absent lover back to you."

"I don't think I'd want to bring that faithless lover back to me." Annabelle leaned against the countertop. "I'd much rather turn him into a frog."

"Girl, he already was one." Naomi began carving another candle. "That was the problem. At least you didn't get warts."

We laughed. Resigned to the fact that the relationship with her ex was over, Gillian was searching for a love spell. As she thumbed through the old book reading ingredients and recipes, I realized that it had taken me a long time to get over thinking of all the props and ingredients, oils and herbs, and other mysterious items that were so often a part of spellcasting, as superstitious mumbo jumbo.

Mystics and shamans, Witches and quantum physicists all know that, ultimately, everything is energy. We don't work with supernatural powers, but rather with the natural, rhythmic energies of earth, moon, sun and stars, and our own bodies. The next step was coming to accept that other aspects of the natural world—the ingredients used in spells—can lend their energetic properties to our efforts.

If plants have the power to heal the body, such as digitalis, which is the source of heart medicines, why can't a plant help heal the emotions of a broken heart? If you pay attention, Nature teaches that creation is organized in harmonious relationships that reveal divinity. Wiselore, as the old wisdom is called, is the way to understand, honor and work with these relationships that we call correspondences. Thus, water is the element of love, compassion, deep emotions and dreaming, and corresponds to the direction of west, the colors of water such as blue, sea green and turquoise, and the creatures of the water such as dolphins, whales, seals and otters. And there are divinities of water such as Poseidon and Neptune, Yemaya and Oshun, Venus and Aphrodite, who each year bathed in the ocean from which she was born to purify herself and restore her autonomy. And there was the voluptuous Indian goddess Lakshmi, who also arose from the primeval ocean, holding the lotus of divine revelation, wearing perfumes and jewels to bestow all the pleasures of prosperity.

Though much of our work was intuitive, correspondences had to be learned, for they are the palette with which we practice the art of rituals and spells, charms and potions. But finally, it seemed to me that one of the most important purposes of all the ingredients and items, potions and props, was to physicalize the Sacred, to facilitate our experience of, and enable us to encounter, divinity through the gift of our senses. And this spirituality was wonderfully sensuous.

The risk was that all the props and accoutrements might become receptacles into which we projected and thereby lost our own, sacred power. Over time I had come to the conclusion that ultimately, it's the power of our connection to the Divine that makes a spell work. But for whatever reason it had manifested, the fulfillment of my love spell had reconvinced me that magic was very real.

Two days later, on Saturday morning, Gillian sat in my apartment, keeping me from jumping out of my skin with first-date jitters, by describing the love spell she'd done last night.

"It's an old Irish spell. I cut up one of my grandmother's old, white Irish linen pillowcases and then I stitched a small bag from the fabric. I filled it with primrose and hawthorn, pink malva and lily, a red rose and a stalk of yellow yarrow, and violets. And a sprig of rosemary, which went in separately."

"Where did you get all that?"

"Some of it came from the shop, and I got some from my parents' garden in Southampton." She poured us more tea and paused as she devoured a piece of a Greenberg's sticky bun. She licked her fingers and continued. "So, I had to start as the moon rose. I stirred the bundle, and the rosemary, into a pot of simmering springwater—"

"Where—"

"Poland Spring." She shrugged and we laughed. "I let it boil for about ten minutes, and then I pulled out the rosemary sprig and I let the potion steep until it had cooled. I poured the strained liquid into my goblet, and I put the goblet on my altar, in front of my Venus statue, and then I raised the cup to the moon and tilted it so that I could see the moon floating in the cup, and then I drank a little bit of the potion."

"How did it taste?"

"Okay." She smiled. "I wouldn't bottle and sell it. Unless it works." We laughed. "And then I chanted:

'Beautiful Venus and shining moon,
By my heart's desire I ask a boon.
Let this potion I drink bring to me
The love that is mine and meant to be.'"

"That's lovely."

She nodded. "I changed it a little from the original. But this was the really hard part—every three hours I went to the altar, said the spell and drank some of the potion. I finished the last of it at midnight, chanted the verse one final time and then I went to bed."

"That's a lot of focused energy. Any dreams?"

"Nothing I remember. So now how long do you think I have to wait for true love?"

"Ask me again tomorrow." I looked at the clock. "I've never felt like this before. Gillybean, I'm so nervous."

"Don't be nervous. Well, how can you not be?" Gillian sighed. "You deserve true love. And so do I. I know doubt can kill a spell, but it's really hard not to ask myself, *What if it doesn't work?* And I don't think I can bear another broken heart. Ever since I broke up with Chris, I just don't know." Gillian got up to leave, staring out the window to the fog-shrouded bridge. "I mean a lot of spells work; yours did, but I'm always sort of surprised when they do."

I laughed. "I know. Me too. Actually, I'm still stunned." I hugged her and looked at the clock over her shoulder. Derek would be here in a few hours. A rush of adrenaline shot through my body. "Don't worry—it'll work."

I checked the clock again. I couldn't concentrate, couldn't shake the nervous anticipation that had been building all day. After Gillian left, I'd finished everything on my list and even had time to soak in a tub with lavender, roses and chamomile—but nothing helped. I'd thought it wasn't possible to feel more excited than when Derek and I had met, but it was.

I filled the room with red candles rubbed with Venus oil, lit them and stood surrounded by a fire of fragrance. But as the room grew hotter I felt as if I were exposing some private side of myself, some force of Nature, and magic, not meant to be seen. At least not in this way. I blew them all out and stashed them away, but the scent lingered in the room.

I checked the clock again—suddenly I was running late. I tore into the closet of gray, brown, black, and navy blue suits. There had to be something feminine that revealed instead of concealed my figure. Had I become what I so dreaded—a conservative workaholic? I pulled out the few dresses buried at the back, but they were either too formal, or just not right. Although careful about how I spent every precious penny, I wished I'd gone shopping.

I had just pulled on my tightest jeans and a snug black sweater when the doorbell rang; my stomach fluttered, then dropped like I was falling from a cliff. I checked myself quickly in the mirror, paused to catch my breath, then walked to the door. I hesitated, feeling the cold curve of the doorknob and the rapid beat of my heart. I knew that on the other side was more than a man, or magic, or even love. I was about to open the door to a future I could not see and could not stop. Whether I was ready no longer mattered. The spell had been cast, the magic was manifesting.

I took a deep breath and opened the door. My stomach fluttered again as Derek, bundled in an old motorcycle jacket, leaned against the wall, smiling. He handed me a small bouquet of pale peach-colored roses and shyly crossed my threshold.

"They're beautiful. Thank you." I dipped my face into the soft petals.

He gave a quick nod, smiling again, and my heart stumbled. I felt the cold he brought in with him and the warmth that emerged as he took off his jacket and draped it across the back of my desk chair.

"Warm in here." He peeled off his sweater and the quick movement made the studio apartment contract around his large frame. No matter where I moved, I was aware of him, seeing, hearing, feeling his movements and his body, as if we were submerged in water together and every gesture created waves that rippled against me. I recognized the heightening of senses but this was something more, something so overwhelming it was almost too much to allow. I wondered whether he was feeling it also.

"Let me just put these in water." I escaped to put the flowers in my only vase. I caught a glimpse of myself in the mirror, smiled slowly, and set the roses on the end table. There was a drop of water on one petal and I wanted to bend down to catch it with my tongue. I touched it with my fingertip, and lifted my finger to my lips.

"This is nice," he said. I watched him study me as he studied the room, taking in the misty view of the bridge, reading the titles of my books, surveying my modest collection of WPA art, kneeling to flip through my record collection. He pulled out Patti Smith.

"She's amazing, especially live."

I smiled. "I always think of her as a poet who chose music as the medium to express her words, instead of a musician who writes great lyrics." I felt momentarily awkward, as if I was back in high school being the brainy girl with the cool guy.

"Mind if I put it on?"

"I wish you could. Unfortunately, I haven't figured out how to hook up the stereo. And that receiver's so heavy it's really hard for me to move."

"Well, if you've got the cables, I can do it."

"I'm not sure." I pulled out the box with all the stereo stuff and he dug in.

"You've got everything you need. Although you might want to get better cables. But this is a good system. Bang and Olufsen, good turntable." He got to work and within minutes had the whole thing hooked up. I watched the muscles in his arms and his back as he bent, lifted and maneuvered the heavy pieces into position. He moved quickly, clearly at home in his skin. I was mesmerized and aroused by the swift display of masculine skill and grace. But even more, it was a gesture, a token of what it might feel like to have someone help me, to have a man who, on occasion, even took care of me. It made me feel safe. I wanted him to kiss me.

He placed the record on the turntable and for the first time in a long time, music that was more than random radio filled the room. He lowered the volume.

"It makes such a difference to have music again. Thank you so much." I smiled at him, thrilled by more than just the music. "It probably would've been sitting forever without you."

"Good speakers," he said, smiling back, shy again but clearly pleased.

"Okay, you've earned a reward. Would you like something to drink? I've got a bottle of wine." As I brought it to him, I realized I was moving very differently from how I moved when I was in an office, or alone. The movements were curved, softened, slower and flirtatious.

He took the bottle and studied the label. "This is a nice Bordeaux. Good choice. Cabernet Sauvignon's been called the Clint Eastwood of grapes—muscular and bold when it's young, but with age it becomes very complex, you could even say it becomes . . . charming. California's still suffering the aftereffects of phylloxera, but once they get going they're going to make some superb Cabernets. It'll be interesting to see what happens in the next twenty years." He stopped short, looking sheepish and very sweet. "Sorry. Did that sound pretentious?"

"Sounds like you know something about wine." I was impressed, even more so because he didn't seem to be trying to impress me.

Derek nodded. "Something."

I smiled and he looked happy, like a kid. I realized I was probably behaving the same way. "I've been known to use my teeth, but I'd just as soon use a corkscrew." He gave me a quick grin and I laughed.

"Oh, shoot, I lent it to a neighbor," I realized as I poked through the drawer. "You'll have to use your teeth."

Derek laughed, warm and relaxed, and all the nervousness evaporated. He reached into the pocket of his jeans and pulled out a Swiss Army knife. "You may not believe it, but I was once an Eagle Scout." He unfolded the small corkscrew from the red handle and swiftly opened the wine. I handed him the glasses and his hand brushed mine; the current between us arced. He poured; the wine flowed downward and rolled up the sides of the round glasses, the laws of Nature ruling the mellifluous action and reaction, and finally the inexorable pull of gravity. I watched him hold the glass to the light, swirl, and sniff.

"Yup." He handed me a glass and tapped it with his. "To you."

It was a small gallantry that made me blush. Every gesture seemed to generate a subtle friction, a texture of unseen sparks collecting to ignite. Every movement, every word exchanged was intentional kindling, and I felt a needle of anxiety, instinctually aware that once started, the blaze would escape my control.

I brought out bread, some *rillettes* and cheese, and we sat on the floor with the picnic. The sun blazed orange and then crimson as it set, and the room around us withdrew into pale then charcoal gray.

"Got any candles?" Derek asked as I turned on a lamp.

I smiled. "A few." I walked to my desk, knelt and leaned forward, pulling open the bottom drawer. I arched my back, reaching to find the magical red candles, and instantly realized I was offering him the most primally suggestive posture. My cheeks were flushed as I turned to see him staring at me, my hands full of candles, head full of confusion.

I rescued myself as I always did from emotions and situations beyond my control—I busied myself with thinking and tasks, finding candleholders, striking matches, watching how thoughts turned into actions and actions into results. Laws of energy. Laws of Nature. *Of love?* Finally seated in the candlelight, desire and fear dancing around the flame, I realized he really *was* here, casually beside me on the floor, on the spot where just weeks ago I had cast my spell for love. *Should I tell him?* What man would accept that his presence was the result of magic? I bit my tongue.

Instead, we shared stories of self-revelation. I told him about the Libyan Sibyl. He told me about a month he'd spent hiking and traveling to ancient sacred sites in Ireland, and the way the land seemed to shimmer with energy. Tales blended seamlessly with quick jokes, giving rational justification, or perhaps something more, to the instinctual connection between us.

The candles melted. It was close to midnight, the Witching hour, when he reached down and took my hand. We sat quietly, palm to palm, mine so small in his, my senses inflamed by the feeling of skin upon skin. His fingers interlaced with mine, locking my hand in his.

My thoughts darted erratically, fluttering toward the light of something unfamiliar, while all my instincts stretched, sensing mysteries as distant as the origin of the Universe pouring into the room. I was sure I knew what mattered—how could love not be real when it had taken form?

He leaned forward, touching my mouth, gently tracing the rim of my lower lip with his thumb. Suddenly afraid to look at him, I closed my eyes, but there was nowhere to hide as he ran his fingers along my chin. Afraid to give myself away, I pressed my lips together, swallowing the pleasure that pushed for expression. But there is no dissembling in the language of touch. I opened my eyes. He smiled at me and brushed the hair back from my shoulders, exposing my neck. I shivered as something else, long hidden, was exposed.

He leaned slowly forward, his arm slid around me, and I held my breath, felt my heart slamming against my ribs, expecting the shock of his first kiss. He tilted his head and I gasped as his lips, warm and soft, kissed my neck, his tongue stealing my breath away as it traced a path to a point just at the edge of my ear. He exhaled gently and flames fanned out through my body, burning away the past, incinerating any doubts or thoughts or inhibitions.

"Come to me, come to me, climb down from that tower and let me have you," I heard as if from far away, and then as close as a whisper in my ear. I was summoned back to life.

He drew me close into the heat of his body. A feverish pulse raced through me. Leaning down to kiss me, his warm breath touched my face and I tasted the wine on his lips, on mine. His tongue pressed me to open myself and I felt the spinning intoxication of contact.

I drew back to catch my breath, to look at him, to hide in plain sight from his onslaught. His eyes held mine and I was unveiled. He smiled and I was safe. Again he took my hand, placing it against his. My senses swimming and my reason drowning, I longed for the moment when the last walls of thought that held me hostage crumbled, and I could fall into the teeming ocean of my rebirth.

His fingers interlaced with mine, locking my hand in his; he pulled me tightly to him. Twin serpents of fire exploded through my body, rebellion and arousal, battling as they merged. But my body knew its own truth. His arms cradled me as I fell backward to the rug. He tugged at my sweater, pulling it from me. Quickly stripping away my bra, his eyes darkened as he stared down at me. I reached beneath his shirt and slid my hands slowly along the heated skin of his chest.

He tossed his shirt aside and lowered himself to me as my arms wound around his neck, our legs intertwined. He traveled slowly across the unfamiliar landscape of my longing, his lips on the soft hills of my breasts, gently conquering as he persuaded me. A moan escaped my lips as desire whirled between us, filling the small room with a potion of dizzying anticipation. I drank through every pore as it flowed between us, creating a hunger it satisfied with every nuance of connection. My blood was racing, my breath quickening as my mind, intoxicated, released its imprisoning grip. There was magic in his touch, and I ached for more.

His weight bound me to my body, his hand gliding into hidden hollows, fingers cupping, encircling, stroking. Slowly cherishing the moist yielding of my lips, he kissed me, his tongue sliding down my body, penetrating the grotto where Aphrodite bathed, inhaling the dusky fragrance of flowers crushed upon her wedding bed.

"You taste so sweet," he murmured, looking up at me. My fingers tangled in his hair as he licked and kissed and probed and brought me to a fever of need, pulling back and then returning, keeping me poised at the edge of ecstasy. He looked up at me, smiling at the flush that colored my cheeks, the trembling that I could not control. His mouth moved slowly up my body until he had returned to my lips. He smiled and reached down, holding me tightly as he touched me, stoking the liquid fire he'd ignited until it blazed uncontrollably and I cried out, clinging to him.

He whispered softly in my ear.

I nodded. "Yes."

He lifted himself above me and my hands gripped his arms as slowly, carefully, he pushed forward and I arched to meet him. I could smell the sea on his fingers, taste the salt on his damp forehead, on his lips, his tongue a darting fish as whirlpools and swirls of pleasure urged us to rhythmic motion. A small and sudden bite startled me with pain that was more sweetness than distress. Currents rushed in and swiftly tugged away, a tide of sensations surging through all our cells and consciousness, which altered in arousal.

We caressed, plunged, dove and then together rode the mounting waves of desire until he exploded with a groan and shudder, his sudden dissolution fulfilled as I followed in breathless surrender.

He walked in from the shower wrapped in a towel that I immediately wanted to pull off. His blond hair was wet and dark, slicked back from his forehead, a small trickle of drops running down his neck and shoulders. His chest was sculpted and all I wanted was to feel it pressed against me again. I sat on the rumpled bed, my hair tousled, my heart enraptured. He smiled at me and the pleasure plunged through my stomach and into my womb.

"If you don't get out of that bed now, you're not getting out of it at all." He started toward me. I leaned back into the pillows, curling my legs out of the tangled sheets, and bit my lower lip. My heart began beating its new, quickened rhythm. His hands shot out and I squealed with surprise as he grabbed my ankles and dragged me down the bed. He flipped me over, pulling me by my waist so that my legs were hanging over the edge.

His hands reached around and grabbed my breasts, squeezing my nipples hard, then slid down my sides to grasp my hips. I could feel him pressing against me, his legs nudging my thighs further apart, his hands sliding to my bottom, gripping hard and pulling me open and into him as he thrust himself into me. I was wet and swollen with need as he pounded away any memories that were not of him.

We lay, sleeping, dreaming, wrapped in each other's arms, the sun moving from one end of the sky to the other. The moon rose and set and the sun rose again.

"I've got to keep my strength up." Derek stood at the bathroom door, already dressed, waiting for me to finish my shower. "Let's go to breakfast."

I padded out of the bathroom, wrapped in my robe. The bed was made and he'd made us tea.

"Milk and honey." He handed the cup to me and I took it in both hands. "It looks like a beautiful day. I want to take you to my favorite part of the park. It's up at the north end and hardly anybody goes there. Wear boots you can hike around in and dress warm."

I scrambled into my clothes.

The sun was blindingly bright as we stepped out of my building's dark lobby. His arm was draped around my shoulders, but even the weight of it couldn't keep me grounded. I wrapped my arm around his waist and dug my hand into the hip pocket of his jeans, feeling the tight muscles of his butt moving with every step.

We walked up Columbus Avenue to a coffee shop, and I blinked and stared, wondering at the sudden, miraculous beauty of the busy street. It was as if everything and everyone were glowing with golden light. And I began to notice that every man we passed was staring at me.

"Do I look okay?" I asked Derek nervously.

"You're beautiful. Radiant." He smiled and leaned down to kiss me.

It was summer and the night was balmy as I climbed out of the stifling subway. Even the taxi fumes and the bus exhaust couldn't detract from the sensuality of the breeze that lifted my dress and drifted over my bare skin. The moon was waxing and almost full, and it was Friday—

named for Freya, the Scandinavian Goddess of fertility. Friday was also devoted to other Goddesses of love—the Roman Venus and the Greek Aphrodite. It was perfect timing for tonight's ritual celebration of fertility, love and sexuality, and I was in the mood to revel in it all.

I was in love with Derek. It was like a fairy tale, as if I'd been kissed and was now awake. Happier than I'd ever been, I noticed a subtle shift in the way I lived in my body—I felt more alive. And there was a sway to my walk, a softness in my voice. I'd suddenly realized how much of my energy—the way I carried myself, the personality I projected, the way I tackled life—was composed of hard edges. I'd never really noticed until it began to melt away. And beneath that toughened surface, that impervious armor, I was finding an unfamiliar joyfulness.

I headed straight to the temple and found the circle of ten women already busy. Amid animated talk and laughter, I helped set up the altar, covering it with a pink cloth. I filled it with statues from all over the world, all of them Goddesses of love and sexuality, and I surrounded them with spiraling shells, ripe fruit, roses, lavender and lilies. Beneath the altar we placed bottles of wine, mead, water and juice, bread, cakes and more fruit, along with scarves, jewelry, makeup, hairbrushes, fans, rattles, tambourines, finger cymbals and drums.

Onatah spooned the incense she'd made onto a burning charcoal. The smoke spiraled around her long, curly black hair, caught in her long lashes, making her dark, almond-shaped eyes blink, then quickly filled the room with clouds of delicious perfume. Onatah was a provocative yet innocent beauty, a voluptuous example of a little-known but not uncommon blending of Native and African American, who was putting herself through college as an exotic dancer.

"What's in the incense?" I asked.

"Lavender, cinnamon, rose petals, orris and ummm." She paused and bit her pink-rouged lower lip. "And orange peel, and the oil."

"And what's in the oil?" I opened the little bottle and inhaled its richness.

"Patchouli, almond, sandalwood and musk."

Onatah handed Naomi the bottle of oil and together they sat on the rug, rubbed the pink candles with the oil, then put them in the four directions and on the altar. Everyone else put mirrors of all shapes and sizes around the room and Maia lit the candles. The flames reflected in the mirrors and the hazy temple glowed with the dancing light of huge fire-filled diamonds.

When everything was ready, we undressed. I was an only child and so when we first began working skyclad—naked—it was an unfamiliar intimacy that made me very self-conscious. Like most women, I couldn't help but compare myself to the relentless displays of impossible perfection that bombarded me from magazines and movies, billboards and television, and I felt inadequate. But working skyclad had, mostly, freed me from those imprisoning images.

I stood surrounded by naked women, not one of them bearing even the remotest resemblance to a centerfold. We had large thighs and round bellies, small breasts and breasts that had fed babies, full figures and thin ones, dark skin and light, muscles and fat. And each was beautiful in her own unique way. Laughing and full of light, the radiance shone forth from within.

Maia rang the bell and our rite of love and pleasure began. "Maiden, Mother and Crone—the Threefold Goddess. Tonight we honor Her powers of love and sexuality, beauty and pleasure. These are also aspects of ourselves, for the Goddess is within each of us. So, let our celebration begin."

"Hand to hand, I cast this circle," Nonna said, smiling and taking my hand as I stood to her left. I smiled into those warm eyes, took her hand and turned to Gillian on my left. Moving clockwise, we cast our circle hand to hand and heart to heart, in a form that was both a symbol and an embodiment of the Goddess and her generative, erotic, magical womb. The four directions were called, and then Nonna invoked the Goddesses of Love.

By the standards of Western culture Nonna was "past her prime" because she could no longer bear children. Walking down the street, with her silver-streaked hair, her face with its soft lines recording years of happiness and sorrow, she would be invisible to most of the men who searched for the Goddess of Love in mortal guise. But as she moved gracefully around the circle, she reminded us that the Crone contained the sexy mother and the youthful maiden within her.

"Goddess of Love, you who emerge shimmering, clad only in glistening water and filled with light. You dance upon the waves, your undulating curves returning lovers to their senses. You whose hidden pearl of rapture rests within the briny rose. Laughter-loving Goddess who is worshipped by entwined bodies with damp and salty skin, probing tongues and sensuous fulfillment. Goddess of pleasure, teach us the blessings of our bodies and the secrets that open the gates of heaven on earth."

We consecrated each other with the oil, leaving glossy triangles that connected the fertile realms of breasts and Venus mons. We poured the wine and offered libations to the Goddess, then sat on velvet pillows and artfully painted each other's faces like ancient priestesses of erotic, sacred love with kohl-lined eyes and ruby lips. I inhaled slowly, drawing in the heady fragrance of incense and oil, perfume and flowers, and the passionate energies that were already flowing through the room.

Annabelle, with the body of a young girl and the face of an angel, had been making up for lost time in the romance department. She wanted to teach us a spell she used for sexual pleasure and for love. "While I chant the spell, I weave and I visualize what I want—tonight me and Ray making love. Passionately." She brushed and then, chanting softly, slowly began braiding the enchantment into her long, raven hair.

"I am yours and you are mine,
as I weave our loves entwine.
Our bodies, souls and hearts are one,
as I weave let it be done."

Smiling as she wrapped a red ribbon to hold the braid in place, she told us, "When I get home tonight, right before we make love, I'll unbraid my hair in front of him and that will release the charm to work." Her eyes were full of mischief, and Onatah immediately began to braid her own hair.

The room filled with hazy smoke and soft murmurs as the mirrors caught fragments of divine beauty incarnating, remembering, rejoicing. The landscape of love was reflected back to us from the looking glasses in which we were encircled, revealing the subtle slope of a shoulder, the ample curve of breasts, the sensuous flow of calf and thigh and hip, the soft glow of skin and the sway of hair, full lips moistened by a tongue, flushed cheeks, the nape of a neck and the small hollow of the throat waiting to be kissed.

We wrapped silk and velvet around our hips, and hung bracelets around our wrists and ankles and jewels about our necks, from our ears and our nipples. The circle stood, hips swaying, arms around each other's waist and shoulders as Nonna picked up a sistrum, shaking it as she walked, slowly and sensuously around the circle of beautiful women.

"I call to you, erotic Goddesses, ancient and ever present—Aphrodite, Cybele, Bast, Inanna, Ezulie, Freya, Shakti!" She chanted the names like a song of summoning; chills flowed along my skin and down my spine and I felt my nipples harden and my womb begin to thrum. "Come to us, restore the divine blessings, the pleasure and wisdom and power of our bodies. Teach us that we are temples of spirit and love and beauty."

With the last line, she danced swiftly around the circle, rattling over our heads. Lovemaking is the most sacred form of worshipping these powerful Goddesses, and I could feel the electric pulse that shot around the circle. Maia turned the music up louder and drums pounded beneath its sinuous surface.

Nonna began to sing, repeating the phrase over and over: "I am the Goddess, I am the Mother, all acts of love and pleasure are my rituals."

The line was from the *Charge of the Goddess*, and Maia and Bellona quickly added harmonies. Nonna began to move, her hips thrusting, her shoulders rolling, arms undulating like rippling waves of energy, her body becoming her invocation. The other women picked up the chant, singing and whispering, calling and laughing, clapping and shaking tambourines, slapping drums, shaking rattles.

"I am the Goddess, I am the Mother, all acts of love and pleasure are my rituals."

We wove the chant with harmonies, spinning, turning, connecting, separating and joining again. Onatah placed her hands on my hips, showing me how to swivel and pivot. She stood back and watched as I gyrated, awkwardly at first, and then as if some ancient sense memory were flowing through me, my hips smoothly circling an unseen center of ecstasy. I watched Maia and Bellona dancing together as if no one else in the world existed, and Nonna as she moved with easy beauty, her hips making an up-and-down and then side-to-side motion. She took me by the hands, pulling me to dance with her.

"Keep the small of your back relaxed," she advised, "and your feet a shoulder's distance apart. Point your toes straight forward, relax your knees. That's it, now just lift one hip, and lower it, lift and lower. Very good," she encouraged me as I began to loosen up. "And when you're ready, I want you to add your Kegels." She winked and spun off to dance with Jeanette.

I squeezed and molten desire spread upward from my womb through my circling hips, my stomach and into my heart. I was on fire, and I longed for Derek. I danced, burning, surrounded by dancing women, their hair flying, eyes full of joy, their bodies supple and seductive. We danced and we remembered our bodies were sacred. We danced and we knew that we were luscious and sensuous. We danced and we rejoiced as our sexuality rejoined our spirituality. We danced, filled with divine desire, and we filled the room with sex, sweat and certainty.

We lost all sense of time, the energy building and finally peaking, directed not outward into some visualized goal, but inward to ourselves, to each other; it was like being plugged into the Universe's main power plant. We finally collapsed, laughing and struggling for breath. The Goddess's cup was passed and more libations offered. Our jokes were bawdy, our stories full of sex, heartache and wisdom. I watched this circle of radiant women, knowing that tonight our circle had become a shining mirror of the Goddess, a reflection into which each of us could look. There we found an image that confirmed our own divinity—seeing Her in each other, we could see Her within ourselves. We had come home to our bodies, our souls, our authentic and sexual selves.

Finally, the Goddesses were thanked and the circle was closed. We hugged and kissed and carefully changed our appearance from sacred, sexual priestesses who danced between the worlds to luminous, beautiful women who lived and worked in this demanding city.

"I had a feeling you'd be getting done about now." Derek was leaning outside the shop's front door. *Magic!* My heart leapt downward, landing right in the delta we'd just been celebrating. He kissed me warmly. "Look at you." Grinning, he stepped back and stared at me. "I don't know what you're doing in there, but it sure is working."

I threw my arms around his neck, pressing myself against him, feeling my softness against the hardness of his body. I lifted my face and kissed him again, deeply, the fire in my womb spreading quickly through the rest of me.

"Mmmm, you smell good," he mumbled against my hair as I hugged him. "And you feel good. I was going to take you to hear that trio at Sweet Basil, but let's go home."

"Sounds perfect. I want to take you to heaven." I smiled up at him and we kissed again, long and slow and sweet.

It was Saturday morning, and like a typical New Yorker who worked all week, on my day of rest I had a list of errands a mile long. But I knew that I'd be seeing Derek later and so I had the energy of Wonder Woman. By mid-afternoon I found myself burdened with bags and in the neighborhood of the Magickal Cauldron. The shop was unusually quiet for a Saturday afternoon. I spotted Gillian in the back talking to Nonna, who was facing away from me. Tiptoeing down the aisle, I gestured to Gillian not to give me away. I snuck up behind Nonna and covered her eyes with my hands.

She immediately started laughing, reached around and tickled me. "As if you could surprise me. I could smell you coming the minute the door opened." She gave me a hug.

"Well, that's a lovely thought. And here I'm meeting the guy tonight." I hugged Gillian. "Do I smell?"

Gillian laughed, shook her head.

Nonna chuckled. "No, no, not like that. It's different—something else. The way mothers know their children. Better, it's part of the attraction between men and women." She crooked her finger, and we followed her to the Oil Office.

"So, what's this about?" I asked Gillian.

She shrugged. "I asked her about love potions."

"Gilly, you're going to end up dating a different guy every night, and they're all going to want to marry you if you don't watch out."

"And the problem with that would be—?" Gillian grinned.

Nonna pulled a large brown bottle from the shelf. "What's one of the most common ingredients in love spells?"

"Patchouli," Gillian, the new expert, quickly answered.

Nonna nodded. "And something else." She twisted the cap off the bottle and handed it to me. "What's that?"

"Musk?" I offered, sniffing cautiously.

Nonna nodded again. "Artificial. And do you know why we use it so often?"

"Because it smells sexy?" I offered again. I loved these weird Socratic lessons of Nonna's—they always led somewhere I never expected.

"To animals. Originally, musk came from the sac beneath the abdominal skin of a male musk deer. It was used since ancient times as a perfume fixative, and also as an aphrodisiac. It's the pheromone of the animal, the chemical it produces to attract the opposite sex."

"You mean if I put that on and go into the woods, I'm going to be pursued by some horny buck?" Gillian giggled. "No, wait—if it comes from males, I'd be attracting does. Too confusing."

Nonna chuckled. "We use an artificial musk. So those horny bucks should have two legs instead of four. But it may or may not work. There is something else, however, which actually does work."

She went to her purse and pulled out a small blue bottle. "I have friends in France doing some experiments with artificially created pheromones," she opened the bottle and handed it to me, "that duplicate human ones."

I sniffed. "I can't smell anything," I said, disappointed.

She looked over the top of her glasses at us. "No, you wouldn't. It doesn't have an overt scent. But we all have a gland in the nose that's sensitive to pheromones. This one is a woman's. And when she wears this, a man will sense it."

Gillian looked at me and smiled. "A love potion."

Nonna nodded. "One of Nature's many. And one that enhances sexual attraction. Sexual, not necessarily romantic. I'm going to combine a few drops of this with a traditional formula for love." She quickly mixed oils of almond, vanilla and ambergris, adding two other oils we couldn't identify into the bottle. And then very carefully she added just a few drops of the precious liquid. "Shake it gently before using it, and only use one or two drops." She swirled the bottle delicately, then poured the mixture into two small, clear bottles and handed them to us. "This will attract a wide range of men. It will be up to you to find the one who's right for you. Remember, use too much and it will have the opposite effect."

"I don't need to attract more men, Nonna," I said, surprised that she had given it to me.

Nonna lifted her hands, refusing to take the bottle back. "It can also work a deeper love magic, releasing the passions that are hidden beneath fears or inhibitions. Take it and use it," she said firmly. "In fact, why don't you put some on right now?" I looked at her quizzically, and she just winked at me. "You can think of it as an experiment. And you," she turned to Gillian, "will know when it's time to use it."

I shook the bottle gently, opened it and applied one small drop beneath each ear. "Well, it should make this evening interesting. Thank you." I grinned and Nonna pinched the end of my nose.

"Have fun." And with those words Nonna sent us out into the utterly average Manhattan Saturday afternoon.

Gillian headed off to meet Jeanette and I set out for my last destination, a big, old hardware store on the East Side. I pulled open the door and inhaled. Ever since I was a little girl and accompanied my father on his trips for nails or washers, tools or other strange things, I had loved hardware stores. Wandering the aisles with all the odd and unfamiliar sights and smells and sounds, and all the things made of metal and glass and rubber and wood that were so mysterious and so very male, I felt like I was in another world.

"May I help you, miss?"

I turned to find a round-faced fellow in his forties with a smile that reached from ear to ear. I blinked, thinking he looked familiar, blinked again and realized he looked vaguely like the Cheshire Cat.

"Thanks. I need some molly screws, and some boric acid. Um . . . let me get my list." I smiled, fishing around in my purse for the list Derek had made for me.

"I can take care of this, Hal." I looked up to see a young man pointedly inserting himself between us. Hal looked annoyed but backed down and away. "How can I help you?" He gave me a grin bigger than Hal's. "I'm Glen."

I pulled the crumpled paper out.

"Let me just check that for you." He gently tugged the list from my hands and in best gentlemanly fashion gestured for me to precede him. "Now, let's just see where the plungers are." His chest seemed to puff a bit as he smiled at me again.

Within moments of arriving in plumbing supplies, I noticed that the aisle had begun to fill with men. Smiling men. And when we moved to pest control, they all showed up seconds later, crowding the narrow area, as one, then another quickly offered his expert advice on the best way to kill cockroaches. And all of them were smiling, except not at each other. They were smiling at me. I followed Glen to flooring materials, and they followed me. Smiling.

Standing at the cash register with a long line of smiling men behind me, some of whom had nothing in their hands to buy, it suddenly dawned on me—Nonna's potion was apparently working. I left with a smile on my face, the door quickly opened for me by Hal.

Within minutes of returning to my apartment, the phone began to ring. I dashed for it, hoping it was Derek, hoping as if it were the first week of dating instead of months later.

"Hello," I answered breathlessly.

"Hey." That single syllable made my heart flip over. "Listen, I was thinking, I know we were supposed to catch a flick tonight, but the guys wanted to get together. You know how hard it is to find a night when we're all free . . ."

I was disappointed, but didn't want to pressure him. "That's okay . . . How about I come along? I'd really love to hear you play." He'd recently started playing with some of his old band members and I'd asked him several times if I could go, but he'd been reluctant, telling me they were just messing around. I'd dropped the subject, but had begun to feel a little uncomfortable that I was being excluded from something he clearly loved.

There was a long pause. "I'm not sure . . ." He suddenly sounded withdrawn.

"I'd really love to." I tried again. "But I don't want to push you . . ." My voice trailed off.

"Why don't we just get together later?"

"Okay. Do you want me to meet you somewhere?" I tried not to sound disappointed.

There was another long pause. And then a resigned sigh. "Okay, you can come."

"Great! I'll meet you there," I replied, thrilled.

"The neighborhood's a little rough, but it'll be daylight when you get there, and we'll leave together."

"No problem." I was a New Yorker; I was also used to taking care of myself. I wrote down the address on the lower, Lower East Side. We hung up and I danced around the room changing my clothes. I decided to leave Nonna's potion right where it was, under my ears. I added one more drop—between my breasts.

When I walked into the cavernous brick-walled space, Derek's normally sweet kiss lasted twice its usual length, maybe three times. And it was a lot more passionate. In fact, he seemed oblivious to the four other musicians in the studio. But I was enjoying myself too much to stop him. A little dizzy when he finally let me go, I was glad he still had his arm around me. I'd met the other members of his band before, but I immediately noticed that instead of their usual casual nods or quick, distracted grins, they were staring. And they were smiling. Two of them offered to get me a chair, another offered me a beer, and the fourth told me how great I looked.

Derek pulled out an old folding chair and I sat listening, completely spellbound by him and by the music, a sound that was very deconstructed. My eyes were fixed on Derek, on his relaxed self-confidence, his comfortable interactions with the other guys, and what seemed like an amazing mastery of his saxophone. I watched his fingers on the round, golden keys and his lips around the mouthpiece, watched his tongue sliding on the edge of a new reed and I shivered. I watched the way his hair kept falling in front of his eyes, the way he'd drag a hand through it, pushing it back from his sweat-slicked forehead. And how incredibly James Dean sexy he looked in that white T-shirt. I sighed, and watched how his chest appeared through the thin material as the shirt slowly soaked through with sweat, and how the muscles of his arms bulged from beneath the short sleeves, not too much, just enough to make my thoughts wander to images of his carrying me to bed. I decided I loved the sax.

And I couldn't help but notice that every time they took a break, Derek would come straight to me, looking at me like he was a hungry man and I was filet mignon. He knelt beside me, held my hand, kissed me, stroked my thigh and promised that they'd be done soon. After two of the planned three or four hours had passed, Derek suggested that they knock off for the night. The other guys stuck around to keep jamming, but Derek packed up his instrument, grabbed me by the arm and whisked me into the subway as fast as my feet would carry me.

He slung his arm over my shoulders, pulled me close and nuzzled my ear. "God, you smell so good," he muttered as the subway rattled uptown. "Can't this thing go any faster?"

The door of my apartment slammed behind us and Derek backed me against it, pinning me, his mouth on mine, hard and insistent. A tidal wave of need rushed from between my legs into my blurring mind and I threw my arms around him. We knocked over the armchair and he pulled at my blouse, struggling with the buttons, finally pulling it over my head. My bra disappeared and his hands closed over my breasts. I yanked at his T-shirt and wrestled it over his head. The phone crashed to the floor and files spilled everywhere as we slammed into the desk; the dial tone buzzed like a swarm of mad bees. Stumbling through the scattered papers, hands roaming, grabbing, kissing wildly, I heard him, felt him inhaling me as if he were breaking the surface of the water after a deep dive. I tugged at his belt and fought with the button of his jeans, finally pulling down the zipper and shoving my hand inside to stroke him.

He pulled my skirt up. "I want you so bad," he growled. His hand grabbed my backside and pulled me up. I wrapped my arms around his neck, my legs around his waist, and he carried me to the bed. I clung to him, inhaling his scent, kissing and biting his neck, tasting the salt of his sweat. He dropped me onto the bed and I watched, carnal and dizzy, as he stripped off the last of his clothes. I reached for him and he came into my arms. I pulled him to me, his skin hot against mine, my mouth meeting his in a kiss that made what was left of my mind reel. His hand slid up between my thighs, mine slid down between his, and as he rolled on top of me, I let myself be swept away.

6

A New God

Blessed, blessed are those who know the mysteries of god,

Blessed is he who hallows his life in the worship of god,

he whom the spirit of god possesseth, who is one

with those who belong to the holy body of god.

—EURIPIDES

Nonna's Shalimar perfumed our hugs and kisses. We linked arms to walk the windy, cold Lincoln Center courtyard to the Metropolitan Opera House, its modern facade glowing like a square-cut diamond. It was always a thrill to attend the opera, any opera, and tonight we were meeting Gillian and Naomi for a production of Strauss's comedic *Ariadne auf Naxos*. Although I'd barely given my daemon a thought since Derek had appeared, an opera about Ariadne and Dionysus was a synchronicity I had noticed immediately.

And we had the added pleasure of using Gillian's parents' season tickets. That they were also center parterre box seats was directly correlated to her father's substantial annual contributions in an amount that well exceeded my first salary as a public interest lawyer. A few rebellious years ago I might have wanted to pull the screws from those seats. Tonight, I couldn't deny it was going to be fun.

"I haven't seen much of you lately. What's up with you these days?" Nonna asked.

I smiled. "I'm in love. I took Derek to meet my parents this weekend and my father actually told me he was glad I'd finally brought a real man home." I beamed, and then frowned. "And my mother seemed to like him . . ."

"Seemed to?"

"Well, she's worried that he already has a child. And he isn't divorced yet."

"But he's been separated for, what, two years?"

I nodded. "I would never have gotten involved with him if he wasn't already out of that marriage." I paused. "But it's true, he's not divorced. Yet." My mother's concerns echoed my own occasional anxiousness. I held open the heavy front door for Nonna and we stepped into an alternate universe, immediately wrapped in the ebullient warmth of the Opera's grand foyer.

"So how do you feel about her worrying?" Nonna stared at me over the top of her glasses. I helped her remove her black cashmere clutch coat, beneath which she was wearing a ruby silk evening suit.

"You look stunning."

"Thank you, dear. Armani. Since I've lost weight I'm having such fun with clothes again!" Nonna was one of the few people I knew who could put a positive spin on having battled cancer a short while back. "So, where were we? Oh yes, your mother's concern."

"She's my mother, it's her job." We laughed. I shrugged off my coat and fluffed the full skirt of the vintage black taffeta dress I was wearing, one of my mother's. It was such a rare pleasure to be able to dress up and I was happy. "Anyway, with a separation he had to wait at least a year before he could file for a no-fault divorce." And then I dug deep, wanting to pull the weed out of the garden of my hope. "There are times when I worry that it's too good to be real, that something's going to ruin it. But it's been less than a year, I'm not going to pressure him." Memories of making love last night flooded back and I smiled. "He just hasn't gotten around to it. But he will."

"So the rest—good?" We moved off to one side and away from the crowd pressing toward the ticket takers, watching for Gillian and Naomi as we talked.

I smiled happily. "Very good. My dad's right; I mean all the other guys I dated seemed so . . . young. They were just looking to score, they weren't ready to fall in love."

"And he is?"

"Derek's fourteen years older than I am, Nonna. It's wonderful to be with a man who knows what he wants." I was talking very fast. I took a deep breath. "And he wants me. It's so sexy."

"Why, thank you." Naomi was standing behind us, grinning. She looked great in a tailored, figure-hugging tuxedo.

"Well, don't you look sharp!"

"No Gilly?" she asked, surveying the crowd. "That girl's always late. So what'd I interrupt?"

"Love, sex, Derek, the usual."

"You are just besotted." Naomi rolled her eyes. "But I've been there. Marcia and I are so different but, man, when we met it was like the earth moved."

Nonna nodded. "There's no desire without polarity." She opened her small black evening purse, pulled out a handkerchief and her opera glasses and gave the lenses a quick cleaning.

"You mean, like opposites attracting?" I asked.

"Most people think that opposites are repelled by each other, that there's a fixed separation between those poles. But actually, those opposites are constantly interacting. That's what polarity is—the force of attraction binding opposites together, in a kind of magnetic, creative dance. It's the way energy moves, from the most infinitesimal level of subatomic particles to the infinite scope of God and Goddess."

"Well, not just male and female." Naomi looked surprised.

Nonna nodded. "You're absolutely right. We mostly refer to polarity in terms of masculine and feminine genders because that's the most obvious expression of our human polarity. Some folks prefer the terms *active* and *receptive*." The opera glasses went back into the purse. "But whatever you use, polarity exists between all couples, regardless of gender."

"And how do we know what masculine and feminine really are?" Naomi asked defensively.

"Isn't it just culture that ascribes certain qualities to one gender or the other? You know, women are illogical, men are unemotional. Stereotypes," I offered.

"Well, there's nurture, but there's also nature; we may never know exactly what's innate to each gender because we may never escape the influence of culture," Nonna replied, pulling out her lipstick and a small mirror. She applied the ruby-red color like an artist, pressed her lips together and continued. "But there's no arguing that there are differences between the sexes."

"I don't know, I think we're more alike than we're different." I shook my head.

"I don't know, I think we're more different than we're alike," Naomi jibed.

Nonna laughed. "Yes, well, you're both right. You've had a real struggle to be accepted as a woman lawyer." She smiled at me. "And you've had a struggle as a lesbian." She nodded to Naomi. "You've both had to break down the barriers of gender stereotyping." She pulled out a small white bag and offered me a butterscotch. I shook my head but Naomi took two. Nonna's tiny purse was beginning to remind me of those clown cars at the circus and I wondered what she'd pull out next. "But there *are* differences. Not that one is better than another—just different. In fact, those differences are valuable, we need them. At the same time, each sex has an aspect of the other within—what Taoists call yin and yang; Jung called it anima and animus. We each mix up all these qualities in our own unique way. Speaking of which, Dionysus was disguised as a girl to protect him when he was young."

"One of the earliest cross-dressers," Naomi quipped.

Nonna smiled. "And it's said that he was the only God who never cheated on his wife."

"Ariadne?"

Nonna nodded. "His grandmother, the Goddess Rhea, initiated him into her Mysteries—women's Mysteries. For us, the most obvious opposites are gender-based. But we don't ever want to get trapped in gender stereotyping again. And you've also got polarity in all sorts of other ways—active and receptive, or shy and outgoing, calm and volatile, serious and funny, nurturing and adventurous."

"Butch and fem." Naomi wiggled her eyebrows. "I gotcha."

"So it's about . . . complimentarity, not opposition?" I asked.

Nonna nodded. "Relationships always involve the balancing of all sorts of polarities; each partner is an energetic pole, and how well a relationship works reflects how well two people have integrated and balanced their energies. But balance isn't static; it's a movement back and forth between the two. A dance if you like." She paused and we watched a young couple walk past, wrapped in their own bubble of obvious pleasure. "Polarity is the erotic magnetism between partners; it's what makes the pulse race; and in sex magic, it's the way the energy flows between partners. Ultimately, love is the unification of polarities. That's the love story of the Goddess and God, in all religions. That's all love stories." She nodded toward Naomi.

"We've mostly worked with the Goddess, and that's fine with me. I mean, what's the God got to offer me?" Naomi asked. I could hear the tinge of defensiveness in her voice return, and Nonna answered her gently but firmly.

"If you exclude one gender, you're making the same mistake the biblical religions have made. And you're out of balance. Fem *and* butch remember?"

Naomi nodded.

And Nonna looked to me. "The God has been working with you from the very beginning of your journey. It was Pan piping that led you to the Goddess. And now it's up to you to find him."

It was true that since I'd met Derek, the signs and synchronicities had stopped. Or I hadn't noticed them. It felt as if Derek had filled that place in my life, and my heart.

"When was the last time you read that favorite poem of yours, 'Kubla Khan'?"

"It's been a while."

"Well, as I recall you said it was a road map for you."

I nodded. "Yes, by deciphering its meaning I realized how my life really had become a spiritual journey. And how much it resembled the story of the Goddess Persephone. Her abduction into the Underworld, and her journey back."

"But she also falls in love—with Hades—and that changes how you view what happened, and why. Go back, read the myth again. And go back and read that poem. I think you'll find that it also contains hints about the God."

"Does Derek have anything to do with the God?" I asked suddenly.

"Only you can answer that question. But all paths that lead to discovering divinity *in* the world know that your lover embodies the God. Or the Goddess." She smiled at Naomi. " 'When a new God comes along, we're dumbstruck.' Now, let's see if we can find Gillian, I'm getting very tired of standing in these elegant and painful shoes."

We worked our way back to the edge of the milling crowd, craning our necks to see over the mass of people. "There she is." I pointed to Gillian, stunning in a long, black velvet evening coat with a fuchsia silk scarf and matching gloves, on the far side of the crowd. And just as I spotted her she looked straight at us and waved.

"It's great being a Witch." I grinned.

"Yes, it is." Nonna smiled and pinched my nose.

Later, sitting in my wonderful seat, watching Dionysus finally rescue Ariadne, I recognized the last line of the opera: "When a new God comes along, we're dumbstruck."

I was heralded into the spacious Brooklyn loft. We'd been invited to a circle with Derek's Wiccan friends. I'd attended many seasonal celebrations with men, but this was the first small, mixed-gender circle I'd ever been to and I was curious to see what it would be like to work so intimately with men—and with Derek.

An older gentleman was setting up the altar—a small table sitting in the center of the large room. "Richard," Derek called out loudly. "He's a bit hard of hearing," he explained to me. Derek was across the room in a few quick strides, tapping Richard on the shoulder.

"Derek!" he exclaimed, grabbing him in a bear hug. "How long has it been?" He was salt and pepper, with closely cropped hair and a neatly trimmed goatee. His elegant gray cashmere sweater and herringbone blazer carefully disguised a small paunch. A small pink triangle pin festooned his jacket's lapel, the discreet but emphatic declaration that he was gay. I was also welcomed with a gracious hug, and Richard, who I learned was the group's priest, immediately began introducing me to the diverse gathering—a Ph.D. in math, a psychologist, the manager of a bookstore, an electrician's apprentice, a fireman, a secretary and an advertising executive.

Having men in a group didn't seem to alter the usual gabbing and catching up, but when it was time to start, everyone quickly swirled into action. Morgana, the group's priestess, a petite, maternal brunette, laughed and chattered as she bustled about her narrow kitchen extricating ritual tools from the drawers and cabinets and ingredients for the incense from her spice rack; pine, sandalwood, valerian, cinnamon, and frankincense, into which she mixed drops of civit and musk oils. I noticed that the altar was set up as it was in my circle, with the four elements and the usual tools and statues of Horned Gods—Gods of forest and fertility that combined the animal, human and divine—from several cultures. And there were also natural expressions of the Divine Masculine—pinecones and stalks of ornamental corn, a branch of brown oak leaves and a small sprig of sharp-pointed holly. Instead of a wand there was a thyrsus, the staff topped with a pinecone carried by Dionysus and his priestesses, and a gleaming cere-monial sword. Lastly, Richard placed a pair of antlers around the God-dess's chalice.

Beneath the altar were the usual bottles of wine and juice, and corn cakes shaped like phalluses, which were met with laughter. Although the group usually worked skyclad, because there were guests tonight they wore simple, floor-length cotton robes, most of the men wearing green, the women red or white. All the men, including Derek, had drums, and the women had rattles, which they placed behind them. The incense and can-dles were lit, transforming the living room into a serene temple, and we stood holding hands in a circle.

Morgana stepped before the altar in the circle's center, and an extraor-dinary metamorphosis occurred as gregariousness gave way to regal com-posure. She led us in grounding and centering, then purified and consecrated the elements. After dipping her athame into the water, and then the salt, she handed it to Richard, who cleaned the ritual knife with a quick stroke across his thigh.

We were each purified and consecrated with the four elements— Morgana blessed the men, Richard blessed the women—a simple method of working with polarity which I felt as soon as I stood before Richard. I was used to the energies of my teachers and the other women with whom I worked, and I immediately felt a noticeable difference in the texture and quality of the energy with Richard.

The circle was then purified and consecrated as each of the women carried an element around its perimeter. Morgana stood silently, eyes closed, breathing deeply. When the Goddess had awakened within her, she smiled and her eyes opened. She lifted the heavy sword sitting at the altar's edge and, holding it in the upturned palms of her hands, offered it to Richard. He bowed to her as he took it.

Richard walked decisively to the east, lifted the sword before him and strode swiftly around the circle, casting as he spoke: "By the power of Lady and Lord, by the power of mind, by the power of will, by the power of love, by the power of manifestation, I cast this sacred circle to preserve and to contain the energy that we shall raise herein . . ."

I shivered as Richard encircled us. Just as Morgana seemed possessed of some greater sense of her true self, Richard exuded an aura of deeply grounded power. His forcefulness seemed to have an extra measure to it, and something else that I could not name, but I could feel. And there was something profoundly stirring about the sight of a man holding a sword as he did.

He finished, standing beside Morgana, bowing again as he returned the sword to her. Receiving and returning the sword to the hands of the priestess expressed a conscious, moral choice not to use the power of man's superior physical strength to harm or oppress, but rather to serve the Goddess as she was embodied in women, the land and its people, and therefore to serve life—as a hunter, warrior and protector. And it harkened back to the ancient rites by which a man was made king only through his union with the Goddess's priestess.

Morgana handed Richard his athame, the more facile counterpart of the great sword, and he invoked the powers of the four directions. Already, I could feel the intense vitality of this circle cast by a man. But the chivalric cadence had only begun. Richard knelt before Morgana. Bowing his head, he addressed her: "May the power of the Lady descend into you and bless the work that we shall undertake tonight."

Morgana placed her right hand at the back of his neck and replied: "Receive the blessing of the Great Mother who is served with power and compassion, honor and humility, mirth and reverence even by the Lord of Death who is also the Lord of Rebirth. Rise and let the power of the God be drawn into you that those gathered tonight may be blessed."

Richard stood, reached out his arms and invoked the God by his many names: "Lover, hunter, trickster, Lord of the Dance, God of the fiery Sun that makes the Earth grow, God of creation and fertility, of forest and field, Horned God, God of the wild. Descend, we pray, into our circle, into our lives, into our souls and our bodies. Let us bid you hail and welcome!"

Like Morgana, he spoke in a style that had an unfamiliar formality, but seemed utterly suited to the archetypal flow of energies that I was witnessing. There was a sense of mutual acknowledgment and honoring at the core of their interaction. As they worked, Morgana was becoming softer and more feminine—yet vividly powerful—and Richard seemed stronger and more masculine—yet genuinely tender. And as they engaged one another, they also seemed to be engendering a palpable energy that began to pervade the circle.

Richard crossed his arms over his chest, closed his eyes and again bowed his head. In one hand he held his athame, in the other the antlers. Morgana faced him, holding the thyrsus. They stood for just a moment, and then he lifted his head and she touched the wand to the center of his forehead, his third eye, and began to invoke the God:

"By hoof and by horn I invoke thee, by hide and by bone I invoke thee, by the power of love I invoke thee to descend into this the body of thy High Priest. See with his eyes, speak with his tongue, kiss with his lips that your children may be blessed. Mighty Horned God, Spirit of forest and glade, piper at the gates of dawn, Lord of the Dance, wild one, intoxicator, beloved Consort, arise and come unto us. Come to us, touch us, bless us."

Electricity raced across my skin as she spoke, and as I watched, Richard seem to grow taller, his shoulders broader, his stomach disappearing, years dropping away from his face. His voice was not his own, but deeper and tinged with strange inflection:

"I hear your call and I come. Await the sound of hooves upon the earth, the scent of the woods as I approach, the rustle of leaves and snapping of branches in the moonlight that makes your heart leap with fear and desire. I bring you what you seek—the dangers of passion and love."

His voice seemed to fill the room as if coming from all around us, rather than from Richard's lips, as he continued:

"I am Herne the Hunter and I am Cernunnos, stag of seven tines, I am Pan, lustful goat foot God and I am Osiris, bull God, lord of death and rebirth, and I am the blessed Dionysus, bull-faced God conceived in fire."

A pulse of excitement raced through me as I heard the name Dionysus. I wondered if, because I had begun to think about my daemon, he was returning to me.

"Embrace me and I will give you the greatest ecstasy you have ever known. Run from me and I will gore you with the agony of madness. Come to me through the labyrinth. I am with you at every turn and I wait with open arms to dance with you at the center."

Richard's eyes suddenly opened. He dropped the athame and held the antlers high in the air. The men seized their drums and sought a rhythm. They found it quickly and the beat steadied; the counterpoints rose and fell, and drumming saturated the space and all my senses—not just my hearing and sight, but also my sense of touch when the floor beneath my feet began to vibrate.

Richard and the women began to dance within the circle of drummers, singing a song that I recognized, the old Quaker hymn "Simple Gifts," but with unfamiliar lyrics.

"Dance, dance, wherever you may be
I am the Lord of the Dance, you see!
I live in you, and you live in Me
And I lead you all in the Dance, said He!"

The candle flames leapt and flickered, casting our dancing shadows upon the wall. My self-consciousness quickly disappeared and I began to move. The beat was strong, and sweat already glistened on the drummers' faces as they played. Richard danced and leapt, chasing the women with his horns lowered before him, darting between the drummers, urging them on.

The song disappeared into the relentless chanting of the ancient name of Dionysus once sung by his priestesses, the Maenads, who roamed through the mountains of ancient Greece clad in the skins of panthers, bedecked with wreaths of ivy, playing drums and tambourines, wild in their physical abandonment and spiritual ecstasy: "Evoi! Evoi! Blessed be!"

I spun and skipped and whirled, surrendering myself to the drummers' rhythm, to the power the men were raising, to the ecstasy they conjured and to communion with its mysterious origin. Again and again as I circled around the altar, I found myself in front of Derek, and I realized that the Aphrodite circle weeks before had been preparation for this encounter.

Our eyes met and I felt the drumbeats enter and arouse me from within. The tops of my breasts were exposed as the straps of my dress slipped from my shoulders, and the full skirt flared and spun, revealing my legs. I watched Derek watching me, saw the heat in his eyes, his hands flying across the top of his drum. I could no longer tell whether I was dancing for the drummer or he was drumming for my dance.

The room was growing hotter and our exhilaration heightened. The women rode the energy the men and drums were building; our dancing urged the men on. They seemed to merge with their drums, and the rhythmic force the men generated pressed against the walls, shattered my inhibitions and drove all of us to push through the exhaustion. We caught a second wave, riding a primordial cadence, dancing faster and faster, until the drumming peaked in frenzied cacophony.

Richard stood in front of the altar, antlers aloft as the women grabbed hands and the energy we had raised whirled about the room, spinning around and between us. The air itself seemed to dance from my lungs as the chant rose to a final, gasping, exhilarated shout. We threw our arms into the air, releasing the spiraling light that flew from our fingertips. Then we reached earthward, kneeling and laying our palms flat against the floor, feeling the power flowing from our hands into the ground far beneath us.

We collapsed on the floor, with the pairs of lovers in each other's arms. The air was soaked with an erogenous potion we had chanted and sweated, danced and pounded from a part of ourselves that knew the meaning of life. I felt Derek's breath hot and fast against the back of my neck, felt his lips and then his tongue on my slick skin. His teeth nipped my shoulder and a shudder of desire seized me. I leaned back against his damp chest, oblivious to everything but the pleasure of his arms around me and his mouth on mine. A searing cord of lust bound us as we kissed hungrily, and I wrapped my arms around his neck, inhaling his earthy smell, wanting to pull him into me, wanting the room empty and my body filled by him.

He pulled back, eyes darkened by desire, his hand sliding up the inside of my thigh. I heard people talking, laughing, and the shell of ardor that had surrounded us thinned. I pulled my eyes from Derek's and looked around at the group. They were no longer ordinary folks with day jobs, but beings of light charged with grace and joy and holy delight who had drunk the milk of Paradise.

We were all smiling, laughing, talking, passing bottles of wine and water. I had danced and chanted many times to work with the ecstatic energy of the Goddess, but tonight was different. We'd abandoned ourselves to a different kind of physicality—graceful dancing replaced by erotic inspiration, and beautiful harmonic singing giving over to percussive chanting. And we'd chanted louder, danced faster, and done both longer. There was less subtlety and more robustness, and it felt good. Though I reclined exhausted, I was energized with joy.

And then the courtliness returned. Richard knelt before Morgana as she sat upon the altar, holding the silver chalice. He raised his athame, saying the familiar words that now seemed charged with deeper implication:

"As the athame is to the God . . ."

"So the chalice is to the Goddess," Morgana replied.

"And conjoined they bring blessedness," they said together. Richard plunged the blade into the chalice that Morgana lifted to meet his thrust. Ritualistically, they expressed the relationship between God and Goddess, man and woman, as one of generative polarity and sacred union. The chalice was passed, libations offered, bread consecrated and shared, the God and Goddess thanked and the circle closed. Derek came up behind me as I was helping to clean up, wrapping his arms around me and suddenly sweeping me up off my feet. Holding me in his arms, he kissed me and I floated in weightless contentment.

Polarity. I wanted more. As Derek kissed me I sensed that, just as I had learned to find the Goddess in myself, my next challenge was to recognize the God in Derek. And to surrender myself to the fire that burned beneath my skin.

"*Hey gorgeous*, what're you reading?" Derek leaned down and kissed me. A rush still hit me whenever he came into view, and especially when he kissed me. I was happy—radiant was the word everyone in circle used. When we were together there weren't enough hours in the day, and when we were apart the day was too long. He filled my thoughts, my bed, my life. We spent almost every night in each other's arms and it was as natural as breathing. There were no doubts, no uncertainties about my feelings, or his—just the way it was supposed to be.

He dropped into a chair, dumped his knapsack and a bright yellow and red plastic bag on the floor. He'd been shopping for records at Bleecker Bob's and we'd decided to meet at the Riviera. But what caught my attention was the big black sax case. He pulled my book to see the cover. *"East of Eden,"* he said.

I nodded. "A present from my parents. It's a first edition, so I probably shouldn't carry it around." I slipped it back into the padded envelope I carried it in and put the envelope in my oversized purse. "Every once in a while I just get this urge to reread it." Since the opera, I'd been thinking about my daemon, and though he wasn't appearing as he used to, the ritual with Derek's friends had certainly seemed like a nudge from him. Looking at his handsome profile, I wondered, again, if perhaps my daemon was living inside Derek.

"It was a movie, wasn't it? With James Dean?" He reached over and picked up my coffee cup. I nodded, surprised and instantly alert.

"His first; he played Cal. Cain, cast out of the American paradise. There's something about that . . . archetype, the son cast out by his father, wounded, betrayed, wandering. Longing for love."

"The scapegoat," Derek said frowning slightly.

"Bearing someone else's sins. His father's."

"I used to think we were a generation of that estrangement."

"You mean Vietnam?"

He nodded and stared out the window at the rushing yellow river of cabs.

"What did you do?" It had been years since the war ended, but it was still the formative event of our generation, and though I knew that Derek hadn't served, I didn't know why not, or what he had done.

"I got lucky with a college deferment. But I was going to move to Canada if I had to." He paused for a minute and I was silent, wondering what he would reveal. "My father and I've never fully reconciled. You know that Springsteen song, 'Adam Raised a Cain'?"

I nodded, remembering how often I'd played it the year my daemon first appeared.

"I never understood where Cain's wife came from," he said, unexpectedly.

He startled me with those last words. "Actually, that's easy," I offered. He looked surprised. "She came from the pre-biblical Goddess cultures that Adam and Eve's storytellers invaded. I was always sort of intrigued by the book, and the movie and the song. And by him—Cain. I went back and reread the original story and it blew me away. If you look at it in historical context, God accepts Abel's offering of a slaughtered lamb—the offering of the nomadic invaders, the people of the Old Testament. And he rejects Cain's offering of wheat, which was the traditional offering to the Goddess. It's because of that invasion and the forced shift from Goddess to God that Cain fights Abel."

He looked at his watch. "Listen, I talked to the guys and we're going get together later, do a little playing, no big deal. Why don't you come along?"

I was jolted by the swift change of subject, but I was also getting accustomed to it as something he did with frequency. And the mystery of the sax was solved.

"I'd love to." I was happy that he was playing again, not just because I enjoyed hearing him, but because it made him happy.

He smiled at my excitement. "Great, let's go." He shrugged on his motorcycle jacket, then held my coat for me. He took my hand as we flagged a cab to the Lower East Side. "Finish the story you were telling me about Cain and Abel."

"You're not bored?"

He shook his head and laughed. "This stuff is fascinating; it's like the explanation for a mystery that most people completely miss. Go on."

I smiled. It was such a weird pleasure to be talking like this with anyone, let alone with the man I was madly in love with. "Okay. So when Cain fights Abel, he's actually defending the civilizations of the Goddess against the invasions that were happening at the time. Jahweh puts a mark on him, so that, supposedly, the earth won't bear her gifts for him, and he's cast out. He's turned into a scapegoat. But God can't separate Cain from the earth, because the earth *is* the Goddess. So he goes and dwells on the east of Eden, in the land of Nod, where he falls in love with his wife. She'd been waiting all that time for him to find his way home to her. And they lived happily ever after, and had a lot of children."

"Interesting, but I don't know if a passel of kids makes for much of a happily ever after." He shrugged. "My own interest tends to run towards the Gnostic Gospels. St. Thomas. Jesus as the mystic, the shaman who returns from forty days and nights in the desert. Ever spend any serious time in the wilderness?"

I shook my head. "Not like that."

"I've never done more than a lunar cycle. But that's a long time. Very intense. It changes you, and the way you see the world. No one ever talks about what that must have done for Christ's spirituality."

"That would be interesting. But I don't know, I've never been comfortable with the idea of the crucifixion, the brutality of it—a father sacrificing his son." I shook my head. "The martyring, it seems so . . . anti-spiritual. And we just seem to be repeating the pattern."

"It's supposed to be a lesson in compassion." He sighed. "Somehow the message of a love so strong it will make the ultimate sacrifice became an excuse to sacrifice without love. Most people don't realize it, but it's almost easier to understand the message of love if you understand the historical context. Like you did with Cain. Christ was following in the ecstatic footsteps of Dionysus."

"Dionysus?" I asked, surprised, not only with the parallel, but to hear the name coming from Derek's lips. I watched him intently.

He nodded. "Lot of parallels. Both were hailed as the 'King of Kings.' They're both Gods of love and visionary ecstasy. Both claimed to be the son of God, and neither was believed. Both challenged the religious establishments, both were persecuted by political authorities, both were scapegoats, like Cain. And both were accompanied by outcasts and women."

"That's a lot of similarities."

He paid the cabbie, grabbed his stuff, and I followed him out of the cab and onto a street filled with fabric stores and kosher meats, leather jackets and luggage all on the ground floor or basement level of very old redbrick tenement buildings. He took my hand again as we walked, and I could feel its warmth spreading through me.

"There's more. Both were sons of divine fathers and mortal, virgin mothers. Christ rose from the dead, Dionysus emerged from the underworld. Both mothers ascended—to Olympus, to heaven."

"I didn't know you knew so much about Dionysus." I was fascinated.

He shrugged. "Well, I started with Jesus and that actually led me backwards. I mean, the whole thing can't be taken out of the historical context of the time, and at the time that whole area was very much under the influence of Greek culture. Anyway, both die and both are reborn. Both embody the spiritual lesson that life doesn't really end. Dionysus ascended to Olympus, Jesus to heaven, and both sat at the right hand of their father."

His words were weaving an enchantment, a bridge between worlds and cultures long believed to be divided, and somehow between us.

"They're both archetypes," I offered, and he nodded.

"Divinity," he responded. "And of course, there's the wine. Dionysus was constantly creating wine and one of Jesus's most famous miracles was turning water into wine. Both are honored with communions of flesh and wine—the most famous Christian chalice, the Antioch chalice, is inscribed with Christ on a swing of grapevines. Just like Dionysus, Jesus said, 'I am the vine.' Drinking the wine, the blood of God, the Eucharist, is an ecstatic ceremony where you literally become one with the Divine, if only for a moment."

"But Christianity has ended up being the main force of repression *against* experiencing divinity within yourself. And certainly not through loving another person."

"That wasn't Christ's teaching. Christians do speak of feeling the spirit within all the time, and they speak of loving each other as an expression of God's love. You experience God's love through loving another. God *is* love. That may not be true of some of these crazy fundamentalists, but mainstream Christians believe these things."

"Yes, but I mean sexually. Finding divinity within another . . . by making love." I was thinking about Nonna's teaching and about making love with Derek. "It's taken a very long time for sex to become socially acceptable again. It's still very taboo and *very* threatening to the social order. People are just starting to accept healthy sex as part of psychological health."

"And creative energy," Derek smiled. He'd been playing more often.

"So the culture repressed Dionysus, but he returned as Jesus." I finally saw the pattern and the connection.

Derek smiled. "You can't suppress the ecstatic, it's who we are."

"It's our connection to divinity." I thought of my conversations with Nonna, and my experiences with Derek. A pulse of desire ran through me and I smiled up at him.

"And to each other." And then he leaned down and kissed me. "This is it." We stood in front of a very old brick tenement building on the corner of Ludlow. As he held the door open for me, just one of his many courtly gestures, I felt closer than ever to him.

"I've been walking in the park every day, but I need more Nature and a lot less people! Could we take a drive out to the Delaware Water Gap this weekend?" Derek agreed. It was a beautiful day, cold but clear as we drove through the state forest and then into the federally protected Gap.

"Oh!" My hands flew out to the dashboard as Derek slammed on the brakes. A huge buck leapt from the brush onto the old road just feet from the car, its hooves sounding like small explosives against the old asphalt, and just as quickly it disappeared into the woods. I was thrilled at the sudden reminder of the Horned God.

We pulled the car to the side of the road and climbed out. It was cold enough to see our breath, but we warmed as we tramped through the woods, then through harvested, corn-strewn fields, finally climbing the high ridge into the returning forest. I inhaled the damp musk of decaying leaves underfoot, like grapes in a winepress, transforming from one thing into another in the original alchemy of time, death and rebirth.

Nonna had sent me in search of the God, the divine masculine, the untamed power of male sexuality, ecstasy and fertility. The Horned God—Herne with the antlers of a stag, Dionysus and Osiris, both bulls, Pan of the goat hooves—unifies spiritual, human and animal natures, all three of which are essential to a man's wholeness. And I was learning that He always had an important and erotic relationship with the Goddess as Her lover and companion.

Years ago, the Church had falsely accused the Horned God of being Satan, seeking to undermine and demonize this ancient God of the Old Religion. But I'd learned early on in my introduction to this spirituality that Satan is a personification of evil who belongs strictly to the biblical faiths. The Horned God is a god of love—physical and holy.

"Let's stay overnight," I pleaded. "It's so romantic."

We stood outside a quaint stone inn built in the 1800s that had one room left. Derek was grumpy and full of trivial reasons why he had to get back to the city. And then the mystery of his moodiness was solved—he didn't have the money to pay for the room.

"I'll pay for it. It's not a problem. Really. It'll be wonderful." I hugged him and we went in to register. At dinner, I smelled and tasted and felt the God of wine and ecstasy, red and intoxicating in the wineglass, on my tongue, in my blood, and on our lips as we kissed, moaned and grappled.

I could see the waning moon through our bedroom window, and as if I could hear Pan piping in the woods, I was lured from the warmth of our bed into the frost-hardened field beyond to dance, laughing, beneath the moonlight. He came to me as the Great God Pan, he came to me as Dionysus, or even by a mortal name as Derek lifted me in his arms, threw me over his shoulder and carried me laughing and squirming from the field back to our room and to the exquisite *petite mort* of bodies firm and yielding.

"I love you," I whispered as I heard his breathing grow slow and even. He rolled over and threw an arm around me.

"Love you," he mumbled.

I had a hard time falling asleep.

"I'm in a kind of cave and there's a man, with dark hair, and dark eyes. He looks a little like Springsteen, and his wrists are wrapped in cloth. There are markings on the cloth, runes, but I don't know what they mean."

A few weeks later, I woke to the sound of Derek snoring. The room was cold and I tiptoed quickly into the bathroom, closed the door, and jotted down the dream, and the symbols, in my journal, finishing with a simple line: *"And then I woke up. It feels important, even though I don't know what any of it means."*

I stared at the symbols I'd drawn. They were runes, the ancient Scandinavian alphabet obtained by Odin that was said to have magical and divinatory powers. After breakfast. Derek left to see his son and I dug out my rune book. The first was called *Ansuz,* meaning God, or ancestral god. It was also called *ansur,* which means mouth. *The mouth of God.*

Stunned, I stared at the sacred letters. My heart was racing as I quickly returned to the book's explanation, carefully writing as I read: *"Divination, inspiration, transformation, enthusiasm."* Enthusiasm comes from the

Greek *en theos,* meaning to be filled with the God! My sense of excitement began to mount—it was the rune of inspired, magical speech and ecstatic incantation. *"The rune of the Wild Hunt, of gods who ride the howling winds."*

The other was *Eihwaz,* the yew tree, the rune of wisdom; it symbolizes movement and communication between the worlds, between different levels of reality.

The dream was a message from my daemon. But what *were* the words of God? Where was I to find them? I listened to the wind howling, not just outside my leaky old windows, but inside the building, wailing down the elevator shaft like a banshee's remorseless cry.

I waited for a cledon, for a synchronicity, for another dream, another message. And then, one snowy night when Derek was not with me, I turned on the television and found myself watching a strange, romantic fairy tale called *Sweet Hostage,* starring Martin Sheen as another Cain-like antihero. A demon lover. It had been such a long time since I'd felt the cinematic presence of my daemon, and I watched, rapt and transported. But when he began to quote "Kubla Khan," an arrow of shock struck my heart.

And I remembered Nonna's forgotten advice. When the movie was over, with shaking hands, I pulled the old volume of poetry, with its broken binding that fell open to the poem, and I read.

> But oh! that deep romantic chasm which slanted
> Down the green hill athwart a cedarn cover!
> A savage place! as holy and enchanted
> As e'er beneath a waning moon was haunted
> By woman wailing for her demon-lover!

Demon-lover. I shivered, reliving the desire and fear those words had summoned the first time I'd read them. It was never that he was literally demonic, but rather that she, that I, longed for a lover who was dangerous and forbidden and consumingly erotic because of his rebelliousness. And now I understood my instinct was correct: The reference was not to evil,

but to the taboo, for the origin of the word *demon* was *daemon*. The daemon always stood in opposition to what was socially acceptable—so many
stories about Dionysus were challenges to kings and rulers. It was *he* for
whom she longed. And I had longed for his human counterpart. I read on.

And all who heard should see them there,
And all should cry, Beware! Beware!
His flashing eyes, his floating hair!
Weave a circle round him thrice,
And close your eyes with holy dread,
For he on honey-dew hath fed,
And drunk the milk of Paradise

It was Dionysus who fed on honey and drank the milk of Paradise,
Dionysus whom I honored in circles cast three times around. But what was
the point of longing for a daemon lover—a magical, taboo-defying, erotic
lover—if I could never feel his kiss, his arms around me, his body pressed
against mine? Without his physical presence, he was no lover at all. But I
had Derek. I heard Derek's music playing in my head, saw the ecstatic way
he played and how he had drummed, the unrelenting passion with which
he made love, his refusal to toe the line and join his father's company. And
his love of wine. He *was* Dionysian. Was that why I was so smitten? Had
Derek taken the place of my daemon? I stared down at the text and the
question rose from hidden depths. *Was Derek my demon lover?*

It was another long and sleepless night.

7

Fantasies

Love is a smoke made with the fume of sighs.

—WILLIAM SHAKESPEARE

Love was its own potion. I placed the ace of cups from my tarot deck, the Holy Grail, symbol of overflowing love, in the center of my altar. In this season of darkness, light ascended from holy waters and the world was enchanted. It was February, the bleakest part of winter, but in the Celtic tradition this was the season of Imbolc, of life stirring in the belly. In China, it was the Spring Festival, the oldest and most important celebration of the year, when the earth is once again planted with seed and new life begins. Tonight was also the second new moon after the Winter Solstice, the Chinese New Year, the year of the dog.

We had gone to see a Shaw Brothers Kung Fu movie—one of Derek's favorites, filled with fights in midair and magical spirits—down at the Movie Palace in Chinatown, but it was closed and so we wandered, politely pushing our way through the labyrinthine streets. We were strangers in a foreign city, a ruby Oz. Glowing red paper lanterns were festooned across the streets and illumined all the windows, the shops were ablaze with light, and long scrolls of gold-trimmed red paper hung everywhere.

"They're called Red Couplets; they're for luck in the New Year. The writings are prayers for health, long life, and wealth, and they praise Nature's gifts. It's an old practice—originated with hanging peach-wood charms to keep ghosts and evil spirits away," Derek explained, gripping my hand tightly as we wove through the jostling crowd. He'd studied martial arts and was familiar with many aspects of Eastern cultures and religions.

"Really? Peaches are the fruit of Kuan Yin. She's the Goddess of compassion." I spotted a pair of ornately embroidered red silk slippers in a shop window. "Why all the red?"

"Red's considered the most auspicious color, and it frightens off the monster Nian." My stomach leapt into my throat as a string of fireworks exploded just a few feet away, filling the narrow street with deafening, echoing sound. The gutter was already filled with colorful mountains of shredded paper, and a smoky haze—of incense burning everywhere, in honor of the ancestors, and the raw, sulfurous residue of hovering gunpowder—drifted around us as if we were entering a dream.

Derek pulled me through the packed streets as body-stunning M-80 firecrackers flew from windows into back alleys, exploding with the firepower of a quarter stick of dynamite. He pushed open the door of a steamy, crowded restaurant and all heads turned to look at the *lo fa*, the round-eyed foreigners. "The owner," Derek said to me as he nodded to the thin, milky-eyed man at the cash register, who smiled and waved back.

We squeezed into a table by the window and quickly shed our coats. "*Gung Hay Fat Choy!*" The harried, overweight waiter and Derek exchanged New Year's greetings as the waiter set down a pot of tea and two small thick cups. There were no menus, but Derek was already ordering, in Chinese. He turned back to me with a huge smile.

"So who's this monster everyone's trying to scare off?" I asked.

"Nian—the name actually just means year." Derek switched to a storytelling voice and I sat back, delighted as he began to perform for me. "Nian was the biggest, scariest monster of all and every New Year he would suddenly appear and terrorize people." He made a scary face and I laughed. "He'd destroy the crops and people's homes and he became so fierce that finally he threatened to destroy all of mankind." He grabbed the teapot and started filling the small cups.

"Well, what happened?" I asked impatiently, enthralled as a child by a bedtime story.

"Well, the people were in an uproar, so the emperor summoned a wise man who challenged Nian." His voice sounded like an old man's: " 'Why do you choose to destroy the humans who are no match for your strength?' he asked the monster. 'If you were truly powerful, you would prove it by destroying the other monsters of the earth.' "

Derek said something in Chinese and the waiter laughed as he filled the table with small plates and round wooden baskets filled with little rolls and dumplings. "*Dim sum.* Looks fantastic." Derek loaded up our plates. I looked, discreetly sniffed, tasted warily and then started devouring everything.

"So what happened?" I asked. "Did Nian fight the other monsters? Or eat all the people?"

Between bites, Derek resumed his story. "Well, Nian was a very proud and ferocious monster, and he was not about to be humiliated by a human, so he took up the challenge. In just a year, he destroyed every monster on earth, but then he had nothing to do so he decided to go back to picking on mankind. But the day he returned there were kids playing with firecrackers and Nian was so frightened by all the noise that he ran away."

I jumped as a string of firecrackers went off right outside the window. "Did you arrange for the special effects?" I asked, laughing.

He nodded, grinning. "From then on, firecrackers and fireworks have been used every New Year to scare away the last remaining monster on earth. And the last of last year's negativity."

I was charmed, but felt a quick kick of sadness. "We've become our own monsters, and gunpowder's used for killing."

"Come on, this is a very magical day. You know—you've got to give yourself over to it or it won't work. You can't think negative, you can't use any bad or unlucky words." Derek put a dumpling in my mouth. "And you can't curse. That's more for me than you. And there's another one I'd like to manage—you're supposed to have all your debts paid off before the New Year." He smiled and stared out the window as the street filled with another series of rapid-fire explosions. "And you don't talk about the past because everything's supposed to be about a new beginning."

The concussions pushed through every molecule in my body, leaving me breathless and open. It *was* a new year—a new life! I studied Derek's handsome profile, still amazed at how much he resembled the kingly warrior from my spell. He was archetypally heroic, though his background was typically American. His father owned a medical publishing house and had moved the family—one wife, one boy, one girl, no dog—to one of those 1950s Adam Sykes movie towns in Connecticut. Lots of manicured green, lots of wives drinking before noon and playing bridge after. But Derek had escaped, he'd gone away to college and never looked back. He'd made his living as a musician until his son came along. And then, after stints in wedding bands that made him depressed enough to drink, he'd gotten a job working as a surveyor, supporting himself and the child he was rarely allowed to see.

Derek ordered *Jin Dui*, a special New Year's cookie made from sweet potatoes, red bean paste and rice flour; we sat watching the river of people, their edges blurred by the smudged air and the foggy window. Derek had grown quieter as the evening progressed, until finally he sat silently. The harsh fluorescent lights accentuated the hollows in his cheekbones and around his eyes as he stared at the passing crowd.

"I know it's only been a year, but do you know how much I care about you?" His words sounded more like a plea than a question. I nodded, reaching across the Formica tabletop to touch his fisted hands. Even when we were together, when I knew he was happy, he seemed haunted. He'd been wounded, he'd sacrificed his dreams, he'd had his heart broken. It was a romantic story, a hero who had suffered, who wouldn't settle for less than true love, who wasn't afraid of hard work. He wasn't a working class poet with dark hair and darker eyes, but he was my white knight and I was ready to be carried off.

I nodded. "It's hard to believe it's been that long. It feels like no time at all."

"You know I wouldn't do anything to hurt you."

"Of course." I nodded, smiled, but his words made me anxious and I pulled my hands back and crossed them in front of me. A tendril of uneasiness began to twist its way around my heart.

"I've dated, but it was all just pretty casual stuff. And sex. But with you it's different." I breathed more easily, watched the flexing of his fists as he pushed our messy dishes away and flattened his palms against the tabletop.

"It's gotten serious. And, well, I've been thinking about the future and what I need to do."

Finally. I exhaled and it felt like thousands of pounds were lifting from my body. "I didn't want to say anything. I mean, I didn't want you to feel pressured. But I'm so relieved." I was smiling as if I'd swallowed the moon. "There's an attorney in my office share that handles no-fault divorces. Actually, if you wanted, I could help you draft the papers, and file them yourself to save the money, since you're already separated."

He looked startled.

A small wave of apprehensive embarrassment began to rise from the pit of my stomach. Maybe he wasn't going to get divorced. "I'm sorry, did I misunderstand you?"

"No, no, I'm separated, like I told you."

"But you don't want to file for a divorce?" I heard the question leave my mouth. I felt as if I were floating away from my body.

"Well, it's not that simple. I'm separated, just not legally separated."

"It's not legal?" I asked, stunned. "I just assumed." My voice was a crumpled murmur. A legal separation closed the door on a marriage. Without one, that door remained open to a reconciliation. Was that what he was trying to tell me? "I thought it was over." My voice was flat and hard as I struggled with my feelings.

"You know it's over between Paula and me." He sounded angry, defensive.

"Over? Even if you wanted out now, your wife"—the word sent a wave of agony through me—"would have to agree to the terms of a sepa-ration agreement, or you'd have to go through a divorce battle. Either way, it could take years before you'll be free." I kept my tone even and low, struggling not to sound angry. I stared blankly at the table, unable to look at him.

A whirlpool of bewildered despair and anger twisted inside me. But I wasn't going to engage in a public display of emotions, especially hurt. "I can't be the 'other woman.' I won't be," I said, finally looking into his anx-ious eyes. I got up, knocking over my chair as I grabbed my coat and purse. I felt my cheeks flush as the restaurant turned its eyes upon me. "I'm sorry," I mumbled, straightening the chair and rushing out the door.

I raced up the street praying for a cab, for an escape from the tangle of pain and confusion. I ran past the Buddhist temple, trying not to bump into people, looking over my shoulder, hoping to get away, hoping he would catch me. I spotted Derek just as a huge, monstrous dragon puppet flew around the corner, snapping its jaws. It pinned me to the wall, dipping and rising, undulating and thrusting and blocking my path each time I tried to move away. The musicians laughed, banging a gigantic drum, gong and cymbals, as firecrackers burst at the creature's leaping feet and shattered the last of my self-control.

A strong hand gripped my arm and I looked up to see Derek staring at me, his eyes hard with anger. He steered me down a small side street and away from the crowds, abruptly pushing me into a darkened alley.

I jerked my arm away but he remained standing so close I could feel his agitated breathing. "I don't want to be the reason you leave your marriage, your child. I won't be," I snapped at him.

"Who said you would?" he replied angrily and my heart shriveled to a stone.

"And I won't be your . . . your cunt on the side." I shocked myself and his face contorted in fury. I winced as he grabbed my shoulders and shook me.

"If that's what you think of me I should've just let you go," he spat and released his grip. I stumbled back against a pile of empty wooden crates that rocked precariously. A sob and a sudden rush of tears escaped me. Derek hauled me against him.

"You should have—" I tried to push him away.

He clamped his mouth over mine. The kiss was brutal, frustration fueling his passion. He backed me into the shadow of the building, pressing me up against the brick wall, his hands pulling open my coat and shoving my sweater up. He jerked aside my bra and squeezed my breasts, leaning into me, pinning me with his hands, with the strength of his hardened body. I gasped for air, pushing ineffectually against him, tears rolling down my cheeks. "No . . ."

He took my mouth again in a harsh kiss that slowly gentled, his tongue pushing deeper, silencing me, plundering, stealing my breath, my resistance. One arm held me tightly around the waist while the other hand tangled itself in my hair, pulling my head back as he ran his lips along my exposed neck, biting just hard enough to make me weak.

"Let me go," I protested feebly, squirming against him, my pride launching a last, trivial defense against his relentless abduction; he held me fast. He was merciless, driven by a desire that quickened again, pushing his passion beyond his control, or mine. His hands roamed, grabbed, pulled wildly, his breathing harsh and fast, his kisses hard and consuming, sweeping away my protests as his need became mine.

I softened to him and his touch gentled, penetrating the last of my defenses with words. "If you cry on New Year's, you'll cry all through the year. I can't let you do that," he murmured, burying his face against my neck. His warm breath sent chills through me as he gently kneaded my breasts, his fingers stroking my skin. "You don't want to be angry at me. Tell me what you do want." His voice was husky. "Tell me."

"I want . . . I want you to be free to love me, to have a future with me." My voice was choked with longing.

"I *am* free—my heart's yours, you *know* that."

I stared into his eyes and stopped pushing against him, gripping his shirt instead, leaning into him, trembling. I wanted him to kiss me, to hold and reassure me. He pulled me tightly against him, sliding a hand beneath my skirt and along the back of my thigh. I moaned. He spun me around and wrenched my skirt up, ripping the thin stockings and tearing away my flimsy underpants. I gasped and, pitching forward, I reached out to steady myself, my palms scraping against the pitted brick wall. I was exposed to him, to the cold, and to the conspiring, dangerous city that snaked around my naked skin.

"What else do you want?" His voice was low and penetrating. "Do you want me to touch you . . . here?" He pressed up against me, wrapping an arm strongly around my waist, his other hand slipping into the wetness that had extinguished the last of my fiery anger. His fingers moved in slow, small strokes seeking the hidden prize that released my ecstasy. "Is that good? Do you like it?" His words were stripping me as bare as his hands had. I nodded. "Tell me," he muttered against my ear.

"Yes, it feels . . ." The words were lost in slow, spreading pulses of pleasure. "It feels good." His soft fondling won the response he wanted. The fight was over as my mind's protests gave way to my body's pleading.

A muffled firecracker exploded in the distance. His hands were warm as he pressed down on the small of my back, arching me against him. I heard him unzip his pants. He pulled me open and, in silent certainty, entered me. I moaned as he leaned forward, stroking me inside and out with feral assurance.

"You know it's going to be okay." He was relentless, firm. "Show me that you know, baby. Show me."

The orgasm exploded through me in wave after wave that showed him I knew, that I believed everything he wanted me to. He thrust himself into me, hard and deep.

It was a very different kind of sex magic.

I woke up alone, in his bed, the next morning. I stared at the raw, pink scrapes along the fleshy mounds of my palms. A quicker beat began in all my pulse points as images of last night rushed back. I could hear Derek in the kitchen, humming, heard his footfalls down the hall, smelled the coffee he was carrying. He was dressed only in jeans and I blushed as he sat on the edge of the bed, smiling, and handed me a cup.

"Sleep okay?"

I nodded. "Thanks. I'm in kind of a daze." I wrapped my hands around the warm cup. "This should get me to the desired heart rate."

"I can think of something else that might help." He put his cup down and climbed into the bed beside me. His hand slid under the blanket. It was cold against my thigh. I looked down at the coffee, suddenly uncertain and confused. *Why didn't I want him to touch me?*

His hand slid along my thigh, but when I didn't respond, he eased back. He picked up his coffee, sitting quietly for a moment. "Listen, you need to know, I'm going to get divorced."

"It could take years." I felt a remnant of last night's disillusionment resurface.

"I don't care how long it takes."

I hesitated, but it seemed the moment to put our cards on the table. "You're fourteen years older than I am." I paused and he jumped in.

"I thought you liked being the younger woman?" he teased. "I sure like it."

I smiled shyly. "I love that you're . . . a man. But, well, you've already got a child." I stopped, looked at the pale blue winter sky through the small bedroom window. "Derek, I want to have a baby." I had to pull the words out—as if expressing what I wanted somehow made me needy. Or vulnerable. But I had to know. "Not right away, I mean, I've got to get myself established with my career."

He stiffened and moved back on the bed.

"I do want a child, when the time's right. And I want to have one with you," I said softly, waiting, exposed. Why didn't he answer me? Dread began to rise like acid through my stomach and into my heart. I stared at his averted face.

"I never thought I wanted to have another kid," he said slowly. I hung in agonized suspension. "But with you," he continued, looking into space, "I could see myself having another child."

I exhaled and the fears that had been squeezing my heart, like the monster that had crushed me during my love spell, eased. I nodded, smiled; it was a small smile. His tone had been flat, and I was afraid of the consequences of having asked and forced an answer. But it was the answer that I wanted to hear, that I had to hear if we were to have a future. "That makes me very happy," I said quietly. I shivered.

"You cold?"

"A little."

"Damn boiler. Listen, I know this place is not the greatest." I raised my eyebrows, stared at the dingy gray wallboard, the grimy windows, the piled-up boxes. I thought of the little mouse I'd found running through the kitchen. "Okay, I know it sucks." I smiled. "But it's a huge amount of space for the money."

It was the only reason for remaining. But he wasn't fixing it up, and it was doubtful, after already living there for several years, that he was going to start now. It was a disastrously depressing space in a run-down and remote section of the city, and size was just not reason enough to remain. Not for me. I tilted my head and stared around me.

"It's not permanent. It's just hard right now what with the support payments, and the debt I need to pay off. But I'll find something better."

"You need to find work that pays better." I stopped myself. I didn't want to pressure him, but it was hard seeing him so tired and depressed at the end of every day. "Work you enjoy. I mean you're so smart." I wanted him to know I had faith in him. "And you're so talented. You shouldn't give up your music."

"Well, that's not the way to make a living." He shrugged dismissively and started to rise.

Everything in me kicked into high gear. I knew he had dreams of pursuing his music, and with my love and support I knew he'd succeed. I reached out and grabbed his hand. "I know you can make it. You're an amazing musician. You can do anything you put your mind to." I smiled at him, tugged him toward me. "I love you. I believe in you." I wrapped my arms around him and kissed him, softly, then insistently, pushing my tongue into his mouth, teasing and poking.

He pulled back and smiled at me. "Well, you never know." He kissed my upturned palms. He loved me, he was getting divorced, he wanted to have a child with me. I slipped my hand into the top of his jeans and tugged. He leaned forward and I unzipped his pants. I knew everything was going to be okay and would only get better.

"*So there I am sitting* on the plane next to this incredibly gorgeous guy; he's got a great job, he's funny and smart. We talked the whole way back, and the chemistry was just amazing. I was wearing the potion you gave me, Nonna." Gillian smiled. "Anyway, the plane's about to land and he looks at me and he says 'Can I just tell you *je t'aime*'? I mean, my heart stopped beating. So it's been three weeks and really it's been incredible." Gillian had returned from a trip to Paris for the magazine, and along with her usual fashion stash, she'd brought home a lover.

"Why can't I find a guy that fantastic?" Onatah pouted.

"That's exactly what everyone's asking me. It's fantastic all right, until it blows up in my face." Gillian frowned.

"Oh, Gilly, you shouldn't think like that," I looked up from my candle carving in surprise. I had a pile of orange candles that I was inscribing with the symbol for the sun and for success, which would be part of our ritual later in the evening. "You'll just create what you're afraid of. Magic rule number one—energy follows intent. Thoughts have power. Lots of power."

Gillian shrugged. "I'm just kidding. Really, it's going great. I guess sometimes it's just that old 'if it's too good to be true, it probably is' thing. But he's the first guy I've been with, since Chris, who really seems to be in touch with his feelings, you know? Willing to express them." She sighed, and smiled. "He's always saying *je t'aime*."

"It's always good with a get-well guy," Naomi scoffed. "Just have some fun and don't get too carried away with Mr. *Je T'aime*."

"A *get-well guy*?" I asked, grinning.

"Yeah, you know, her transition relationship."

Nonna had been sitting, listening quietly. She folded her reading glasses and started to talk, very slowly, almost as if telling a bedtime story to us. "Many years ago, on my thirty-fifth birthday, I cast a love spell that changed my life. I'd been alone for too many years, and I wanted someone to share my life with. I cast my circle, and I could feel my heart open and my need lifted out of me like a crane floating in the morning mist. I called to the Goddess asking Her for three things: Bring me the love that's right for me, bring me a man who wants to be with me, and give me a sign so I'll know it's him." She paused and sipped her tea.

"What did you do?" Onatah asked breathlessly. "Did you get a sign?"

"I let go, I just surrendered my fate to the Goddess." Nonna smiled at her patiently.

"What was he like, the man you asked for?" I asked, fascinated by her unexpected tale.

"I hadn't made a long list of qualities I wanted in a man and I didn't try to visualize all of his physical characteristics. I didn't create an elaborate potion of herbs and oils and I didn't chant ancient incantations of enchantment. I simply opened myself to the infinite wisdom of a holy universe; I offered my longing on the altar of promise, and I gave thanks." Nonna put her glasses carefully away in their case.

"And then what?" Onatah pressed again.

"Almost a year went by. I tried not to get discouraged, but of course it was difficult. I finally decided to stop dating."

"Altogether?" Gillian asked. "But if you wouldn't date, you weren't allowing the opportunity to present itself."

Nonna shook her head. "I was waiting for the sign I'd asked for. Without it, I knew I'd be dating the wrong man. I also stopped dating to open space in my life for him to manifest. And then, one night, I had a dream so vivid it was as if I was awake. I was at a very crowded club, trying to leave when a man stepped into my path and asked me to dance. He was wearing a motorcycle jacket, and he was very sexy."

"Nonna, a guy in a motorcycle jacket? I asked, astonished. "You had a thing for bad boys?"

"Lots of good girls do." Nonna shrugged and smiled. "Anyway, I couldn't really see his face, but he seemed very attractive. He took my hand and insisted that I dance with him. It was a slow dance, and when we put our arms around each other, I knew he was the one I'd cast my spell for. And then he whispered in my ear that he wanted to marry me. I woke up to the sound of my phone ringing. It was a friend asking me to go dancing with her that night, and of course, I agreed. After a few hours of dancing, I gave up looking for him and decided to leave. I was almost to the exit when a very handsome man—in a motorcycle jacket—stepped in front of me and asked me to dance."

You're kidding." Gillian expressed the surprise that was on all of our faces.

Nonna smiled again. "I'm quite serious. We danced until dawn. A few months later we went back to that club and while we were dancing, he proposed to me."

"Was that your second husband?" I asked.

She nodded. "We had our share of happiness and problems, as all couples do. But I wanted to have a child, and when it finally became clear that he didn't, we divorced. I saw the dream, and not the reality," Nonna explained to us. "I asked for what was right for me at the time I cast the spell. And it was right for that time in my life. I was happy, I was sad, most importantly I learned what I needed to." Nonna looked away from us, and it was one of the few times in all the years I'd known her that I could feel her give in to sadness. "But I was too old to have a child when it ended."

"But how could a love spell that started so right turn out that way?" I asked.

Nonna shook her head. "The spell didn't go wrong. Spells are organic; like all living things, they live for their time, fulfill their purpose, and then they end. And spells don't always work the way you think they will. Our families, our culture, the movies, the songs—they all create such unrealistic expectations of love and romance. And what we absorb from our parents' relationship—all their struggles and heartaches, their fears and disappointments—it all creates powerful undercurrents of emotion in us. There are hidden forces that can influence a love spell's manifestation. And there's danger in certain spells, especially love spells, that practitioners of magic rarely talk about it. You must choose your dreams carefully."

We were quiet, absorbing Nonna's words. I wondered about the sleeping dragons that could emerge from the cave of my unconscious, the dangers aroused by longing, by passion and by conjuring. I thought of the dragon that had wound itself around me as my love spell began, and I wondered if it had been a warning of the unexpected problems with Derek.

Derek had filed for divorce, but the legal bills added to his financial stress, and it was impossible to leave his job. His son was already a pawn and seeing him had become a terrible battleground, along with countless other disputed details about the divorce that seemed to have invaded our life together. Sometimes it felt like things were getting worse instead of better. Yet for all those difficulties, and even the loss and disappointment Nonna had suffered, and her warnings, I couldn't help but feel my own longings had been fulfilled. My mother continued to worry, but I told her everything was going to be okay. We were going to be okay. I was sure of it. I gave Derek a long hug when he arrived at the shop to take me to a movie.

A buzz of joy hit me when I spotted Derek waiting for me at a little Indian restaurant on Second Avenue in the East Village. He rose, wrapped me in his arms and, indifferent to the smiling staff and diners, kissed me slowly. We sat across from each other, enclosed within ruby-colored walls hung with paintings of courting couples, and beneath strings of colored Christmas lights, feeding each other with our fingers and drinking spiced tea. The table was cleared, and as we waited for the check, Derek reached across, taking my hand in his. A flash of memory struck me—the last time we had been in this position was at the restaurant in Chinatown. But tonight was different—the fears that had separated us had been banished.

Derek smiled and looked shyly down at the table. "So why don't you move in with me?"

I wasn't sure if I'd heard him correctly. "Did you just say move in? Are you sure?" He nodded. "I'd love to," I replied without hesitation.

A few days later, I packed up my books, files and clothes, rolled up the Chinese rug, and in a few hours had moved my life from the Upper West

Side of Manhattan to a part of the city that didn't even have a name. Love had swept me away.

"*Well, there wasn't much room* for him to move in with you." Nonna wasn't the least bit surprised when I told her I had moved in with Derek. We'd met for coffee at Café Reggio, my law school haunt which turned out to be an old favorite of hers. It was early in the day and the café was empty, so we took the window seat with the ancient, carved ebony chairs.

She watched me intently. "I'm sure you have a lot to tell me."

"I just feel very lucky, like I've been given so much. I mean, to cast a love spell and have it manifest." I shook my head. "It's still hard to believe. Even waking up with him every morning, I have to pinch myself. I'm so blessed. And then I looked around me, and there's so much suffering." I nodded out the window at a homeless man who had been on these same streets since my first day in law school, and probably before that. "And there's all the suffering we don't see—it's an endless list: migrant farm workers who pick my food, child labor in foreign countries making my clothes, entire ecosystems destroyed to provide our apartment with heat. It's all connected. *We're* all connected. The people out of work—there but for the grace of Goddess, and the sacrifices of my parents, go I. I feel like I've been given so much, I want to give something back. But there's so much suffering. What can one person do? What can *I* do?"

"Of course it's overwhelming. The problems are vast. And most people feel they can't make a difference. It can be very discouraging, very depressing. But you're right to realize that there's also so much to be grateful for—you're able to make a living, you're healthy and loved."

"Gratitude." I nodded. "But I became a lawyer to help people, to pursue justice. I feel so frustrated that my work's confined to my own financial survival."

"So, you want to help others."

I nodded. "What's the point if I can't help people? It's why I became a lawyer in the first place."

"Then you will. But remember—there are many ways to help the world. You love movies—do you know that old film *Sullivan's Travels*?"

"Preston Sturges." I nodded. "It's set during the Depression. There's a film director who wants to make meaningful movies that help people, so he dresses up like a hobo and sets out to find America." I paused, sensing what Nonna was guiding me toward. "It gets pretty rough for a while, but along the way he realizes how much he *is* helping people by making movies that make them laugh, that ease their sorrows."

"Joy, laughter, love—real magic that changes things. Actions must be rooted in love, not in anger, even at injustice. To feel those things, you have to heal yourself, and help yourself, before you can truly help others. Change yourself and you change the world around you." She waved to the waiter for two more cappuccinos. "So, tell me about life with Derek." Nonna changed the subject lightheartedly.

I talked about going to sleep with him at night and waking with him in the morning and how easy it seemed to intermingle our daily lives. I even described his awful apartment, where we—I paused as I said *we,* feeling the tiny rush of joy—lived. "I love him."

She patted my hand gently. "Of course you do."

As spring arrived, Nonna's prophecy was fulfilled. I was approached to represent a number of Wiccan priestesses and priests, pro bono—for free. Though few people were aware of it, Wicca had been a legally recognized religion in the United States since the early seventies. In New York City, unlike the rest of the state, clergy were required to register with the City Clerk in order to perform legally binding marriages within the city. But the Clerk had been refusing to allow Wiccan clergy to register.

This was a simple First Amendment right that required defending. But it was more, for winning public acceptance of this elegant and empowering spirituality had become increasingly important to me. *Act locally, think globally,* I said to myself as I prepared for my meeting with the City Clerk, David Dinkins. I looked at myself in the mirror—gray suit and pink blouse, pearls, high heels and briefcase, a modern-day gunslinger seeking justice. I smiled at myself; some things certainly had changed.

The meeting was brief and to the point. The reason for not registering my clients merely confirmed the discrimination—"that other religions would be offended." We decided to give the City Attorney's Office a chance to remedy the situation before initiating a lawsuit. Finally, after months had passed, the Clerk was ordered to register Wiccan clergy. We beat City Hall. To a small fanfare of positive publicity, my clients signed the old, oversized registry book and weddings were scheduled.

I had defended not only an important constitutional right but also, I hoped, the power of love expressed by couples who had the courage to commit themselves to each other. Seeing the article in *New York* magazine, I realized that perhaps I had made a small difference. My work, at least for a brief moment, had become more meaningful again. I had also emerged from the broom closet. But as I sat with the magazine in my lap, I wondered, Would I ever be able to take advantage of the rights I had just won for others? Would Derek ever propose to me?

Naomi was on me the minute I walked through the door. "So I hear you're giving away the milk without his having to buy the cow."

"Oh, that is so old," I moaned. "And who says I want to sell the cow?"

"You have a cow?" Onatah asked, genuinely confused. "How can you have a cow in the city?" She had just arrived and was juggling a huge load of books, bags and flowers.

"Who's a cow?" Jeanette bristled as she emerged from the temple's secret door.

"Look what you started." I poked Naomi. "Me."

"Hathor's always depicted as a cow," Jeanette said. "Sexy *and* maternal. Now that's a combination."

Naomi widened her eyes, made a little motion as if she was milking, grinned and waved a small bottle of oil under my nose. "Whadaya think?"

I inhaled deeply. "Delicious, like intoxicating delicious. What is it?"

"It's a Nonna formula—a love potion."

"Who's it for?" Jeanette leaned over and sniffed.

"A couple that's going to be handfasted."

"Who?" I asked, feeling my heart jump.

"Don't know. Nonna just told me to get to work."

Was it possible? Nonna always knew before I did—was Derek going to propose? Coming of age in the sixties, I'd always sworn I would never marry, but I'd also always known that there was one man, one great love meant for me. I inhaled the potion again—if Derek asked me, I *would* marry him.

A handfasting was an old Scottish rite of marriage in which a couple made a sacred commitment to love each other and to live together for a year and a day. At the end of this time the couple could renew their vows, or if love had departed, they were free to part. If they separated, they were to do so in peace and without ill will; but if the woman had become pregnant, or a child had been born, the commitment remained binding.

The term itself came from one of the key elements of the ritual: During the rite the couple tied their left—heart—hands together with strips of their clans' tartans to symbolize the commitment they had made to each other, and the union of their families. It also symbolized that they would now help each other to do that which they could not do alone.

Handfasting had become the favored form of wedding ritual in the Wiccan community, for it also lent itself to a couple's unique creativity—there was lots of room for personalizing. Instead of strips of tartan, satin ribbons were used and each of the colors symbolized a blessing for the couple. The ribbons were usually tied first by the officiant, then the couple, and then by those attending the ritual. When the ceremony was over, the couple had the fun of wriggling out of them without untying them. The bundle was then kept someplace safe and sacred. It was a beautiful ritual, and I wondered if Derek would be willing to be handfasted.

It always took about an hour for everyone to arrive and catch up with one another. Tonight we were running even later. Finally, Maia rang her little brass bell and the circle quieted down.

"We have an announcement." Her voice was filled with excitement and Bellona's usually stressed expression had given way to a broad smile. "Bellona and I have decided to handfast."

The circle erupted in cheering and applause. Nonna had been talking about Maia and Bellona. I was thrilled for them but I also felt a small pang of disappointment. I pushed the feeling aside and went to hug the happy couple.

Derek lifted the last box onto the van we had rented. We were moving. I watched the muscles in his arms flexing, the strength it had taken to move dozens of heavy book-filled boxes, the easy way he moved even after hours of working, and a pulse of desire struck me. I handed him the last item, a floor lamp, which he wedged between the couch and the van's wall. There wasn't an inch of space left.

After what seemed like forever, Derek was finally divorced. He'd cut back on his hours as a surveyor and, after a lot of urging, was rehearsing regularly with his old band. I was practicing real estate law, working with an attorney from my union democracy days who lived and worked out of his Brooklyn Heights brownstone. I finally had a mentor I respected and a way to make a more secure living. And since he was planning to retire and I would be taking over the practice, each week my responsibilities increased. But so did my income.

Derek and I had decided to buy a place together and now we were moving in. It wasn't just a romantic desire anymore—with this joint financial commitment, it was certainly sensible for us to get married. At least I thought so. Although things weren't quite as easy as I had imagined they would be, I was convinced that I, that *we*, could handle whatever challenges lay in our path. I waited, and hoped, but Derek still hadn't proposed.

It was dark by the time we pulled up to the building. We filled the hand truck dozens of times, finishing around midnight. We made the bed and were asleep the minute the light went out. The next morning I awoke to the sun streaming through the windows and into my face. Derek was already making coffee in our kitchen. *Our kitchen*—it sounded so good. As good as the coffee smelled, as good as I felt as I stretched and sat up.

"Morning, Sleeping Beauty." Derek smiled and handed me the coffee cup. "The cabinets are going to be delivered next Tuesday. Would you call some plumbers today, get some quotes?"

I nodded. "Can we have our coffee on the terrace?" It was heaven. The air was soft and warm and Central Park stretched out like a sea of green beneath us. "I'll call about the appliance deliveries, and I'm going to start painting the living room today."

"Why don't you wait 'til I get home and we'll do it together?"

He leaned over and kissed me. *If only he'd ask me, everything would be perfect.* I leaned back against the building's brick wall, running my hand along its rough texture, remembering. It had been a while since making love had the intensity of that night in Chinatown. I would plan a romantic dinner, with candlelight, and if he didn't, I'd bring it up then.

"*That was great.*" Derek's plate was clean. "And nice wine. Good choice." He poured the last of the Sancerre into our glasses.

I'd drunk just enough to be ready to bring up the subject of marriage. Calmly, sensibly, without pressuring him. I began cheerfully, casually. "So, do you think you'll ever want to marry again? I mean it's been a while since the divorce . . ." My resolve suddenly weakened.

Derek emptied his glass and stared out the window. My stomach clenched when he lifted his eyes to mine. *What if he doesn't want to?* I started to put on my protective armor: *We'll just live together. I never wanted to get married anyway.*

"When I left Paula, I thought I'd never make that mistake again."

My stomach stopped clenching and started churning. He stood up and carried our dishes into the kitchen. I sat waiting and his silence pulled the acid into my throat. He came back and sat down. I sat, unable to look at him, with my hands in my lap, wishing he'd take them in his own.

"I want to be with you. I wouldn't have bought this place with you otherwise." He stared at the wall as I glanced up at him. "Sure, we can get married if you want to."

I struggled with my emotions—an unexpected mixture of relief, happiness and disappointment. It wasn't the proposal a girl dreams of, no bended knee, no declaration of abiding and passionate love, no breathtaking ring.

I pushed the yearning for a more romantic proposal aside, and heard myself replying, "I always swore I'd never get married." I knew I was being defensive. I took a deep breath and focused on the positive. *He's said he wants to get married.* "But I love you. Yes, I do want to get married. Yes."

He leaned over, gave me a quick kiss and smiled.

"Okay, so when should we do it?" I asked cheerfully.

"How about the fall?"

"That's pretty quick." I was surprised at how calm I felt.

"Well, it doesn't have to be too big or elaborate."

"Simple, tasteful and not too big." I got out of my chair, and sat in his lap. We were getting married. The spell was still working.

8.

Perfect Love and Perfect Trust

Love can turn an ordinary life into a fairy tale.

—ANONYMOUS

"*You're getting married*—you should have a proper engagement ring," my mother said as I opened the black velvet box. "Consider it a tradition of the women in our family." I stared at the diamond ring—the jewel was one of three diamonds, each taken from a necklace my grandmother wore to the opera, and each made into a ring. My mother had one, her sister had the second one, and now I had the third.

I had waited for an engagement ring from Derek. I didn't want anything large or expensive, just a token of love, but Derek had never given me one.

My mother swiftly brought all her business skills to the planning of the wedding. Derek was amiable, and in just a few weeks, we picked a date, made arrangements with the country club in Connecticut to which Derek's parents belonged, and found a quartet—friends of Derek's—a florist, a photographer and a beautiful, tea-length, silk organza dress. Derek bought a handsome dark blue suit. We got his parents' guest list; the invitations were printed and sent. Now we just needed to write our ceremony, which we had decided would be a legal handfasting ritual—and decide about the rings.

Derek didn't want to wear a wedding ring, saying that it would be uncomfortable when he played the sax. I'd pushed him to play again, and it had been a long struggle to convince him, so how could I insist on something that would make it more difficult for him? I did wonder to myself why he couldn't just take it off when he rehearsed or performed, but I accepted his decision.

Since he wasn't going to wear a ring, I decided I didn't want to wear one. Looking at my grandmother's ring on my finger, I realized that to some it was an old-fashioned symbol of my status as a soon-to-be-married young woman, but to me it was a symbol of my connection to the women in my family, and so to my independence.

After Derek rejected my suggestion that we both hyphenate our last names, I decided not to change my last name to his. I was a liberated woman, a professional woman known by my given last name. If anyone asked, I replied that it was all fine with me, but deep down inside, his decisions had planted a tiny seed of doubt about his commitment to me. I told myself, I told the world, that what was important was that we loved and supported each other. That's what partners did. And that's what our marriage would be—a modern partnership.

I was bringing home most of the income. He did the laundry, shopped, and cooked, usually more than I did, as I was often late in getting home from work. But then, there were evenings when Derek had a class or rehearsals. Except for our very private spiritual practices, we were a very typical New York couple. It was a busy life. It got busier as the day of the wedding approached.

And then, one morning I awoke to find that something inside of me had shifted, a boulder in front of the cave of uncertainty had rolled away, and I was filled with doubt.

"I don't know what to do," I said anxiously to my mother. I had taken the train out to see her. I hadn't slept much for the last few days and I was upset, worried if I was making the right decision, feeling that there was no turning back, concerned about the money she had spent. I watched her expression, and she was utterly calm as the fears tumbled out of my mouth.

"He hates his work, but he hasn't done anything to find something else. All he's done is cut back on his hours, so he can play more often, which I want him to be able to do. I mean, it was such an effort to get him to start playing again. But it's going to be a long time before he can support himself with music, if ever. Of course, I want him to pursue his dream, but it's hard carrying so much of the financial burden. And I want to have a baby, so he needs to do something where he can make enough money so that I can eventually quit, or at least cut way back."

"Everyone has doubts. I'd worry if you didn't have them." She stroked my hair as I sat on the steps into the kitchen, a rare gesture of affection that reassured me more than words. "You don't have to go through with this if you don't want to. It's only money."

"But it's so much money . . ." There was something more, a sense of being haunted by something I felt but couldn't see, a ghost that beckoned me away. How could I explain what I didn't understand?

"Nothing's more important than your happiness."

I was filled with relief, and gratitude, by her reaction. But I was still confused. "I don't know—I mean, I love him, and I know he loves me. Is it just jitters?"

She hugged me. "Why don't you sleep on it for a few days? Just remember, the way things are at the beginning is the way they're going to be. You can't change another person."

I nodded. *I could always get divorced.* I shook off the thought, and the specter of restlessness.

"*Nothing's different,* but I look at him and I don't know if I'm doing the right thing." I now confessed to Nonna, the first to arrive for my Aphrodite ritual, an evening of purification and preparation for my wedding, and more importantly, for my new married life. My mother's words haunted me. "How much is really going to change?" And yet, overnight, it seemed as if my feelings had done just that.

Nonna sat quietly, waiting.

"And when I talked to him about having a baby, he just said we had plenty of time; he wanted more time with me. I understand, but if he doesn't start making more of an effort to find a better job, we won't be able to afford to have a baby." I could hear how anxious I sounded. "When the time is right."

Nonna reached across and took my hand in hers, placing her thumb in the center of my palm, her third finger pressed firmly into the middle of the top of my hand. "Breathe. Slow, deep."

I did, and felt the tumult begin to recede. But the doubts remained.

"Your mother is right. You don't have to get married. You could just live together."

I nodded. "I thought about that, but we've made all these plans . . . No, it's more than that. We're at a crossroads, and I'm either going to leave or I have to give it everything I've got."

"You're the one at the crossroads, *mia figlia*." She squeezed my hand and released it. "There's no wrong choice. There's only the choice that will bring you the lessons you need."

"I do love him, it's just that . . ." I paused, took another deep breath and finally heard Nonna's words. "The lessons I need?"

She nodded. The doorman buzzed me from downstairs; everyone was arriving. It was time to begin. I allowed myself to get caught up in the giddy playfulness, the jokes, and the gifts they had brought, tokens from all the Goddesses that each woman represented—a mirror from Naomi and the Goddess Diana to see myself clearly, a red candle marked with sigils of passion and love from Jeanette and Ezulie; Mindy brought a large French enamel casserole for Hera's blessings of the hearth, and of course, there was a Venus oil from Annabelle, an aphrodisiacal incense from Onatah and Yemaya, and a love potion from Maia, Bellona and Shakti. The purification potion I would use in my bath was from Gillian and Aphrodite, and Nonna and Ariadne had given me a statue of Dionysus.

It was the last gift I unwrapped and I held it tightly, feeling a current run from my hands into my heart. I gave Nonna a hug and she whispered in my ear: "No matter what happens, you always have your daemon. Don't forget him." I looked down at the statue, feeling both confused and reassured.

Jeanette and Gillian started giggling and tugging at my clothes, while the rest of them went to work in the bathroom, transforming it into a sacred grotto. They filled it with flowers and with white, pink and red candles, and ran a bath with Gillian's purification potion—peppermint, chamomile, sage, lavender, and sea salt. I was escorted into the tub with laughter and singing, and as I bathed, one at a time they each used the potion to wash me. I was bundled into a towel while Naomi emptied and refilled the tub, this time with a Goddess of Love potion—rosemary, myrtle, red roses, white mums, a cinnamon stick, almond, musk and patchouli oils. The bathroom was crowded with women, singing to me as they washed my hair—*"I am the Goddess, I am the Mother, all acts of love and pleasure are my rituals."*

And then they left me to soak, to meditate and to honor the romantic destiny that I felt within my heart. As I bathed, I knew that every step had led me here. Where the path would lead next I could not know, but I sensed it was to that great love nurtured within me. I stepped from the bath like Aphrodite, and they attended to me like the Muses, drying and styling my hair, applying makeup, dressing me with silks and jewelry, and then they brought me into the circle they had created.

I stood in the center encircled by beautiful women, chanting my name, laughing and smiling. The energy built and peaked as they extended their arms toward me, opened their hearts and sent their joy and blessings to me in wave after wave of love. And then we feasted.

My doubts had been washed away and I knew that I was going to marry Derek.

It was late in May. The sky was overcast, but it was warm. The trees were green, lilacs were blooming, and a soft breeze lifted my hair as I got out of the car. *I'm not nervous. I'm happy.* Derek wrapped his arm around me and we walked up the stairs of the country club and into its high-ceilinged foyer. There was the elegant little sign announcing our wedding in the Hollister Room and adjoining terrace. We hugged and I was suddenly pulled away by the women from my circle. Fussing, joking and crying, they helped me dress. When I was ready, they gifted me with something old, new, borrowed and blue and then left me to myself as they went off to bless and consecrate the circle. I picked up the small bouquet of lilacs, rosemary and lavender tea roses I would carry.

I stepped out onto the terrace to see a hundred and fifty friends and family smiling, standing and sitting in a circle in the manicured courtyard adjoining the terrace, the club's busy golf course in the background. *A perfect spot for a handfasting*. My mother beamed at me, quickly dabbing her eyes with an embroidered handkerchief. And there was Derek, smiling, his eyes holding me, drawing me to him in the center of the circle. In moments, my dream would be fulfilled.

It was time to join him in the circle. A pang of sadness struck me—the only thing that wasn't perfect was that my father couldn't walk me down the "aisle." He had passed away. Standing on the brink of a new life, all I could think about was how much I missed him. My cousin Matt took my arm—he would walk me down the brick path.

"You don't have to do this, you know," he muttered as we walked toward the circle. "I've got my motorcycle right outside, we can just make a run for it." I laughed and the photographer snapped a shot. Derek took my hands as I joined him in the center of the circle. I was lost in the love I saw shining in his eyes.

The wind picked up and the gray clouds flew across the sky. I held my breath as a sprinkle of rain fell. It stopped after a few light drops and blue sky began to appear from behind the scattering cover.

Nonna walked slowly and gracefully around the circle. As she moved, everything around us seemed to recede, growing fainter and quieter. I heard her speaking as if from far away. "I cast this circle as a sacred place between the worlds, a place where the worlds meet, a place where lovers meet, a place where two will become one. I cast this circle as a circle of love to encircle love. I cast this circle by the power of all that is sacred, by the power of love that is divine. So mote it be."

I looked at the happy faces that surrounded us and I could feel the unconditional love that was being sent to us from everyone, even Derek's parents, who looked like their shoes were too tight. It was like floating in a sphere of light, and it was the safest, most nourishing and peaceful place in the universe. It was also the most powerful magical circle I had ever been in, and when I looked at Derek standing with me at its center, I knew I stood at the point where heaven and earth met.

Onatah stood in the east, lifting the burning sage stick so that it left a swirl of pungent, purifying smoke floating in the air. "Spirits of air, bless this couple with the ability to speak clearly and honestly to each other, and bless them with the ability to hear each other and to listen respectfully. And bless them with laughter and insight."

"Spirits of fire." Jeanette stood in the southern quarter of the circle and called out in a strong voice. She lifted the burning red candle as she spoke: "Bless this couple with passion for each other and the courage to express their feelings for each other. Give them fire when they touch each other. Bless them with determination and bless them with the power to transform their challenges into rewards."

Gillian stood in the west and lifted a shell as she sprinkled water. "Spirits of water, bless this couple with love and compassion." Her boarding school grace was apparent in every word and gesture. "Give them the ability to be tender with each other and the generosity to nourish each other's dreams. And let them play together like otters in the sweet waters of life."

"Spirits of earth, bless this couple with the power to make their dreams come true." Naomi, in the north, scattered seeds from a basket as she spoke. "Give them the strength to work hard and the creativity to work well—together. Bless them with the prosperity and pleasures of the earth, the body and spirit made manifest, and with a happy home."

"Father Sun, Mother Earth, bless this couple and all who gather here today to witness this sacred union." Nonna addressed us. "Goddess and God of love, by all the names with which you are called, Aphrodite and Ares, Shakti and Shiva, Isis and Osiris, Ariadne and Dionysus, Freya and Odin, divine couple who fills the stories of our ancestors, who fills our dreams, dwelling within us and all around us. Goddess and God of holy union and the mystery of love. Bless this couple who come today to enter into this union. You have something to say to each other?" Nonna smiled at us as she asked.

Derek spoke first. "Phyllis, will you marry me? Will you be my wife?" There were tears in his eyes. It was the proposal I had been waiting for.

"Oh, Derek, I love you! Yes, of course I'll marry you. And I promise to nourish your dreams and help you make them come true." With the utterance of the last syllable, two barn swallows flashed through the sky above our heads.

Nonna handed me my silver chalice, smiling, her dark eyes blessing me. "The chalice is the womb of the Goddess, the vessel of new life, the Holy Grail of rebirth. It is within you and it is love." She handed Derek his athame. "The athame is the power of the God, the seed of new life, the lance that protects the land. It is within you and it is love."

I can see his heart, that's what's shining in his eyes. I can see his love for me. I brushed the quick rush of tears away with the back of my hand, and smiling at Derek, I held the chalice before me. Our eyes never leaving each other, he lifted his athame and plunged it into the cup. I could hear a little gasp from the circle, and some light, startled laughter.

"As the blade is to the God," Derek said, his voice resounding as if from a stage.

"So the chalice is to the Goddess," I replied.

"And conjoined they bring blessings," we said together and to each other. We leaned forward over the united blade and chalice and kissed, briefly, tenderly and as a vow.

Nonna took the tools from us, tying a gold and then a silver ribbon around our joined left hands. "May the Goddess and God bless you with love and joy." And then my mother stepped into the circle and wrapped a purple ribbon around our hands. "A long, healthy, happy and prosperous life together." She was beaming as she kissed and hugged us. Even Derek's parents, who had been more than a little uncomfortable about such a non-traditional ceremony, especially at their club, tied ribbons around our hands and wished us happiness.

One by one, friends and family wrapped the silk ribbons around our hands and offered us good wishes and love. We were laughing, well bundled together as Nonna finished our ceremony. "And now by the powers invested in me by the State of New York, I pronounce you husband and wife. You may kiss, again," Nonna said with a small laugh.

Derek took me in his arms. I raised my face to kiss him as he pulled me closer. He lowered his lips to mine and his tongue pressed softly against my lips, which opened to his touch. My heart jumped as I inhaled and he dove deeper into my mouth. For that endless moment, there was only the two of us, as one. We separated to the returning sound of applause and laughter.

And then came the hugs, and kisses, and slaps on the back.

"I gotta tell you, when you raised that knife you gave me quite a scare, young man," Sam, one of my parents' friends, laughed. "I thought you were going to stab her."

"Well, that was certainly an original ceremony, very unique, just like you, my dear." My aunt hugged me. We had moved to the terrace as the waiters circulated with hors d'oeuvres and cocktails.

"What was the meaning of that thing you did?"

"You mean you don't get that? You've been married too long."

"That was so lovely, just beautiful, simple and profound."

As people floated into the dining room, Derek looked down at our bound hands. "Now how do we get out of this?" He suddenly jerked his arm sharply down toward the ground, my own arm flung harshly along with his; then he did it again, and the third time he shook off the ribbons. They fell to the ground, which I saw for the first time—the dirt, the wandering ants and green shoots between the worn bricks, the smudge of dirt on my white silk pump. He picked the tangle of color up and handed it to me. I stood, stunned, confused by the violence of the earlier gesture. He leaned down and gave me a quick kiss.

"Come on, we don't want to miss our own party." He took my naked hand and we walked into the reception to the sound of the song I'd requested the musicians play, "It Had to Be You." I smiled, pushing the shock away. *It didn't mean anything. It was just a quick, efficient way to get us free for the party. It was . . . a guy thing.* I put the ribbons on our table.

Derek led me out onto the dance floor for the first dance. We had never danced together before. There seemed neither time nor occasion for it in the lives we led. Until now. I rested my cheek against his shoulder and closed my eyes. His fingers spread out against the small of my back, pressing me into him as we moved. He felt good, strong and real. *Fears are only that, this is what matters.* In that moment, dancing in his arms, I had never felt more feminine or cherished. *Everything is going to be all right. I've done the right thing.*

We danced, turning in a slow circle, as love spun around us. I lifted my face to look into his eyes and he kissed me. I kissed him back, closed my eyes and returned to blissful certainty.

Derek unlocked the apartment door, and I laughed as he picked me up and carried me over our threshold. He put me down and went back to retrieve the few small pieces of luggage we'd had for the wedding, and I headed straight to the answering machine filled with messages.

"Italian?" I asked pulling out a stack of take-out menus. I left Derek to order and headed for the bedroom. We had decided not to go on a honeymoon. Derek wasn't going to ask his parents for the money, and he couldn't afford it on his own. I'd thought about paying for it, but decided it would be a mistake. "It's really all right," I had reassured him. "We've just bought the apartment. We need to save money. We can have a honeymoon later."

It's called a honeymoon because long ago the bride was given mead, created from fermented honey, to drink as an aphrodisiac and to make her fertile. Abducted by her would-be husband and his companions or clan, and then hidden away, the bride drank the ambrosia every day for a full cycle of the moon—long enough to become inebriated, uninhibited and pregnant. I thought about Persephone—and how she had fallen in love with her abductor. At some point in her life, every woman's heart is stolen and she becomes intoxicated by love.

Flipping on the bright, overhead light I stared at the barren bedroom. Derek put the suitcases against one empty, pale blue wall, as I walked to our bed. Our marriage bed. I picked up a pillow, holding it to my chest. It was more than where we would sleep together for the rest of our lives, more than a place to dream. It was the place where the most important dream of my life would come true, where our new life together really began. It was where, someday, we would create a new life, a baby that embodied the love we felt for each other. This bed was an altar at the center of the labyrinth, the point where heaven and earth met, where sex was most holy.

We were too exhausted to make love that night. I lay with my head on Derek's chest listening to his heart, to his rhythmic breathing and his rumbling snore. A police siren wailed, a bus roared, the subway far below screeched to a stop, noises infiltrating the dark room. Lying awake in the bed, my mind too stimulated to sleep, but my body too tired to get up, I decided that I would transform the austere bedroom into a temple of love, a place that was sensual and sacred. Love required the earthiness of sex to fulfill itself, and that fulfillment had the power to transport one to a heavenly ecstasy beyond the realm of the senses. I wanted that sexuality and that ecstasy to be part of our marriage.

The next day I sat down with a calendar and found a Friday when the moon was waxing to full. I sent Derek a romantic invitation to a night of ecstatic love, and he happily accepted. I practiced my Kegels, I ran the energy through my body, I talked to Nonna about sex magic and sacred sex, and using a mirror to work with, I practiced the techniques of sending erotic energy with my eyes, my breath, my mind and heart. And I would use the rest of my body with Derek. I even chose a simple goal into which our energies could be projected—that our dreams should come true. And I meditated upon Derek as the embodiment of an erotic God, one that I adored.

When the day came, I left work early, shopping on the way home. I poured a glass of sherry, flipped on the stereo, danced and hummed as I washed and scrubbed, chopped and baked, making love magic with aphrodisiacal food. The world *was* a different place when I experienced it as an expression of desire. I hung diaphanous white silk from the bronze cube bed frame and remade the bed with new, white linens. I put the red candles I'd collected all around the room—but far from the drapery. All afternoon I burned an incense of musk, vanilla, almond, ambergris, patchouli and sandalwood in the bedroom, which left just a hint of scent in the air, on the drapes and the linens. Enough to enhance, not mask, my natural aphrodisiacal pheromones.

As I ran my bath, I moved the coffee table into the bedroom and filled it with the feast. In the middle of the table I put a red rose and a small statue of Shiva and Shakti making love. I scattered the petals from five other red roses into the bathwater as I stepped into the warm tub. I closed my eyes and my mind drifted toward the evening. I ran my hands over my body, feeling the water stir and slide around me. I imagined Derek's lips kissing me, his hands touching me and I drifted.

It's time. I rose from the bath, feeling the warm water trickle down my skin, seeing the white porcelain beneath my feet shimmer like the iridescent shell upon which Aphrodite rose from the sea. I massaged the Venus oil into my skin at the pulse points so that by the time we made love, Derek would taste me and not the oil, and the fragrance would not overpower my own. I wrapped myself in a silk robe and went to finish my preparations.

I made a path of tea lights and rose petals scooped from the bath, leading from the front door of the apartment to the bedroom. Rose petals scattered down the path to the wedding bower were a remnant of one of

England's oldest love spells that I was adapting for this evening's rite of
love.

As dusk approached and just before the moon rose, you were to drop
the petals of five red roses from the front door of the one you loved to your
own, softly whispering the loved one's name as you returned home. There
you were to call his, or her, name into the flame as you lit a beeswax candle.
Next, one at a time, you were to burn five petals from the sixth rose in the
candle flame, as you chanted the ancient spell:

> *Burn a pathway to my door, five rose petals now are four.*
> *Four to three in candle fire, bringing closer my desire.*
> *Three to two, I burn the rose, love no hesitation shows.*
> *Burn two to one, till there are none, the spell is done.*
> *Come, lover, come.*

The sixth rose was to be put in a vase in a window that looked toward
the home of your beloved, and the candle was to be set, safely, nearby so
that its light fell upon the rose, and was left to burn itself out. The rose was
buried when it died, and if your lover had not come to you, the ritual was
repeated with six new roses.

I glanced at my watch. Derek would be home soon. I took the oysters
from the refrigerator, and put on Rimsky-Korsakov's *Sheherezade* while I
dressed. I lit the path of tea lights, returned to the bedroom, lit the red candles, turned off the lights and stood in the center of the room. It was
beyond any expectation or imagining—beautiful in the daylight, in the
light of countless flickering flames it was ethereal. It was fire magic.

This was the inner realm of our marriage, a sanctuary where the
ancient rites of a sacred union would be enacted. It was here that love
moved from heart to body, from fantasy to reality. And it was here, in this
bed, that we would truly make and consummate our marriage vows. I
heard the lock turn and the door open and then Derek's laugh and excla-
mation.

"Well, what's this?"

A ripple of nervous excitement shot through me, just as it had the very
first time he'd come to my door. That was why I had done all this—to
rekindle that energy. Like most couples, we had fallen into an unimagina-

tive pattern of lovemaking. I'd begun to wonder if he was bored. Over the years, I had come to realize that men had a tendency to repeat what was successful for them—the same restaurant, the same old pair of sneakers, the same way of making love. They didn't seem to realize the elements of surprise and spontaneity were some of the greatest aphrodisiacs for women. Of course, maybe our own malaise sent them the wrong signals. *Well, if you want something done, do it yourself.*

I heard him put down his keys and the bag he always carried. I pulled the pin from my hair and shook it loose. I had planned to lie on the bed like an odalisque, but he was already standing in the door frame.

"You look like a Goddess," he said in a low voice that immediately sent a shiver through me. "I think I'm about to enter heaven."

"Or an earthly paradise." I smiled at him. "Fit for a God."

He smiled at me and I could feel a spark of desire fly between us. "I should shower."

"Not unless you were doing heavy manual labor today, and maybe not even then," I replied.

"Well, that works for me." He was grinning as he approached me. "So this is what you've been up to. Maybe you should quit your job."

I laughed. "I'm afraid we couldn't afford this if I quit my job." I pressed myself against him and lifted my lips to his. It was a slow kiss, soft and searching. He wrapped his arms around me and I softened, letting go of the get-it-done drive. "Do you like it?"

He nodded. "Very sexy, just like you."

I didn't realize how much I needed to hear that. "You must be hungry."

"Starving. Looks like quite a feast." Derek studied the wines, nodding with approval. "Champagne first." He held the bottle of Bollinger and slowly rotated the cork, gradually easing it out until it hiccupped quietly. He found the flutes, poured and handed me one. "Two into one," he toasted, tapping his glass against mine. We drank and kissed again, the wine on our lips.

Kiss as if he wants to kiss you. I felt myself open, immediately becoming more receptive to him. I pulled him toward the bed and gave him a little push, enjoying the surprised look on his face as he sat back. I stood between his legs, rested my hands on his shoulders and kissed him. Eagerness ran from the sudden contraction in my womb straight through my belly and into my heart.

In one fluid motion, Derek pulled me onto the bed and rolled on top of me. There was no hesitation in his kiss, or his hand as it traveled a deliberate path along my body. His fingers found the soft under curve of my breast and he fondled me slowly, enjoying how he touched me as much as I enjoyed his touch. Even through the fabric, my skin came alive. He flicked his fingernail back and forth, gently teasing my nipple into hardening. I inhaled, feeling the pleasure spread through my body.

"Why don't we start with dessert?" he asked, smiling down at me.

I felt the gathering passion in his body, and remembered the old expression that men were like blowtorches and women like ovens. I knew that if I didn't slow us down now, in minutes I wouldn't be able to. "I'd rather start with an appetizer." I smiled up at him. "I want to take our time tonight." I pushed myself up onto my elbows and wiggled away from his searching hands. "I promise, you can have whatever you want . . ." I flirted with him, something I realized I hadn't done for a long time. "Later. I worked so hard, can we just eat a little first?"

He groaned and rolled away. "Food and sex, every man's dream, just not in that order."

"I want you to have all your dreams—and your strength." He laughed and I handed him his champagne as he settled back into the mass of pillows.

"So, we begin with the oysters."

"Oysters, eh? I don't think I'm going to need those." He licked the corner of his mouth with his tongue and I blushed.

"Next, with the burgundy, *crostini de truffi bianchi,* white truffles. And for dessert, lots of yummies—almonds, which are sacred to Aphrodite, and vanilla pudding with shaved almonds."

"Vanilla pudding is sacred to Aphrodite?"

"You keep this up, you'll be lucky to get a peanut." I tried to retrieve an air of seriousness, but he was having none of it. "Figs, stuffed dates . . ." His eyebrows went up and he grinned. I rolled my eyes and continued. "That's mango and papaya." I pointed to the pink and orange slices. "Apples and grapes. And lots of chocolate." I nodded toward the candy and strawberries dipped in dark chocolate.

"If I didn't know better, I'd say you were planning to feed me a meal of aphrodisiacs. Not that I need them; the dress is more than enough to whet my appetite. Why don't you take it off and let me eat . . ."

I put an oyster in his mouth. We fed each other, licking each other's fingers, savoring the flavors and textures of food and kisses. I fed him the *crostini* and Derek ran his tongue over the palm of my hand, sending arrows of heat shooting through my body. He put a piece of chocolate in my mouth, then dipped his finger in the champagne and ran it along my lower lip. I pulled his finger into my mouth, sucking on it slowly, watching his face. He moaned, his eyes growing smoky.

His breathing quickened as I slowly unbuttoned his shirt, kissing and licking between each button. I pulled it off of him, the sight of his bare chest touching off a rush that made my heart bang against my ribs. He was so Nordic, with no hair on his chest. I reached up to tease his nipples with my tongue.

Derek cupped my breasts, squeezing, fondling, eliciting a shudder as he drew a willing response, my nipples caught in the gentle squeezing of his thumbs and forefingers. He let out a low groan as my hands slid down and dipped into the top of his pants. He grabbed the hem of my dress, pulling it swiftly up, and reached between my legs. My mind and my body were working at a slower pace.

"Please, I don't want to rush."

Derek let out a long sigh. He slid down the bed and rested his head on my heart, wrapping his arms around my waist, and we lay together, very still, breathing softly. I could feel his heart beating against my thigh. "Are you happy?" he asked, staring up at the silk canopy. It was the question I usually asked him.

"I've never been happier." I wriggled down the bed until we were facing each other, looking into each other's eyes, something it seemed we rarely did anymore.

It was one of the first practices in sex magic and sacred sexuality, yet when we had first tried it, it had felt contrived and Derek had clearly been as uncomfortable as I. But now it was happening naturally. I let my self-consciousness surface and then ease away as I saw the love in his eyes. I knew he could see it in mine and I could feel it beginning to flow between us like warm honey.

I took my hand and placed it over his heart and placed his hand over mine. Our breathing slowed as the excitement subsided; the heat didn't expire but instead became a slow burn, and gradually we began breathing in synchronization. The energy swirled between us, through our eyes, our breath, our hands on each other's heart, until our hearts seemed to beat as one.

"I love you," I said simply. Slowing down had allowed my feelings, my mind, my body to align and to open to love. "Can you feel it?" I asked softly.

He nodded and smiled. "Can you feel this?" he asked as he kissed me. Fire swept through me—I could feel his desire, I could feel *him*. The deeper his tongue probed, the deeper I could feel him within me. And I could feel my desire for him. I opened to him, and opened again, and longed for him to fill me.

My hands slipped around him; he buried his head between my breasts. His breath was warm and moist, his lips soft and seeking. His hand lifted my skirt, slowly tracing an incendiary path up my thighs. I kissed his neck, his jaw, his lips. Derek tugged the shoulders of my dress, lifted it swiftly over my head and tossed it aside, and I lay beside him, naked. It was incredibly arousing to be completely nude while he was still, at least partly, dressed, my bare skin against the coarse denim of his jeans, the cold belt buckle pressing against my belly. He gazed at my body, his appreciation stripping off my inner veils. His eyes followed his hands as he ran them slowly over me, around my breasts, stroking the backs of my thighs, making me squirm. I arched and writhed and sought to pull him to me, but he just smiled and gently placed my hands down on the bed beside me. I struggled not to move, kiss and touch him as I always did.

"Slowly," he said quietly, then kissed me deeply. "Let me pleasure you." I was intoxicated by his relentless, probing caress. I could feel his enjoyment electrifying my skin as his hands roamed freely. All the while he watched me, never taking his eyes from mine, except to enjoy my body's reaction.

"You're beautiful," he said softly. "I feel like I'm making love to a Goddess." For a moment, I couldn't accept what he had said, but as the words resonated in my heart, they swept away the last of my uncertainty. His lips and hands visited neglected parts of me that were awakening to exquisite sensitivity—he kissed the inside of my elbow, turned me over and kissed a trail down the backs of my thighs, lingering behind my knees. He ran his hand back and forth along the inside of my thigh, kissed the curves of my backside, licked the spot at the base of my spine where the

Kundalini arises, sending wave after wave of excitement through me. I moaned and stretched as he explored every inch, finally wandering into the secret garden of my soul. I was quivering.

I rolled into his arms and he kissed the sensitive hollow in my collarbone and then my neck, whispering in my ear what he was going to do to me and what he wanted me to do to him. My fingers curled in his long hair as he slid down my body. His tongue ran along the subtle curve inside my hip and down into the furrow, caressed and stroked and tasted until I couldn't bear another moment. I was surrendering, opening, receiving.

Every molecule ached for him. Derek stood up, unbuckled his belt and whipped it through the loops. I shuddered, not with fear, but with anticipation. He unsnapped his trousers and slid the zipper down, the sound creating another pang of hunger between my legs. He stripped off his pants and briefs, threw them aside and turned back to me naked, as glorious as a God.

It was my turn now. I sat on the edge of the bed, my hands moving along his hard thighs. He stepped closer, smiling down at me, heat in his eyes. I took his burly weight into my palms, feeling the silky skin and rigid hardness. I flicked my tongue along the opening in the crimson head, and then along the ridge of skin behind it. I kissed and licked and he groaned in ecstasy, threading his fingers through my hair.

I began sucking slowly, running my tongue up and down the shaft as my mouth moved back and forth. I drew on him with just a small amount of pressure, then licked with none. I looked up to see that his eyes were closed and his head thrown back.

This is how to worship a God. How to worship God. As he had with me, I gave myself completely over to adoration, and as I did, my own arousal intensified. He trusted me, relaxing, knowing that I would be careful not to nick him with my teeth, while receiving the pleasure I was giving him. And it was exhilarating to see how much pleasure that was. My mouth was an act of devotion, moving back and forth with a sure and steady rhythm, taking him deep against the back of my throat. The momentary loss of air was my offering of trust to him, the receptive willingness a silent erotic supplication. I could feel his passion mounting and it swept into me.

He put his hands on my shoulders. "You've got to stop now," he rasped, "or I won't be able to do this slowly." He fell into the bed and took my mouth with his. His tongue plunged into me as he raised himself over me. I expected him to thrust into me, but instead he nestled the head of his cock at the edge. Looking into my eyes, he pushed gently, ever so slowly opening and entering me. He stopped, waiting with only the head resting within me. He matched his breathing to mine and watched me.

My hunger to feel him inside of me surged. "Deeper. *Please.* I want you. I need to feel you inside of me." I moved my hips to bring him deeper inside of me. Carefully, deliberately, he pushed the full length of himself deep inside me and I was suffused with the sensation of opening to him. I began to move my hips in circles around him, and he waited rather than thrusting. As we kissed, I could feel a rush of ecstatic energy, from womb to belly, to heart and lips, and to him. *Give, receive and respond.* I fell backward into pleasure as his energy pressed forward into me.

My arms wrapped around him, my hands slid down his back to pull him closer, deeper. We were a vessel, our passion building, spinning between us, pressing to merge.

I was ripe and moaning with eagerness. He thrust hard and deep inside me, then withdrew. I squeezed as he entered and released as he departed. He grasped me strongly, holding me to him as we rolled over. I was now on top of him and able to move freely, to find the rhythm that would bring me to a climax as I rubbed against him.

He looked up at me, pulled my face to his and held me in a kiss. I began rocking my body over his as my thighs straddled his hips. The feel of his hands grabbing my ass, squeezing hard, holding me firmly against him, unleashed another surge of excitement. I felt it rushing through me and back to him.

I was gasping, while the currents of abandonment carried me and I felt myself lifting. I deliberately slowed my breathing, and, inhaling deeply, squeezing my Kegel muscles, I drew the energy up through my spine, through my stomach, my heart. I exhaled, sending the energy to Derek. Together, we rode toward the crest of the wave, then sent the spiraling, spreading energy through the rest of our bodies and back and forth between each other. I felt his presence deep within me, urging me to ecstasy. Derek gripped me tightly, thrusting into the very center of my paradise, exploding with a moan from deep within. I cried out as uncontrollable bliss undulated, immersing me in radiance that flared infinitely outward and within, the pulsating merging of love complete.

Let our dreams come true. The energy flowed into a spinning luminous orb, from my body, heart and mind out into the hallowed sanctum that enveloped us. I could feel Derek's heart beating as if it were my own. We lay entwined, blissfully languid, floating. Perfect love and perfect trust. *Let our dreams come true.*

The spell was cast.

9

Spellbound

Love is that condition in which the happiness of
another person is essential to your own.

—ROBERT HEINLEIN

The apartment was dark. I flipped on the lights, dropped my briefcase, hung up my coat and kicked off my heels. *Why should he be here? It's after ten and I'm just getting home.* A note was propped against the telephone: *Rehearsing. See you later. Love, Derek.*

I checked the phone messages. *How late is later?* I wondered, rummaging in the junk drawer for the worn pizza menu. Standing in my stocking feet in the cold kitchen light, I was too tired to dial, too tired to eat. I stripped down to my underwear and wrapped myself in my velour robe that Derek had left on top of a pile of clean, carefully folded laundry.

I rubbed the velvety surface of the cuff, like the child I used to be, stroking my very first stuffed animal, Hoppy the rabbit. Years later when he was nothing but tatters, his mysterious disappearance sent me into my first memory of devastated tears. He'd been thrown in the garbage by a great-aunt who thought it was just a rag, but I still saw Hoppy.

I pulled on a pair of Derek's wool socks, curled up on the couch and turned on the television to fill the silence while I shuffled through the week's mail. My ACLU membership renewal notice, my Brown alumnae magazine, next month's *Vogue* and this week's *New Yorker*, the usual bills—credit cards, phone, electric, health insurance, monthly condo maintenance, the mortgage. It was normal for a young Manhattan couple to have so many bills, but only one of us was working full-time and able to pay them.

I'd supported Derek's decision to cut back on his hours. He was finally pursuing his dream again, and he wanted more time to devote to it. There was just enough for him to pay his child support and something toward our expenses; the rest, and any pleasures or unexpected necessities, came from my income, and I was stretching it as far as it could go. I was afraid that with just one unexpected tug it would snap like a broken rubber band—sudden and painful. But I couldn't complain—after all, I'd been pushing him to go after what he loved to do.

I believed in him, in his talent, and I'd been unswervingly supportive. But last week I'd suggested he try to find work, at least part-time, as a musician—studio work, weddings, anything that would allow him to play, but also bring in some more income. He said he was looking for other work, but he wouldn't go back to playing weddings. And so I worked harder, longer hours. Someone had to.

I fell asleep in front of the television.

"*Well you should've asked me*. I'd've been happy to tell you. The quickest way to kill your sex life is to get married." Annabelle laughed.

"Well, it's not dead, it's just . . . ," I said defensively. Derek was rehearsing so I was free for the evening. It was just as well; I needed some girlfriend time. We'd met at Violet's, as Naomi's shift ended. Gillian had joined us, and Mindy too—a rare event for a working mother of two children. Marcia wasn't coming. Her absence said it all—she and Naomi were having problems.

As my eyes adjusted to the dim, smoky light, I thought I'd walked into the wrong bar. I might as well have been walking the gauntlet at a hard-drinking hetero haunt like the Blarney Rose. But midway down, my mind stumbled in a quick blur of confusion—what was *he* doing here? We stared at each other, me and the woman standing at the bar thinking she was James Dean. But why couldn't my daemon be a she appearing as a he—after all, Dionysus was raised in girl's clothing, a he appearing as a she, so why couldn't a girl dress in his? *Take a walk on the wild side?* her eyes asked as I walked past. I kept walking.

Chemistry. I laughed to myself. I headed to a booth and spotted Naomi flirting with the new bartender she'd been training, a pretty blond with close-cropped hair and a rose tattoo on her right bicep. I sighed. *Love stinks.* Naomi caught my eye, grinned and sauntered over. We hugged and she tossed her cigarettes on the sticky tabletop and slid into the tattered green Naugahyde seat. I gave her the evil eye, but it didn't stop her from lighting up. She took a long, relieved drag and blew the smoke away from me. The smell of spilled beer and cigarettes made my nostrils pinch, but this was exactly where you had this kind of conversation—whether you were gender bending or not.

Naomi grinned at the bartender and Annabelle pressed on. "Honey, I don't know why you'd want to settle down with one man when you can have as many as you want. I mean, New York is a single girl's sex buffet. Why you want to have hamburger every night . . ."

"Derek's not hamburger," I straightened my shoulders. "What did Mae West say? 'It's not the men in my life. It's the life in my man.'"

"Men. Life in my *men*," Annabelle corrected me with a stretch of her usual drawl.

"Anyway, I might not be happy with our sex life, but nobody has a right to criticize him but me."

The table erupted with laughter.

"Honey, you just made the same mistake most women make—you're lettin' your feelins get all mixed up with sex. Just enjoy yourself and then get on with your life." Annabelle wasn't about to concede the argument.

"Just because you have a sex life like a guy—no fuss no muss no heartbreak—doesn't mean the rest of us want to," Gillian responded. "Women want love and sex and romance to go together."

"And heartbreak." Annabelle chided her.

"I don't know about you all, but I'm tired of taking a step toward some guy and having him take a step back."

"Been there. It's the yo-yo dance," I offered.

"What?" Naomi asked as the table of women laughed.

"Cutter explained it to me. He said men are like yo-yos: You reach towards a yo-yo—it spins away. Jerk your hand back, and it'll snap right back to you."

Annabelle gave a curt nod. "Conditioning or wiring, or both. They want to be the hunter, not the hunted. Or they want what they can't have."

"Don't we all." Naomi stared over at the new bartender.

Gillian wasn't giving in. "I like having my head and my heart and my body connected. Now, if we could just get more men rewired . . ."

"I need another." Mindy waved to the waitress. She'd cut her hair again, as short as a boy's, but it worked with her pixie face. She also kept her nails short and her clothes simple—she tried to keep everything as simple as possible because she never had enough time. "A stiff one . . ."

Naomi and I burst out laughing. Mindy shrugged her shoulders and sighed. "I need a potion that makes me feel like twenty-five again—and I want the tits and ass of a twenty-five-year-old."

"Well, there are plenty of those at the bar," Naomi quipped and ducked as Mindy slapped at her. But I looked over at the image of my old guide, still standing at the bar. *It had been so long—was he surfacing again? And why here, and now?* I shook the immigrant thought from my head.

"So, I actually get a night off and we meet here? Where are the cute waiters to make me grateful I'm single again?" Annabelle stared at the crowd of very handsome women.

"I need to call home, make sure Ted's okay with the kids. Amazing how a grown man can't find his way around a kitchen." Mindy was a hardworking pragmatist, the consequence of eleven years of life married and raising children in New York. But she didn't move. "Okay, so where's my potion?"

I slid my glass of wine over to her. "Drink and know the truth."

She slid it back to me. "Give me something for my sex life and I'll buy a round for the house."

"I told you the cure for that." Annabelle smirked. The magic of laughter with friends was working.

"How about a love potion?" I asked.

"Oh, don't go there—please!" Gillian rolled her eyes. "You all remember Gary?"

"Mr. *Je T'aime?*" Naomi cocked an eyebrow.

Gillian nodded. "Well, after all that, he actually said to me, '*Je t'aime* also means *like* in French.'"

"*Like?*" I exclaimed. "What did you say?"

"I told him, '*Go fuck yourself* means *Go fuck yourself*.'"

"Well, Nonna did say the potion would work, but it was up to you to choose the right guy," I reminded her.

"You're a fine one to talk." Naomi stared at me.

"Listen, just 'cause things aren't so hot in the sack doesn't mean things are bad," Mindy said. "You can't have mind-blowing, magical, tantric sex every night."

Mindy's words immediately conjured an image of my magical night with Derek. But that special evening had been months ago; now it seemed we'd swung back to the opposite pole and somehow we'd gotten stuck there.

"I take it that's experience speaking?" Annabelle jibed as the waitress arrived with the drinks.

"There are other things just as important. And having kids does change things," Mindy said and turned to me. "Speaking of which, missy, any news?"

I sighed. "Derek's not working enough. I can't take time off, and we'd need his income to have a baby. He's waited all his life to make this dream come true. He had to give it up to support his first family. I can't make him do that again."

"Well, that's very generous of you. But what about your dreams? When are they supposed to come true?" Naomi stubbed out her cigarette.

"You could just get pregnant."

"I couldn't be dishonest with him, especially about something that important. I want to do it when he wants to."

"Men are always afraid that having a kid means losing their freedom, but once they're holding their baby in their arms, they're happy." Mindy tapped her watch. "You do have a biological clock, you know."

"We've got time. Once he gets his first real break and starts to make some money, we'll be able to do it."

"Having kids is expensive," Mindy sighed. I'd seen her wearing the same wool coat for the last five years.

I nodded. "And I feel like, well, like I have to give birth to myself before I can give birth to a child. Would you do it again?" I asked.

Mindy stared into her Merlot as if she was scrying, and the long silence seemed its own answer. "Sometimes I think about how different my life would have been if I hadn't," she said very quietly. "Your life isn't your own anymore; for twenty years you live for someone else. And their needs always come first. That can be very hard. I mean, it's just a small example, but how often do I get to hang out with you guys? It's a miracle I can get to circle as often as I do. And unless you've got live-in help—and how many of us can afford that?—it wreaks havoc with your love life. But there are ways to keep marriage sexy after kids."

Annabelle looked at her sideways and shook her head.

"No, really, you just have to be very creative once you've got kids. Showers together are great. You just pop in the video while you're cleaning up." Everyone laughed, but I wondered if it wasn't out of fear. "And then there are sleepovers and when they're at school. Love in the afternoon is *very* hot—Daddy just has to come home for lunch once in a while." She took a sip of her wine and smiled, and then her expression softened. "I've never felt as much love as I do for my kids. And the way they love me, I can't explain it, it's just the most incredible feeling in the whole world. It's true love."

"And Ted?" I asked.

"I love Ted. And he loves me. It's hard work, but it's worth it. It doesn't have that same thrill it did in the beginning, but it's richer now, deeper. It's more . . . real."

Annabelle knocked back the rest of her beer and waved to the waitress. "I'm telling you, there's a reason love is blind, at least at the beginning. And why it isn't afterwards." She startled us by reaching for one of Naomi's cigarettes. "Love's a mystery, and it always will be, potion or no potion."

"So a relationship is learning how to cope with whoever the hell it is you fell in love with," I said, not sure if I was joking, but we all laughed.

"The real question is whether you're in too deep once you find out." Annabelle wasn't laughing.

I scanned the bar, the other tables, the dance floor for James Dean. She, he was gone. I remembered—Dionysus appears from the dark places, the places of uncertainty and ambiguity, where there is love and then there is none, where desire was and is no longer, where women are men and men are women. He abides in the place between the worlds, moving easily between them, unifying them, all the while drawing us into the dance along the shadowy and razor-sharp edges of possibility. And so, from the liminal and the labyrinth, he had, for just a moment, returned to me. *But why?*

"Come on, let's dance." Naomi pulled Mindy out of the booth and the rest of us followed. We headed to the iridescent jukebox vibrating against the back wall. "How about a little Joan Jett?" Naomi dropped the quarters in the slot.

"Have you phoned the studio yet?" I called to Derek from the kitchen. "I thought they gave you a great price." His success had become the shared focus of our lives. We talked about it every day—how much it would cost to do a demo, which studio to use, which clubs to try to book, which agents to pursue, even the music itself. I poured my energy and my love into him, encouraging, prodding, constantly coming up with ideas and strategies. But he couldn't do anything until his group had a demo, or he had a solo one.

"I'll get to it."

I heard the television go on. I put the rest of the dishes in the dishwasher and the pots in the sink to soak. I leaned back against the counter, closed my eyes and felt the frustration and the exhaustion wash over me. If he wasn't going to push a little harder, he needed, *we* needed, him to get a full-time day job. I'd already brought it up; I couldn't do it again without sounding like a nag. Worse, I'd sound like I didn't have faith in him.

I sat down beside him on the couch, letting myself get lost in the movie. It ended and he flipped to the late night talk shows. I stood up. "Are you coming to bed?" I asked.

"Sure." He turned off the noise. I heard him in the bathroom; we passed in the hallway and he leaned down and kissed me. I kissed him back, feeling a small pulse of excitement. Hoping it would grow, I followed him into the bedroom. We stood on either side of the bed, removing our clothes. He climbed in, pulling up the covers, and I stood, hoping he would look at me and that I would see his desire for me in his eyes. Instead, he closed them.

I turned off the light. The bedroom was cold and the draft leaking in through the air conditioner sleeve made me shiver. I longed for things to be as they once were, to be swept away by desire and the certainty that we were meant to be. I wanted Derek to know that I loved him, I wanted to know that everything would be all right.

"Shit!" I hissed.

"What's wrong?"

"I banged my knee on the bed frame." The beautiful, elegant, romantic frame of our marriage bed. I pulled back the covers and slipped between the cold sheets. Derek leaned over and kissed me. I kissed him back, still hoping for the intoxicating, heart-stealing rush.

"Tired?" Derek's opening gambit, so different from the lost magnetism that once merged us with such charged erotic force. I wondered what it would be like to be able to look into each other's eyes, to breathe together, to be touched slowly, with sensitivity and passion as we made love, to feel desire for the man I loved rise and carry me to the wild abandonment of an orgasm. It had been too long since I'd been able to feel enough arousal to climax.

"No, not tired at all," I responded, hoping.

Derek kissed me again, his tongue plunging into my mouth. I wanted to feel swept away, but instead I felt invaded. I kissed him back, sending my tongue back into his mouth. He rolled quickly on top of me, still kissing me, kissing my nipples, then sucking on them. He was heavy and I was pinned beneath his weight, my breathing squashed into short gasps. I wrapped my arms around him. I kissed him back. I slid my hands over his back, down his backside.

What's he feeling? Can he feel me? I could feel his body pressing against mine, hear his breathing, but I couldn't feel *him*. I felt a quick laceration of despair.

He rolled to the side, and I inhaled deeply, then exhaled. He slipped his hand between my legs. I wanted to respond but it was too soon. I murmured, "Not yet, wait . . . ," but whether he didn't hear me, or he chose not to, his hand stayed where it was, his fingers moving back and forth, suddenly dipping into me—a gesture, like his first kiss, that felt intrusive rather than arousing. I inhaled slowly, tried to focus only on the feeling of his fingers between my legs.

Am I taking too long? Why can't I respond? Uncomfortable just lying there, I reached up and kissed him, trailed my hand up and down his wide back, stroked his hardening cock as he stroked me. "A little slower," I said softly. "Gently."

"Is it in?" he asked.

"No."

"Would you put it in?" It was not a question.

I rose from the bed, almost as if escaping, and darted through the cold to the bathroom. I took my diaphragm from its plastic case and filled the rubber cup with viscous contraceptive jelly. I carefully squeezed the wire rim together, hoping it wouldn't explode from my fingers and shoot across the bathroom or drop into the toilet. I shoved the messy thing in; it felt like a capful of snow. I shivered and sighed, wiping off the excess left behind as it slid in. I washed my hands and returned to the bedroom.

If I'd been honest, I would have said I needed to start over, to slow down, to spend more time on foreplay. But I didn't say a word. It's not like I hadn't asked him before. I had, carefully, using positive language to reinforce how much I enjoyed, and needed, more foreplay. But it didn't seem to have registered, and how many times can you say it before you're a nag?

I should be ready. Derek was far more experienced than I and I didn't want to seem inappropriately demanding, or less than . . . what? *Good enough.*

Derek kissed me firmly, confidently, his tongue once again filling my mouth. I kissed him back. His hand went instantly between my legs to continue his efforts to make me come. *What if I can't?* I pushed the thought aside. *Let yourself be swept away. Concentrate on your own feelings.* Suddenly, he was on top of me, pushing my legs open and then back, folded tightly against my chest, pinning me so I couldn't move as he plunged inside of me. He pulled back and pushed in more deeply with each stroke. It was hard to breathe and I felt myself stretched and reshaped as he moved in and out.

It feels good to be filled, to be taken. I love his intensity, I need it. His passion can ignite mine. It can.

He panted, he moved, supporting his weight above me, caught up in his own excitement until finally he buried himself in me, coming in two, three silent spasms. I felt a quick, rolling wave of energy within my vagina. A spark to light a fire that had ended.

He collapsed and I lay pinned beneath him as he drifted to sleep. I synchronized my breathing with his, my arms still wrapped around him, clinging to him like an invisible rope above an abyss.

How do you love when your heart's been broken? Use hope to bind it back together again, to fill in all the cracks and crevices. And with hope you can take actions. Or at least you *act as if* until it becomes so. That's how you do it, with the other kind of magic—with a glamour, the magic of creating an illusion.

"*I'm so confused,* Nonna." I exhaled raggedly. "And I'm scared. I love Derek but I think I'm not *in* love with him anymore. And I don't think he's in love with me. It's like the passion has just evaporated, for both of us. I know that things change in relationships, everyone says this happens, but it's awful." I got up, walked to the old casement windows at one end of Nonna's living room and stared into the maze of Greenwich Village streets far below. We'd just closed on her purchase of the apartment she'd lived in for the last twenty years, as the building converted from rental to a co-op. It had been fun for me to be her attorney, and we'd returned to open the bottle of champagne I'd given her.

Photographs of her first and second husbands and several glasses of champagne had triggered my confession. Nonna listened with her usual calm attention as I turned back to her. "It's like I'm numb, like I'm suffocating." As I spoke, I could feel the pain winding its way up through my guts and around my heart. "When I do feel, it hurts so much I feel like I'm dying." I couldn't breathe.

Nonna took off her glasses and rubbed her eyes. "So, the spell's worn off."

"Worn off?" My heart tightened with fear. "Is that possible?"

"Oh yes, indeed it is." She rose and went into the kitchen. "I'm going to make us some Irish Breakfast tea. Lots of caffeine. And you should eat a little something."

I tried to shove the panic down. "Is it because I used magic?" I was afraid to hear her answer and my breathing came quick and shallow as I stood in the kitchen doorway.

"Take a deep breath." Nonna put the kettle on the stove and came to me. "It's natural for you to have that fear, but you didn't manipulate him with the spell, did you?" She rested a hand in the center of my back and I could feel her grounding me.

"No, I didn't even know him." I clung to the belief that if I could figure out what was wrong I could fix it. "I know the spell brought us together, but when we fell in love it felt like the real magic was just beginning. The whole world felt magical. I was so happy, so full of energy, and my feelings for him were so powerful. I mean, just seeing him gave me such an incredible rush. I felt like we could deal with any problem as long as we had each other. And whatever we did was fun, even dumb little things like going to buy the Sunday paper on Saturday night. The sex was so intense. But it's all changed. I can't feel it anymore." The words rushed out of me. "I just want things to be the way they were before."

"I know how hard it is." Nonna put an arm around my shoulders and squeezed. "They can't be the way they were because you can't go backwards. But you can go forward."

Embarrassed to be crying, I inhaled deeply and quickly wiped away tears. She tucked her arm in mine and for the first time in months I felt a small glimmer of hopefulness. "Come in here and make us some cinnamon toast." Nonna set me to work. "There's some wonderful Irish butter in the refrigerator." It was a small thing to do, but it was calming. We settled back in the living room and Nonna gestured for me to sit beside her. After I'd eaten and had some tea, she patted my hand and returned to my worry.

"I know this is painful, but the magic has run its course," she said.

Her words smashed my regained control and I began to cry. She rubbed my back in slow, wide circles just the way my mother had done when I was a child. I rarely cried and I hated crying in front of anyone. My mother was strong, my grandmothers were strong, *I* had to be strong. But my fear pushed up like a sea monster through the waves of sorrow and frustration and I was afraid that even Nonna wouldn't be able to help me. She gave me a handful of tissues and waited patiently for the emotion to ebb.

"I must have done something wrong."

"It's not *your* magic that's worn off," she said softly.

"Not mine? What other magic would there be?" I knew that I had acted precipitously when I'd cast my spell. There were many things I hadn't learned, skills I hadn't mastered, and I knew that Nonna had been concerned. Now, finally, so was I.

"Blow."

I made an awful noise, wiped my face, and we both laughed.

"Better?"

I nodded.

"Good. Drink some tea." I picked up the thick blue mug, felt its comforting warmth between my palms. Nonna handed me her other universal cure—a cookie—and continued. "Even before you found your way to the Goddess, you embarked on the path of love. It's a path everyone takes at some point in their lives, at least they try to. Love is the greatest and most difficult magic, the holiest magic. But whenever you make magic, especially love magic, you don't do it alone."

"No, I've realized, it's the way I . . . co-create my life with divinity."

"And what's Nature?" Nonna asked patiently.

I wasn't expecting the Socratic approach to heartbreak, but I answered. "Well, I've experienced it as . . . the embodiment of divinity."

"And?"

"And it's our greatest spiritual teacher—when we pay attention."

Nonna nodded. "So Mother Nature makes her own magic. It's Nature's magic that's ending for you."

"I don't understand."

"Your spell worked. You and Derek found each other. You were very attracted to him—for many reasons that you'll need to understand. But as soon as you two met, Mother Nature stepped in and dosed you both with a very powerful love potion of her own."

"How? You mean metaphorically?"

Nonna shook her head. "Literally. Everyone's searching for a love potion and it's right inside of them. Like Dorothy running through Oz trying to get home when she has the power with her all along." Nonna smiled. "The body produces very powerful chemicals that saturate your brain and create specific effects on your emotions, your behavior and your libido—what we recognize as falling in love. Some call it the love cocktail, which makes sense since we're in the realm of your intoxicating pal Dionysus." She gave a little laugh again and it reassured me more than her unexpected explanations, which I was still struggling to grasp. "It's so powerful, you were in an altered state of consciousness."

"You're saying that being in love is just being under the influence of brain chemicals? *And* the great sex?"

Nonna nodded. "I know what it feels like, *mia figlia*, don't you listen to all that nonsense that you lose your sex drive after menopause." She smiled mischievously, and winked. "Not true."

I finally smiled too. "So Nature's love potion is what made me so hot for him. All I could think about was making love with Derek, and the sex was so great." Then my smile faded. "But it hasn't been that way for a long time."

"The potion stimulates your sex drive. But it's only at full power for about six months and then it gradually diminishes. After that, you're on your own. That's why so many people break up after a year or so—they're chasing that initial high. And that's also why love and tragedy always go together in so many myths and plays, movies and songs and books. What we think of as romantic love only lasts for as long as the potion lasts. Who wants to watch a couple get bored, take out the garbage, argue about bills, and lose interest in sex?"

"So when the potion ends, the spell ends," I said quietly, the realization giving way to despair. "And love ends."

Nonna shook her head. "No, it's when the spell ends that real love *begins*."

I sat silently, wanting to accept her reassuring words, but wondering how it was possible. "But what *is* love without that feeling of romantic connection?"

"Ah, that's the danger. We confuse true love with that initial flare of passion and euphoria."

"So Derek isn't my soul mate after all?" I asked in a whisper, afraid to speak the words, as if in speaking them I would break the spell of true love. But I had to know the truth.

"When the potion's in your system, it's easy to believe you've found your soul mate. It's also very easy to completely overlook the reality of who you've fallen in love with. You know the expression 'Love is blind?' Well, the potion blinds us. Even the bad seems good. In fact, danger and risk stimulate the cocktail—that adds to my theory about the fascination of bad boys and also why some men cheat. Love can be very dangerous. You'll do anything, lose yourself, and not even know who's stealing your heart."

"So you're saying I don't know who I fell in love with?" I shook off a shiver.

"There were stars in your eyes." She nodded. "But now you can discover who he really is. And you can also figure out *why* you fell in love with him."

I felt myself getting angry, pulling back, resisting her words. "But why does Nature do this to us?" I demanded, as if I expected an answer that would make it all different, that would take away the haunting sense of hopelessness that was growing instead of diminishing. "If that feeling isn't real, if it's not meant to last, then what's the point? Just to get you crazy enough to make babies? Then what?"

Nonna laughed. "It's about babies and much more. Remember, this is divine magic at work here. Don't underestimate what's happening—even what you think is *not* happening is important. Nature strikes the match of passion and starts the fire of love. But as a very wise woman said: 'To keep the fires burning, *you* have to fan the flames.' "

"Nonna, I've tried, but if we're not soul mates, I don't know what we are." I shook my head, still confused.

"It's natural for love to shape-shift, to become something new, different. All living things grow and change," she said firmly. "What you experienced with Derek was just the first stage of love. But it's not just the love potion that makes the beginning so wonderful. It's also the way you treated each other—and *here* is the rest of the divine magic at work. Tell me, how did you behave toward each other in those early days?"

I sat silently; images flooded back of the first time we met, the first time we made love, and all the happy times afterward. "We loved being together, doing things together, having fun—we made time for each other. We were affectionate and we showed it. We figured out how to tackle things together, how to make things happen for our future together. We had sex a lot more often, and it was more . . . spontaneous, less mechanical. I think we were just more of a priority for each other, and the relationship felt like it was more of a priority." I began to feel a little better as I talked. "And we flirted a lot more. I can't remember the last time he brought me flowers. Now it feels like we're taking each other for granted. It's like that old cliché that getting married is the death knell of romance."

Nonna smiled. "But it doesn't have to be. The potion shows you how to keep your love alive *and* exciting *and* romantic: You continue to treat each other the way you did at the beginning, when you fell under the influence of Mother Nature's magic. It requires effort now, which it didn't when you were intoxicated, but it'll become second nature if you really do it."

"So romantic love *can* lead to true love?"

Nonna smiled. "True love is not just those intense feelings of being swept away, it's not just desire and passion and rapture. It's a commitment you make to each other every day to treat each other with love. Act with love and you'll create love."

"I want true love, Nonna, the kind of love that lasts."

"And perhaps that's what you will have. Only time will tell. It's up to you and him—*that's* the secret of real magic. It's always up to you. But just remember, you can't have a soul mate until you have your soul."

I hugged and thanked Nonna and took the racketing subway home. Staring at my reflection in the train's dark windows, I thought about the last time Derek and I had made love, of how lost I'd felt and my decision to "act as if" I could have the love I longed for with him. It wasn't so far from Nonna's instruction to act as we had when we'd fallen in love. Act as if we were in love, and we would create that love. But I sighed, realizing that at some point I'd have to figure out whether we had succeeded in creating real love, or had just spun a glamour.

I had trouble getting to sleep that night, wondering how much of what I'd felt for Derek was real, or just the consequence of chemicals. I opened the blinds and searched for a star in the overlit, urban night sky. The nightingale that lived in the park began to sing and I began to think: Nature's magic had shown us *how* to love. Now it was our choice whether to love, or not. But to love truly, you must know the truth about who it is you think you love.

I stared down at Derek, lying on his back, his eyes closed, his mouth open, snoring, oblivious to the stars and the turmoil, the magic and its consequences. *Who is he?* I closed the blinds and climbed into bed.

The cab pulled up in front of the World Café, an inconspicuous restaurant on the Upper West Side that had become the confidential watering hole for Hollywood's down-dressing glitterati. I'd arrived early but Dale was already sitting at his usual table in the window, usual tuna salad, usual signature denim hat. How could he be such a creature of habit when his films were so spontaneous? But perhaps because of the risks he took as a filmmaker, he stuck to his rituals and routines.

"I love that scarf." He eyed the violet silk draped about my neck. The one sartorial extravagance Dale allowed himself in a relentlessly simple wardrobe of dark trousers and stone-washed silk work shirts was fabulous scarves. A quick hug and kiss and I slid into the seat opposite him.

It had been almost a year since we'd seen each other. Dale was an independent filmmaker long before that was a remote possibility, let alone a term of vogue. He was a maverick, determined to tell the truth in film, refusing the siren song of hollow Hollywood fantasy. Though often compared to Woody Allen, he worked in an utterly collaborative, cinema verité fashion, making actors' films that used their unique gifts to improvise not just a scene but an entire story. His films further blurred the line between reality and story, real life and film by dealing in a semidocumentary way with Dale's life, the actors' lives and issues of concern to women.

We'd met years ago, at a planning meeting for one of the massive antinuclear demonstrations in New York, and had become friends. Dale lived primarily in Los Angeles, but also had an apartment in Manhattan, and periodically we'd get together when he was in town. He came from a family of great privilege and since childhood, he'd explained to me, he had always been more at home in the world of emotions inhabited by his mother and her friends—sitting with them at their tea parties, accompanying them shopping, and most of all listening to their conversations, which fascinated him—than in his father's realm, the "men's world" of business and external events. A man who loved women, he'd laughingly described himself as a lesbian in a man's body, and though he was still far more male than he would acknowledge, he was very much a wonderful girlfriend.

"So, still enjoying your handsome husband?" he asked after I ordered.

I nodded and sighed. "Things do change. He's been pursuing his music."

"He's older than you, isn't he?"

I nodded. "Fourteen years."

"Good, you're just who I want to talk to! I'm thinking about my next film. I want to look at the attraction between older men and younger women."

His words caught me up short, for although I knew Derek was older, I rarely gave it any thought.

"Three young women in New York City, sharing an apartment, and their relationships with each other and with men. I've got someone very special for the lead—very gifted. Beautiful long black hair, so now I need a blond and a redhead."

"Modern version of *How to Marry a Millionaire*?" I asked.

"*Plus c'est change, plus c'est le meme chose*. The desire to marry for money or for love—which is stronger? In the fifties, they started out for cold cash, but love won in the end."

"Well, plenty of women still marry for money. But now women have careers, we don't need men for financial support. In fact, sometimes we support them—even if they're older. But we still need them for love, and for a different kind of security—emotional security."

"Well, our trio may start out with a desire for love, but who knows what they really want?"

"Dale, what do you think romance is, what desire is?" I thought about my early attraction to Derek—it was true that his age had lent him an air of confidence that had been very seductive. But that confidence had been a thin veneer behind which was a man uncertain about his talent, his abilities and his future. "The heroine with a young man—we think it's passion, right? With an older guy, we think it's the need for security. But it's not necessarily financial. It could also be . . . ," I hesitated as the thought surfaced, "for the love she never got from her father. Is that a cliché?"

"They're clichés because they're so often true."

"Well, is it love, or lust?" I paused and stared at the older man with the younger woman standing at the bar together. "Or the need to heal a wound?"

"Why couldn't she have passion with an older guy? A lot of women have told me they prefer older men because they're more in touch with their feelings; their hearts are finally connected to their sexuality."

"Yes, that's one of the things that attracted me to Derek." *At the beginning*, I thought, but didn't say.

"And he's a musician, isn't he?"

I nodded. "Definitely connected to his feelings." I kept my voice even, but caught my frowning reflection in the window.

"Moody," Dale said sympathetically.

The word echoed out of the past. A nod was all the reply I could muster as an image of Derek sullenly polishing off a good Bordeaux all by himself last night flashed past my inner eye.

Dale sensitively steered the conversation away from me. "So the plot—they've sublet an apartment—we'll use mine. And there's confusion about the date the lease is up and the next tenant, a guy in his forties— me—arrives in the middle of the farewell New Year's Day party they're throwing for themselves. What happens when he shows up? Who is he? Will the heroine get back together with her young ex-boyfriend, or will she fall in love with this older guy? Who does she really want?"

"*What* does she really want?" I said quietly. "What does true love look like—is it what we're raised to expect? A knight on a white horse? Or something totally unexpected?"

"Yes, that's it—can you trust desire to guide you to true love or is it just self-deception and cultural indoctrination?"

"All those fairy tales and movies and songs about romance and love at first sight and strangers across a crowded room. Are they on to something real or are they just fantasies that ruin the chance of finding real love? I mean, do you ever really know who it is you're falling in love with?"

Dale looked up from his sandwich. "Speaking from personal experience?"

I shrugged. "I'm trying to figure out who I married. Then maybe I can figure out why I married him."

"Love's a mystery. You've seen *Always*." One of his early films, it was about his divorce from his first wife.

I nodded. "Well, if you can answer those questions, every woman in America will want to see this film." I laughed. "*I* want to see it."

Like Dale, I'd grown up believing I would live the romances movies had shown me. When I met Derek, I thought my movie had begun, that my knight had finally arrived to sweep me off my feet. I wasn't the sort of person that kind of thing happened to, even if I was a Witch living in a world full of magic. I was a lawyer, an independent, hardworking, self-reliant woman. Not the sort who gets swept away, no matter how much she might secretly long for it. And Derek, erratic though his progress and his moods might be, was busy building his own career, not whisking me off to some fairy-tale kingdom.

No, the romantic magic of the movies had not turned out as I'd expected. And I sensed that Nonna's explanation was only a small part of the reason.

I puffed hard to keep up with Derek. I took huge steps to fit into the trail of footsteps he had left in the snow before me. It was early Sunday morning and the long, light-filled field stretched before us glistening, dreaming and undisturbed. We tromped quietly along the edge, close to the line of pine trees, until we found a sunny bench sheltered from the wind.

We sat, his arm around me. "There aren't many birds in winter," I said, staring out at the splintered light. I looked into his eyes. But almost immediately, I felt uncomfortable, and so did he. I smiled self-consciously, looking away with relief.

This weekend walk was one of our routines—and after my talk with Nonna I had come to realize this love of being out-of-doors, in as much Nature as a city could provide, was something we shared. It was a common value, a bond. It was more than a routine. It was a ritual, and nurturing those rituals was a way to nurture our love as real love.

I had taken Nonna's words, and Nature's teaching, to heart and devoted myself to rekindling our romance. I hoped that the most important expression of my commitment was my continued support of Derek's career. He'd been playing more gigs, which didn't pay well but gave him good exposure, but other than that, nothing seemed to be materializing, and I continued to worry that he wasn't doing much of anything else to manifest his goals.

He sighed and let go of my hand, and stared off across the snow.

"What's the matter?" I asked. I'd become very attuned to the slightest shift in his emotions.

"Nothing." His voice was flat.

I hesitated for a moment and reached for his hand. "You can't get discouraged. Look how far you've come—you've gotten some good gigs. And soon there'll be better bookings." There was just enough happening with his music to keep hope alive. And hope was all we needed. I applauded and I was endlessly optimistic. Partners are there for each other when they're needed. That's what a marriage is—actions taken every day to express your love. That's what would keep the romance alive and nurture true love. "Don't worry about making money right now. We're getting by okay." Money wasn't important, as long as we could support each other in pursuing our dreams.

He stood up. "Let's head back."

I followed him slowly back to our apartment overlooking the shimmering park. By the time we got inside, my feet were wet and frozen. We read the Sunday *Times,* had soup for lunch, cleaned the apartment, made some phone calls. He'd seemed annoyed when I tried to talk to him about his schedule for the coming week and so I dropped the subject. We had dinner in the living room while we watched television. We kept watching until bedtime. A typical Sunday, shared by countless other urban couples.

I locked the front door and turned off the lights. Derek was asleep when I came to bed. I climbed quietly beneath the covers, trying not to wake him. Lying in the dark, listening to his breathing, I realized I was relieved that he was asleep, glad that I would not have to make love with him. That I would not have to have sex with him. Because that's what it felt like, and while I could *act as if* in all sorts of other ways, it was impossible to act as if I was satisfied when I really just wanted to cry.

10

Breaking the Spell

There is no happy ending for true love, for true love will never end.

—ANONYMOUS

"*Hey there,*" Derek said from the couch. "I wasn't expecting you back so early tonight." He turned down the volume on the television.

"I'm almost done going over the files." I dumped my coat and cumbersome briefcase. "I needed a break." The real estate attorney I'd been working with had finally retired and I'd taken over the practice. I plopped down on the couch next to Derek and gave him a quick kiss. His eyes were drawn back to the flashing images behind me. "I've got great news. I might have a positive reaction from one of the A and R guys." I had been trying to reconnect with some of my old contacts in the record business to see if they could help Derek.

"That's great!" I had his complete attention. He clicked off the television, looking like I'd told him he'd just been nominated for a Grammy. "Who was it?"

"Jackson, from Polygram."

"Did he tell you what he thought?"

"Just that he's interested in what you sent him. He wants to see you live." I smiled seeing how excited he was. "You just need to find the right club. But don't let too much time go by." I bit my tongue after I'd said it, but Derek's procrastinations had made this journey feel as long and labored as the one in the *Odyssey*. "My neck's so sore—I'm going to take a bath."

I went to the kitchen and put together a relaxation potion, grinding together chamomile, valerian, peppermint and lavender. I inhaled their clean scent then bundled the mix into a cotton handkerchief and dropped it, with a cup of Epsom salts, into the hot tub. I sank into the water up to my chin, feeling my muscles slowly succumb. I closed my eyes, and images from Derek's last gig played across the screen of my eyelids like a movie.

I'd watched the way a young woman had flirted with him, her femininity curling around him like a cat's tail in the sunlight. She played a girlish coquette, her body communicating every intention. It seemed so brazen, the way she arched her back just enough to make her breasts jut forward, the way she angled her head to one side, the little laugh, the parted lips, the eye contact. If I behaved like that I'd feel so . . . obvious. He'd refused when she'd offered her phone number, but he had flirted. I'd felt jealous, but there was something else bothering me.

No one observing us would ever suspect, but for all of the efforts to re-create our initial passion, something was still missing. Nonna had explained to me that though the love potion wore off, the body provided another enchantment—it was called oxytocin, and it was the chemical produced by the brain after an orgasm. It was part of the delicious high, not only making your skin more sensitive to touch but most importantly creating a deep emotional and spiritual bond between a couple. No orgasm, no oxytocin, no bonding—at least not in that all-important way.

I already knew that my sexual frustrations were contributing to the distance between us. I had to do something before it was too late. If rekindling the sexual heat of our relationship was going to take more work, then so be it. Like all the other challenges, I rolled up my sleeves and got to work.

I began by finally confronting the haunting fear that I was frigid. Gillian had laughed when I'd talked to her about it: "A dry spell doesn't make you frigid. It means you're traveling through a desert." Her laughter was a temporary balm. But the terror that I would remain unable to respond gripped me as I returned to my barren marriage bed. My heart and body were numb, and if I wasn't frozen, I was dying in a desiccated landscape. I was desperate to fix my lack of arousal, a problem I'd learned was shared by a majority of women in America regardless of age.

I read everything I could get my hands on about women's sexuality—everything from *Cosmo* to Lonnie Barbach, *Our Bodies, Ourselves* to medical journals. I read about how it takes a woman about twenty minutes to get fully aroused whereas men are aroused almost immediately. I read about angles of penetration and the inability of most women to have an orgasm when they were underneath a man because of lack of clitoral stimulation. Again and again, I read about low sex drive.

The books and magazines were all saying exactly what all the women in circle had advised, and a little more: "Figure out what you like, what you need and want, and tell him. Show him if you need to. Take charge of your own pleasure. And if all else fails, fantasize." I put the advice to work.

Don't just lie there like a dead latke! I was always active when we made love, I was always moving, doing, touching, sticking my tongue deep into his mouth and tangling with his, thrusting my hips, wrapping my legs around him. But something just wasn't working and I couldn't figure out what it was. I wondered how he was reacting and whether I was doing it right, because I just didn't seem to be reaching him, or reaching my own orgasm.

Take responsibility for your own pleasure! Okay, sure, I tried that. I was good at taking responsibility in all the other areas of life. And I'd been trying in the bedroom, but obviously I'd been missing something. I began by attempting to rediscover what turned me on. Alone in the apartment, I explored my body with my own hands, touched myself slowly and carefully, learning what felt good and where. And I thought about what used to turn me on about our lovemaking, about Derek. But . . . there was still a problem.

Focus on your feelings! I had to acknowledge how difficult it was to think about myself, to concentrate on my own feelings instead of worrying about Derek's. I practiced masturbating to try to get in touch with my body's responses. Unlike making love, there was no fever of excitement, but I learned what I needed—I paid careful attention to the rhythm, speed, motion and pressure so that I could communicate them to Derek. And I noticed that slowly moving my fingers in circles, and then gradually speeding up, seemed more arousing than the quick back and forth I was familiar with. But it was obvious right away that just mechanically touching myself wasn't enough to get me off.

Your biggest sex organ is between your ears! It was the fantasy of being touched by Derek that pushed me over the orgasmic edge. Although sometimes it was a mysterious stranger who made love to me—but everything I read said that fantasy was *Perfectly Normal and Perfectly Okay*, even though I did feel a little guilty. One thing I was sure of was that I had to stop the self-reflecting, self-doubting voice in my head or I would never be able to relax and just feel.

Communication is the key to GREAT SEX! He's not a mind reader! It was true that somehow I'd expected him to know what I needed and how to do it—it seemed to have started out that way. And that, to some extent, had been the love potion. I had spoken up long ago, but he never seemed to take in what I was saying, much less remember it. I'd given up because I just didn't know how to say it in a way that got me what I wanted, and needed. I was also concerned that what I said would be taken as criticism, which would in turn damage his confidence and his desire for me. And I was afraid of being a Xanthippe.

Communicate in a positive way, without being critical! Affirm what's good! "Oh yes, like that, that feels wonderful. I love it when you kiss me slowly first, when you kiss me right there, when you surprise me, when you take more time . . ." Okay, here was something I could try: accentuating the positive.

And be specific! "I need more foreplay. I need to take more time. It really turns me on when you fuck me from behind with your hand on my clit." Okay, I could be precise.

Show, don't tell! I'd learned that we each make love to the other the way we want to be loved. I decided to show him what I liked. I'd guide his hands to where I liked to be touched, and I'd touch him and kiss him the way and where I liked to be kissed. And I would try to slow him down for me while simultaneously attending to his need for speed.

It was time to talk to Derek.

Pick a relaxed time and place! And create a sexy mood! Saturday night, when the pressures of work were behind us, I cooked dinner and uncorked a Châteauneuf du Pape. I filled the bedroom with candles while he washed the dishes—our division of labor dictated that whoever cooked didn't clean. And then I nervously initiated the conversation, trying to use all the communication skills I'd read about.

Begin with the positive! "Sex with you has been really incredible."

He beamed. "It's been great."

I took a deep breath. Would he still feel that way after I finished? "You've always really turned me on." *Be specific!* "The foreplay is so great—it really gets me . . . hot." I hesitated self-consciously, then plunged ahead. *Be enthusiastic!* "Really hot! I would love it if we could spend more time . . . making out before we . . . have intercourse." That word sounded so technical, but at least I'd said what I wanted. I waited nervously for his reaction.

"Well sure, why not?" he replied. I felt as if I'd been sprung from jail. It was so easy! Why had I ever hesitated? "I want you to tell me what you want. I want you to be happy." He smiled and gave me a quick kiss.

We made love and he took more time. The wine helped me relax, and I did what had become most difficult of all for me and what was most important—I focused on my feelings instead of worrying about his. *Get on top!* I did. *Guide his hands!* I did. *Moan and let him know when he's doing it right!* I moaned and sighed and said *"Yes!"* After some initial self-consciousness, I was able to enjoy myself and have a heavenly orgasm as my fantasy of fulfillment came true.

And then, as if we'd never talked, within a week we were back to the same perfunctory, mechanical pattern. He seemed locked in a world of his own sensations, and so I began to create a world of my own, inside my head. I began to find my fulfillment through fantasy—which, I reminded myself, all the books and articles said was *OKAY!* But although it sometimes worked, it also made me feel more distant and disconnected. It made me feel unfaithful. Was Derek living in his own fantasies? We were having sex, but not with each other.

Tonight had been no different. I lay in the darkness listening to his steady, grumbling breath. We were so far from the exquisite merging, the heated surrender to love. I drifted back to my daydream, to the images that silenced the voice in my head. Desire for the stranger—a man with dark hair and darker eyes, a man with callused fingertips, a man who knew how to sweep away my doubts and fears, who knew what I wanted and needed, who was strong enough for me to finally be soft—desire for that man flooded me and I reached between my legs.

My fingers moved in the wet remnants of unfulfilled desire, separating the swollen, battered petals. I gently circled the neglected plunder of excitement and release, rhythmically drawing forth the pleasure I could no longer find with Derek. The knowing fingers were no longer my own; they belonged to my ghostly lover. The cadence finally caught me and pleasure coursed through me.

I was free and the wave of released fulfillment rose, carrying me over to the other side where an explosion of light shattered the last of my resistance and I found myself floating, suspended out beyond the boundaries of body and conscious control.

I am a point of light, in a vast web of light. I felt a wonderful ripple of joy as I saw a strand of the web leading to a glowing orb that was my mysterious stranger, and then he shape-shifted, staring at me with laughing eyes from another point on the web. I saw a stream of light that tied me to a shining sphere that was Nonna, and radiant strands leading from her to other points of light; bright bands that led to my parents, who were connected to each other, and their parents, who were connected to each other and to my parents, and through them to me. I was surrounded by countless shimmering stars connected by paths of light, stretching out above, below and all around me into infinity.

This is what I am—I am a sphere of light in a vast web of energy. This is life; this is what it truly looks like. I floated in silent bliss.

I was haunted by Nonna's words. *Only when the potion ends can you see the person with whom you have fallen in love.* Not who you want him to be or fantasize he is, but who he *really* is. If I could see Derek clearly, maybe I could begin to understand *why* I had fallen in love with him, and maybe I could figure out how to reconnect sexually. It was like peeling back layers of an onion—I knew I had to be prepared for tears. But I had already found myself crying over the differences between what I'd expected and what I was experiencing. I needed an oracle.

I chose the tarot. I didn't use divination very often, at least not to fore-tell the future. I'd realized that I preferred living my life as an adventure. But it was a way to better understand Derek and our relationship. Having worked with both, I knew that an hour with a good tarot reading was often more fruitful than six months with a therapist.

I was ready to ask—I needed to look into the obscure heart of what had drawn me to Derek.

I sat cross-legged on the bed, staring down at the kaleidoscopic cards spread out on the white duvet. I was working with the classic Ryder-Waite deck, painted by a woman artist, with text written by a member of the Golden Dawn, the ceremonial magical group to which the poet Yeats and Lady Gregory belonged. But as I studied the answers, I wasn't sure I was ready to receive them. There were cups, the symbol of love, fallen with their contents spilling out, and swords, the symbol of the mind, including the unconscious, representing woundedness and hidden forces.

The king of swords, a man whose occupation was linked to communi-cation, appeared reversed, meaning he was not holding his power. And the queen of swords was crossed by the ten of wands—a woman was shoul-dering a very heavy load, believing it was her responsibility to do so. In the past were kings and queens, and reversed tens of pentacles and cups—all showing the damaging impact of parents and their problems within the family. And in the future I saw the empress reversed, a woman without children, and the eight of cups, someone leaving to search for true love at its source. Memories of another reading where this card had appeared rushed back.

I wrote everything down in my journal, searching the images carefully for all of their hidden meaning. And I waited, knowing that, having been given a pathway to the light of awareness, more was going to surface. I held the diary to my heart. I should have felt empowered by the insights, but I wondered: like Nian, dragons and demons were ascending, roiling the waters of love as they approached—would they bring their hidden treasures with them, or would they destroy the life that I had built?

"*It was so powerful*—it *was* love at first sight. From the first moment I saw him it felt like we'd known each other before. I *recognized* him." I handed Nonna the curfane, the small white hilt knife used for practical purposes like carving a candle, which is what she immediately proceeded to do. The shop had just closed and we were alone.

"Almost like déjà vu."

I nodded. "Yes, he was so . . . familiar, so comfortable. Mindy said it was a past life connection." I wasn't completely convinced that past lives were real, but given the relativity of time and space, facts could be stranger than science fiction. "She had a dream in which Derek and I had been married, hundreds of years ago, in India. We had six kids." My eyes widened at the image.

"Let's hope you don't run into *them*." Nonna smiled. "But I suspect there's something besides past life memories going on. You said you were going to ask an oracle—did you?"

I nodded. "It was very hard to look into that mirror. But you were right. I have to know who it is I fell in love with. Whether it's just been self-deception."

"Or self-revelation," Nonna responded.

I took a slow breath in, remembering the images. "I saw our parents. What's that old saying—when you make love with someone, there are six people in bed together. I've given it a lot of thought, and I've done some reading."

Nonna laughed. "Of course."

"It's so obvious really, but we don't see what's right in front of us. *In* us. We're reflections of our upbringing. We learn how to love from our families. Good or bad, whatever their problems were, in one way or another they become ours. A lineage of love and confusion and pain that's passed from generation to generation. *Adam raised a Cain.*" I could hear the song playing in my head as I said it, and it tugged a small shudder of sadness from me.

Nonna surveyed her handiwork. She'd carved a sigil—a sun with an unfamiliar symbol in its center—into a fat orange candle. "Where's that oil?" she muttered, foraging around the shelves. "Ah!" She dabbed some on her fingers and began rubbing the candle. "So, you saw love and wounds. What does that mean in terms of being drawn to Derek?"

I paused, picking up the small knife, cleaning off the orange wax now stuck to the sharp blade. "I think that when we're drawn to someone in that powerful, instantaneous, romantic way, it's because they resemble some aspect of our parents. It's all unconscious, of course. But that immediate attraction is the soul seeking to heal its wounds, trying to resolve the obstacles to love that were suffered in childhood."

"So you each long for the other to help you complete the process of learning to love."

"Yes, I guess that's it. Derek's mother never really mothered him—he said she smothered him, and treated him like her 'little' husband. She heaped all sorts of responsibilities on him because his father was never around. He never got to play. So now, I guess, he's playing—and I'm taking care of him. He also said she was very overemotional, and I'm so . . . well, reined in. And his father was never around to show him how a man takes care of someone else, a woman, or a family."

I had been thinking and speaking in a methodical and detached manner, but a quick flash of insight hit me like a small detonation. *Talk about yourself*. "Is that what happened with my love spell? Is *that* why we were drawn together, why we were so attracted?"

"Women can get careless, even desperate, when they long for love." She pulled a small bottle of gold glitter from a drawer. "But so can men."

"What is that?" I stared as she sprinkled it onto the slippery candle.

"It's called a Solar Blast candle. For divine insight and healing. And it's very fast, very powerful—really has a kick to it. So, what else was going on with your love spell?"

I spoke slowly, each word feeling like a stone lifted from an excavation site of some ancient burial ground. But I didn't know if I'd find corpses or treasure, or both. "My mother once told me that I had a pattern: I loved wonderful men who hadn't reached their full potential, I poured my love and energy into helping them reach that potential, and then I was drained and I would leave."

"Was she right?" Nonna slipped the candle into a long, clear glass and wiped the oil and golden flakes from her hands.

"I didn't really understand, couldn't feel the emotional consequences when she said it." I thought about all the energy expended trying to help Derek manifest his dream. "But yes, I think she was right." I felt a growing clarity, and with it confidence, as I spoke.

"To see what is true is the first step." She put the candle on the shelf behind her and began to work on a blue one. "Now, do you know *why* you do that?"

I didn't hesitate in answering—it was as if a light had been switched on inside my mind, and my heart. "Because that's what I learned. I watched my mother with my father. He was a brokenhearted hero—he was in the Navy, and the Merchant Marine during the war, he helped found the NMU during the thirties, he was Harry Bridges's bodyguard for a while fighting the mob from taking over the Longshoremen's Union on the West Coast . . ."

Nonna looked up at me, surprised. "Those were your first jobs as a lawyer, weren't they? Fighting to clean the mob out of unions?"

I nodded. "I became a lawyer because that's what my parents wanted. But I wanted it too. My dad was very Nordic, very withdrawn. Moody I guess." I paused, surprised that it had taken so long to see the obvious. "My mom had to be so strong; she also worked, stayed focused and positive, *and* encouraged him, and held it all together." I sat silently, a little rattled by what had spilled out of me. "It seems so simplistic, but I guess I've been the strong one, trying to find and fix my broken hero. To fix my father," I said quietly.

"Look in my eyes." Nonna put down the knife and the candle and leaned toward me. "Go ahead, look. Now what do you see?"

I felt silly leaning over to stare into Nonna's black pools, but I did as she asked and immediately understood. "I see myself."

Nonna nodded. "We are mirrors for each other. We see what is missing in ourselves, and we seek to fill that hole with someone else. Jung called it 'projection.' And it works in another way. You are actually drawn to someone who has qualities you also share, but that you won't embrace or acknowledge in yourself. Until you learn to be fully yourself, you will attract others, in love and in friendships, with the energies you most resist and need to integrate into yourself."

"I don't know if I understand." I shook my head.

"I want you to use the scrying mirror in the temple, just ask yourself what it is he's reflecting that you don't want to look at. Use this." She handed me the orange candle. "Go, and take your time."

I closed the temple door behind me, lit the candle and placed the round mirror with its black rear surface at an angle behind the flame. I grounded and centered, and when my mind was still I stared into my dark brown eyes, which ever so slowly turned into Derek's blue ones. I lost track of time as the energy began to flow slowly upward from the dark well of my past. Finally, I closed my eyes, resting, allowing myself to absorb what I had seen. A gentle tap on the door and the soft creaking as it opened roused me.

"So, how do you feel?" Nonna asked gently. She handed me a glass of apple juice and a piece of cheddar. As always after doing this kind of work, my senses were more acute and appreciative, and the smell, taste and texture of the food were very intense. It was also grounding, and I needed the fuel to process what I had experienced.

"By fixing him, I'm trying to fix what's wounded inside myself. A wound I inherited from my parents. Sins of the father, the parents—it's part of the Cain thing."

Nonna nodded. "But you can't heal someone else. Yes, you can support him, but ultimately he must do it for himself. As long as you persist in projecting the wound outside of yourself, you will never heal." Nonna spoke very gently, as if she knew that each word was pulling a brick from the foundation of an edifice I'd been trapped in for longer than I could remember. "You work to make his dream come true, but you don't work on your own. You try to give him the courage and drive to find his fulfillment, but you don't give those things to yourself. You will have to face those fears, *mia figlia*."

"By trying to fix him, I'm *avoiding* fixing myself," I said slowly. "If all my energy is going into him, and I'm focused on what's wrong with him and his career, I don't have to look at myself, or confront my own fears. I'm too busy dealing with his." I stared at the orange candle with the crazy marking and the Mardi Gras sprinkles. It made me smile. "People think that's what magic is," I nodded to the candle, "but it's really all in here." I touched my chest.

Nonna nodded. "And in here." She tapped my head. "It's all around us. And it's in that candle. You've achieved quite a bit of illumination these last few hours."

"The last few years. But I have a long way to go. The question is how am I going to get there?"

"When was the last time you called your daemon?" Nonna winked.

"Hmmph," I nodded. I blew out the candle and made a wish.

That night, alone in the apartment, I relit the candle, pulled out my journal and recorded our conversation. *Be careful what you ask for when you cast a spell—you just may get it*, Nonna had warned me long ago. But there was so much more to that axiom—unrecognized truths that were critical to the casting of spells, and particularly love spells. And it was equally true to the way we all lived our lives—for if we didn't cast spells, we prayed or

wished, visualized or fantasized, planned or expected, pursued or projected.

Like everyone else yearning to cast a love spell that works, I had cast
mine by carefully visualizing what I thought I wanted, just as I lived my
life as I thought I should. I had cast my spell to make my dreams of love
come true. And love can make an ordinary life into a fairy tale. But just like
Sleeping Beauty, I too was asleep. I was dreaming, and the dreams pre-
vented me from seeing what was really true.

Dreams are one of the creations of the unconscious. Our conditioning,
our programming by family and culture—all lie buried deep beneath our
conscious mind. And from beneath the surface of our awareness, these
ingrained patterns assert their power over us, the choices we think we make
freely, the life we lead, the love we fall into. As long as we remain unconscious, they also control the magic we make, our prayers and plans, and
their outcome. I was beginning to understand that powerful, unseen forces
had manifested in my love spell.

I had needed to understand how my love spell could have been fulfilled
so precisely and yet not fulfill my deepest longing. I began to understand
another of magic's most important lessons: spells work in the way that they
are meant to, not necessarily in the way anticipated or intended. When a
spell does not work as expected, or at all, there is a greater force—a divine
destiny—at work. Spells that facilitate this destiny manifest swiftly; those
that lead us down a diverging path materialize—but not in the way we
anticipate. Instead, they teach us the lessons we must learn to lead lives fulfilled with the gift and power of real love. I remembered Nonna's words—
it seemed so long ago—that *I would learn what I needed to.*

As the Oracle at Delphi commanded, before entering the temple where
magic is made, and love is found, you must know yourself. I had used divination to remove my blindfold—and to see my partner and myself as we
truly were, rather than as I wanted to see us. I used divination as a mirror
to look deeply into my heart, and into the unconscious influences at work
in my love spell, and my life. The limits of our ability to love each other
are learned. Now the question was, could we love beyond those limits?

I had the day to myself and I'd gone to the bookstore, coming home loaded with treasure. I needed to know myself, I needed to know

Derek, but the need I had been feeling most powerfully since my conversation with Nonna was to know my daemon. I felt as if somehow, in the process of falling in and out of love with Derek, I had lost my daemon. It was as painful to contemplate as the loss I was feeling in my marriage.

I sat surrounded by the *Bacchae* by Euripides, Homeric hymns, Kerenyi's book on Dionysus, Robert Johnson's *Ecstasy*, and in my hand a book by W. F. Otto. I closed it, and closed my eyes. I always preferred to let the magic come to me; it was far more compelling to find an explanation for an event *after* it happened, rather than to try to create an event, or magic, out of thought and information. But my instinct had guided me to the bookstore and books were always filled with magic.

I was hoping that somewhere in all of these pages, in a phrase, a fact, in the myth of Dionysus I would find a guide revealing the events in my own life as a journey to love, and if Nonna was correct, to the God. It might also bring me to the knowledge of who my soul mate was, for though I was afraid to acknowledge it, I wondered whether it was Derek. I pulled out my journal and wrote.

Though the people adored him, kings feared and attempted to persecute and drive Dionysus from their cities. They dreaded the freedom, visionary experience, ecstasy and eroticism that he inspired, particularly in women. The most famous tale was of King Pentheus, who refused to permit his worship, and whose mother and aunts, driven mad by Dionysus, ripped Pentheus to pieces, mistaking him for an animal. A lesson to all that if one resists and denies the ecstasies of Dionysus, he will instead bestow the dangerous gift of derangement.

His murder by the Titans, and persecutions by kings, earned Dionysus the title scapegoat, and some of his rites became the origin of theater—the tragedy, derived from tragoidia, *which means 'goat-song,' of his death, as well as the comedy of his birth. A God of life and death, feminine and masculine, mortal and divine, Dionysus is the 'God who comes,' who appears unexpectedly bringing rapture and terror—uniting two poles of the same reality, and with them, visions and transformation.*

His worship grew and spread throughout Greece to Rome, celebrated in ecstatic rites and mysteries held on the borders between wilderness and civilization. But of all the places he traveled, it was said that his greatest pleasure was found on the island of Naxos.

I stretched and checked the clock. Derek and I were meeting friends for dinner. I made a quick final note to myself: *"James Dean, Martin Sheen, Cain, check movie listings, Darkness on the Edge of Town, Kubla Khan. Find the pattern."*

Dale was back in town and we were having lunch, at the World Café, same time, same table, same lunch, same hat. But it was a very different discussion. "You're still practicing law, aren't you?" Dale asked between bites of his tuna sandwich.

I nodded and shoveled in another bite of poached salmon.

"But you can set your own hours?"

"I have a lot of flexibility. Why?"

"I'm going to shoot the next film—the one we discussed, relationships between older men and younger women—here in New York. Over the holidays. I want you to produce it."

I stared at him, speechless.

"Well?" He smiled at my obvious surprise.

"I've never worked on a film, how could I produce one?" The air around me was charged in a way that always meant magic was afoot. I could feel the electricity skimming across my skin, covering me with goose bumps, the atmosphere slowly thickening, sounds softening and time stretching. These were feelings that always induced wonder, as a portal opened between worlds and the extraordinary permeated the ordinary.

Out of nowhere, Dale was materializing my childhood dream. I grew up inside the movies. In the afternoons after I'd finished my homework, waiting for my mother to come home from work, I would lie on the floor in front of the black-and-white television. I would enter the world of Fred Astaire dancing with Ginger Rogers in gowns that I was sure I would wear someday. I all but took notes as Lauren Bacall asked Humphrey Bogart if he knew how to whistle, and I learned about bravery as Ingrid Bergman left Humphrey at the foggy Casablanca airport. I cried during *The Grapes of Wrath* as the "Okies" were forced from their homes, and I fell in love with Tom Joad. I pictured myself standing by Gary Cooper in *High Noon*. And I felt, I *absorbed* all those endless, romantic, cinematic moments when eyes met, breaths quickened and the heart's destiny manifested, no matter the odds.

James Dean. Was my daemon returning? I sat very still, feeling my heart race, realizing that what I sensed opening like a rift in time or space was an initiation into his realm of immortal light. I was desperate to accept Dale's offer, but how could I? I had no film experience and this would be a huge responsibility—what if I failed?

"I've got Jennifer back in L.A. who'll take care of a lot of it, but I need you here, on the set, as line producer. You'll be great—you're smart, you're good with people, you'll do a terrific job. I'll give you an associate producer credit and I'll pay you what I can. But I need to know right away."

I nodded, still dazed, but certain. "Okay, if you really think I can do it, I will."

"Good. Lunch tomorrow, bring a notebook—loose-leaf—and we'll get started." Dale disappeared behind his newspaper, leaving me to wonder what a line producer was supposed to do. I thought back to our conversation about the romantic magic of the movies—my marriage had certainly not turned out to be the enchantment I'd anticipated. But then, magic usually doesn't deliver in expected ways. I recalled my work with the scrying mirror, and suddenly I remembered the sex magic I had done that one amazing night with Derek. *Let our dreams come true.*

I had focused entirely on making Derek's dream a reality. Perhaps now it was my turn. I was about to make a movie. My heart was pounding with excitement for the first time in a very long time.

I couldn't wait to tell Derek.

"That's fantastic! I'm so proud of you!" Derek opened a Pinot Grigio. "When's he shooting?"

I spooned the saffron rice and garlic shrimp onto our plates. "Probably over the holidays. I won't be around much while we're in production—we'll be working through for several weeks solid," I said with a touch of anxiety.

"You have to do it, it's an incredible opportunity. We weren't going anywhere over Christmas anyway." There hadn't been enough money for a vacation. "Think he'd need any music?"

"I don't know, but I'll ask him. Wouldn't that be great?" I put down the spoon and gave him a hug. Maybe that was part of what was wrong, I suddenly thought to myself. Maybe I just needed to have something that I enjoyed as much as Derek enjoyed his music. If I was happy, maybe our sex life would improve and that missing connection I was so acutely aware of would knit back together, *we* would knit back together.

I hadn't looked forward to the holidays with such excitement since meeting Derek.

The phone was ringing with belligerent insistence as I struggled to wake up. I looked at the clock—1:30. I was momentarily confused—how could I have overslept? But it wasn't the afternoon, it was dark out. *Who was calling at this time of night?*

"Hello," I mumbled, trying to sound awake.

"It's about time you picked up. I left you a half a dozen messages at your office—don't you call in?" It was Dale sounding put-upon.

"Not after hours." I sat up, suddenly alert. It was three hours earlier in L.A. "So, what can I do for you?"

"I hope you're going to have time for this because I'm going to need you a hundred and fifty percent. Do you have comfortable shoes? You need comfortable shoes—no heels, you're going to be standing for sixteen hours a day. I need you there before anyone else gets on the set, and you're going to be the last one to leave. Sneakers, you need sneakers. You can get black ones, they don't look as bad."

I smiled at his fashion sensitivity, not yet realizing what critical advice he was giving me. "Okay, I will. Thanks."

"I want you to order the film stock. Jennifer will call you with what I want."

Derek rolled over and pulled the covers over his shoulder.

"Can you hold on while I switch phones?" I threw on my robe, ran to the living room and yanked the notebook from my briefcase.

"Call the d.p. Get her budget and make up a crew list. You need to talk to her about the equipment she wants and call the rental places. Don't commit to anything until you get back to me with the rates. Try to get us a good price for shooting during the holidays. You'll need to call the lab and make arrangements with them. I'm going to want to screen dailies, but while we're shooting there's not going to be much time, so we may have to do it in several long sit-downs instead of every day."

I was writing furiously as he talked, my mind racing with anxious anticipation. He was speaking a foreign language, but so far I was managing better than I'd anticipated, and in the middle of the night no less.

"Make sure they can do it that way. But I'm going to need to know that the film's okay, so they'll have to check for me. Oh, before I forget, you have to find a caterer—it's a tight budget, but it has to be good, and there are going to be vegetarians and special food needs. We'll talk about that later."

He continued on with endless details. Suddenly, glamorous filmmaking was all about numbers—the number of feet of film, of sound stock, the costs per foot to purchase, to develop, to print, to transfer and synch up; figuring out not only who to work with in terms of best prices, but also how to pay them.

"Okay, I've got a million things to do. Call me tomorrow when you've got the info." And he hung up.

He had a million things to do! And by tomorrow! I looked at the clock. Tomorrow was today. I looked at my list. I was not going to panic, it would all get done, it *was* getting done. *Just stay focused and keep pounding away. After you get some more sleep.*

Dale was in town again but only for a few days and wanted to meet. *Where was my notebook?* I spotted the red loose-leaf full of phone numbers and price quotes, petty cash accounting, endless lists and leads, grabbed it and a coat, kissed Derek and ran. I hailed a cab and skimmed my notes as we sped down Columbus Avenue. I'd amazed myself by successfully accomplishing most of what Dale had given me to do, but one completed task brought on a myriad of others and the stress of unfamiliar territory.

I ordered lunch, pulled out the notebook and readied myself for Dale's usual barrage.

He proceeded to run down the details of insurance, releases and other paperwork which, as a lawyer, was right up my alley. "There was something else. Oh yes, about casting. The ex-boyfriend is going to be Wendy's real ex," Dale said, clearly pleased with the concept. He wanted his films, and his actors, to be as real and in the moment as possible, blurring the line between the fantasy of film and the reality of the film's participants, and vice versa. The basic plot and ideas he wanted to explore would be presented and discussed with the actors—but not too extensively.

"Well, that's a dramatic bear trap waiting to spring. Is he an actor?"

"He's studying acting at Yale. It'll be great—they just have to be themselves. I wrote his name and number somewhere." He fished around in his shirt pockets, pulling out a scrap. I added the name and number to my actors list.

"If you're ready, I want to talk to you about the rental package I've been negotiating."

Dale nodded and I turned to my equipment notes. I was filled with optimism for the first time in a long time. It was time for *my* dreams—and perhaps that was why I had entered the realm where my daemon had first appeared. This was real, it was magic, I was making a movie.

11

Dark Desires

A sudden blow: the great wings beating still

Above the staggering girl, her thighs caressed

By the dark webs, her nape caught in his bill,

He holds her helpless breast upon his breast.

W. B. YEATS

I'm alone in a small room painted deep crimson. There are murals on the walls—*women and men, dancing and seated, as if watching what goes on in the room. I notice that one of the frescoes is an angel with a raised whip in her hand and it startles me, makes me feel off-balance.*

A very strange, high-pitched whirring noise fills the room, getting louder and louder, and it begins to sound like some kind of animal roaring. It fills me and I'm immersed in it; it's captivating, and somehow arousing. I hear sounds coming from outside, a crowd of people laughing. I'm nervous because I realize I'm naked and I don't want them to see me. I'm looking for a place to hide when suddenly a door opens. There's a man standing in the door frame.

He's bathed in light, lit from behind, so I can't see his face. I'm suddenly scared, but I'm also aroused. The door closes behind him; he approaches me and I try to cover myself. He draws closer and I back away. I can hear him breathing, thick and heavy; it's almost like he's part animal, and more than a man. I'm staring at him, mesmerized, filled with fear and excitement.

He's right in front of me, he's naked and I'm afraid to look at him. But I do and feel a penetrating shock when our eyes meet. His are dark eyes, but full of fire.

He reaches out to touch me—his hands are large. I slap him and he grabs my wrist and I hit at him with my free hand. I'm hitting him as hard as I can because I think that I should, that I shouldn't be feeling aroused and I don't want him to know that I am. He makes a guttural, grunting sound—is he angry or amused?—as he grabs me. He flings me to the ground and the room is again filled with the strange whirring noise. I feel as if I'm in the midst of a whirling tornado. I look up and he's spinning a long, dark rope, in the air above his head—that's what's making the noise. I'm watching it whirling in the air above my head when suddenly I feel this sharp, stinging sensation, a pain that's also, somehow, pleasure.

He stands over me as the air ripples and bends, and from between its undulating waves I hear strange music, a chthonic magic birthed from the caves of time but older than time itself. The energy pulses and throbs with ancient drums reverberating the rhythm of infinite yearning, countless wailing, blaring horns summoning the goat dancers—young men dressed in skins like Pan, with wild, light-filled eyes who answer the call to run through the hills and into the towns, into the cities and into the dreams of women who long to be filled with life.

The men run with their whips of goat hide, of woven grape vine, of green spring branches, whirling forbidden lust above their heads, piercing the air, piercing the veils of time, piercing the shrouds behind which women have waited, hidden and wet with desire. The air hums and roars as the cords of life circle endlessly, spinning the sound of immortal passion; bulls run and women wait upon altars, their clothes left behind in the streets. The drums pound, the horns blare, the whip falls, one blow to end the benumbed waiting, to unleash a power so holy and vast that it will re-create the world as ecstasy.

The walls of the room break open, like an egg cracking, and light pours in, making the red walls glow as if on fire, and the shining fire pours into me. I'm burning with heat and desire, and the moment I realize how I feel, he's on top of me, kissing and biting and touching me. I'm not fighting him anymore, I'm not afraid. I've surrendered to how much I want him. There's no fear, only desire. We make love and it's wild, sensuous and passionate. I have never felt so free or fulfilled.

———

I awakened, awash in a tide of pulsing, rippling pleasure. *I'm coming.* But the feeling began to slip away as my mind followed my body to waking. I sat up, remembering, still feeling the dream, scared and upset that I would find such disturbing images so incredibly arousing.

Where's Derek? I thought desperately, wanting the reassurance of his familiar face. He'd left early in the morning to meet someone about buying a new sax. I scrambled out of the bed, as if it were a guilty accomplice, and yanked open the blinds. My hand was shaking as I fought my feelings of guilt, shame and excitement. I found the notebook I kept beneath the bed, and quickly wrote down what was still affecting me.

I stared at the words, at the images—so clear, as vivid as the feelings that were reclaiming me. I wanted to touch myself, I wanted *him* to touch me. Mortification at the mixture of violence and eroticism stopped me. I threw the book across the room, rushed to the bathroom and washed my face in hard-running, cold water. Staring into the mirror, I saw his eyes, remembered being entered with just a look, felt my pulse racing between my legs.

It was monstrous to have a dream about . . . something so close to being raped, about being overcome, even whipped—because I realized that was what the pain had come from. How, *why,* would I have an orgasm in a dream like that? I turned on the shower, running it as hot as I could stand, and climbed in. I leaned my forehead, then my whole body against the cold porcelain wall, shocking myself with the extreme change in temperatures, feeling the burning water pound against my back, trying to scrub away the dream's effect on me.

It was wrong. I'd had too many friends who'd been raped. I knew that the reality was nothing but a terrifying nightmare. As far away from a dream as could be, they were in pain and afraid for their lives every minute—there was nothing erotic about it. *Nothing.*

I rejected the claim that many women had rape fantasies. But I couldn't reject what I'd just dreamt or how I'd felt. I told myself it was just social conditioning coming back to haunt me. I turned off the water and again stared into the lost eyes in the mirror. The dream felt like an indictment, a failure to free myself.

I picked up the notebook, struggling, torn between my sense of morality and the undeniable carnal craving. I gave myself to righteousness, to embarrassment and determination. But I didn't tear the pages from the notebook, didn't set them to flame. Instead, I carefully hid the diary beneath the bed.

Relentlessly, like something summoned that I could not banish, the brute from my dream stole back into my thoughts, arousing and tormenting me. He even pushed his way into my mind as fantasy while making love with Derek, triggering orgasms that rent my resistance and my conscience. Despite shame, I called Nonna and told her I needed to talk to her—in person.

She immediately invited me to her cottage on the North Fork of Long Island. I took the morning bus, and after two hours we drove through Riverhead and out onto the Fork, past Jack's Bait and Tackle, the Modern Snack Bar with its huge 1950s neon sign, and the Magic Fountain homemade ice cream parlor. Even in the barren winter, the landscape and its small towns were bucolic.

I climbed off the bus at the last stop, the whaling town of Greenport. Nonna stood beside her old blue Volvo station wagon, waving wildly and then hugging me as if I were a refugee from war-torn and foreign shores. And in a way, I was, but I carried the war within me. She drove slowly so I could enjoy the views of water, boatyards and farms, finally turning onto a winding road that cut through a venerable four-hundred-acre orchard. When the road forked, she pulled into the driveway of her cedar-shingled, green-shuttered English cottage. It faced west, on the shore of a wide sapphire estuary filled with migrating, resting waterfowl.

Even in the dead of winter Nonna's gardens were beautiful—an earthy abstraction of brown, gray and surviving green textures of evergreens and holly trees. A small statue of Pan playing his pipes sat beneath the bare Japanese maple and there were numerous bird feeders, all being visited.

The back door was sheltered by a vine-covered trellis, adding to the sense of a magical cottage. We walked through a small mudroom and into a huge country kitchen. A large bow window at one end was balanced at the other by a big wooden farm table with a green ceramic bowl filled with lemons; behind the table a wall of elegant, leafy, pale yellow and green wallpaper brought the garden into the house.

Nonna gave me a tour; the house was not at all what I'd expected.

I realized that after all these years even I was still susceptible to the stereotype—there were no bundles of herbs hanging from dusty rafters, no cats scooting underfoot, no crowded altars dominating the living room, no cauldron in the fireplace. Instead, I was greeted by a refined mixture of contemporary and French country furnishings in earth tones and butter yellow that glowed as the house filled with sunlight pouring through the many windows. And through those windows, from every room, there were views of the water in front and the garden in back. I drifted to a round, intricately carved rosewood table filled with family photographs and stared at the pictures of Nonna as a radiantly happy younger woman.

"Come, let's sit outside." Nonna led me out to the front porch with its white-framed windows that stretched from floor to ceiling. Warmed by the sun, it was as comfortable as a day in May. "I'm going to put on some tea—how's jasmine? I love that flavor in the afternoon." She smiled as I nodded and turned back into the house. I could hear her in the kitchen as I watched a pair of swans floating in water that danced with shimmering light. It was so warm I tugged off my sweater. Within minutes I realized it was *quiet*, the only sound a barely discernible hum of occasional and distant cars. I pulled the notebook from my bag and nervously opened it to where I'd written about the dream. It seemed the antithesis of this sun-filled serenity.

"They're beautiful." I nodded toward the swans.

"Yes, they live here all year round. They had babies last year." Nonna set down a tea tray with a plate of sandwiches and we settled into white, deco rattan chairs. "Don't worry so much. Pour some tea." She put on her glasses, picked up the notebook and began to read.

I poured the tea, put honey in mine, picked nervously at a sandwich. I felt as naked as I had in the dream, but this time I would be seen not by an erotic phantasm but by my mentor, my Nonna, my spiritual grandmother. *Who gives her grandmother an erotic dream to read? A kinky erotic dream?*

I wanted to disappear. I watched the swans, counted clouds, wondered why it was taking her so long. Went to the bathroom and returned. It was hard to make eye contact as Nonna closed the journal and set it on the small table, folded her reading glasses, and smiled at me.

"First, no one can, or should, interpret your dreams for you. Only the dreamer knows their true meaning. But since you've asked, I'll give you my perspective." Her tone was reassuring, but I still felt uneasy and exposed. I nodded, setting the cup and saucer down so that it wouldn't rattle.

"It's not easy to talk about, is it?" Nonna continued. "In my generation, any discussion about sex was completely out of the question, even between mothers and daughters, and *never* in public. Things have changed so much, but still there are so many inhibitions. There's a veneer of acceptability, but sex is still forbidden fruit."

Her acknowledgment helped me relax. She lifted a spoonful of honey into the sunlight, then stirred it into her tea and continued.

"Women still have a hard time talking honestly to each other about sex, and I suspect it's even harder for men. We all think that everyone else is having such a marvelous time, when the truth is most people aren't. But they could. So, the dream—why this dream?" Nonna asked matter-of-factly. "What's its purpose for you?"

I shifted in the chair, stared out at the water. "I don't know. Maybe it's just some dark, unhealthy part of myself."

Nonna shook her head and sighed. "Dreams and fantasies like this are very common. It's so difficult for women. They judge themselves for having them, and they feel ashamed and guilty. You think there's something wrong with yourself?"

"I do. I feel very . . . ashamed. That's why it's so hard to discuss. Or to allow." I picked up the journal and put it back in my bag.

"But there's no reason for shame." Nonna poured more tea in our cups and I clung as much to the reassurance of that simple gesture as to her words. "It can seem very frightening, and it antagonizes many feminists who feel that such thoughts are the result of thousands of years of domination. And in a sense they're quite right—if women were completely free to embrace and enjoy their sexuality, perhaps we wouldn't require such scenarios to experience our feelings. These days, so many young women approach sex the way you approached work—on a man's terms, thinking that's liberated," Nonna sighed and shook her head, "instead of making up new rules that reflect what women feel, and need and want. But for all of our liberation, real or imagined, women are still very inhibited in their sexuality."

I nodded. "It's true. I've had a hard time just letting go with Derek, giving over to my feelings. I've been very active in trying to take responsibility for my own pleasure but . . ." I stopped, unable to explain.

"Maybe the dream will help you."

"Help? It seems like just the opposite."

"Stop judging, start discovering," Nonna said firmly. "First, it shouldn't be taken literally. Dreams and fantasies like this are messages from another realm, from your unconscious and your soul. They serve an important purpose—they help you to recognize the ways in which your erotic energy is obstructed. Even now, women are taught that surrendering to sexual feelings is shameful, so they fantasize about being forced to surrender—the fantasy circumvents the inhibition and guilt of accepting pleasure."

"So these fantasies are a way to have our inhibitions overridden?" The tightness in my chest eased.

"It's like the secret solution to the good girl's dilemma—being forced to have pleasure absolves us from responsibility and allows—no, *requires*—us to have sexual feelings."

"But the violence, the sort of dominance-and-submission tone, it makes me so uncomfortable," I admitted, still feeling ashamed.

"I understand why you feel that way, but you shouldn't, *mia figlia*. Much of the relationship between sex and violence remains mysterious, but mysteries are not without their points of revelation, or why else would they fascinate us so? There are always clues to the bigger pattern. Your dream is filled with mystery. But also with clues, and here's one of the most significant: Who needs cultural police when they're inside your head? The dominating power is actually a part of yourself seeking to free you."

"From what?"

"From the jailer in your psyche who enforces the cultural inhibitions and blocks your pleasure. The dominator forces the jailer to surrender to pleasure, and opens your mind, body, and soul to sexual ecstasy."

The sun was dropping toward the horizon, and its honeyed light was reflected in a path shimmering on the water directly before me. "If I could just give over, the need for that kind of force would evaporate." My sigh was cut short as the two swans exploded into the air with thunderous flapping. It reminded me of the sound from my dream. I watched as they glided silently on wide-spreading white wings, their long necks stretching toward their destination—the beginning of the trail of liquid light on our side of the lake.

"You know, all the swans in England belong to the Queen." Nonna smiled as they landed with barely a sound. "That's because the Queen used to be the High Priestess of the Goddess, and the swans were messengers between the worlds. Your dream is a message from a sacred realm."

"But it was so close to rape . . . ," I mumbled.

"There's something else very important to understand—the rape in fantasies is nothing like the reality," Nonna said firmly. "The reality of rape is about power, anger, dissociation, disconnection. But in fantasies, sex is always pleasurable, a woman is always swept away with desire and fulfillment. These fantasies are actually about experiencing deep, erotic, sexual union."

"Yes, yes, that's so," I said, exhaling. It felt as if I'd been holding my breath since the dream weeks ago.

Nonna smiled. "They're about *ravishment*, not rape. Sometimes the words are used interchangeably because they both involve the idea of being seized and carried away, but *ravished* is very different from *raped*. There's a dictionary in my study; bring it out here and we'll look it up. And while you're up, why don't you put the kettle on for another pot of tea?"

I put the water on to boil. Nonna's study was filled with books, boxes of papers, and endless objects of fascination. I found the heavy book beside her electric typewriter on the long inlaid library table that was her desk, brought it back to the porch, and found Nonna with the tea and a plate of chocolates.

I read aloud: "rape—from the Latin, to seize, snatch, carry off by force, the crime of having sexual intercourse with a woman or girl forcibly and without her consent." And then: "ravish—to seize and carry away by force, and to have sex without consent, to rape." But what I found next confirmed Nonna's use of the word: "to carry away with emotion; to fill with great joy or delight, to transport, to charm, entrance, captivate; being carried away with delight, joy, rapture, ecstasy."

The moldering degradation began to crumble. "Ravishment! *That's* what it is—being swept away, being overwhelmed with rapture and ecstasy. The sex wasn't forced; the only force was the energy required to overcome my resistance to enjoying the sex."

"So, this is all theory, but the dream—what does it say to you?" Nonna asked.

I stared out at the water, thinking suddenly of the dark depths beneath the sparkling surface. I struggled to dive beneath the covering of rational explanations to the reasons hidden in my heart. "It's very hard for me to . . . surrender." That was the word: *surrender*. I was uncomfortable even saying it—like the fantasy, it was charged with conflict. To surrender was to be weak, but it was also a word conjuring forbidden pleasure.

Nonna nodded again. "Yes—surrender. A strong, liberated woman never surrenders, eh? You must always be self-contained, inviolate. But how can you experience love if you're so shielded? Surrendering means letting go of your resistance to love and pleasure, and to who you really are. It means letting down your defenses so you can be fully present, so you can show yourself, and what you feel. That's the purpose of the exercises I gave you—so your body is relaxed, your mind is quiet and you can open yourself to feel, to receive. To surrender is to be fully present in your body and your heart. You have to surrender to be free."

"But why is it so hard to surrender to pleasure?" I asked softly. I had come to the core of my difficulty. And I remembered how intensely erotic that night in Chinatown had been for me—because my doubts, my fears, my resistance had been swept away.

"That's a question we all struggle with, whether we realize it or not, men as well as women. For all of the public displays of nudity and sex, the culture is still very repressed and very afraid of sexuality. At a deeper level, it's a fear of *Eros*. But without surrender there can be no ecstasy. A man also has to surrender to pleasure, to receiving love, to his feelings, especially at the moment of orgasm. And imagine how difficult it is for them to give up control! It's one reason that very powerful men often seek sexual gratification with dominatrixes. They need and want to give up control, but it has to be forced from them, because their grip is so tight."

"It's very frightening to give up control."

"Yes, it is. And women have become very much like men these days—in order to succeed, they've become self-sufficient, very self-contained, very in control of themselves and their feelings. Passion with a stranger is easy—he can be anything you want him to be; you're free to live out your fantasy, and he can live his. There are no obligations. But it's short-lived gratification, based in unreality, and there's no love. We can treat each other like objects, or like deities. It's a choice."

"To surrender is to be so completely vulnerable." I stared at the crimson sun floating just above the water. "I'm afraid of getting hurt," I said softly, pushing away the pain of the heartbreak that surfaced as I spoke.

"If you get hurt, you won't die—you'll learn, and you'll heal. To live trapped in your defenses is to remain perpetually wounded. Surrender means opening past your emotional and physical limitations, allowing yourself to move beyond the sense of self you're trapped by. We hold the keys to our prisons. It takes great courage to surrender. And it requires great trust and love to overcome fear. You need time and a partner who can be fully present to earn your trust and love."

"I'm afraid that I'm not good enough somehow, that if he saw the real me in some out-of-control, erotic frenzy he'd turn away."

"There's nothing more beautiful, more powerful, than a woman possessed by passion. Without surrender, sex can never be truly fulfilling because there's no love. To surrender to love is to experience sex that is sacred; love is unbound and that is where divinity dwells."

"But what does my dream have to do with divinity?"

"Everything. The room you described sounds just like the Villa of the Mysteries near Pompeii. It's where women were initiated into the Dionysian Mysteries."

"Dionysus?"

"You wrote that you saw an angel in the room?"

I nodded.

"A *pneuma*—fiery divine breath. A winged messenger through whom Dionysus speaks—and she's holding a whip. It's the divine soul force come to release you, and by force if necessary, because you cannot deny Eros any longer. The pain shocks you out of your numbness, breaks open your resistance."

I sat quietly, trying to absorb the relationship of Dionysus to my dream.

"Tell me the line from the Coleridge poem, about the demon lover," Nonna asked.

I stared out at the glowing sky and the darkening horizon before me, speaking softly:

"A savage place! As holy and enchanted
As e'er beneath a waning moon was haunted
By woman wailing for her demon-lover!"

"The word *demon* always scared me until you explained it was originally *daemon*." I smiled at Nonna, beginning to trust what was unfolding within me.

"This dream is about the struggle, and the dance, between your soul and the Sacred. That dance is always erotic because it is the dance of life. In the presence of the Sacred, the soul longs to surrender, to receive, to be the vessel into which the Divine is poured and carried into the world. You said the room broke open and flooded with light?"

I nodded.

"So, to surrender is to break open, to give yourself over to divinity— this is the experience of ecstasy. Can you surrender? Can you give up the control of your conscious, inhibiting, jailing mentality and accept that you don't know what is going to happen next? Can you trust that you will be all right? Ultimately, to surrender to the Sacred means surrendering to your own true and holy Self. It doesn't require anyone else. But sexuality with your partner can be a way of surrendering to God, or the Goddess."

The sun had disappeared behind a silhouette of black trees and the sky was streaked with clouds of blazing salmon, pink, and purple, all reflected in the water below.

"The struggle and the fulfillment in your spirituality and your sexuality are the same. Something sacred within you has challenged the voices of shame. You have begun to discover, to free, your true nature and your true sexuality."

"It felt more like I was meeting a monster, not a God."

"The Minotaur has always been encountered, at first, as if he were a monster. Dionysus always arises from darkness. Does it feel dangerous? It should; without that edge, life, sex, even love becomes tepid." Nonna rose and began to gather up our tea. "Oh! And before I forget—the sound you heard, and what you saw, it was a bull-roarer. It's a very ancient, mystical instrument used all over the globe in rituals and initiations; it's full of sexual meaning and is usually played by men. The Greeks called it a *rhombus* and it was an important part of the Dionysian Mysteries."

"Nonna, all that from one dream?" I sat stunned in the gathering darkness.

"All that and more. The rest you will have to live. Let's go inside and light a fire."

After years of training, now a High Priestess and legal clergy undertaking covens and congregations of my own, I had organized a large public Winter Solstice celebration. It would be one of the first such Sabbat rituals in New York City, and it was happening just a week before Dale and I were to begin filming his movie. I was frantically busy, excited, and nervous.

Regardless of modern commercialization, the season of cold and darkness is illuminated by a universal celebration of light, hope and rebirth by many of the world's faith traditions—Chanukah, Christmas, and in recent years, Kwanzaa, are all celebrated in proximity to the Winter Solstice, which was honored by the Old Religion. This Sabbat, from the Greek *esbaton,* which means holy day, was one of eight sacred, seasonal holidays. I had been fascinated to discover that all eight holy days had been appropriated by the Catholic Church and were now the basis for the Christian worship calendar.

In the Old Religion, the Sabbats show us how Nature makes Spirit visible by honoring the sacred wisdom in each seasonal shift and transformation. And celebrating the Sabbats is one of the most powerful ways of attuning our minds, bodies, lives and spirits to the rhythms of the earth. By living in harmony with Nature, we learn to live in harmony with the Divine. It is a simple but profound lesson.

Although there are various interpretations of the Sabbats, there is also a common, archetypal pattern mythologized in the courtship of the Goddess and God that leads to their sacred union. Their relationship is the dance of life choreographed through the cycle of the seasons, revealing the erotic mystery of the Spirit ceaselessly changing forms. At the Winter Solstice, the longest night and the shortest day, the Goddess gives birth to the Sun as the God of the Waning year departs.

Tonight, I would enact the role of the birth-giving Goddess, and Derek had agreed to take the part of the dying God. I pushed opened the massive, dark wooden doors and stepped into the Unitarian church we were renting. It was simple and serene, almost stark, constructed of pale gray limestone with huge columns and flying buttresses high overhead, an inlaid marble floor and a few distant, narrow windows. I stood in the center of the dark, chilly cavern. Had I been overly ambitious—what if people didn't come? I closed my eyes and opened my heart. *Let the light of truth burn brightly, may the light of love illuminate our paths, may hope and kindness be reborn, may all those who suffer find solace. And may everything go well tonight.*

I opened my eyes to see Naomi and Nonna smiling at me, and heard the sound of laughter and happy voices as the circle, friends and family began arriving to set up. A few hours later, I stood surveying the transformed space—the simple tartan-draped altar, placed in the center of concentric circles of pews, held a large cauldron, symbol of the Goddess's regenerative womb, surrounded by deer antlers, pine and mistletoe. There were pine and fir trees everywhere, baskets filled with candles, and everyone was dressed after a final run-through.

"Time to open the doors." I nodded to the volunteers. A small chorus sang the haunting refrain, turning it into a hypnotic round: *"Listen to the Lord and Lady call their children in the moonlight."* As they sang, the church began to fill with people. I watched with endless gratitude as people filled dozens of huge plastic bags with donations of warm clothes that would be given to charities. But I was completely unprepared to have every seat filled and to have people standing all along the walls. It was time to begin.

Nonna stepped into the center of the circle.

"We greet you on this longest night. Come turn the Wheel that brings the light. 'Tis the season of darkness and rest, of new life that stirs 'neath the Mother's breast. 'Tis the time of rejoining Sun and Earth, the moment of mystery, joy and rebirth. We gather on this longest night, to dance and sing, to share and bring . . . the Light! Let us unite our voices and our energies, our hearts and our souls, let us sing the sound of the beginning of form: *Om.*" She began the chant alone, standing in the center of the circle of hundreds of strangers, in the vast space of the cathedral. The sound grew, tentatively then stronger, gathering fullness, form and power. It swelled, filling the space with vibrant joy that peaked and then in sudden silence departed, like a prayer, into the realms of mystery.

Nonna smiled and walked to the east. Derek and I entered the circle together. My stomach filled with butterflies and my palms were simultaneously cold and clammy. I was afraid I'd forget everything I was supposed to say and do. And then, on cue, the music began—an exotic, joyful old English tune with fiddle, bagpipe, guitar, bodhran and harp—and all my nervousness vanished. I was exactly where I belonged. Standing before the altar, we looked at each other and smiled. My heart filled with gratitude and the sudden sense that real love was still possible for us.

The music rose, filling the space, gathering everyone in its web. Walking in pairs, the women stood in each of the four directions at the edge of the circle. I handed Derek the staff that rested on the altar. He lifted it high into the air and spoke in a voice that filled the space, drawing it tightly in around us: "We are gathered on this darkest night to cast our circle with sacred light." He began to walk clockwise around the circle, holding the staff high above the heads of those seated, casting as he went: "We cast this circle by air and fire; we charge this circle with water and earth. Here we circle and are encircled, to share the wisdom of rebirth."

And then Derek began a chant, buoyed by the chorus and the musicians, that was quickly picked up by the hundreds of people who had come to celebrate: "We are a circle, within a circle, with no beginning and never ending." As the chanting peaked, he moved to the center of the circle, lifted the staff high above his head and then touched it to the ground.

The women of my circle called the quarters. And then it was my turn. Projecting my voice so everyone could hear me, I said the words I had memorized and now, without self-consciousness, remembered: "I am the song in every heart. I am every mother's gaze, I am every wife's embrace, I am the circle of infinity where every change takes place. I am the faith that never falters and the love that never fails. Let the journey of new life begin again!"

I faced Derek and moving slowly and opposite each other, as if in some ancient, instinctual dance, we circled three times around the altar. We looked into each other's eyes, speaking as we moved. Derek spoke first: "I am the power of transformation without which there could be no life. I am the force of time, I wear the holly crown. I am the spark of regeneration."

And I replied, "It is I who give birth to the light."

"Feel her around you."

"Feel him within you." A rush of extraordinary energy hit me as I finished and I felt my entire body tingling as if electrified. Derek held out his staff to me. "My power came from you and now I return it to you."

I took the staff from him and placed it on the altar. "May your rest be sweet and peaceful and may your power return renewed." I lifted the cauldron and held it out to him.

He struck a match and lit the candle. "The time of endings has ended. Behold, I offer you the spark of new life."

I responded, "And, for your love, I will nurture it to flower and fruit in season." We kissed softly.

"I am ready!" he said with a shout, backing swiftly away from the altar. The air filled with shouting and the music of a lone fiddle as six Morris Dancers—a troupe that performed the traditional, seasonal, sacred dances of pre-Christian England—burst into the circle, their swords waving wildly in the air. They were tall and short, fat and thin, dressed in black shirts with flying black ribbons and black pants. And their faces were painted black.

They encircled Derek, dancing madly around him in intricate patterns, their feet flying, their arms holding swords that interwove, separated and reconnected with the fearsome sound of clashing metal. They locked their swords together into the shape of a six-pointed star held aloft to the cheer of the crowd, and then all six held the star horizontally above Derek's head as they danced, faster and faster, around him. The music accelerated as they lowered the star down around his neck. Holding the deadly nova around his throat, they whirled about him.

Just as rehearsed, but without warning to those gathered, the cavernous space was filled with the hideous sound of scraping metal as the black-faced dancers wrenched their swords from his star-enclosed neck. Derek dropped and the cathedral plunged into darkness.

Gasps and anxious murmuring rippled through the blackness. Derek rose slowly, so slowly it seemed as if time were slowing with him, and without a backward glance, he walked out of the circle, flanked by the dancers. There was absolute silence in the black adumbration. The space had been emptied.

It was all as we'd rehearsed a dozen times. And although I knew Derek was perfectly all right physically, I stood in the sudden vacuum, a sob of shock and sorrow rising in my throat. I felt myself tumbling into a dismal hole of vanished light. *What had just happened?*

I stood, alone, in the center of the emptiness, but I was surrounded. They were waiting and like me they were lost in the darkness. I looked down, seeing the heavy cast iron cauldron in my hands. And in it was the light, small, fragile but burning. I lifted it above my head, my arms trembling. "The light returns! The dance continues! The Sun is reborn!" I called out with as much faith as I could summon.

The cry was taken up by my circle and then by one more voice and then another until it became a chant shared by all, reverberating, building, filling the space with rekindled joy. "The Sun is reborn! The light returns!"

The ritual proceeded, the new Sun bursting joyously into the circle. The candles were passed to everyone as the musicians began to play a favorite chant adapted for the Sabbat. The chorus began to sing, followed soon by the celebrants: "We all come from the Goddess, and to Her we shall return, like the growing light, shining in the darkest night."

The first candle was lit from the cauldron and then the light was passed from person to person until the entire church glowed with hundreds of dancing lights. I returned to stand in the center, turning slowly, watching all the bright novas being born, seeing people—the smiling stuff of stars—stand together as a single illumination of hope and thankfulness, an eternal circle of glorious light filling hearts and minds and souls with wonder. I stood quiet, knowing that despite the loss that had come to me when Derek left the circle, "love is what light *feels* like."

Finally, I lit my own candle, and as the chant softened to a whisper and then disappeared into the future, I said: "See your dreams, your visions, wishes, goals, your new life clearly before you, manifest and shining like the newborn sun. Call them out."

Voices of all ages called out from the glowing ring of fire, sending their intentions into the realm of Spirit and into the world. Some called for strength, many for peace, others for wisdom, happiness, hope, and healing; one asked for tolerance, another for compassion, and many called for love. When the voices stopped, I said: "As you go out into the world, carry the light of the Sacred within you, let it shine so that others may see. Let the light of divinity illuminate the holiness of your life and the world in which you live. Now blow out your candle as you make your wish; take it home and relight it and let it burn through this longest night. The time of rebirth is upon us. The Wheel has turned." Electricity prickled across my skin, and a sense of purpose, peace and happiness animated every wave and particle of my being.

Each of the four directions was thanked, as was the power of the sun, the earth, and the Spirit. I spoke the final words and scores of people joined in with irrepressible glee: "Our circle is open but never broken. Merry meet and merry part and merry meet again!" A raucous cheer reverberated through the church as the music played, the revels and the feasting began, and I found myself encircled by hugging friends.

But no Derek. I searched the crowd but couldn't find him anywhere. I had been left to handle all the socializing, to clean up and manage all the final responsibilities, and to worry about him. But, I reminded myself, it was my ritual and they were all my responsibilities. Nonna worked with me, remaining after everyone else had gone.

"Don't be concerned about the emptiness. You're supposed to feel it." Nonna tried to reassure me as she tied the top of a black plastic garbage bag. "Something else will come to fill that space."

"I hope you're not using that as a metaphor." I eyed the bulging bag, trying to joke my way out of what she knew I was feeling. I dragged the final black garbage bag to the back hallway, put on my coat and tried not to let the wonderful evening sour. Derek was standing outside the locked front door, awash in Glenlivet, having taken off with the Morris Dancers.

"Hey, ready to go home?" he slurred slightly, leaning lopsidedly over to kiss me, a hand groping my bottom. Resentment hit me. We took a cab home and he passed out, in his clothes, on the couch. I stared at him, the image of his "decapitation" replaying in my mind, the obliterating darkness and sorrow it had summoned returning to my heart.

Bundled against the cold, I sat on the terrace, looking out at the slumbering city and into the empty womb space within myself. It felt worse to be lonely with someone I couldn't reach than to be lonely and alone. At least alone there was hope; the way we were, there was nothing but hopelessness. I cried, feeling the cold and salt water make my cheeks burn. I was still there as the sky began to shift from black to gray to icy blue. It had been the longest night.

As the sun rose, I wondered if the love spell had been broken. Worse, I wondered if love and magic were even real. I shivered, wishing the light would warm me, and when it didn't, I searched for the little flame within. I wasn't ready to give up, not yet. Somehow there had to be a way to save our relationship.

"*Dale wants you for the next scene*, so let's get your makeup freshened up." I put my arm around the actress's shoulders and gently steered her into the kitchen and away from Dale. I was immersed in filmmaking. There was an occasional call that had to be made to my office or a client, but since we were shooting over the holidays, I was virtually free from my work as a lawyer.

We were about an hour from lunch break, so after depositing the actress with the makeup girl, I checked on the food setup. It was a relief to see the vegetarian and the wheat-free meals—which they'd forgotten yesterday—along with the rest of my order. I checked my notes to see who would be needed on camera after lunch. Despite a tight budget, Dale had the luxury of shooting most of his scenes in sequence as the story progressed, which big-budget films rarely did. But it was still like conducting a four-ring circus—most of it from Dale's scribbled notes on the back of a large manila envelope.

"Phyllis!" I heard Dale shouting. I was supposed to be at his side at all times, an impossible feat unless I managed to split myself in two, or better still five.

"Right here!" I hollered back, dodging actors loitering about and jumping over cables and power boxes as I rushed back to the living room.

"Where are my notes?" Dale snapped anxiously. I immediately feared he would erupt. *He's just worried*, I reminded myself. *Time is money, lots of money*. It astonished me that he was able to remain as calm as he did, and that he could weave the magic that he did, in the midst of so many technical and pragmatic concerns and confusions.

I was there to alleviate as many of those as possible so that he could concentrate on the actors and their performances, and the discussions with his cinematographer. Considering that we were into our tenth sixteen-hour day, I thought we were all doing great. Exhausted, but great.

I spotted the envelope—it had fallen beneath the twinkling Christmas tree. I started for it but his barked command halted me immediately: "What are you doing on the set? Stay out of there!"

"Your notes." I pointed.

He sighed. "Thank God. Okay, let's go. I need Wendy and Jake." He retrieved his notes and it was time for the next scene. "I need quiet on the set," Dale said curtly, and the camera assistant shouted Dale's command in a voice that carried through the entire ten-room apartment. "Day ten, scene three, take one," he said, using our unique marking system. The sharp sound of the clapboard striking snapped everyone to attention. The soundwoman nodded to Dale. Dale nodded to the actors. "Action."

The bell jar descended over the apartment and we slipped into that strange place between the worlds of reality and fantasy. The apartment was tropically warm—a humid heat generated by the radiators, dozens of bodies and the huge, hot lights required by the camera. We couldn't open the windows because of the street noise, and so the sultry, hothouse environment thickened. I leaned back against the wall, watching in fascination as the scene began.

"I don't think there's anything to say." Wendy's voice was stubborn, sorrowful and exhausted, and yet she was pleading with her ex-boyfriend. Her long black hair was pulled back, revealing a voluptuous profile, wounded dark eyes, and full lips that spoke a truth countless other lips have spoken.

"Anything that I say is just bullshit. I just have to act." His words were rushing together. Jake leaned in closer, his voice getting louder, desperation and aggression mixing. "It's not saying. It's showing. You just have to give me some time. Now I know it's important."

"You've had lots of time. *We've* had lots of time. I know everything there is to know about us. I don't think there's any reason for us to do this again . . ." Her tone wasn't angry; it was beseeching and confessional. He pressed the emotional opening she had given him.

"I just need one more chance."

I arched my aching back; my feet were so sore I couldn't feel them anymore, and my nerves were frayed. Although I'd quickly grown a skin as thick as an alligator's, I still felt vulnerable to the ever-present threat of disastrous failure. But I'd hit my stride and I knew I was running a tight ship, as my father would say. The shoot was going well.

I was also having the most fun I'd ever had working. I was bone tired and yet I'd never felt so alive, so sharp, so connected to what I was doing. I'd realized early on that a film set was an almost ideal working environment for me. Sure, there were egos and prima donnas, but this was drama and theatrics were to be expected.

But what I hadn't expected was the amazing way in which everyone worked together. Each person had his or her job and everyone was essential to the success of the film, including the guy who delivered the food every day. And even though there was tension between some of the cast members, and some of the crew grumbled at Dale's style of working or occasional flares of temper, they all gave it a hundred and ten percent. And I gave a hundred and fifty—I was the first one to arrive in the morning putting on the coffee and the last one to leave at night taking out the garbage. If it needed to get done, I did it.

Watching the story emerge from the lives and the imaginations of the actors, and Dale, I began to understand what Peter Guber, one of the heads of Columbia Pictures, meant when he described filmmakers as modern shamans, telling the sacred stories in the darkened cave of the movie theater. Antonin Artaud had said that films had a unique ability to depict our dreams and fantasies, and to explore the deeper layers of inner life, and so had Australian director Peter Weir. But Anaïs Nin observed that movies had abandoned that magic power, telling only "one dimensional" stories.

Despite budgets that were often more than the gross national product of some countries, most films were vacuous, overbudgeted, overblown cartoons, filled with mindless violence and exploitive sex. Hollywood was still a magical place where dreams came true, but it took a rebel like Dale to make that special kind of magic. And I was making it with him, in the process making my own dreams come true.

I watched the dream playing out in front of me. The actors sat, looking into each other's eyes. And then she relented, allowing him to stay, agreeing to talk more after the party was over. Jake leaned in, kissing her tenderly, saying something intimate and inaudible as his lips touched hers; she kissed him back.

"Cut," Dale said, beaming. "Great. How was that?" he asked the cinematographer. She gave him a thumbs-up. "Okay, let's get the close-ups. First Wendy, then Jake. Quiet, please," Dale demanded. The two actors sat on the floor leaning against a couch, their heads almost touching, talking quietly, then suddenly laughing. They were at ease with each other, they were at ease moving between realities.

"He sure is something to look at," one of the older actresses said to me quietly as she stared at Jake. "He reminds me of Richard Gere—he's going to be really big. You can't always see it, but with him you sure can."

And sometimes you can't see the truth until it slaps you in the face. That was the next scene we'd shoot—Wendy finding Jake in bed with her roommate, and their confrontation.

I was completely immersed and living in the realm from which my daemon had first appeared. Although I couldn't see him in any of the actors, not even in Dale, who also went to the Actors Studio and who adored James Dean, I could sense his presence. It was as if he were standing right behind me, whispering in my ear, *Enjoy it, every minute of it.* I did exactly what he told me to do, and the empty place inside of me felt full again.

"*It's a wrap!*" Dale called out. We were done shooting.

After the wrap party I came home and fell into bed for twelve hours, but I didn't have time to rest. I had a long list of postproduction responsibilities, and the chance to watch the dailies, to see the wizardry I had participated in. I had clients to represent and work to do. But I also began to have the blues.

"It's call postpartum depression. You've just given birth to a film. It was your entire life for weeks. Of course, you feel empty now," Dale tried to reassure me as we waited in the screening room at Du-Art. It had been one of the most intense experiences of my life—an initiation into the world of drama, the temple of Dionysus, the realm where life and light, illusion and authenticity merged, mixed and became confused. But one truth united this realm—the truth of the heart, of our emotions, our feelings.

To act was to express those feelings, courageously, fully and publicly, where others could see, feel, vicariously experience and perhaps undergo a catharsis that might transform their own real lives. Working on the film, I had found a truth in my own heart: I had to find the courage to feel and to express and act upon *my* feelings.

Watching what we had filmed, I made a decision and with it my depression began to lift. I couldn't wait to tell Derek, who was meeting me for dinner at Mario's, an inexpensive neighborhood Italian restaurant on 56th and Ninth. He was late but I had brought work to do.

He leaned over and kissed me. "Did you see the rest of the dailies?" he asked.

"Not yet." I smiled at him. We ordered and I returned the plastic-covered menu to its place between the wall and the salt and pepper shakers. "There's something important I need to discuss with you. I started thinking about it while we were shooting but now I'm sure."

Derek poured the inexpensive red table wine, *tinta* my father called it. I almost knocked over the glass as my hands flew like birds into the air from where they were folded over my heart. "I've decided to go back to school—to film school. The intensive graduate program at NYU."

"But you've just produced a feature—why do you need to go to school?" Derek asked, more concerned than I'd anticipated, and a bit of my excitement evaporated. "Can't you just work?"

"Working on the film made me realize how much I have to learn. Sure, I can keep working if I just want to be a desk jockey, but then I'd have to go to L.A. I'm not a shark—I don't see myself in the studio system. And it's brutal on women. Anyway, I don't think either of us is ready for that kind of move. You've worked so hard to reestablish yourself here." Why wasn't he excited for me?

He sat quietly, his own wheels starting to spin. "I don't know, maybe a fresh start's a good idea." I knew he was thinking about his band getting turned down by the record company.

"If I want to pursue independent filmmaking, I need a better grounding and this is the best way to get it." I could hear the plea I was making. "But I need your help. I can't go back to school and work full-time. I can work part-time; it'll be hard 'cause it's like being on a shoot for six months, sixteen-hour days, seven days a week, but I can do it." I paused watching his implacable expression, took a deep breath and continued. "I really need you to get some kind of regular part-time job so there's enough money to pay the bills. Otherwise, I can't do it. Will you?" I asked, anxious but certain he'd agree. After all, I'd been carrying most of the load while he pursued his music full-time. Now it was my turn to follow my heart; of course, he'd reciprocate.

He nodded. "Sure, I'll see what I can come up with."

I looked at his tentative smile as he looked distractedly away. Suddenly, Derek seemed as remote as an image on a screen. But I brushed the shadow of isolation away. I *was* happy and everything would be all right—feeling good meant I could give more to making the relationship work. At least that's what I told myself.

.12.

Freedom

Who has ever been betrayed by real love?

—ANONYMOUS

I stretched the rubber band and then released it. The thin strip snapped back against the inside of my wrist, sending a sharp explosion of pain straight into my gut. And my brain. One of the old definitions of magic is that it's the art of changing consciousness at will. It was working. I didn't say a word as Derek lounged on the couch.

I had to stop obsessing about Derek's career, and more importantly his lack of drive about getting a part-time job. I had to stop giving him advice, ideas or suggestions. It wasn't helping him or me or our relationship. After months of being unable to control myself, I'd come up with this crazy idea and it was working. The pain sent a clear, quick message to my brain that what I'd been doing was hurtful. The way to stop the pain of my Sade-ian self-help strategy was to break my old pattern.

Snap! It had been a huge struggle at first, my insides twisting as I wrestled myself into silence. *Snap!* That was followed by anxious emptiness when I didn't know what to do or say. *Snap!* I learned to say nothing, and then a simple "I have faith in you. You'll figure it out." And now, finally, I could feel all that energy that I'd been devoting, fruitlessly, to Derek's passivity. I rubbed the sore spot on the inside of my wrist.

As the fog of obsession lifted, I was discovering a deep pool of enthusiasm and vitality waiting for me and I was using it. I was keeping the focus on myself, accepting that the only person you can change is yourself. Nonna had been right—it was time to face my fear that I couldn't make my own dreams come true. I'd filled out my application to NYU, received my acceptance letter, sent in my registration fee and was looking forward to starting film school in the fall.

And I still believed that Derek was going to come through for himself, and for me. He'd worked briefly as a cabdriver, but we both agreed he should quit after he'd been robbed at gunpoint. That was followed by an odd job here, an occasional gig there. I was sure he'd find something by the time my classes began. With a resurgence of optimism, I found myself, again, thinking about having a baby. We'd certainly have to wait until after Derek found a job and I'd finished school and at least begun to establish myself, but then there'd be nothing holding us back. I also knew I had a biological clock ticking, although I did think I could wait until my forties if circumstances required. I wasn't having that mad baby fever Mindy had described, but I was sure that once we were both working together as partners, supporting each other's dreams, that overwhelming emotional urge would kick in.

It was a good plan, and it wouldn't require a rubber band. There was no reason why it couldn't work.

"*I decided not to* take the job. I know I said I was going to do it, but the hours really suck. I'd have to work the weekend shifts and then at least three nights a week. Anyway, it's ridiculous—I'm not going to be a waiter, not at my age." Derek was putting the groceries in the refrigerator as he gave me the news. "I've got a rehearsal in an hour, so I won't be here for dinner."

"Of course you don't want to wait tables." I leaned against the counter shuffling through the pile of mail. "There's so much more you can do." I put the mail down. "Did you call Paul?" I asked, trying to sound casual.

Paul was a friend and real estate broker I'd done a number of deals with who'd said that if Derek passed the exam, he'd hire him as a sales agent. Brokers made great money, had flexibility with hours, and with Derek's looks, charm and background, it was a natural fit.

"No, I'm not comfortable asking for a favor like that."

"It's not a favor—he said he needs agents." I could feel a shot of adrenaline make my heart beat faster. School started in less than two weeks. "It's the perfect job for you." I reached for the rubber band around my wrist and pulled. It broke, striking my fingertips. "*Ow!* Shit, that stings!"

Derek didn't say a word. And then, like the rubber band, the last of my control snapped. I was hurt and angry. No, I was finally furious. "How are we supposed to pay the bills?" I said quietly, seething, looking from him to the torn piece of rubber lying at my feet, so thin, so ridiculous, just like all my optimism.

"Don't get upset. We'll manage. Besides, I've got a much better shot at getting gigs now."

I watched as he put the expensive rib-eye steaks into the meat drawer, an indulgence he wanted that we couldn't afford. A wave of nausea hit me—I was going to have to bow out of the film program. Another grenade of anger—and fear—detonated in my stomach. "There's always a reason why you can't take a paying job. You've promised and promised but you don't *do* anything, except what you want to do for yourself." My voice got louder.

"Don't get so worked up."

"It's *so* unfair! You've had nothing but support from me and now when I really need you, there's nothing!" I struggled to think clearly, to speak plainly, to make my arguments logical, not emotional. I lowered my voice, trying to control my feelings. "You've known about this for months. We've talked about it endlessly. You've made me endless promises. And you've had plenty of time to find something. *Anything*. But there's always a reason why you can't. It's all just bullshit, just meaningless words." My voice had risen again.

He remained silent, his back to me as he rearranged the food on the refrigerator shelves.

"You know how much this means to me. Is it too much to ask? I've always supported you pursuing your dream. Don't I deserve what I gave you? What about *my* dreams? I'm always thinking about you, about *us*. You didn't even consider me when you made your decision." It made me feel invisible, desperate, to talk to his unresponsive back. "Doesn't *my* happiness matter? Damn it, Derek, I'm sick of this." I was filled with fury and I let it all out, trying to break through his shell. When he didn't respond, I stormed out of the kitchen.

Derek emerged a few minutes later, picking up the mail and looking through it. A dark Goddess with a string of skulls around her neck danced her black tongue into my own. I could feel myself losing the last of my control, heard myself shouting, not caring if the neighbors could hear. "I can't believe how selfish you're being. I'm exhausted—I can't keep carrying the load by myself. I need your help. You've got to take some responsibility. Don't you get it? This is *real*. It's not some damn rehearsal. I need you to be a grown-up. I need you to be a man!"

There. I'd said it. The one thing a professional, liberated, thirty-something woman should never think, let alone admit. But I did need him to be a man. I needed him to rescue me, to rescue *us*. I wanted him to be my White Knight, at least this once. But the minute it was out of my mouth, I knew that because I'd said it with anger, he'd never respond the way I needed him to. He wouldn't come to me, put his arms around me, reassure me that he would call Paul, or take the job, or get a loan from his parents. Or sell his motorcycle. There was also some deeper part of me that knew it wasn't my anger stopping him.

"Maybe if you were more of a woman, I could give you what you need," Derek tossed back at me, his voice like frozen steel. "I've got to go. We can talk about this later."

I felt as if he'd slapped me. I escaped out to the terrace, gasping, trying to breathe the cloying, overheated summer air. I *was* a woman, I thought desperately. I looked down at my suit. I was a woman warrior. Of course, we didn't want to have sex anymore. I was married to a little boy, and he'd turned me into his nagging, caretaking, world-battling mommy. But surely he would do something, now that he saw how upset I was.

My hands were shaking, but I was calmer as I pulled open the terrace door and stepped back into the over-air-conditioned apartment. Derek had left for his rehearsal. I sank to my knees and I cried. Finally empty of tears and exhausted, I numbly realized I had looked into the mirror of my mother's anger and my father's withdrawal, and was living the reasons for both.

It was almost 3 A.M. I lay on the living room floor, a single candle providing fragile illumination, the headphones snug against my ears. I'd made an excuse every night since the fight, saying I'd come to bed soon, knowing I would creep in silently long after Derek had fallen asleep.

My mind was no longer able to protect me, and the blues I'd had after the shoot ended were back. I couldn't return to the cold and abstract realm of the law, of constraints and financial responsibilities without some hope for something that challenged and stimulated my creativity. More important, I couldn't bear to leave the realm of my daemon. Film school had been my route back—a chance that Derek had taken from me.

I recognized the restlessness, the longing that was rising within me. From the first moment he'd appeared, I'd looked for my daemon everywhere I went, in the eyes of every man I met, hungry for the feel of his arms around me, his lips against mine, for a strong, penetrating, masculine love that entered and filled me. When Derek arrived, I thought my daemon had finally taken form. I was wrong.

Deep inside, I knew that it was over between us and somehow I was going to have to accept that. I had been afraid to let go, to be alone, afraid that for all of our problems I would never feel for anyone else what I had felt for Derek. I was still afraid, but the pain was becoming greater than my fear.

I wanted an impassioned life; and I wanted a partner who would honor and protect my dreams, not sacrifice them. A man whose love I could feel in the vigor and direction he brought to his life *and* ours, and the sensitivity and sensuality he brought to our lovemaking. Most of all, I wanted a man whose love I could feel in my soul, because I knew that unless I felt it there, I wouldn't feel it in my body.

Are you there? Oh please, be there. I longed for my daemon. Waiting in the silence, I knew I had to find a way to him. I remembered Shakespeare's wisdom: "Make passionate my sense of hearing." I began riding the music the way shamans rode their drums—the shaman's horse, the mother's heartbeat—into the liminal, harmonic space of sound, emotions and energy where a daemon moved with ease. Like filmmakers and actors, whether they are aware of their role or not, musicians are the priests and priestesses of Dionysus, troubadours coming through time, working shamans of the modern world. They tap the power of the daemon and the muse and release them into the world. And they enact the rites, sing the sacred songs that carry us into the sphere where spirits dwell because the heart has reasons that reason knows not of.

With their help I was breaking through to the other side—to the realm of possibility where a heart can heal and life can begin again. But there was more to the magical power of music. Whether randomly caught on the radio, or through the mysterious connection to a particular artist or piece, music can be a *cledon*, a message from the Gods.

I rode their magic into the center of my tornado of need. I was lost; longing for my guide, and I wept, knowing I was the woman wailing for her daemon lover. And when the storm had passed, the tower of excuses broken and tumbled by the winds of wanting, I was quiet, clear and free inside. I turned up the volume and continued the long walk to the bright side of the road, to his front seat, windows rolled down, hair blowing back, ready to pay the price to continue the journey down Thunder Road to Xanadu.

I shifted my heavy briefcase into my other hand as I stepped into the street and flagged down a cab. "Twenty-first and Fifth," I instructed the cabbie. It was the new office I shared with my new law partner, and it was a good address, right in the middle of the literary district. Although it was stretching my already thin budget to transparency, it was a necessity. The individual offices were small but their blond wood decor and packed library conference room said we were up-and-coming, and charged reasonable fees.

I hung up my jacket, appreciating the downtown views from the office we shared to keep our costs down. *Messenger the purchaser's check to my client, finish the closing statement, check phone list—calls.* I pulled out the check for my fee. It was enough to cover my tuition for the film program at NYU; instead, it would pay next month's bills.

It was still light out when I finished my work. I started to pick up the phone to call Derek, then realized that I really didn't need to check in with him. We were living in the same apartment, but we were acting like roommates. No, like strangers.

Naomi would be working at the shop, and if I were lucky, Nonna would be there too. I grabbed my purse, left my briefcase and headed out. Summer was ending, and though the days were still hot and sticky, at dusk the city gentled into an almost tropical balminess. The shop was a short walk from my office, but instead of turning onto 19th Street, I found myself continuing down Fifth Avenue, finally walking beneath the Washington Square arch and into the crowded park.

I collapsed on a bench near the chess players' corner, across from the law school and a block from the film school. Slipping off my high heels and wiggling my toes, I watched the occupants of the city's most densely used park—old and young, musicians and street performers, dope dealers and law students, lovers and the lonely. Tonight, there were drummers and they made me want to get up and dance. But we don't do that in this culture of ours, except maybe in the movies, or with a lover. I sighed. Being with a lover reenchants the world. It gives you license to be joyful, to break the rules and play. You can dance in the park, kiss on a street corner, sing to each other in the middle of the supermarket—and everyone, including you, will smile. The world is full of magic when you're in love. *Where has all the magic gone?*

I closed my eyes and let the last of the summer sun shining down Third Street bathe me in consoling warmth. I'd caught it at just the right moment, when the buildings and sidewalks and all the occupants were glowing as if made from liquid gold. The light penetrated my skin and then my heart, giving me the courage to let my mind go where it needed—to things I'd been afraid to look at but could no longer avoid.

How was I supposed to be soft, receptive, feminine and beguiling in bed when I had to spend the rest of my time working, struggling, cultivating the exact opposite qualities? Masculine qualities. Goddess knows I tried, but I couldn't get the armor off. Why wouldn't it come off? What was wrong with me?

"So, this is where you are."

My eyes flew open. Nonna was sitting on the bench beside me, smiling.

In her vivid vintage Pucci blouse, black slacks and sunglasses, she looked like she should be strolling through Anacapri rather than New York.

"What are you doing here?" I leaned over and gave her a kiss and a weary smile.

"I came down to do a little shopping at Balducci's and then I was going to Murry's for some organic parmesan. But a little voice suggested I go for a quick espresso so I detoured, and now I know why. So, when are you starting school?" She pulled an orange from one of her shopping bags, releasing an invigorating perfume as she started to peel away the skin.

"I'm not going."

"Why not? You've been looking forward to it for so long!" Nonna slid her sunglasses down her nose and stared over them at me.

"We can't afford it." I shrugged and answered dully. "I can always go next year."

"No, you can't, you have to go now." The glasses came off.

I was startled by the urgency of her tone. "I wish I could. I mean, what am I supposed to do? Wave my magic wand and make it happen?"

My cynical crack earned me a look. "If that's what you want to use. You can work with anything you like—that paper cup over there." She pointed with her sunglasses to an empty coffee cup tumbled by the evening breeze along the cobblestone path. "Or this orange, or a song, or your heart. At this point in your work, it's not about the accoutrement of magic; it's about your life. You have to *inhabit* it, not confine it to the technical. That's the real magic. You know that."

I sighed. "Yes, I know—my life is my magic. The Great Work. But life doesn't feel very magical right now. Anyway, my life isn't just my own, it's all tangled up with Derek's. He hasn't found a job, so I have to keep working or the bills won't get paid." I could feel myself hardening bitterly, and then collapsing into depressed resignation. "Nonna, am I hard?"

Nonna shook her head and sighed. "You're strong. It's natural, it's feminine to want to do more for him. But the more you do, the less he does. He's not fulfilling his responsibility to you. He's not being your partner. You have a right to expect that he will and he has an obligation to do so." She handed me a piece of orange. "But he's not holding up his half, so you'll have to figure out what you're going to do, regardless."

Is it just that simple? I stared disinterestedly at the piece of fruit.

"Eat that," Nonna prodded.

I bit into the slice, licking my fingers quickly as the juice ran between them. *It's sweet.*

"Good?"

I nodded.

"But money is only part of the issue, isn't it?" Nonna asked.

I sat silently, waiting for the answer to surface, and I sighed as it appeared. "It makes me feel . . . like he doesn't really love me. I told him I needed him to be a man for me, and he said I'm not enough of a woman for him." I wanted to cry, another thing you don't do in public, alone or with anyone. Except Nonna. "He's right. I know it's not all his fault."

"Did you tell him how you feel?" Her eyes were deep pools of sympathy.

I nodded. "I got angry."

"Did you cry?"

"After he left. Nonna, every night I've been running to my daemon, and I wonder, if . . . ," I hesitated, as if saying it would make it true, "if the reason I can't make my marriage work with Derek is because my daemon is leading me away. I'm afraid that maybe I can't love a real man because I have this ideal in my head. In my heart."

Nonna patted my cheek. "Your daemon can't take you *from* love. He's leading you to what you need in order *to* love. You're reacting to Derek's lack of purpose, his lack of self-knowledge and self-discipline. You want a man with strength of purpose. It's only when a man is being true to himself that he can truly love. If you're carrying the masculine energy in your relationship—supporting him financially, handling the responsibilities of your lives together—you won't be able to feel him as a man, because he's not contributing any male energy to the relationship. It's all on you."

"But he's very masculine. I mean it's taken a long time, but he's totally directed towards his career." I stared into the sun.

"That's good—he's doing what he should. But he also has a responsibility to bring those energies to your relationship, to you, and he's unable, or unwilling, to do that."

"I poured so much of myself into encouraging him and he's giving nothing back." I heard the edge of bitterness in my tone. "It was so hard for me to ask for help. I feel like it makes me . . . weak, dependent. But I asked, and he didn't respond." I turned back to her, momentarily blind.

"Maybe he has nothing to give. You can't help a man find his strength; he has to do that for himself. To him, your needs are just a constraint on the freedom he needs to find. Your needs are a burden." Nonna shook her head.

A cold little shiver skidded across my skin.

"It sounds like he still has a long way to go before he can be whole as a man, and until then, he can't give you what you need." Nonna tossed me an orange.

I dug my fingers into the thick rind, grateful for the sharp smell as I pulled the skin away, and grateful for the fruit that I was liberating. "But it's so unfair!"

"Yes, it is. We all have a wide range of qualities that go from one end of the spectrum we call masculine to the other we call feminine. Polarity, yes? The journey to wholeness requires us to develop what's missing in ourselves, usually for men the feminine, for women the masculine qualities. We used to suffer from gender stereotyping, but now we also suffer by being confined to the opposite pole. We're restricted in ways that are very hurtful and debilitating. A man who refuses to bring strong male energy to his woman forces her into the masculine role and traps her there."

"I'm glad I've learned how to be my own White Knight, but I'm tired of being his too. I'm so exhausted, Nonna. I have to spend every day in a man's world, cultivating all my assertive, take-charge qualities. And that's fine for the workplace, and for lots of other things. I mean, it's part of who I am and I'm proud of it. But I don't want to live my whole life like that. Parts of me are missing and I want them back. I just can't be the husband all day and then come home and suddenly be the wife. I want a husband!"

Nonna smiled. "*Mia figlia*, you're not alone. Most of the working women in America, and most everywhere else for that matter, feel the same way. The world values the masculine, and to succeed that's what we've had to cultivate. It's *very* hard, sometimes impossible to let go of that energy when you've been locked in it all day, year after year. If you're happy there, more power to you. But you also have a right to experience the fullness of who you are—as a woman. Remember, the Goddess is far more than just a warrior."

"I've tried, but I can't just flip a switch and presto I'm a Goddess of Love. It's hard even feeling like a woman." I stared down at my short, broken nails. "For a while I didn't even notice anything was missing. But for whatever reason I feel . . . empty. Off-balance, like I'm walking a tightrope without a center of gravity."

"Without the feminine parts of ourselves we can't be whole, or happy, or sexy. And neither can the world. The culture traps you, but so has Derek. He's carrying the feminine energy in your relationship. It was probably one of the reasons you were drawn to him originally—because in some ways he completed those missing parts of yourself—he's sensitive and emotional, creative and instinctual. Just as he was drawn to your masculine energies—your strength and courage, determination and control. But people can't finish each other. You have to find your own inner balance. And ultimately, if that energy is not in alignment with your deepest needs and nature, you'll be unhappy and unsatisfied, and the sexual polarity will vanish."

I thought about my nightly ritual of summoning my daemon until Derek fell asleep. "It's true—I'm not attracted to him anymore."

"No, because his lack of masculine energy turns you off. The polarities have reversed in your relationship and so you're losing your desire for him."

"I was counting on him, and he let me down. Either he's not competent enough to go out and make a living and contribute to our life together, or he's choosing not to. Either way, it's destroyed any attraction I felt." A last chunk of despair floated to the surface. "I don't trust him."

"How can you trust him if he doesn't have it together enough to handle his life as your husband? You don't feel safe, and without that you're not free to be feminine."

"But how do I escape being trapped in the armor?" I felt my life depended on her answer.

"Be true to yourself and the way will present itself."

"I'm not sure how; I'm so used to putting his needs first." We sat silently, finishing the last of the orange. "And Derek?"

"You have to focus on yourself now, on your journey to wholeness. It's time to pull back your masculine energies—they don't help him anyway. Just as his feminine keeps you trapped, your masculine traps him. Trying to solve his problems for him, telling him what to do, taking on all the responsibilities—it emasculates him. Keep that energy for yourself—use it to pursue your dream of creative work, find a way to go to film school. Use the masculine skills that you have developed to protect and fulfill those dreams and that woman. Use them to rediscover the feminine parts of yourself that you've neglected. The rest will take care of itself. The dynamic with Derek will sort itself out, one way or the other, if each of you retrieves the parts that are missing."

I sighed and I felt lighter, less afraid of the future, less trapped in my armor.

"So, what did you learn from the orange?"

"The orange?" I laughed. I looked down at the pile of bright thick peel, tasted the sweetness, felt the stickiness and smelled the juice on my fingers. "There's a reason for its armor. It needs the strong outer skin to protect the soft, inner fruit. It takes energy, focus, effort to pull the skin off, but as it comes off, the peel releases a fragrance that's . . . like an invitation to the satisfaction within."

Nonna smiled and nodded. "Anything else?"

"I need both protective outer shell and inner beauty. And the process of shifting requires strength, and courage, but the effort is rewarded with pleasure and nourishment. And once freed, there's nothing to fear. What else? It brought me into my body, it reminds me of Eros, and feminine sensuality, and life." An image of the God placing his sword at the feet of the Goddess flashed through my head. "And something else—the masculine force within women serves the feminine, protects it and the life and beauty that it offers. And the feminine rewards the masculine with love, eroticism and joy."

"And so it can be with all couples, in all the ways they choose." Nonna gathered up the pieces of rind, cocking an eyebrow as she smiled. "So, I like to think of that as orange magic. I'd say it worked. One more thing, you're much further along in this journey back to yourself than you realize."

I nodded.

"Come, let's walk. There's a beautiful pair of earrings I've had my eye on. I want to show them to you."

I picked up her Balducci bags and we strolled down MacDougal Street to the dusty window of an old jewelry shop. We stopped and stared at the display of artisanal pieces.

"Look at those." She pointed at two long, slightly curving lines of silver. Beside the earrings was a beautiful gold band of tiny flowers and leaves.

I stared down at my left hand—with my grandmother's ring but no wedding ring.

Nonna took my hand and rubbed it between hers. "Perhaps there's another reason you never wore Derek's ring, *mia figlia*. Legend says that the very first wedding ring was given by Cain to his wife. I remember you told me, several years ago, that when your journey began you felt that you were Cain's wife, waiting for him to find his way home. It might be that you are meant to wear someone else's ring."

I felt my stomach jump.

"Did you know that Masons are said to be the descendants of Cain and his wife? They built the temple of Solomon and the great cathedrals of Europe, but long before that masonry began in order to protect the Goddess's grain. Masons built the foundation upon which civilization rests. And in Italy, Witches are called the children of Cain. There are many clues as to who he is. When it's time you'll know. Let's go to Monte's. I could really go for mussels." Nonna changed subjects happily. "And you can chew on what we discussed."

I took a last look at the golden ring. *The Divine will use whatever is available to communicate with you, to teach what you need to know—if you will pay attention. And that is real magic.*

When I woke the next morning. I was relieved to find that Derek was already gone. He'd slept on the couch. I showered and dressed for work. Staring at myself in the mirror, something I'd been afraid to do for the last few months, I saw my confusion, and I heard Nonna's words about Cain, the ring, and . . . Was it really possible that there was someone else? I pushed the thought away. Or perhaps Nonna had meant my daemon. Letting the library angel guide my hand, I randomly grabbed one of my journals. Sitting in the subway, I let it fall open and began to read a section describing a dream I'd had several years ago:

I'm naked, with long dark hair; standing on a swing and facing me is a man, tall and blond. We are both holding onto the ropes of the swing and as we swing back and forth together, rising into the sky and then falling backwards to the earth, each movement giving power and momentum to its opposite, a powerful surge of desire flows back and forth between us. With each downward and then upward surge, the energy circulates from his groin to mine, then up to my heart and from my heart into his, descending from his heart into his groin and then back to mine in a continuously circling connection of desire and fulfillment. And then I woke up, still feeling the current running between us, still feeling the pendulant motion of my dream. He's nowhere to be seen—but I seem to feel him within.

I closed the journal and headed to my closing.

I paper-clipped the six-figure check to the inside of the manila file and slipped the file into my well-worn Mark Cross briefcase.

"Nice doing business with you, Counselor." The purchasers' attorney, a seasoned lawyer with silver hair, wire-rimmed glasses and a tight little bow tie, extended his bony, age-spotted hand. I reached across the gleaming mahogany table and we exchanged a firm handshake. *Opposites with so much in common.*

I stood alone in the bank attorney's well-upholstered conference room staring out at the glorious Manhattan skyline. It was extraordinary—a stunning testimony to man's drive, ambition, and yes, his greed. For all of its imperfections, it was magical—like a seductive, silver Oz. But where was the magic in the misery I'd been feeling all week? Where were my ruby slippers? I wanted to go home, but the man I wanted to go home to wouldn't be waiting for me. And neither would Derek.

What I wanted most of all was to go to film school. It was Friday afternoon. My classes began on Monday. I watched a single red-tailed hawk circling over the park with Nonna's words echoing in my heart: *Find a way to go to film school.*

I'd been raised to expect that I couldn't count on a man. And so I had a man I couldn't count on. But I could count on myself. *Magic is how you co-create reality with the Divine.* It wasn't in some spell or potion. It was in *me.* My life was the magic. I made up my mind—*whether Derek gets a job or not, I'm going.* A rush of joy hit me and my spirits lifted as if seized by that sublime raptor floating above the city. If I had to take money out of my retirement account or get a loan to pay the bills, that's what I would do. Somehow, I'd pull it off. I was going to be my own White Knight, once again, but I was also going to be my own Princess. *Was it that simple?*

"*When we get back from break,* we're going to vote on which of your screenplays will get filmed. Okay, fifteen minutes. We start whether you're here or not. Why?" The head of the film program sat with one hip hoisted onto the desk at the front of the room. He was one hundred percent male—tall, square-jawed, with a head of thick, curly auburn hair, squinting green eyes and a bad cigarette habit. And though he came from a famous Italian filmmaking family, his enlisted stint in the Navy and a life working as a cinematographer had given him a hardened edge. I loved watching his hands—it was the first time in a long time that I'd been attracted to another man.

I answered: "If you're not on the set when you should be, you're fired." I was one of the older students, and unlike my classmates who cut or blew off their assignments, I was enjoying every minute and had an easy rapport with my instructors. It was like being on a shoot again and it felt great.

Smiling, he nodded at me. I smiled back, grabbed my briefcase and ran out the door. I didn't have time to think about sexy professors. I had less than fifteen minutes to get downstairs to the bank of pay phones and call my clients, various attorneys and banks. I was working too hard, but I was pulling it off. I took out my leather change purse filled with quarters. It was heavy enough to knock a grown man unconscious, and by the end of the day—after the coffee, lunch and dinner breaks, all of which I spent on the phone being a lawyer—it would be light as a feather.

"Hi, Joan. Yes, sorry I couldn't call sooner. I was in a meeting. The seller's holding out for a higher bid. I think we should push the broker to try to make this deal happen. I know he wants his fee." I wondered if she could hear my charm bracelet, a golden bracelet filled with charms I'd been collecting since my sixteenth birthday, as I took notes. I wore it every day—a small gesture with huge psychological impact. It made music as I moved, glinted in the light and reminded me that I was not just a hardworking lawyer, or hardworking filmmaker, but also a woman.

I scratched Joan's name from the list and moved to the next one. *Shit!* I'd meant to call the insurance broker about the damage caused by a water leak from our upstairs neighbor. And I needed to make sure that the health insurance company hadn't canceled the policy because I'd sent the premium in late. I spotted my classmates returning with their coffee and checked my watch. I could squeeze in one more call. But as I waited for the broker to pick up, I found myself thinking about the screenplay I'd submitted, wondering if it would be one of the few chosen for production.

It had been prompted by an undeniable bit of magic. I'd been toying with the idea of a modern-day fairy tale—the unexpected love affair between a busy, young career woman and the erotic daemon whose appearance changes her life. And it would have a hot love scene. But last week, after crumpling another effort and lobbing it into the wastebasket, I'd given up.

I'd turned off the computer, slit open the pile of bills and written checks. I took a bath to unwind, and then I climbed into bed with the enormous September *Vogue*. It weighed almost as much as my change purse, but it wasn't the Armani suit that made my heart jump. It was an ad for a new Calvin Klein perfume—a full-page black-and-white photograph of a young woman with long dark hair and a tall, blond young man, both of them naked, and both of them standing, facing each other, on a swing. *It was the exact image from my dream!*

There's an old saying that three's a charm, and this was a triple play of signs: On the subway to school every day, I was reading a book about my daemon called *Ecstasy: Understanding the Psychology of Joy*, which had been sitting, unread, on my bookshelf for two years. I had been so stunned the other day to find an explanation of the dream, I'd almost missed my stop: The book described how Dionysus was commonly depicted on a swing, suspended between heaven and earth, joyously connecting them, just as I had been doing in my dream. And now with that understanding, the dream and my daemon had materialized before my eyes. I tore out the image, propped it next to the computer, sat down and wrote the screenplay for my eight-minute film.

No answer. I hung up the phone and raced back upstairs, hoping that mine would be one of the scripts chosen. It was. I was going to make another movie—my own.

The film program had ended, and thanks to the efforts of one of my filmmaking team, my short film was screened at the Cannes and Sundance film festivals. But there weren't any opportunities in independent filmmaking, unless you made your own. So, at least for the time being, I was practicing law full-time. I was also looking for ways to make movies.

But I had another challenge facing me. Nonna's words about wearing someone else's ring had lingered in my heart. I'd tried to ignore them to deal with the reality of the man right in front of me. The reality was, however, that I'd put off dealing with my problems with Derek while in school. Now, despite my fear, there was nothing stopping me. Film school had brought me to a better sense of inner balance; Derek was more committed to his music than ever and, I hoped, finding his way back to his own power, but he was still not my partner. Things hadn't changed; in fact, they'd gotten worse. Derek and I rarely saw each other while I was in school; we were living separate lives and I'd finally accepted that we needed to find a way to save the marriage, or I needed a way to end it. I stood staring into my closet, considering what I would pack if I walked out the door.

I struggled with the commitment to Derek, to our marriage, that had felt sacred to me—it was why I was having trouble walking away. But maybe, I thought, it was also the love spell I'd cast. I would have to talk to Nonna about that, but in the meantime I sought out someone else to help me in other ways—a therapist. Everyone in New York had one, and now I did too. Derek had agreed to go with me.

Just before our session I consulted my tarot deck, and drew the tower card. I was momentarily frozen by the image of divine lightning striking the fortress and bodies falling into the tumultuous sea below. Whatever was going to happen would obliterate what we had been. And it seemed to my weary soul that perhaps the force of destiny was approaching. What I did not know was whether we'd survive as a couple.

We sat in the waiting room, a small, windowless white space with old *National Geographic*s and older *New Yorker*s piled on a small end table. I flipped nervously through magazines I'd already read while Derek sat with his eyes closed.

The door to the inner office opened and a very downtown, older couple, both dressed in black, emerged. Her mascara was smudged; his face was bleak. The door closed quickly behind them. I buried my face in the magazine, avoiding the denuding eye contact that would strip us all of our cloaks of invisibility. Worse, I sensed it would somehow acknowledge what we were all trying to ignore—that we were rearranging the deck chairs while the *Titanic* was sinking.

The door opened again. A man with a face that seemed to be melting nodded at us. "You can come in now."

Derek held the door for me and I followed our psychopomp into his cave, eyeing the leather patches at his tweed jacket's elbows with suspicion. He sat facing us in an armchair in front of his desk, a view of Seventh Avenue out the huge plate glass window behind him. We sat together on a couch that needed new springs. My knees were higher than my ass, and I felt as if I were going to disappear down some dark hole, instead of being helped out of the one I was already in.

"So, tell me why you're here." He smiled professionally, the folds in his face contorting slightly upward, looking back and forth between us.

I want advice on new slipcovers? I was ready to walk out, but after a moment of endless and awkward silence I plunged in. I'd never felt so uncomfortable or self-conscious. "I guess I've just lost hope. In our relationship."

The three of us sat in silence. I felt guilty for talking to a stranger about my loss of faith. But the desperation that had brought me here, brought *us* here, pushed the words out of me. "No, I've lost faith in *Derek*," I admitted. "I can't deal with being the one who has to handle all of the responsibilities, all of the time. I don't have anything left to give, and I'm not getting anything back. I'm worn out. I need him to be a real partner."

It was a struggle not to climb into my head and analyze, but, with prompting, I managed to describe how I *felt* about the last few years. Derek sat silently, stone-faced, having been told that he'd have a chance to speak uninterrupted. Every negative word felt like a nail being hammered into the coffin of our relationship. But you can't fix it if you can't face it.

"I need him to be strong enough so that, at least sometimes, I can be soft." I sat, empty and flat, stunned by how much despair had spilled out of me.

The therapist asked Derek how he felt about what I'd said.

"Shitty," Derek said defiantly. I couldn't blame him for reacting defensively. "It's not like I haven't tried to find work." He went on to explain and defend himself and I felt the oxygen leaving the coffin. Wasn't this guy going to say anything? Wasn't he going to help Derek see how unfair he'd been to me?

The therapist turned to me and suddenly I found myself confessing a fear that, until this moment, in this place of foreign and utter honesty, I hadn't allowed myself to acknowledge. I looked at Derek, who stared at the therapist, to whom I turned. "Derek knows I want to have a baby. He said he wanted to, but he doesn't act like it." I spoke slowly, looked down at my left hand and then back up at the stranger sitting across from me. I'd never felt so vulnerable. "I don't know how we can unless he starts to hold up his end financially."

"It sounds to me like Phyllis feels you haven't been taking the steps necessary to create a family together." He immediately addressed Derek, and for just a second, I felt a flash of hope. "How do you feel about having a baby, Derek?"

Derek was silent. All the air left the room and I was falling down a long, dark tunnel. And then he answered and I crashed.

"The truth is I really don't want to have another child. I've been . . . trying to wait her out."

The hole closed in around me, but instead of being swallowed in darkness, the room bleached white as bones in the desert. As if from far away, I could hear Derek saying that he didn't want the responsibility of a second family. He was at a point in his life where he wanted to finally accomplish his dreams, to enjoy himself and me. He was a stranger.

A stranger had lived with me, and touched me, kissed me, entered me, fucked me. Lied to me. Later, I had no memory of how the session had proceeded or ended or how I got home. Derek's words had exploded inside of me, pulverizing what was left of my shattered heart, leaving me in shock, my inside covered in bloody dust.

For days, I couldn't think clearly, couldn't sleep, and I had no appetite. I moved like a ghost through the apartment, uncertain about what was real and what wasn't, certain of only one thing—I was collapsing into the void that had displaced my life, my dreams.

I awakened to find him lying beside me, the first time in days. I wanted him to put his arms around me and reassure me that the nightmare was over and everything would change, that he had been afraid, but now he knew how much he loved me, enough to have a child with me. He was silent. He put his arms around me and, longing for reassurance, I began to cry.

"I don't understand," I sobbed into his shoulder. He didn't reply. "Was it all just a fairy tale? A hallucination?" I was afraid that I would drown in all the tears, in the devastating grief, that I would die. He remained silent. I rolled away, sat up, wiped my tears, and struggled with the fear and the lethal pain. "I can control my emotions. My emotions won't control me," I said dully, repeating it like an inverted mantra. We were silent and still.

"Why, just tell me why? I need to understand." I reached for a life jacket—a rational explanation that would allow my mind to rescue me.

He shook his head. "I do love you."

A sharp pain cut through the heavy numbness, and my control crumbled. Tears rushed through the laceration. "Why don't I matter?" I pleaded, but he offered nothing, no explanation, no reassurance. Dizzily, I got out of bed, went to the bathroom, and held a cool, wet washcloth to my burning eyes. I sat on the cold tiles, slumped against the wall. It was time to stop lying to myself. I knew I could never trust him again.

I cried without his arms around me. I was mangled, broken, but I heard the small, desperate voice inside me that said I *do* matter, my dreams mattered, if only to myself. Maybe nothing else would change, but that realization, I knew, would change me. I clung to the memory of Nonna's reassurance that the pain wouldn't kill me. I just needed to make it through the rest of the night.

———

I had the apartment to myself. Derek was visiting his parents, or so he said. I stood in the bedroom, staring out at the black, starless night. It was the dark of the moon, the time for banishing. Magic is a simple thing—a prayer, a vision, an offering that requires only the opening of one's heart, even a broken heart, to the Sacred.

Did I really want to do this? Once done, the love spell, the handfast binding and its magic, would be forever undone. And then I heard Derek's words, as if he were sitting beside me, saw his face as he said them, felt the wave of pain and shock. *I was trying to wait her out.* At least, in the end, he had been honest. I took a deep breath and grounded myself. I had been abandoned and left barren, but I was still standing.

I untied the velvet sack from our bed frame and carried it into the living room. I lit the blue candles in each of the four directions and on the altar, and poured a banishing incense of ground sage, lavender, peppermint, bay leaves, myrrh, cinnamon and salt onto the burning charcoal. A tumbling gust of smoke quickly filled the apartment. I stood, turning as I cast my circle, calling the powers of the four directions, summoning the aid of Goddess and God, summoning the Sacred from within.

I washed my face in a bowl of water into which I'd sprinkled the herbs, and then rubbed a wet hand over my heart. I sat holding the pouch. Finally, I took a deep breath, opened and shook it. The knotted ribbons tumbled into my lap along with images of our past—the night we met, our first kiss, our last kiss, our handfasting, memories of making love, and having sex; memories now tainted by a deception. Long before I had lost faith in him, he had broken faith with me. I placed the tangle of ribbons in the center of the altar and rested my hands on them.

"With no ill will towards Derek, with nothing but good intentions for us both"—my voice cracked as I spoke the words—"let us release each other in peace and without animosity, let us part honoring the love that we once shared. And let us heal and be able to trust and love again." I picked up the bundle of broken dreams and softly said my spell, a prayer from my broken heart. "I accepted the loss of perfect love and perfect trust between us."

And then I began to untie the knots, crying and murmuring again and again the soft chant that tasted of salty tears. "I release these ties that bind us to one another. I release the ties that bind us." I plucked and struggled and pulled them apart, and I felt the anger and the pain until gradually my sorrow eased, my tears stopped, my feelings shifted from hopelessness to acceptance. An unexpected wave of peace overtook me as I untied the final knot. "I embrace my freedom. I honor his." And with those final words I untied myself from Derek.

I laid the ribbons out in straight rows upon the altar, smoothing them, running my fingertips over their bumpy surfaces where they had been so tightly tied. I would keep a blue ribbon and give one to Derek—a gesture of peace and healing. I closed my circle and put everything away except the ribbons. I left a blue ribbon on the top of Derek's dresser, put one blue ribbon in my journal, climbed into bed, and fell into a dreamless sleep.

I awoke the next morning with the sun in my face and an unfamiliar sense of lightness. I stared in the mirror, grateful that I'd had the strength to be my own White Knight. Like Sleeping Beauty awakened from her dream of love, for the first time in a long time I could see the truth. And devastating as it was, the truth had set me free.

I showered, dressed in my old leather jacket, a sweater and jeans, grabbed the rest of the ribbons and hailed a cab. "Empire State Building," I said to the driver. I climbed out across the street from the building and in front of a florist that also sold balloons. I was instantly overcome by the smell of roses. The bouquets in the refrigerated cabinet stirred memories of the flowers Derek had brought me. *There will be more flowers in the future.*

"I'd like a red balloon, please. A large round one if you have it, not oval." I thought of my favorite childhood film, a fairy tale called *The Red Balloon*, in which a large, perfectly round, magical balloon befriends a lonely young Parisian boy, following him wherever he goes. A gang of jealous little boys destroys the balloon, but as he grieves, all the balloons in Paris tear themselves from their tethers and fly to him, lifting him aloft over the city.

The young girl behind the counter, with the sweet face of a grown Gerber baby and dressed in a Madonna T-shirt, nodded and disappeared into the back. I could hear the rushing sound of helium. She returned, handing the balloon to me with a broad smile. It was small but perfectly round, and red. I paid her.

"For your child?" she asked.

I shook my head and exhaled the pang of sorrow. "For . . . magic. I'm going to use it to help me release my past." The freedom of telling the truth was liberating.

She looked startled and then her eyes brightened with excitement. "Are you Wiccan?" she asked cautiously.

It was my turn to smile. I nodded.

"So am I! At least I'd like to be. So far, I'm just reading."

"Reading's good. But everything you really need to know about magic is right here." I tapped my heart. "Blessed be!" I used the old salutation and winked. I stepped out into the sunny street. *It's so much lighter than a briefcase!* I smiled and people smiled back. The magic was already working. There were more smiles from all the busy suits rushing to their important jobs as we took the elevator up, the red balloon floating over our heads.

I stepped off on the top floor and pushed open the heavy door to the Observation Deck. A gusty wind grabbed at the balloon and blew my hair wildly about my face. The spectacular city stretched out far below me, the blue sky stretched out just an arm's length above me.

I sat on a bench against the side of the building and out of the wind, enjoying the warm sun, listening to the voices of exhilarated children. *Someday.* Slowly and deliberately I tied the ribbons—silver and gold and all the colors of the rainbow—so they hung like streamers from the bottom of the red balloon. I stood up, feeling a little light-headed as I approached the railing. The wind was strong and the balloon bounced about, tugging at its leash. I was ready.

I whispered my prayer, worked my spell: "May the pain of the past, of lost love and broken dreams be carried off by the wind, breath of life. I release the past." I exhaled. And then, slowly, I inhaled. "And may real happiness, true love and new dreams fill the empty space in my heart and my life. I welcome the future."

It was time to let go. I opened my hand, and my heart, and let the balloon sail free.

13

Pleasure

Nothing can cure the soul but the senses,

just as nothing can cure the senses but the soul.

—OSCAR WILDE

The apartment door closed behind Derek with a hollow, metallic thud. I stood staring at it, numb and unsteady; a bit of the earth's gravity had left with him. *Why couldn't love be enough?*

I walked into the kitchen and punched *record* on the answering machine. "Hi, we're not . . ." I hit *stop*, took a deep breath and started again, slowly. "Hi, you've reached 212-555-5151. I'm not in right now, but leave a message and I'll get back to you as soon as I can."

I listened to it twice, then leaned against the door frame looking into the living room. It seemed the same as it had yesterday, before that door closed, filled with furniture, books, things, as if nothing had changed. Except for all the photographs—the evidence of our past together. They were gone, packed away. I walked to the bedroom and opened the door to his walk-in closet. Empty.

The spell was broken.

I sat on the bed, clutching the teddy bear he'd given me, and I cried.

Sobbing as if the earth itself was tearing open, I was unable to stop. I cried for a month after Derek left, tears pouring down from heaven, rising without remission from a deep well of ancient childhood sorrow, tears I was afraid would drown me but that instead, very gradually, washed away the pain. Like Aphrodite, I was purified by salt water and, restored to myself, I was again a virgin.

I cleaned the apartment, every square inch, every drawer, shelf, cabinet and corner. I put away Barber's *Adagio for Strings* and played a lot of blues—Robert Johnson, Blind Lemon Jefferson, Billie Holiday—while I dusted and vacuumed and scrubbed, first with detergents and cleansers, then with water and salt, the substance of tears put to good use.

I rearranged the furniture, stripped the bed, bought new linens, and with Naomi's help turned the mattress over. I inched my way from the blues to jazz to rock and roll, and finally I turned the music up loud and cleaned out my closets. I cried when I found one of Derek's shirts hanging with my blouses, a sweater of his I always wore. And then I tossed them into the pile of clothes that didn't fit, were out of style, or hid me from myself and the world—blouses with little bows and "power" jackets with giant shoulder pads. I thanked this old wardrobe for the blessings it had helped me create, and then sent the clothes to charity.

Surveying the newly opened spaces in the closet, I realized that the molting and shedding had revealed something distinctly feminine—after years of camouflage, the clothes that were left showed my figure. I tried things on, stared in the mirror, but every time I looked I also saw the emptiness inside.

Nonna came to visit, bringing flowers and pastries, and she showed me how to accept what I was seeing. "Losing someone you love leaves a hole in your heart that never goes away. But in time, you'll learn to grow a larger heart around that hole."

I tried to have faith in her advice, and on the Spring Equinox, when the Goddess returns from the Underworld and when life returns to the earth, I burned sage to purify the space and opened all the doors and windows. I picked up a broom and, sweeping along the floors and ceilings, brushed away any remaining dregs of sorrow and heartbreak. And then I burned a gentle mixture of orange, lavender, basil and hyssop to bless the cleansed apartment, carrying it through each of the rooms, and the closets, until the apartment smelled fresh and full of hope. I put flowers in every room. I slept in the middle of the bed. And I stopped crying.

Somewhere in this harvest of sorrow I could sense the seed of a new life. I couldn't control events, anyone else, or my feelings. And ending my marriage had taught me that I couldn't live life without pain. But I'd begun to realize something deeply liberating. Within every loss there's a lesson, and once discerned, that wisdom frees you from the pain. Even more, it empowers you, makes you stronger and more self-aware. And in time my heart would grow larger. At least I hoped so.

"*I've been thinking* about you all week." Nonna hugged me, then stood back and studied me. "You're smiling. That's a good sign. But you look tired and thin. Are you eating?" She hugged me again, then settled into one of the client chairs.

I shrugged. "I haven't had much appetite. I'm still . . . sad that I didn't get my happy ending."

"Give it a little more time. You'll have a happy beginning. It's time for some self-care." She reached across my desk, picked up the phone and called Mindy, getting the name and number of a massage therapist, whom she called next. "You have an appointment at four this afternoon. Here's her address." She handed me the information.

"I can't, I'm having dinner with the founder of the film school, and I've got a lot I should do before then." After months of meetings, we had decided to form a production company together to make independent films.

"You have plenty of time. Now, let's go to lunch." She hustled me out of the office, telling the receptionist not to expect me back this afternoon. "She'll call for her messages."

The elevator opened and we descended to Fifth Avenue. It was the kind of unexpectedly warm spring day that made everyone giddy with relief and anticipation. I shrugged off my coat and noticed that people were smiling. Nonna took my arm as we strolled south toward the returning sun.

"So, tell me how you *really* are," she demanded.

I had been so concerned about Derek's feelings and needs that I'd lost track of my own. But now when I asked myself how I was feeling, and paid attention, I could begin to feel my own emotions stirring and stretch-ing like an underused muscle returning to life. I did that now, and answered carefully as the impressions slowly rose to the surface of my awareness.

"With Derek gone, there are spaces in my life. That hole used to frighten me—it felt so huge I was lost in it. And I thought Derek was going to fill me. But now it's like . . . a portal, like an opening into a realm of possibilities that I'm just discovering. And it's as though I can hear music playing, like Pan piping, or the wind singing, through that hole in my heart. But parts of me *are* missing. How do I find something if I don't know what I'm looking for?"

"You already have what you're seeking. You don't need to pursue any-thing, you just need to realize what already is."

"You sound like a fortune cookie."

Nonna jabbed me in the ribs with her elbow, and as we laughed I real-ized that it had been a very long time since I had.

"You need to get back into your body. That's how you'll begin to find those missing parts." We'd arrived at our destination—One Fifth, a bistro on the corner of Fifth Avenue and Eighth Street, with decor and music that made me feel like I was in a film from the 1930s. "You also need to cele-brate your freedom." She studied the wine list. "How about a Nebbiolo?"

"Great."

"Good, as I recall they have a lovely Giacosa Barbaresco." Nonna ordered the wine as I alternately studied the indulgent menu and the dining room—all women.

"You need to reward your senses, immerse yourself in pleasures—good food, great wine, wonderful music. Enjoy the view from your apart-ment, dress in clothes that make you feel beautiful, start exercising again—and do your sensitivity training."

"And get massages." I smiled.

"Exactly. You have to remember what your body feels like. It's more than just a contraption to carry your brain around. *A la vita!*" Nonna toasted me and we touched glasses. "Remember the conversation we had about the wine . . ."

"Desiring me." I nodded and smiled, inhaled the wine and sipped slowly. It rolled over my tongue, warm and full of the earth's generosity. *The sacrament of Dionysus.* "I've felt so . . . dead for such a long time."

"When you're grieving, your senses shut down. Eat slowly. Savor it. Don't talk, just taste," Nonna instructed as the food arrived. We ate in silence for a few minutes and I realized how many meals I had wolfed down in a rush to move on to the next task. How much of my life I had wolfed down to move on to the next responsibility. "Right now, eating this wonderful food, how do you feel?"

"It's delicious . . . I feel happy."

"You're connected to your body and what it's experiencing through your senses. This culture isn't comfortable with sensuality as healthy, even necessary. Which is insane, since pleasure is one of the most powerful evolutionary forces, and the best reason for being here. The older I get, the more I realize that you shouldn't do anything you don't enjoy."

"Well, wouldn't that be a lovely way to live."

"Precisely. Denying the joys of life is an old part of the creed of salvation. Puritanism denounced spices as too sexually arousing! Denial of the feminine, denial of pleasure—they're joined at the hip."

"Well, I've been eating a lot of chocolate," I said, eyeing the dessert tray being wheeled to a neighboring table.

Nonna chuckled. "There's a theory that it's full of the same chemical that gives you that falling-in-love rush. The body knows what it wants. And so does your soul." She refilled our glasses. "It's been rising to the surface of your awareness for a long time now. The parts of yourself that you feel are missing are the feminine qualities that you've neglected. We all have masculine and feminine energies, and we each combine them in unique ways. To be whole you have to go to the opposite pole to master its gifts, but ultimately you have to come back to your center, to your truth, to be happy. For you to be centered, whole, requires the feminine."

"I think I don't trust it. It makes me uneasy—I'm afraid that giving in to that part of myself will make me less . . . competent. More vulnerable. That I'll be trapped back in some Stepford wife nineteen fifties nightmare."

Nonna nodded. "Women often don't value their own feminine qualities. And men certainly don't trust them—in themselves or women, though they're attracted to them. For thousands of years this culture has pounded home the message that the feminine is weak, incompetent, unreliable. The masculine is what's valued—self-discipline, logic, self-control, competition. The whole feminine way of being is suppressed and criticized. As long as you feel that part of you isn't worthwhile, is 'less than,' you can't embrace or honor it properly. You can't enjoy it—and you'll remain unfulfilled."

"I've never accepted that I can't be all the things that men are—and not just professionally, but psychologically. That I couldn't be strong, intelligent or logical, or unemotional. Hell, that's exactly what my mother was, and those are the qualities I've developed. And you're right, I have mistrusted the feminine aspects that our culture doesn't respect. But you have to play by the rules if you want to succeed—you *have* to be in masculine mode." I thought about the work waiting for me back at my office as I sat enjoying my lunch.

"It's not enough for you to play by men's rules in a man's game. The rules of the game, and the game itself, have to change. But nothing will change if *you* don't change."

"I thought I had—by finding the Goddess and the empowerment She gave me. But there's more to that power, isn't there?" I felt the tightness in my chest ease.

"Being feminine and sexy *is* powerful." Nonna tapped my glass with hers. "You need to embrace your capacity for joy and sensuality. They're sources of power, not weakness."

"But women who are feminine, especially in the work world, are always accused of using their 'feminine wiles.'" I thought about the endless cracks I'd heard about successful women, suspicions even I'd harbored. "The more attractive they are, the more overtly sexual, the more they're accused of using it to get where they are."

"All those power suit disguises of yours." Nonna stared at me over the top of her glasses. "Feminine attractiveness is frequently viewed with suspicion. But the power of attraction is a crucial ingredient of the feminine mystique, to borrow the term back from Betty Friedan. And attraction isn't just physical—it's much more complex and magnificent," Nonna continued, refilling our glasses, an indulgence I would never permit myself but for the afternoon abduction. "There's a treasure cave full of feminine attractions—sensuality, love, spontaneity, elation, radiance, a spirit of cooperation, the desire to heal and nurture, the ability to be receptive, and all the ways that creativity expresses itself."

"Heal yourself and you begin to heal the world? Return the lost feminine parts of my self to myself and I return them to the world?"

"Precisely, Grasshopper," Nonna quipped. We laughed.

"That's *Ms.* Grasshopper to you. Pretty tough to hop around in high heels."

"Remember Ginger Rogers—she did everything Fred Astaire did, but backwards and in heels. But you know it isn't about high heels, or lipstick, or anything external. It *is* about beauty—how you choose to create and present it is up to you. Look at her," Nonna nodded to a woman sitting at a table across the room from us. She was in her late forties or early fifties, completely stunning and utterly sexy. "You can buy fashion, but style you have to own. And the older you get the more you realize that fashion and a sense of style are about expressing yourself. It should be creative and empowering and fun. It can also be a lovely way for fantasy and reality to merge."

"Look at you," I said, reaching over to Nonna's vintage Chanel jacket. "It's so soft."

Nonna smiled. "Listen, a lot of men have lost touch with their sense of masculinity; it's hard for them now. They're uncertain about what's wanted and expected from them. And women have lost touch with their bodies. The feminine is very physical, very sensual. It's full of life force and passion—it's very *alive*. But so many women hate their bodies; they starve them, or overexercise them into submission. And how many young girls cut and mutilate themselves? Or they're bulimic or anorexic."

"I guess that was part of my problem with sex—that feeling that I wasn't completely in my body. I guess I really wasn't." I looked around at all the salads being consumed and noticed the dessert tray being wheeled away without having been indulged in. These elegant women were groomed, manicured and dipped in plastic. When was the last time they'd sweated and moaned and smeared their makeup making wild, passionate love? When was the last time I had?

"The relationship you have to your body *is* your relationship to the feminine. The feminine is not about abstract ideas; it's about the immediate, physical realities of life. Sex, blood, babies, getting old, crying, loving."

"I know a lot about crying. But I'm still having trouble with the idea that being receptive isn't a step back."

"You're making the same mistake the culture's made—confusing receptive with passive, and it's anything but." Nonna gave me a reproachful smile. "Try this." Nonna lifted her fork to me.

"Good."

She smiled and nodded. "So just now, when you accepted that delicious food I shared with you—were you passive?"

I shook my head.

"But you *were* receptive—you accepted it, tasted it, enjoyed it."

"But you initiated the action."

"Ah, but I acted because I wanted to give you pleasure. The receptive is a phenomenal power—it attracts, generates, it sets the whole dance in motion. In the Hindu tradition, divinity is symbolized by a yoni, surrounding a lingam. The yoni draws the lingam in just as much as the lingam thrusts. You need both. Receptive energy is magnetic. That is how it initiates—it draws what it desires to itself. It's what you do when you draw down deity, whether you're male or female."

Her words were like klieg lights in a dark cave. "You're right! I've always thought of receptive as inactive, like an acceptance of nonexistence, taking someone else's orders, being unable to take the initiative. But it's not, is it."

"The Goddess, Shakti, animates the energy of the God, Shiva, who's inert until she invigorates and empowers him. And she does it with sexuality, attraction, pleasure. The Goddess is the erotic provoker, and without her the God can't function and the world wouldn't exist."

"You're describing a . . . pulling in, instead of pushing out of energy," I said very slowly, the veil on some of my sexual confusion beginning to lift. "I was always doing, or worrying about doing, when we had sex. Pushing. I don't think I even knew how, *know* how to pull towards me."

"It's like breathing, *mia figlia*. Do it right now, consciously—inhale."

I did. It was simple, natural and I immediately felt the power to draw in.

"When a couple makes love, each of them is being active *and* receptive. How can you experience the gift of love unless you are open and receptive? You wanted a man who was receptive to your energy, your desire and needs, who was sensual."

I nodded.

"*And* you wanted a man who was strong and dynamic, whose presence could penetrate and fill you and give you what you desired. So for this he needed to be, and you need to be, *both* active and receptive. You see?"

I nodded again. I was starting to see into the darkest corners of that cave I'd been trapped in.

"Magnetism. That flow of energy back and forth between partners is critical to sacred sex, sex magic and pleasure. You must have the polarity or the energy won't move."

"It reminds me of the magnetic dogs I had as a child—one black, one white." I laughed at the memory. "If I put them nose to nose they'd repel each other, but if I put them nose to end they stuck."

"How the energy moves is up to you and your partner. It doesn't matter. But you need that tug and thrust."

I sat, finishing my wine, remembering how naturally the energy had flowed between us at the beginning. "I was all thrust and no tug, and so was he. It must have been just as hard for Derek as it was for me." I was starting to understand how it had gone awry.

"When you reject your own feminine aspects, it can be very difficult to enjoy the body's sensual experiences, especially sex. You can't let go and feel. You're locked in that armor and you can't surrender."

"I wanted a man who was stronger than I was so I could be soft. The ravishment fantasies. But after a while, they didn't work."

"Of course. It's not enough for your masculine to be overwhelmed by a greater masculinity. You needed to be balanced by your own feminine energies. But you didn't feel safe to open all the way into your uninhibited feminine. A man has to provide his partner with the masculine energy she needs so that she can share her feminine gifts."

"I suppose he could say it the other way around about me. It wasn't anybody's fault. I think we loved each other the best we could."

Nonna nodded. "You can only do your best. You were part of each other's journey to become whole. So, you're going to learn how to trust and value and relax into your full female-ness. You're going to find those lost parts of yourself. Now, I think we should get the chocolate mousse *and* the profiteroles, and share them. What do you say?"

"Perfect—all of it!"

"*You cut your hair!* And did you perm it?" Gillian spun me in a quick circle. "I love it!"

"No, I crimp it in my hands and use this great stuff that brings out the natural wave." I looked at my reflection in her Venetian foyer mirror. We were meeting at her very Sutton Place apartment for a long overdue girls' night out. "I needed a change. And Nonna said I needed to track down my feminine alter ego."

"Just promise me you aren't going to shoot her when you find her." I followed her into the kitchen and she pulled out a bottle of Veuve Clicquot. "Let's celebrate your divorce."

I laughed. "Between you and Nonna, I'm actually starting to have fun." I had begun to explore and even enjoy the feminine energies that I had neglected, and in the process I discovered that to cast a love spell for true love, I needed to awaken not only my consciousness but also my body. Gradually, subtly, I felt myself reclaiming the feminine power that I'd neglected—without relinquishing any of my hard-won strengths. "I'm creating little rituals—I turn the music up loud at least once a day and dance around the apartment in my underwear, and sometimes I dance naked in front of my mirror."

"Excellent!" She handed me a flute of champagne and we toasted. "To the new you. But there's got to be more."

I grinned. "Lots more. I'm getting very creative in figuring out what feels good and makes me happy. I buy myself flowers every week. I get a massage every few weeks. I even get my nails done! The best one is the simplest and I do it every day, sometimes a couple of times a day. Tantrists called it a micro-practice. It's so simple and it gets me right into my body—I pay really close attention to the pleasure that some daily experience gives me, like eating an orange, or feeling the sun, or watching a bird fly. Or drinking this champagne."

"I get that one. I need to do my makeup." We headed into the bedroom and I curled up in her rose silk boudoir chair.

"It's incredible how numinous the world gets when you start paying attention, even here in the city. Maybe especially here."

Gillian viewed herself in her dressing table mirror, and tapped a postcard of Notre Dame stuck into its frame. "Paris is a great city for that kind of thing."

"It makes so much sense—this is a spiritual practice that helps us experience the presence of the Sacred in the world, in ourselves. You don't always have to cast a circle or invoke a deity to experience it. I'm getting a major hit every day off the littlest things."

"A Zen Witch."

I laughed. "And tantric. Speaking of which, something you'll really approve of, I've bought some new clothes and some very sexy lingerie, and I shortened the skirts I already owned."

"Well, I think you look great. And I love those heels! Whole new look, huh?"

"Still me, but more so." I smiled. "But let me tell you, returning to your body in three-inch heels is a real challenge." I thought about Ginger Rogers and studied Gillian's profile. "So, you look particularly glowing. I'll have what you're having." Gillian gestured toward the champagne bottle. As we laughed, a question popped into my head. "Gilly, did you ever use that love potion Nonna gave us?"

She shook her head. "Not after Mr. *Je T'aime*. I've thought about it, but there's really only one guy I want."

I raised an eyebrow. "Who is it?"

"Chris."

"Chris?" My voice went up an octave.

Gillian nodded, smiling. "I realized I really do love him. And after all the time apart he's finally realized he loves me."

"So that's why you look so radiant! As long as he makes you happy."

"I am happy. But I realized I have to work at it. I had to take a good hard look at myself, and the truth is I always expected to have everything my own way. So now I'm really trying to meet him halfway. I'm listening, I'm compromising, I'm doing stuff his way."

I gave her a look.

"*Some* stuff. No beer on the couch with football on Sundays. But it's working. *We're* working."

"Oh, Gilly, I'm so happy for you."

She nodded. "What about you? Are you going to put that new wardrobe to use and start dating again?"

I walked to the window, stared at the rush hour traffic on the 59th Street Bridge. "Not yet." I paused, suddenly afraid that I might not have cried all my tears. "I'm just not ready to risk it. I'm afraid to believe in dreams of love—what if I make the wrong choice again?" I heard my voice catch.

"Well, it's natural to be afraid after a divorce. But you can't live without love." Gillian turned to face me and I couldn't help but smile—one eye was made up, the other untouched. "Love isn't about playing it safe. Thinking you can control it, that you have to protect yourself is not the way. You can't have love without taking a risk. The heart's the strongest muscle in your body. And you're a different person now. When the time is right, you'll love a different man in a very different way. You'll see."

"I don't need it right now. I don't know how long it's going to take, but I need the rest of me first. I think it's true—you can't find your soul mate till you have your soul."

Gillian stood up and drew me into a hug. "You'll find what you've lost, and then you'll find each other."

"I'm sick and tired of crying. And so's my soggy teddy bear." I took a deep breath. "And I won't feel sorry for myself anymore."

"It's okay to cry if you still need to. It comes with the friendship. And that feminine part you're looking for." She drew back and planted a kiss on my cheek. "You're going to be just fine."

Looking into her reassuring eyes, I knew that a friend was the best mirror I could have.

The phone was ringing and so was my head. I groaned as I rolled over and reached for the telephone. "Hello?"

"Hi, Dale's on the line," a perky female voice chirped in my ear. I looked at the clock—it was 12:30, in the afternoon. I'd been out dancing till 6 A.M., and my much-celebrated, pleasure-indulging feminine self wanted to go back to sleep.

"Hi. I've got great news." Dale sounded happy. "*New Year's Day* was just selected for competition in the Venice Film Festival."

"Oh my Goddess, that's fantastic!" I bolted out of bed, pulling the phone with me. "Congratulations!" I tried not to shout.

"It gets better—it's the only American film in the competition. You should come; it's going to be marvelous. Actually, it would be great if you came because I'm thinking I'll shoot another film while I'm there and you could help."

My head was spinning and it wasn't from last night's fun. The only thing better than having a film in the Venice Film Festival was shooting a film in Venice. "Are you kidding? I'm there!"

"Oh, and before I forget, we're screening at the Toronto Film Festival after that. That's a great festival—it's so fan friendly. Okay, I've gotta run. I'll put you on with Deborah; she'll give the details. Let's talk next week. *Ciao.*"

Magic! Amazing, breathtaking, heart-stopping magic. And it was just starting.

Just minutes outside of Milan, the Rapido sped through fields of high, tassel-topped corn, in the midst of which stood old, ochre-colored stone and stucco houses with terra-cotta roofs. My red-eye flight from New York had landed precisely at noon, just a few hours ago, and now I was on the fast train to Florence. From there, somehow, I would get to the villa in Fiesole, an Etruscan town in the hills above Florence where I would spend a week enjoying myself and Italy before going to Venice for the festival.

The lack of sleep, the heat, minimal language skills, and heavy bags shredded my inviolable shield. It was like being a child again—I had to trust people, communicating with feelings and facial expressions, and mostly with smiles, which had been obligingly acknowledged. Exhausted, I settled back into the blue velvet seat of my air-conditioned first-class compartment.

It was the middle of the afternoon but the sun was still high. Cornfields alternated with vines rich with grapes hanging full and dark. *Corn and grapes.* I could hear the chant playing in my overtired brain: *Corn and grain, corn and grain, all that falls shall rise again.* They rose full of the earth's life, side by side. There was gentleness in the bargain between land and man, a deal still honored that had been made when Rome ruled the world. It was a pact of love. *He lives in the earth.*

I began to cry. But this time they were tears of joy. We flew past a field of sunflowers bending earthward, heavy with seeds.

I sat on the terrace of the magnificent Pensione Treviste. It was precisely six o'clock. I knew because church bells were ringing, first to the right, then deeper and more melancholy from lower in the valley, echoing up from the city of Florence. An evening haze surrounded the still hot sun, softening the view of the city below and the ancient, layered hills beyond. The famous Duomo, the Cathedral of Santa Maria del Fiore and the crowning glory of Florence, was a deeper, rounded gray cone dominating the landscape and the cypresses stood sharp and dark green, piercing the foreground.

Hovering in the liminal space between waking and sleep, I thought of foregoing dinner for bed, but I caught myself. *Look where you are. Look as if you had died and been given this one day, with all its normal problems, to return and enjoy*. It was a trick I'd devised to pull myself out of depression when love ended with Derek. And it worked, immediately shifting my perspective to one charged with gratitude and the presence of grace.

I inhaled slowly, absorbing the details with all my senses—the birds singing, a rooster crowing, the curtains of red and purple bougainvillea, the golden mustard walls glowing in the descending light, the soft fur of the villa's dog, Luna, who had already adopted me. *Eat well and then sleep soundly*.

The next day I explored the city's museums, spending hours with Botticelli's *Birth of Venus* and the famous, supine Hermaphrodite statue. And more hours in gardens, busy streets, outside markets, and elegant shops, succumbing to their erotic wisdom of daily pleasures. I bought presents for my body and my stirring feminine soul—a suit with curves and cleavage in the color of the red-brown earth of Tuscany, high heels, a finely woven shawl. Each day my pace slowed a bit more. I abandoned my guidebooks, wandering through the city of alchemist and priest Marsilio Ficino, who translated Plato, Socrates's speech in the *Symposium*, and the magical work attributed to Hermes Trismegistus, and who knew that we experience communion with God through loving communion with another person. I roamed the streets where Charles Godfrey Leland, the American folklorist, had recorded the spells and incantations of ancient Etruscans, and the tales of Aradia told to him by the mysterious Strega Madgdelena.

I sat in cafés with espresso and *aperitivo* and saw how men, very emotional men, became more masculine around women. And how women, very strong women, also became more feminine around men. In the ardent

Italian light, I rested in the lap of the Goddess, and so I became softer, sensitized and still.

In the evenings, I strolled out to the villa's gardens or stood on the terrace surrounded by romantic young men who ached with love and urgency, and I felt the tenacious longing return. I closed my eyes. *There is time yet; I am not impatient.* Except when the young man leaned forward so persistently into his shy companion, sighing into her, kissing her mouth slowly, sweetly, insistently, again and again.

I exhaled into the seductive, evening breeze: *Dionysus. Because you are nowhere you are everywhere, always watching me. But when will you appear?* As Firenze disappeared beneath the dark blue curtains of dusk, I felt his presence all around me. I heard him in the excited laughter of the couple in the wet grass below the terrace, the dogs that began to howl, smelled him in the damp earth that intoxicated me, felt him in the caress of the breeze as I leaned from my window in the moonlight. *But it's your caress I need, your kisses, your hands. I have no breath without your breath against my skin, no heartbeat without your heart next to mine.*

I returned to my room, undressed and climbed between the cool sheets. I turned out the light, wondering if he would ever come to me. I lay in the darkness—there was no daemon lover to press me into the soft mattress, to open, to capture and to free me.

I awoke to the morning bells. It was time for the other magic I had come for. I caught the number seven bus into the center of Fiesole, had lunch in the piazza and then went to the Roman theater and the ancient temple site.

I was alone, with stone everywhere, broken columns lying on their sides, marble floors crumbled by weeds, remnants of arches, of walls and carvings, of laughter and tears, invocations, prayers and offerings. And there was energy. I could already feel it humming through me.

I closed my eyes and began to ground and center. An unfamiliar current—slow, chthonic, inebriating—pulsed through me, but rather than shooting up my spine as the energy usually did, it undulated along my thighs and pooled between my legs, making me tremble with sudden need. I opened my eyes and tried to catch my breath. I sat on the edge of a column fragment, the fervency swelling, filling me.

I took a deep breath, reached into my purse and pulled out my bundle of blue corn. My hands were shaking as I opened it. I walked the perimeter, slowly, dropping the kernels in each of the four directions. The air grew heavy and close around me. As I completed the circle, I realized the birds were silent, the dogs didn't bark, and the noises from the street had vanished. I stood in the center of the ancient space feeling the invocation rising slowly to my lips that whispered into the realm of holy mysteries:

"Ariadne, Mistress of the Labyrinth, Potent One, guide me to the center of the labyrinth where ecstasy waits. Dionysus, son of Zeus, midwived by fire, delivered by lightning's blast, abandoned I call to you. Where will you stand, a god incognito, disguised as a man? Show yourself to me, come to me, I wait for you at the center of the labyrinth."

I watched the air shimmer and the stones around me throb. And then I made my last, small request, holding my breath and closing my eyes like a child wishing on a star. "There are two men—an actor and a director, their work is full of magic, and I would like to meet them, either of them, in Venice. Please." I exhaled and made my final offering—the wine I had brought in a small water bottle poured between the stones beneath my feet. I watched it seep into the hard ground.

The vaporetto bounced low over the gray waves, rocking steadily through a thick fog. But when the boat approached the dock, the misty cloak was suddenly drawn back. My breath caught—Venice! Piazza San Marco, the manifested vision of the *Serenìssima,* the great seafaring republic, stretched before me glistening in the soft rain. I had entered not just a city, but a dream.

The small crowd of commuting Venetians surged forward and I was caught in their current, concerned about slipping on the wet deck as I dragged my suitcases behind me. I knew it was the wrong stop for my hotel, but the first time I entered Venice it had to be here.

"La Fenice et Des Artistes," I said to a grumpy, rain-soaked porter. He seized my bags and rushed off. I raced to keep up, wading through water that ran in streams through the streets, hoping not to lose my guide through the crowded labyrinth.

My room was a tiny jewel box with walls, drapes and bedspread of golden silk in what had once been a doge's private residence. Every morning, I pushed open the black shutters and leaned into the narrow alley between the hotel and the famous theater, La Fenice. The sun was shining and the air was filled with the sounds of hammers and men shouting to each other as they built sets, or the music of the orchestra rehearsing. I was ready to begin my daily, morning ritual—after cappuccino and brioche at one of the cafés, I wandered through Venice.

Venezia is a city of art and I indulged at the museums, galleries and churches. I climbed the *Sansovino*, "stairway of gold," in the Palace of the Doges, seeking the erotic in the midst of the religious and finding my daemon in Veronese's *Rape of Europa* and Tintoretto's *Bacchus and Ariadne*, considered his supreme achievement. I went up in the *Campanile*, all of Venice spread below me, with my hands over my ears as the enormous, deafening bells called out the hour. And I pushed my way along the Rialto Bridge to a view of the Grand Canal as the vivid, ages-old regatta called the entire city to celebration.

I put away my map. I wanted to get lost, guided only by the serpentine waterways that glistened in the sunlight and twisted black in the shadows. I wanted to find the city behind the glorious facade that attracted the tourists, and gradually I began to recognize two labyrinths—one of water, one of earth. Venice wore two faces, two realities merged as one—islands and sea, natives and tourists, darkness and light, violence and voluptuousness, dreams and daily life, pragmatism and art, life and death. And in all the tourist shops and the studios of artisans there were masks—reminders that we chose which was illusion and which reality.

Every evening, as I returned to my hotel, the city removed its mask of golden light. Ghosts vanished around the corner just a few steps ahead and shadows, living and other, escorted me home. At first I was afraid, but then the nightly sense of being followed became familiar and was accompanied by an equal sense of safety.

I had thought that my daemon would take physical form, dark and handsome, romantic and compelling. But I didn't look for him in the easy eyes of men who watched and prowled and would pounce with the slightest encouragement. Instead, I felt myself surrounded by his presence, and it grew more pressing, more Byronic every day. The sensuality had diffused through my soul and my body. I had fallen in love and the city was my lover.

The captain, in his shiny-buttoned blazer, took my hand to help me step aboard the motor launch. Every afternoon, I used the elegant motorboat of Dale's hotel to travel to the Lido, the small, lush island near Venice where the film festival was held. It was a long, narrow isle, filled with huge, elegant old hotels still frequented by the sun-chasing jet set who enjoyed bathing in the Adriatic. Now it was an Arcadia of film, populated with leading directors and stars from all over the world, heirs to the rites of Dionysus. This was where Dale was staying, where we were doing much of our filming using the rich, natural light and where, whenever possible, I went to screenings of our competition.

Crossing the gamboling green water that changed color every day, I thumbed through the heavy festival catalogue, excited to see my title *Produttore Associato* and laughing that my name was misspelled. I stepped off the launch at the back of Dale's hotel and strolled along the palm- and bougainvillea-lined path, a few steps behind the animated conversation of an infamous Italian director and a famous actress. I inhaled the balmy air—I wanted the magic of Fiesole to cross my paths with the notorious actor or the extraordinary director. But within minutes I was hard and happily at work.

We set up for a scene on the wide and sun-washed veranda of Dale's hotel. I was amazed at how cooperative the hotel and its guests were being. But the magic of movies charmed everyone within range of the camera, no matter which side you were on. A German documentary crew was interviewing Dale while he was simultaneously shooting his film—shooting them shooting him.

It was like the infinite reflections created when mirrors are placed opposite each other. I watched with amusement as the cameras rolled, wondering which was more real—the documentary, Dale's film, Dale in front of the cameras or those of us who sat behind them? Or perhaps, in the end, what the viewers chose to see and somehow created themselves by their interpretations?

"The theme of the film we're shooting now?" Dale repeated the interviewer's question. "The influence of movies on our expectations of love and romance. And the struggle we all have to know if love is real or imaginary. I'm also interested in whether the realities of movies are more real than life." I smiled, thinking of the scene he had filmed earlier in the day where we'd all sat around a huge table having lunch, with Dale again being interviewed and talking about the heightened sense of life the person being filmed experiences in front of a camera.

The interview ended and Dale continued shooting a dialogue between himself and his striking costar. She played a French journalist who has fallen in love with Dale's character, Dean, the man Dale appears to be in his films. The dialogue would be placed over intercut images of the two of them, falling in love, on the canals of Venice, Italy, and Venice, California, where the second part of the film was to be shot.

"The Heisenberg principle is very complicated," Jeanne said as their boat emerged from under a Venetian bridge.

"Who's Heisenberg?" Dean asked.

"Heisenberg says that one particle can be in two places at the same time," she replied. She leaned into him, the Italian sky as gray as the waters of the canal.

"So you and I can be in two places at one time?" Dean responded.

"Yes," she replied as the two paddled a red canoe through a Californian Venetian canal.

"Venice, Italy, and Venice, California?"

"Probably," she replied as he kissed her, a Venetian palazzo in the background.

"Past and future," he mused happily.

"Mmmhmmm," Jeanne murmured, nestling against him as tourists watched them from the bridge.

"Movies and real life." He leaned forward and kissed her, the bright sun of California making the water shimmer as it rolled off the canoe paddle he lifted from the water.

"Why not?"

"It's all possible." He leaned over and kissed her softly as they passed beneath another Venetian bridge.

Filming was occupying a lot of my time, and I was having difficulty getting to the films in competition, let alone any of the rest. But Dale was filming in Venice today, and I was free to enjoy the festival. I headed to the Palazzo del Cinema, waving my exhibitor's pass to gain entrance and escape the swarming crowd.

Cameras flashed and rolled as I stood at the top of the wide, curving staircase looking down into the clamorous, overcrowded lobby. The paparazzi were frantic as a sandy-haired, elfishly handsome actor—the current possessor of the T-shirted mantle of James Dean—stopped and allowed them the rewards of their feeding frenzy. They called his name and he stood ignoring and indulging them in a staccato of exploding lights. Moody and sensitive, tough and libidinous, he was a star, the star I had summoned in Fiesole.

I watched, stunned by his proximity, and then, suddenly, he looked up. His dark eyes locked on mine and he smiled. The lights flaring around him erupted inside me and a jolt of lust from that intense gaze struck me. Desire rushed through me, but within the pulsing carnality I felt a wound so powerful that its trajectory was swiftly carrying him beyond stardom to self-destruction. The suffering and need for love was voracious—a magnetism that tugged erotically, drawing me in.

A year ago the power of that look, and the seduction of subterranean struggle, would have made me wild for more and launched me into action. I stood straight, and without trembling, let the Plutonian fire course through me and fade. I smiled back, then turned away.

My heart was pounding with excitement. *New Year's Day* was about to be screened at the Palazzo del Cinema. Dale was channeling his nervous energy into telling us the order in which he wanted to enter the Grand Salon. A young man with a clipboard asked us in nervous and broken English to wait until the Salon was full.

It was mid-afternoon and so the evening gown I had bought for our screening hung in my closet in Venice. It was hand-crocheted of terra-cotta silk yarn, with a silk underslip of celadon green—the colors of Italy. Each dress was unique and had been named by the New York designer Lo. This one was called *A Radiant Angel. ARadia.* I knew it was mine the moment it slid down over my naked body. Instead, I was wearing the suit I had bought in Florence.

"You look stunning," Dale commented as we waited to enter. I felt stunning; I was also experiencing every detail and sensation so intensely it felt like synesthesia—an altered state of consciousness in which all of the senses seemed to merge. Music has colors and words have feelings, tastes have sounds and touch has them all. There were movie pros for whom this would be just another screening, but I knew this might be the one and only time for me, and I would always remember it.

The door opened, and led by Dale, the small group of actors and I walked out onto the elevated platform at the back of the cavernous auditorium. The audience turned to watch our entrance and a smattering of applause greeted us. Dale waved, the actors waved, and then we sank into our deep, gold velvet seats. The lights dimmed, the screen flickered and then blossomed with energy, light, music, emotion and intention—all the elements of magic.

Il Giorno de Capodanno. New Year's Day. It was fascinating to watch the audience watching the film, missing much of the humor that was lost in translation. They were viewing a serious film. The lights came up and they jumped to their feet, applauding furiously, reacting to a very different movie. *What was real and what wasn't?* It didn't matter—it was all a pleasure.

"*There's a birthday party* for an old friend of mine, a British film critic. If you're free, why don't you join me?" Wilhelm, our European distributor, asked. It was a friendly, not romantic, invitation and I accepted immediately. We'd finished shooting and the last few days of the festival were unburdened by responsibilities. But the work had held its own rewards, for I had managed to be efficient and hardworking without overwhelming the sensuality that Italy was nourishing in me.

I took the radiant angel dress from the closet—I was saving it for the final night's presentations and party. *Wear it tonight*. I held its heavy silken weight in my hands. The dress was Italy; it was Aradia and there were only a few nights left. *Tonight*. I laid it out on the bedspread, took a long, hot bath in the deep marble tub, ate yesterday's sweet fig and slipped on the dress. *Who is that woman in the mirror?* The armor had fallen away.

I set out in the soft, warm, golden-hued light of sunset, the ethereal glow of the magic hour when scenes of romance or enchantment are filmed. Walking was bliss and I felt every swaying step as the gown flowed between my legs and behind me like woven water. Heads turned, people smiled, men stared and, as I crossed one of the four hundred bridges, a gondolier stopped his sleek black craft and sang to me. He finished with a flourish and blew me a kiss. I caught it, laughing, wishing for one of Dale's cameras to hold the moment like a flower in amber.

As I'd been warned, Vino Vino, the wine bar where we were meeting was already "jammed like a *vaporetto* in rush hour." I spotted Wilhelm, casual in a sports coat without a tie, and we walked to the restaurant.

"You look beautiful. Screening later?" he asked.

"Just felt like it." I smiled as we wove through the crowd. A small sign with the name *Al Graspo de Ua* and a bunch of grapes hung discreetly outside the wooden door. We stepped down into the very local, fragrant and laughter-filled dining room. The party was already under way, two seats at the end of the table waiting for us. My wineglass was immediately filled, and my plate moments later from the huge platters of local cuisine—sarde in saor, spezzatino, baccala and one of my favorites, a creamy, rich polenta. Despite the haze of accumulating cigarette smoke, I sat content, my senses saturated with enjoyment, chatting quietly with Wilhelm to my left and a British screenwriter to my right. People began moving around the table, switching seats, and Wilhelm headed to the opposite end.

"That's a beautiful dress. Do you have a screening tonight?" The man sitting across the table turned to me with a smile that lit up a boyish but well-lined face. He could have been Harrison Ford's brother. Soft brown hair fell across his forehead, and full eyebrows crowned warm, intelligent brown eyes.

"Thank you. No." I smiled. "It's just a magical dress and it was tired of hanging in my closet. It wanted to see Venice."

"I've never heard of a dress having magic," he responded affably.

"I think everything has magic—it's really just the way you view the world. But the word *magic* unnerves people. It threatens their sense of reality." I found myself wandering into the realm I most loved, but rarely discussed, especially with strangers.

He nodded, refilling my glass with red wine. "Yes, there's an agreed-upon idea of reality. And people can get very angry at any challenge to what they believe is real." He was soft-spoken, with a steady presence that put me immediately at ease.

"That's one of the things I'm most fascinated by—what's real but unseen. Or unacknowledged. Like dreams, and synchronicities, and all the manifestations that arise from the unconscious. What fascinates me is the resident force of . . . well, divinity that percolates up, spontaneously." Perhaps because he was a stranger I felt myself opening up.

He nodded. "It's fascinating when the forces begin to come together. I did a lot of reading years ago and I began to see how . . . clues begin to form a pattern." He was leaning forward, still speaking softly, gently. He was clearly engaged, and had a quality of observation and interest that almost seemed to pull responses from me. He was fully active in the conversation, very male, but fully receptive in his responses to me, very female.

"Yes, figuring out the patterns is fascinating, and when we understand them, there's all this . . . energy that gets liberated. Life force, creativity. Eroticism." I felt myself blush as the word left my lips and I quickly lifted my glass to hide the sudden flush. "Those other ways of seeing, it's one of my . . . passions. Cultivating intuition, deciphering those clues. Experiencing the . . . other realms of being."

"Art does that." He smiled and refilled our glasses. "It induces a kind of awakened dreaming that bypasses the intellect. And then the rational mind tries to decode the experience, analyze the clues, find the pattern."

This was the most enjoyable, satisfying conversation I'd had during the entire festival, and much longer. "I love the way movies can have that effect." I was thinking about my daemon and the form he first used to reach me.

"Yes, cinema can completely disarm the guardians of logic, tap into the emotions, but even more it gets into the unconscious and frees things up. Are you an actress?" he suddenly asked.

I was startled that the question could feel like a compliment. I shook my head, grinning. "Other side of the camera. I was the associate producer—the line producer—of a film that's in competition. *New Year's Day*."

"Really!" He looked more than surprised; he looked pleased.

I explained how we shot without a script, relying on reality. "And then Dale finds the patterns as he edits. There's always a question about what's real and what's not, what we agree upon and what we don't, and love is almost always at the heart of it all. The chance that's taken, or lost."

"Yes, you've got to remain open to chance, live it rather than make a movie. The film itself becomes a way of moving between realms. So much of the work is intuitive; too much analysis just inhibits creativity. I think a sense of wonder is really what I try to evoke. How you do it is really step-by-step. Practice the craft." I smiled to myself at his phrase. "Tell the story," he finished.

He was obviously in the film business, and I was just about to ask what he did when I heard my name being called by a familiar voice. Dale had arrived and I was unwillingly pulled away from our conversation. Within minutes the party began to break up and Dale whispered in my ear, "I see you were talking to Michael Baird."

Stunned and thrilled, I stared at the man I had just been talking with—the director I'd wanted to meet! I'd never seen a photograph of him, and so I'd had no idea what he looked like. Magic flooded into the room, into me; or maybe now, with this simple revelation, I was simply seeing it.

Our party emptied into the darkened street, the sound of the Grand Canal's rhythmic lapping behind us and the smell of the sea in the air. I stood bathed in a soft amber light that illuminated the little sign, finally realizing the restaurant was called Bunch of Grapes—the symbol of Dionysus!

"Good night," Michael said warmly, extending his hand.

I reached out, felt the electricity as skin met skin. "It was a real pleasure talking with you," I replied. We stood, hands clasped, and I longed to tell him the story of the magical pattern he was part of, but he was tugged away by the group.

"Yes, it was great talking with you. Enjoy the rest of the festival." He squeezed my hand and released it. "Good night."

"*Buona notte.*" I watched him walk across the cobblestones and disappear around the corner. "And *sogni d'oro*. Sweet dreams," I murmured softly. I wanted more. I wanted everything. *It wasn't enough.*

Like the city itself, magic often wears masks. And where better to encounter Dionysus than disguised within the labyrinth of dark water and ancient stone. I plunged into that labyrinth, walking swiftly, feeling the gossamer silk shawl tossed around my shoulders lift and flutter like wings. After three weeks of lost wandering, I knew exactly where I was.

It was more than enough.

The last night of the festival, the night when *il Leone D'Oro*, the Golden Lion, was presented at a televised banquet, was ending. We hadn't won, but I wasn't disappointed. I was happier than I'd ever been. I lifted the hem of the *Radiant Angel* as the captain helped me off the launch at the Piazza San Marco. As my foot touched land, as if on cue, the bell of the clock tower began to strike. I counted to twelve as I walked passed the Doge's Palace. It was midnight, the Witching hour. And as the last strike resounded through the Piazza, the band at the Florian Caffé began to play "It Had to Be You."

I left Venice early the next morning for Toronto with all but a piece of my heart that remained in Italy. It was the body's gift of the senses and the power of pleasure that had made that heart beat again. And it had grown larger around the hole. A heart of fire can't beat unless it lives within a body afire. Eros had reentered my life and, escorted by my daemon, I had found my lost feminine. Desire was once again burning within me.

14

The Great Rite

Keep Ithaka always in your mind/Arriving there is what you're destined for./
But don't hurry the journey at all. /
Better if it lasts for years, so you're old by the time you reach the island, wealthy
with all you've gained on the way, not expecting Ithaka to make you rich./
Ithaka gave you the marvelous journey. / Without her you wouldn't have set out./
She has nothing left to give you now.

—C. P. CAVAFY

"*Bellissimo!*" Nonna tossed the Armani shawl around her shoulders. The silk draped like a cascade of moonlight. "You shouldn't have been so extravagant—but I love it!" She leaned down and gave me a lavender-scented hug. "Now, tell me all about Italy." She filled my plate with lobster salad and baby greens.

It was Indian Summer and we were seated in her backyard, at a wrought iron dining table within a circular hedge of green boxwood. I pulled the cork from a bottle of Prosecco and filled our glasses. An occasional soft breeze created layers of afternoon music—wind chimes, leaves rustling and songbirds that rode the currents into the apple trees guarding the entrance to the outdoor dining room.

Nonna's garden was bursting with color—yellow coreopsis with deep maroon centers, pale hydrangea, burgundy mums, and sedum that looked like scarlet broccoli. Orange monarch and yellow tiger butterflies fluttered around a huge purple buddleia bush, and a thatch of white clematis provided a roof for the lattice-enclosed outdoor shower. And all the herbs were vigorous. While Nonna prepared lunch, I had cut a bouquet that now sat in a green ceramic pitcher in the center of the table.

I rubbed a sprig of rosemary between my fingers, releasing the deep perfume. Since returning from Italy, I was paying careful attention to being in my body, savoring the daily joys my senses brought me. It was as simple as remembering and experiencing how every day began by eating something that had come out of the earth, regardless of what grand goals I intended or spiritual epiphanies I encountered. I was grounded and grateful, and as we ate lunch, I told Nonna my stories of Italy's magic.

"It's very hard to begin again, but it was harvest time over there, and it reminded me we can *always* start over. An end is always followed by a beginning, a rebirth."

"If you have the courage to dream, you have the courage to find new dreams." Nonna smiled and refilled my plate with salad. "So, when you were in Fiesole you asked your daemon to appear, and he did. Twice. What does it mean to you?"

"It was incredible." I watched the afternoon sun illuminate the wine in my glass, swirling light and liquid into a golden elixir. "A long time ago, you told me that my daemon would shape-shift, especially as I changed."

"The mirror changes as what it reflects changes. So what did you see?"

"First, I saw what used to need healing—in myself—and then I saw what was healthy. Creativity and joy instead of suffering and pain. Working on the films, I began to feel like I was finally finding my purpose, who I *really* am, at least in terms of work. I don't know if I'll go on working in film, but I *know* I'm going to work creatively. I can *feel* it now because I'm finally living it."

The ancient restlessness rustled through me, and immediately the wind ruffled the trees around us. "But it's not enough. I want love in my life— passionate, intense, soul-shaking love. Is that asking too much?" I tried to laugh. "I was filled with love the whole time I was in Venice, and that was enough. But when the possibility of having that energy embodied by a man presented itself, even though I knew he wasn't the one, he brought my need to the surface." I hesitated, and then shared what I had realized as I'd watched Venice recede from the departing *vaporetto*. "I've come to think of my daemon as, well, my soul mate, and I can't imagine life without his being . . . human. Without being able to love him that way."

Nonna raised her eyebrows and put down her glass. "The greatest temptation, and maybe the greatest obstacle, in this journey is trying to find one's daemon in human form. It's just another form of projection—of externalizing what's meant to be accomplished inside."

"But he's always manifesting around me, in others, in human forms. When the energy is expressed *through* us, it's so hard to resist trying to find him. It's very hard to accept that he will never become . . . real."

"He *is* real. He's the guide to your soul. All those years ago, in law school, when you first opened your heart to the Universe, when you called out with all that hope and pain, you cast your love spell."

"When I wished on the star? Without knowing it?"

Nonna nodded. "People are always casting spells—every wish, every prayer, every dream, every goal—they just don't realize it. They've been doing it since they were children, wishing on a star, blowing out the candles on a birthday cake, breaking a wishbone, dropping pennies in wishing wells. When you cast that love spell years ago, you chose the path of love, the path of the Sacred Marriage." Nonna scattered breadcrumbs on the bricks for the birds. "The feminine and masculine parts of the self must be united and balanced for your soul to be fully realized. And it's your relationships that hold up a mirror showing you the wounded or unfinished parts of your soul that are missing, that need to be healed, discovered, transformed."

"But what does that have to do with the Sacred Marriage?" I wanted desperately to understand, but I couldn't keep a tinge of impatience from my voice.

"You can't find your soul's mate until you have your soul. Your soul isn't complete until the Sacred Marriage of the Goddess and God occurs—within you. The temple of that union is in all of us. It's here." She tapped her heart. "Relationships between women and men, between lovers of any gender, have become the new Mystery School initiations. Whatever their religious views, people are realizing that we're all undertaking this initiation into the Sacred through the lessons of love."

"But after all these lessons, I'm still longing."

"Of course. You're alive." Nonna laughed. "But it also means there's more for you to do."

I sighed as a gust of wind blew the napkin from my lap. "How much more, Nonna? How long do I have to wait?"

"Until you've learned how to love. You couldn't know the love of soul mates until you learned what it isn't. There's a line from a fairy tale, let me think . . . ah, yes—'It's the failures and the foolishness that lead us to the truth.'" Nonna smiled as a butterfly landed on the bouquet. "The most important relationship is with yourself. You have to love yourself before you can share true love with someone else. *And* you have to marry yourself before you can marry anyone else."

"Marry myself? How?"

"Ask your daemon. Ask your dreams. Patience, *mia figlia*. Your soul mate is coming, probably when you least expect it. Let's bring these things inside." Nonna began piling the dishes onto a painted tin tray. "And then let's walk down to the beach and put our feet in the water."

I spent the evening poking through Nonna's extensive library, unsure of what I was searching for until I found the love story of Dionysus and Ariadne. As I read, it struck me as odd that I had waited until now to pursue this part of the great myth, and I wondered if my divorce from Derek would have been less painful had I known. Things happen when they're meant to. I sat curled on the living room couch, a blanket over my legs, my journal in my lap, telling myself their story:

> *Whether Dionysus appeared first as the Egyptian God Osiris, and later the Christian God Jesus, whether he came first from Crete or Thebes, was worshipped more feverishly in Rome than Greece, what is known to all is that he was most happy on the island of Naxos. It is there that he found his bride, the mortal Ariadne.*
>
> *Ariadne was the daughter of the King of Crete and she had fallen in love with a Greek youth named Theseus, son of Athenian King Aegisthus. Each year a group of young women and men were sent from the Greek mainland to Crete. There they learned the ways of this highly developed, peaceful and prosperous Goddess-worshipping culture. Among its many pleasures was a dance called bull-leaping. But with the passage of time, it was maliciously rumored that the youths and maidens were actually being sacrificed. Deep beneath the palace there was a labyrinth, designed by Daedalus, and in its center was said to dwell a great monster called the Minotaur—a creature with the body of a man and the head of a bull.*

*What actually dwelled at the center of the labyrinth, what secret
trials and tests awaited one with the courage to confront them, was a
mystery. Theseus, believing it to be a monster, was determined to slay the
Minotaur. And so, betraying herself and her people, Ariadne gave him a
sword and a skein of thread by which to find his way back out, although
anyone who understands a labyrinth knows that, unlike a maze, there is
but one way in and one way out.*

*Theseus emerged from the labyrinth with blood on his sword. Taking
Ariadne with them, he and his companions fled over the seas toward
Athens. On the way, they dropped anchor at the island of Naxos. Never
intending to take her home to Athens, Theseus abandoned Ariadne on the
island as she slept.*

*Ariadne awoke, alone. In horror, she looked out upon the wine-dark
waters to see the sails of Theseus's ship receding in the distance.
Betrayed, her heart broke and she was consumed by grief. Without water,
food, hope or love, she was close to dying when Dionysus came upon her.
He lifted her fragile body into his arms and felt the divine spark, which
was his essence, kindled for the first time into a bright flame of love.
Gently, he kissed her and life returned to her dying form. Her eyes
opened and she found herself in the arms of a man who was part God,
part animal and her beloved; she recognized him as the very Minotaur
who had dwelled within the labyrinth.*

*Dionysus made her his wife and as a marriage gift he gave her a
golden crown encrusted with gems of light. They lived a long and happy
life together, had children and endless joy. Dionysus loved his wife
deeply, never grew angry with her and was always faithful to her. Many
years later, when she died, he took Ariadne's crown and threw it into the
heavens, where the jewels glowed so brilliantly they became the stars in a
constellation of immortal love.*

I closed my journal, stood and stretched. I caught my image in the mirror over Nonna's fireplace—years had passed since this journey to love had begun. I could see that I was older. Like Ariadne, I had given myself to Derek's quest, and he had abandoned me. Was I too old to believe that a man I could love like a God would find me? I thought of Nonna's advice—I had to marry myself before anything else could happen. I had to marry the God within myself.

Myths filled with gods and heroes, fairy tales of enchanted princesses and knights on white horses, Hollywood movies with images of romance and love at first sight—all create illusions and expectations about happily ever after. But they also contained archetypes and road maps of every soul's journey.

Every love story reminds us that there are always obstacles to overcome, battles to win, dragons to slay before we are rewarded with true love. I thought back to the dragon that had surfaced when I cast the love spell that brought Derek into my life; and the dragons Derek had to slay for himself. I wished him everything he needed to be victorious, and I knew he would be.

Would I? I had learned so many lessons, discovered how I projected wounds and fantasies on Derek, realized so much about myself. I had learned to live the best possible life I could create for myself, alone, content and at peace. I had freed myself from the past and found my own soul. And my daemon.

The moon was rising above the treetops, and Nonna had turned out her light. I pulled on a heavy sweatshirt and warm socks and tiptoed through the house and out into the garden. The lunar light was almost as bright as the sun—full and brilliantly white, filling the yard with an eerie illumination that made everything appear in shades of silver, but without any detail. It was a ghostly realm, between the worlds of earth and heaven, knowing and dreaming.

I stood in the center of the circle Nonna had created from shells and stones, herbs and flowers. I lifted my arms and opened my heart. *My arms are empty, my bed is cold, my heart is aching. I long for love to fill me with its fire. I yearn for a love that's embodied and shared, ecstatic and erotic and true. You came to me when I called to you at the temple. Please, come to me now.*

There was a sudden upswelling of wind and the towering locust trees encircling the garden began to bow and sway wildly. I felt the winds rush through my lungs and into my blood, lifting me, carrying me high above the shadowy garden. I hovered, looking down at myself, and wondered where the wind would carry me and if I would be able to find my way back to my body. And in that instant I found myself back on the ground.

The wind was whipping the garden into a frenzy, leaves flying from the bucking trees, flowers pounding against the earth as if to be returned to their source, and then I heard his answer. My heart opened and my breath quickened like the wind, blood rushing through me, igniting the secret, inner flames of desire.

I always come when you call to me. It's time for you to come to me. I wait at the center of the labyrinth.

I knelt to touch the shining earth. If my life was a journey through the labyrinth, where was the center?

"I'm exhausted." Oblivious to the fact that she was sitting in the Oak Room of the Plaza Hotel, Gillian pulled off her Manolo Blahniks and rubbed her feet.

"Don't expect any sympathy from me, Gillybean. Only Goddesses can wear those heels without consequences."

"Chanel was right—you never know, maybe it's the day you have a date with destiny, so it's good to be as pretty as possible."

We laughed. It was good to unwind. Between my practice and trying to get the production company off the ground, I'd been working too hard. "So how's it going with Chris?"

"I have some very exciting news." Gillian's eyes lit up. "We're getting married!"

"Oh, Gilly—that's great!" I jumped up from the tiny table and gave her a hug.

"The best part is how it happened. I finally used Nonna's love potion."

"My gosh, after all this time?"

"Well, you remember she said it could bring choices, or the one that's meant for you. It was the weirdest thing—I put the potion in that little perfume bottle you brought me from Venice. And it's been sitting in the center of my dresser for months. Anyway, I came home and the bottle had shattered. I mean, the base was standing perfectly upright, but the bulb with the potion had burst."

"That's so strange!"

She nodded. "I realized I couldn't get it back into a bottle. I was standing there trying to figure out what to do, staring at Chris—he was sleeping—and suddenly it just came to me. I rubbed my hands in the potion and then rubbed it all over him while he was asleep. He didn't budge, didn't stir, not a thing. When he woke up in the morning he asked me what the smell was and I said, 'It's the love potion, and I used it on you last night, and now you're mine. Forever.' "

"What did he do?"

"He just looked at me and smiled and said, 'Okay.' And then he proposed."

"Oh, Gilly, that's wonderful!"

"Yes." Gillian beamed. "It is."

"You can't be serious," my mother exclaimed over the phone. I'd called to ask if I could borrow her car. Sitting beside the window, watching the snow fall, I felt as if I were inside a snow globe being shaken by the Universe to remind me that I lived in a dream, silent and serene until mystery came along and turned it all upside down.

Come to me. Come to me. Come to me. His command had echoed in my heart like an incantation, a summoning that had, for months, made me restless without relief. But where was I to find him? I played music, watched the old movies, read "Kubla Khan." I waited for a sign, a *cledon*, a dream, a synchronicity. And then one afternoon, out of nowhere the idea simply popped into my head. I was going to take a road trip for my birthday. And I was going to find him.

"I don't understand why you have to do this at all—and why now? It's the middle of winter. There's snow everywhere. Suppose there's a blizzard—what will you do?"

"I need to get away. To clear my head, make some decisions about the future." I tried to reassure her. "It's America, the road is where you go to find . . . answers."

"You're a woman alone." Her voice was hard and tight with tension. "It's not safe."

"I live in New York, Mom. I've traveled by myself in countries where I don't speak the language. I need an adventure," I said lightly, trying to infect her with my enthusiasm. Her silence said it wasn't working. "If there's a storm, I'll pull into a motel. A good hotel." I upped the ante and threw a few more chips on the table to sweeten the pot. "And I promise I'll wait till the roads are cleared, and I'll call you." I heard her sighing. "But if I'm going, I have to go this weekend."

Finally, reluctantly, my mother relented. "Promise you'll call me every night."

"Absolutely. You're the greatest—thank you! I'll send you a post-card."

"Just come home in one piece."

We hung up the phone and I began to pack.

It was 6 A. M. and dark as night. I could feel every mile I'd driven for the last two days in some part of my body—my legs felt like Jell-O, my eyes like sandtraps, my mouth like a swamp. *I drove all this way to be here today. I'm going.*

I poured myself a cup of burned coffee in the motel lobby, stuffed an apple in my pocket and stepped out into the freezing Indiana morning. Driving straight out of the snow-covered parking lot, I accelerated beneath I-69 and out of Gas City. A delicate new moon hung in the black sky, hidden and then revealed by flying black clouds. I drove as the dark sky softened slowly to gray and the hidden landscape changed with the heavens, revealed as a vast, desolate dreamscape of frozen fields, invisible fertility waiting for spring.

How many pilgrims had made this trip? What were they looking for? Whether someone hiked the *Camino* in Spain, or a hidden peak in the Himalayas, walked the ancient path from Athens to Eleusis, or made a vision quest in the wilderness, the lesson was always the same: It was the journey that mattered and not the destination. And yet I knew that I needed to reach this destination to understand the journey, and to find the rest of my missing soul.

I was headed to the center of the labyrinth. Or maybe it was just a wrong turn up a blind highway. I turned left onto County Road 150 East and checked my mileage. Anticipation sent a small spurt of adrenaline through me and I pressed down on the accelerator. *It should be coming up any minute.* And just as I thought it, the innocuous black-and-white sign appeared. *Fairmount.*

Founded by Quakers, it was a small farming town of a few thousand people, one of whom had become an icon. The silver sky turned to gold as the sun broke over the horizon. I drove as it rose and the sky turned pale blue and the clouds white. The light began to fill the landscape with color, dimension and detail—a tweed of snow and flapping tan stubs of corn, white farmhouses, gray silos and red barns.

I drove faster; I reminded myself to slow down and watch for my next landmark—the large, white Winslow farmhouse. Almost identical to the old photos, it was set far back from the road. I passed slowly, overlaying the scene with a black-and-white image of a young man in a cap staring in the direction I was traveling, a black-and-white dog standing behind him.

I drove on, following the page of scribbled directions. It wasn't much farther. A modest black iron fence and a simple sign, "Park Cemetery," in large white block letters marked the entrance. I gripped the wheel, took a deep breath and turned in. It was a small cemetery with a scattering of trees and a white gravel road running through it. An almost incidental marker pointed the way.

The gravel crunched beneath the tires as I slowed the car to a crawl. I drove around the curve and up a small incline, saw the cluster of *Arbor Vitae*, Trees of Life, and stopped the car. I was alone. I turned off the engine and sat stone still. It was utterly quiet—no traffic, no birds, no wind.

I stepped out of the car, buttoning my coat and watching my breath emerge in ghostly puffs of white. The hood of the car was warm and I leaned against it, blowing into the palms I cupped over my cold nose, watching, waiting, without intent and oddly happy. *A strange place to feel happy*. I stared at the granite headstones—all of them modest and low to the ground.

Which was his? One was distinguished by a bunch of red silk flowers thrust into the ground beside it.

Why am I here? As my daemon's first incarnation, he had been my guide to a richer life than I had ever imagined possible. He had introduced me to the reality of the realm of Spirit and, equally important, the ecstasies of this mortal plane. Quakers have no saints, nor do they view the reverence of an individual as part of religious rectitude. Instead, the Friends exalt only the living Spirit, believing that all life is sacramental. And that was his rarely acknowledged spiritual background. It had become my spiritual foreground.

I walked slowly over to the grave, surrounded by points of icy light shimmering between the gray slabs. Places hold energy—visit a sacred site of any faith tradition, a historic battleground, the home of someone remarkable, and you feel the energy of presence. Objects, art, music, words, graves, memories, movies, images of the Divine—they are all points of connection, clues to Divine patterns, portals through which powerful, holy and personal energies flow.

The air was sharply luminous as I inhaled. The sound of my feet breaking through the thin veil of ice was like the rending of a seal. I looked down at the humble monument.

JAMES B. DEAN

1931–1955

The same simple inscription was carved on both sides of the stone. Its sides and top were jagged where people had chipped away their talismans. I knelt down and placed my offering, a bunch of sweet, purple grapes, on the lower ledge of the marker, on the side that faced the sun and the vast cornfield across the road. *A symbol to a symbol.*

There were other offerings—pennies, a kiss in red lipstick and a little homemade cross of twigs and twine. There were no huge bouquets, no massing of tokens. Each year thousands of people come from all over the world to visit this grave, but most of them come on the anniversary of his death. I was here on his, and my, birthday, the day he, *we*, entered the physical world.

I've thought of you as my guide, as part of my daemon for so long that it's hard to think of you as simply human. But even as I thought it, he became fully mortal, merely dust buried below me. A quick chill shot through me—he was there. He wasn't there. To be fully human is to be filled with Spirit. I felt odd standing over him, until I saw my footprints visible in the green grass where the weight and heat of my body had dissolved the ice beneath me, and over him. Without conscious intention, a slow, intermittent pulse of energy snaked up my spine, and then flowed back down it. The frost over the rest of the grave began to melt, revealing glistening, wet, green grass. *Good morning.* There was no reply.

I walked over to the graves of his Aunt Ortense and Uncle Marcus, who had raised him, and then to his parents, his mother who died when he was just a boy, the father who had sent him back to Indiana. It was a family plot and the headstones were all of a piece. I walked the few feet back to Jimmy and sat on a large, whitewashed, graffiti-filled rock by the side of the grave, at the edge of the road.

I breathed deeply, grounded, felt my consciousness begin to shift, alter and open, felt time slowing, heard an occasional car passing on the road make a muffled, stretched *whooooshing* sound.

Finally. You did come here to see me, after all. His voice reached me, clear and tinged with humor.

The inner noise dissolved into a sea of slowed silence, the encompassing, thick-aired quiet in which that voice always arrived. Still, it startled me and my heartbeat quickened.

I did. I came for you.

Silence. The quiet slowly became infused with presence as bright as the light all around me. Around us.

It's beautiful here. Peaceful.

Yes. Home. You should see it in the spring. Hasn't changed much really.

Any regrets? The question surprised me even as I asked it.

None. Well, one. It was too damn short. Nobody asked me. I heard the sound of a quiet chuckle. *But then who'd want to visit an old man?*

You'd be surprised. But romantic love always ends in death—either the couple or the love.

I thought greatness would survive death. But it's love that survives.

I fell in love with you but you were already dead. Do you know how frustrating that was?

Another half laugh. *If it's not one thing, it's another.*

I laughed, the sound like a stone tossed into a reflecting pool. I watched the light rippling outward. *Until you showed up. You were proof of . . . realms beyond, and you guided me into them. I was enchanted, enamored and so I followed you.*

Another soft laugh. *And look where you are—Indiana.*

I laughed. *The lengths a girl will go to. You set me on this path.*

You set yourself. You called me, drew me to you, whether you realized it or not.

I remembered how, so many years ago, my heart had opened, crying out to the Universe for love. *I'm still yearning for you—in a form that will . . . love me.*

I know what you're really yearning for. When you know, you'll have it. You have a question.

Endless questions. I laughed and the light purled. *What am I yearning for?*

Ask your dreams. The words startled me. It was what Nonna had said. Nonna had also said to ask him.

You've shown me so much, why can't you show me that?

There are . . . rules. You have to see by yourself, by faith, by love.

I struggled. *How can I love without someone to love?* I wrapped my arms around myself to stave off the chill that was creeping through me. I sat staring at the headstone, the grass, the glowing air, and suddenly remembered—you have to ask an oracle the right question to get the right answer. It had to be true with a daemon as well. *What do I need to know?* The answer came with an onrush of exhilaration.

Feel it all. Feel deeply. Don't hold back from life, embrace it fully, open yourself, give over to it. It's the essential surrender. The more you do it, the more you'll learn not to fear the vulnerability. Guarded, you live a half-life. Only the gentle are ever really strong.

A sudden cold breeze rustled through the trees and cut through the layers of clothing. *I'm cold. I'm going to go warm up in the car. I'll be back in a minute.*

Let's hope not. Take your time. We all get here soon enough. I heard the almost silent half chuckle, and then the sense of presence withdrew, the voice was silent, the air thinned to chilly, brittle texture.

I moved the car to a discreet distance should anyone else come to visit, parking it so I could sit in the sun. I turned off the motor. Looking out the window, I was startled and darkly amused to see an open grave. A car pulled up to Jim's grave, stopping for just a moment without anyone getting out. I watched as it drove away, then pulled out my notebook and quickly wrote, afraid to lose a syllable, a nuance.

Your gravestone casts a long shadow. I saw how the frost remained in that dark patch as the rest of it melted, filling the air with moist, effervescent light. Another car pulled up: man and dog. He got out of the car. He had dark hair, was wearing a plaid shirt and a brown leather jacket but no gloves. He leaned down and placed something at the base of Jim's headstone. Rubbing his hands together, he looked quickly at both sides of the stone, then swiftly climbed back in the car and left. I knew he visited often.

Love is the way light feels. It is a day of shining light. I climbed out of the car and sat back down by the grave. I stared at the color photo of Jim in the simple, wooden frame that had just arrived, and I waited for the quiet and the voice to return. The glittering air began to gather around me and the sounds of the world withdrew. *You spoke of love.*

You spoke of love. Pervasive. There's really only one magic worth believing in—love. I have a present for you. Look down.

I saw a small, black, heart-shaped rock at my feet. I took off my glove, picked it up and rubbed it, feeling the cold stone warm in my fingers. *Thank you.* I held it to my heart. *Before I forget to ask—the rest of your advice?*

I heard the half chuckle. **If you're having trouble feeling, ask yourself how you feel, pay attention. Focus on it. Imagine it if you have to, then feel it more deeply. That's what I did—I just put it on the outside.**

Pretty brave.

It was fun, it was alive, no regrets. Don't worry about the kid, I never had any—that's not how I made my mark. Make yours. Find your voice.

I let the feelings rise. I wanted to cry as his words about the baby I had longed for in vain echoed in the cavity of my chest. But I also felt consoled by his instruction. The sun was climbing, warming the cocoon of air and making it glow. It was always hard for me to ask for help, but I did. *Will you help me?*

I always have. It's time for you to move on.

A sense of panic struck me. *I don't want to move on if I'm going to lose you.*

You don't need to look for me on the outside anymore. It's up to you now. You've got a chance for real love but you have to take the next step for it to happen.

Aren't you my real love? The air trembled around me and I trembled within it.

Am I?

I sat silently, waiting to feel the answer.

You don't need me anymore. There's someone who's been waiting for you, all his life.

But where is he?

On his way.

I have to think about this.

Don't think—feel. What do you feel?

A sudden rush of light flared through me and the ice around my heart melted into hot tears that washed the fear away. *I feel . . . I feel you all around me. I feel you inside me, here.* I slipped my hand between the buttons of my coat and rested it over my heart. *You've guided me to . . . my heart.*

Because that's where I am. I'm the part of you that feels. And creates from those feelings. That's the part that's been missing, that's what you've been seeking. Not your courage or strength or purpose— you've found those. It isn't me you've been waiting for; it's not even him. It's your feelings, your ability to love again without fear.

Is that why you say I don't need you anymore?

I'll always be inside of you, in your spirit. That's never going to change.

The flare of light had left everything in stark, clear outline. *Heaven's here in my heart. And that's where you live.*

I wiped the water from my face, saw the fractured rainbows that had covered the ground sparkling in the palm of my hand. The wind was rising, the frost was almost gone, the sun was at the mid-heaven. I heard cars passing on the road, heading to work, to school, to life. A bright red cardinal landed in the Tree of Life beside the graves. I finally understood, I *felt* it. *You've been my guide to my ability to love. Thank you. I want to say I love you, one last time.*

There is no last time.

I stood, feeling my body as if awakening from a long sleep. I stretched, put the black stone heart in the pocket of my jeans, touched his headstone. *Oh, one more question—anything you'd do differently?*

I heard the inaudible laugh. **To be here now, alive in my body, but who knew?**

Happy birthday, Jimmy.

Happy birthday, Phyllis!

"*Yup*, he used to come back here a lot. Most people don't know that about him. There's some great rare television footage I can play for you if you like," Mike, the gallery owner, offered.

I was leaning against one of the glass display cases in the sprawling Victorian house, chatting with the man who had put the photo on Jim's grave. Suffused with peace, I had driven through the unassuming town, past the high school and then to the Quaker Meeting House, visited the museum and now the gallery with all its mementos, artifacts and talismans.

I had wandered about, looking at Jim's drawings and paintings, his bullfighter's cape and his drums, the records and books he loved, poetry he'd written, and all the racing-related material. And I watched the little animated film he'd made, remembering that Jimmy had said that if he lived to be a hundred it wouldn't be enough time to do all the things he wanted to do.

"Which performance do you think was most like him?" I recognized Mike's alert energy—the sharp watchfulness of someone used to paying attention to clues and manifestations. I wondered what it was like to live one's life as the keeper of a flame, and then I smiled, knowing the answer.

"It's all him. But his aunt said the scene in *East of Eden* where he's running through the field in the spring trying to get the beans to grow faster was the most like who he really was."

Corn and grain, corn and grain, all that falls shall rise again.

He put an old desk chair in the tiny, dark brown screening room for me, turned on the equipment and turned out the lights. The visceral presence that had always leapt from the screen into the space of my desire no longer jump-started my heart. It was already beating.

I watched a brilliant young actor who had died many years ago. And I finally recognized the parts of Jim, and my daemon, and most importantly *myself*, that had been waiting for my discovery. Not the sexiness or woundedness that had first drawn me in, not even the passionate intensity of the emotions he expressed so freely that he had been guiding me to— but the joyfulness, playfulness and unflinching appetite for life. *Eros.*

I drove out of Fairmount as the sun was setting, turning the car toward tomorrow's sunrise and home. *Will I ever see him again? Had he taken the magic with him?*

Remember—feel it all.

How do I feel? I dove deep and broke through the surface of my awareness with the enthusiasm of Dionysus's dolphins. *Enthusiasm!* That was what I felt—the rapture of my life. The true meaning of the word *enthusi-*

asm comes from the root word *entheos,* which means "having the God [*theos*] within." Whether man or woman, conscious practitioner of the ancient Mysteries or one who simply lives with vitality, a life fully lived is one illuminated by the divine spark within oneself. And that God, who is also mortal, is within each of us. He was within me now; grateful and aroused, I was aware of communion in every part of myself—in body, mind and soul. I had found the God, and he *was* love.

I turned the music up loud and pressed down on the accelerator.

I was just outside of Pittsburgh—smelling it before I could see it. I toyed with the idea of calling some of the steelworkers I knew from union reform efforts. I could travel almost anywhere in the country and find someone, some local, unsung hero who had put his, or her, life on the line fighting for freedom and justice. But I didn't want to talk union politics tonight.

The industrial residue tinted the sunset wildly crimson and I pulled off the highway to watch the drama. As light faded to darkness, I struggled to grasp a thought that had been forming since I'd left Fairmount: The Goddess had taught me strength, and my daemon, the God, had taught me how to feel. She had taught me to be a warrior; he had taught me to be vulnerable. She had shown me how to take action, to express love; he had shown me how to receive, to be open to love.

Each had given me the opposite of what was typically associated with the feminine and masculine genders. Sitting alone in the car, wearing my worn blue jeans and old leather jacket, returning from my solitary road trip, I knew that gender was far more malleable than our culture acknowledged. But more importantly, my journey had taught me how much we shared, regardless of gender. I also knew that to be complete, to be whole and in full possession of my soul, I needed both aspects of being, regardless of which gender was associated with those qualities.

I was smiling as I pulled into an all-night drugstore. Searching through the painfully overlit aisles for Epsom salts, the idea struck me. I was going to do a ritual tonight. In the stationery section I found what I would need—a piece of red poster board, a scissors, a black Magic Marker and a roll of Scotch tape.

I turned the electric heater up as far as it would go and surveyed the chilly, indistinguishable motel room. After calling my mother, I flipped on the local TV news, which was filled with universal traumas—murders, fires, drug arrests, followed by sports and weather, all punctuated with ads for new furniture and used cars. I flipped it off. It was time to start.

I had brought a few simple ritual tools with me, but as I looked in the satchel I realized that I didn't need much more than what I already had—myself and the few things I'd bought at the pharmacy. For me, the best rituals were simple and spontaneous. Air was my breath, fire my passion, water my blood, earth my body and Spirit my soul, my life force. *Trust your heart.*

I ran a bath and tossed in the Epsom salts and a handful of lavender. While the tub filled, I put a small candle in each of the four directions and sprinkled a little salt water around the room to cleanse it. Sitting cross-legged on the bed, which occupied most of the room, I surveyed the supplies I'd bought. The red poster board was the color of fire engines, roses in June, Marilyn Monroe's lips. It was the color of Valentine's Day hearts. I took the scissors and cut out a giant red heart. And then, remembering the sorrows of the past, the losses and loneliness, the confusion and lessons, I tore the heart into pieces.

I cried as the paper ripped, but when I finished there was a deep sense of relief. I left the scattered fragments on the bed and went to take my bath, resting in the warm water until the skin of my fingertips was soft, pink and puckering, and my heart was open.

Wrapped in a small, thin towel, I stared in the bathroom mirror. I looked the same as I had so long ago this morning in another motel room. But so much had changed.

Let yourself feel—all of it.

Trust is knowing that I can give up control and that I will be all right.

Tonight my ritual was to acknowledge the lost pieces of my life, my heart and soul, and put them back together again. And then to welcome the change, *feel* it and trust it.

I returned to the room, lit the candles and then stood as close to the center as possible. Turning slowly, I cast my circle of protection and healing. I called each of the four directions, asking for insight, courage, love and fulfillment. And then I heard myself calling, softly but clearly: "Isis, Goddess of the shimmering wings, you who summoned me so many years ago, be with me, guide me in restoring the pieces of my heart to wholeness. Osiris, beloved husband of Isis, made whole by love, which is the greatest magic, charge my effort with your power of rebirth."

For a moment, standing in the mundane little room, the invocations and the divinity I called seemed too vast for the simple action I had planned. But the small symbolic act was the denouement of years of struggle, searching, discovering and, I hoped, transformation. I sat on the bed, quieting myself with several long, deep breaths. When I was ready, I gathered up the shredded heart and held it to my own. I let the feelings of loss and remorse rise up like the Nile when Sirius rises. And then I let the feelings of hope and love wash away the sadness like the Nile overflowing her banks, making the land moist and fertile and ready for seed.

I spread the pieces out on the bed, took the first one, and with the Magic Marker I wrote: *my father's pain*. I took another piece and wrote: *needing my father's love*. I continued writing all the scattered pieces that had been lost along the way—*my mother's hurt, anger and defenses; Derek's abandonment; not having a child; my fear of vulnerability; being trapped in my warrior's armor; living in my head; self-doubt; loneliness* . . . I wrote until I had run out of pieces and things to mourn.

Slowly, I took each piece and found where it connected to other pieces to form a whole heart. I took the Scotch tape and taped all the torn edges, securing them together so that the heart was restored. And I considered all the lessons I had learned. I sought the wisdom that transformed pain into freedom. Magic, therapy, science, most forms of problem solving—all were the ability to flip polarities, to know that the negative pointed you to its opposite.

I turned the restored heart over, and on the back of each taped piece I wrote something or someone I was grateful for: *the love of my parents; Nonna; friends; health; work; strength; self-esteem; the courage to be vulnerable; softness; receptivity; feeling; my body; the Goddess; my daemon, my soul*. I wrote until I had run out of pieces and things to celebrate, and then on the last piece I wrote: *the true love that is coming, that I will give and receive*.

I studied what I had created—loss and lessons, challenges and blessings, suffering and rejoicing, active and receptive, feminine and masculine—and then expressed my thanks and released the circle as I blew out the candles. I crawled beneath the covers and, lying beside the huge red heart, slipped away into a dream.

"Great and wise Isis, lady whose hips are encircled with the bloodred cord of life that binds each of us to you," I heard myself calling out. "Lady of wisdom and magic, of love and mystery, you who speak the words of power, I call to you, be here with me. Guide my search."

There was a mighty beating of the air, as if great angelic wings hovered above my head, and a soft light encircled me. I heard a voice that surrounded me as it also rushed up from within me.

"I am She to whom you call; I come from the realm of emptiness that is full, bearing new life. I come when called to bring the dead back to life. I come bearing the mystery of love to nourish you, but only when your heart is open. Open to receive my love and I will raise you with my words of power."

I journeyed with Her as she searched in deserts dry as dust and bone, searching in darkest nights, lost and wandering among the dead. With her, I gathered the sundered pieces of all that I had ever loved and longed to love. I accompanied her as she returned to the bedchamber of mystery and dreams. She found all but one of the fourteen pieces of Osiris's sundered body. The missing piece, his phallus, she then fashioned from gold.

I listened to Isis sing the incantations of love, a single voice in perfect harmonies. I watched as she lowered her hair like a veil to conceal herself and her beloved Osiris from the world. I was Isis kneeling over him, my body the altar of the holiest magic. I felt my lips moisten his with a kiss. Felt myself breathing life into the heart beneath mine, joined to mine, that began to beat. I felt my hands stroking his arms, his legs, locking my fingers in his, rubbing myself against him to make the red waters of life flow. I stroked his brow with tenderness, traced the ridge of his sharp cheekbone, the line of his strong nose, his stubble-rough jaw. I ran my fingertips over his lips that moved, biting, licking, kissing me. I whispered charms and endearments and ancient promises in his awakening ear.

And I felt the kiss soften my lips, felt the life breathed into my beating heart, felt hands upon my body and my brow, felt her body rubbed against mine, heard songs and charms, endearments and promises murmured in my awakening ear.

I saw his eyes fly open, felt the ground beneath me tremble with the sound of pounding hooves, and the air grow hot and heavy.

"I am He to whom you call, I come from the realm of emptiness that is full, fulfilling the promise of new life. I come to be reborn, nourished by the mystery of love, but only when your heart is open. Open to receive me and I will live again, raised by your words of power."

"Beloved, how long I have awaited your embrace." I heard her voice. "All new life begins first with a dream. Let my love be the power that summons you forth from dreams into life and into my arms."

Barely a moment elapsed before I heard Osiris answer: "I meet with you in dreams. Let your love be the power that summons me forth into life and into your embrace."

His arms grasped her waist, and I heard the murmur of ecstasy as I lowered myself upon him. Straddling him, his hands glided over my face, down my throat and over my breasts. My head fell back, a moan as timeless as the starry heavens escaping my lips. I leaned forward, pressing my mouth to his, drawing his tongue into me, completing the circle of connection. My hands traveled the length of his chest, stroked the dark hair that curled in a line down his stomach, spreading into a dark triangle beneath my own. My hips rocked back and forth against him and I rode the wave of our desire.

His arms wrapped around me and we rolled together like the earth circling the sun until he rose above me. I arched, opened and received him as he penetrated my warmth with fire, my love with life. I felt the joining—all the pieces of a sundered soul restored, the conjoining in love of two into one holy union.

I awoke at the center of the labyrinth in a motel room just outside of Pittsburgh. It was morning and music poured out of the window of a car flying down the highway. I stared in the mirror and smiled. I was going home to get married.

As the music played, I filled my grandmother's cut glass vase with water and placed it on my altar. In the center was a statue of Aphrodite that Naomi had given me. She was no longer confined to my Barbie doll image, but had become an expression of feminine power whose full title I finally understood: "Aphrodite, Goddess of Joy who is beautiful to all." Beside her was my statue of Isis, elegant, life bestowing and serene, a new statue of Osiris and the one of Dionysus given to me by Nonna. In front of the statues was my grandmother's diamond ring.

I placed my journal and a pen beneath the altar, along with a split of champagne and a plate of chocolate truffles. I carried the full-length mirror in from my bedroom and leaned it against the wall behind the altar. It was time to begin. I cast a simple circle leaving an opening through which to exit and enter, and left the circle to take my bath. I used a single drop of Nonna's love potion, floating in the porcelain-contained sea, allowing the waters to wash away the past and then, gradually, transport me into gratitude and anticipation. When I emerged I did so as a woman restored to herself and filled with joy, cleansed not by tears of loss but by the waters of life.

I dotted myself with the love potion, applied my makeup and fixed my hair. I put on my *Radiant Angel* gown. I stood breathing and quieting my mind, grounding and centering my body, opening my heart and soul. I was ready. A gentle current of elation flowed through me as I picked up the small bouquet of red roses and dark green ivy. I felt the softness of the wide red silk ribbon I had wound around the flowers' stems, the kick and bounce of my gown's hem as I walked slowly into the living room to stand before the altar.

I smiled as I unwound the ribbon and placed the flowers in the vase. And then, as I struck a match and lit the red candle, I spoke: "Divine Grace that is present in all, Goddess of Life and God of Love, fill my heart, my body, my soul with your blessings. Guide me to the love that lives within me and sustain me as I vow myself to that love."

I sat on a cushion before the altar and opened my journal to the page on which I had listed all the values and qualities I had longed for in my soul mate, some written long ago, some newly realized. His generosity and freedom of spirit, his refusal to compromise and his strength to stand alone, his compassion, intelligence and humor, courage, drive and creativity, his love of life and his ability to give and receive love were all enumerated in detail. There were no physical descriptions except that I would find him deeply, sexually, heart-openingly attractive. But as I closed my eyes, I remembered my dark-haired, working class poet, felt his kisses awakening my soul from its chrysalis of dreams, and felt his callused fingertips like flint against skin, leaving trails of fire through the forest of night.

I opened my eyes and remembered that my yearning and my seeking would come to nothing until I understood and embraced the mystery—if that which I sought I did not find within myself, I would never find it without. And the rest of the Goddess's charge rang in my heart . . . *for behold I have been with you since the beginning, and I am that which is attained at the end of desire.*

I stood and faced the mirror. I saw the woman filled with radiance, hope and love. Looking into my own eyes, my heart went out to her and I loved her deeply and truly. I spoke the vows that flowed from my soul: "I love you, and I promise that I will always love you, for all time and beyond it. I will honor and protect you, respect and cherish you. I will help you to be open to the pleasures and gifts of life, and I will help you to be strong and courageous in facing its challenges. I will nourish your dreams, your body and your soul, and I will always celebrate the spirit that lives within your heart, and the senses that fill your life with ecstasy, and the knowledge that we live in a world imbued with holiness."

I slipped my grandmother's ring on my finger. There were tears in my eyes as I finished. I poured the champagne into the chalice, smiled at myself in the mirror and drank. It was time for the first dance, the ancient dance within the labyrinth that summons its magic to life. I hit the tape and Van Morrison sang to the "Brown Eyed Girl."

The Final Spell

15

Love

Love is the only prayer.

—MARION ZIMMER BRADLEY

I sat on the suitcase, grabbed the zipper and pulled. Done, and with time to spare. The car taking me to the airport would be arriving in about an hour. My partner and I were going to the Cannes Film Festival to hunt for financial backers for our production company. I checked my brief-case one more time—I had everything we would need to talk to investors. And, I thought as I dragged the second suitcase to the door, I had plenty of clothes.

The kettle whistled in the kitchen. I poured the boiling water over a metal tea ball and stuck my nose in—peppermint, sharp and clean. I took the cup out to the terrace. It was a perfect, warm May day. The park was a patchwork of pale yellow and green leaves and pink apple blossoms, and the sky was robin's egg blue.

Thank you.

I sat and watched a red-tailed hawk ride the thermals, making slow cir-cles overhead. A siren drew my attention down into the maze of city streets; I watched the yellow taxis race, the people go about their daily lives. I had journeyed the labyrinth of my life, and at its center there was no demon, no monster. What shape would such a creature have taken? Fear, loneliness, illusion, ignorance, confusion, anger, blame—I had faced each of those along the way. The Minotaur who waited for me, half man/half bull, half man/half God, half other, was half *me*. What waited for me at the center of my life was self-knowledge and blessings I'd never imagined. What waited for me was *Eros*; it was love.

I sipped the tea, felt its heat slide down my body, felt its energy flow into my blood. The peppermint wanted me, just as I had wanted it. *Sensual desires could bring union with divinity, because all things are manifestations of that divinity*. That was what Nonna had been trying to teach me, *that's* what the practices were for, and where my daemon had been leading me. It was where my instincts, my heart and my destiny had led me. Every sense brought me a flood of reminders, as long as I paid attention. *The body was the temple and divinity resided in the heart*. And my heart was full.

I held up my hand and watched my grandmother's ring fracture the sun's light into rainbows of color. In marrying myself, I had worked another act of divine magic. My intention had been to bring two aspects of my nature together. But with each day that passed it became clearer that a rite of union had also occurred between my self and my sacred self, between woman and God, human and holiness.

It was a natural high. It was like being in love. It was like *being* love, because I was living every day in a world that was one with the Divine. It wasn't a spiritual idea, it was an earthly experience. I still cast circles, I called the Goddess, the God, created rituals, drew down the moon, honored the cycles of the seasons at the Sabbats. I led circles, and when people asked, I shared what I had to offer. And I made time to immerse myself in wilderness where, undisturbed by human intrusion, I experienced the presence of the Divine as palpable. All of it enabled me to feel the ecstasy of that communion.

I loved all the rites and rituals, the ceremonies and spells. But I didn't need them anymore to experience the presence of the Sacred. I understood why Nonna had been moving me away from ceremony. While fully charged with aesthetic and spiritual power, ceremonies could also become a substitute, a formalism that stood between oneself and the Sacred.

Gradually, I had been moving to direct and simple relationships—with myself just as I was, with my teacher, Nature, others, with divinity. With magic. The practices and rituals had guided me through the labyrinth; they had helped me remove the blindfold tied on by a world that couldn't see the Sacred. They had prepared and opened me; now it was up to me to embrace my life, and to live it deeply. *My life was my magic.*

I inhaled slowly. *Air, my breath.* I looked over to the sun shining in the sky, making everything grow, felt its warmth on my skin. I lifted the cup and drank the waters of life that flowed red through my veins. I stretched my body and felt the flash of anticipation for the trip that I was about to take. *Earth, my body. Spirit, my soul.*

Everywhere I turned I saw the face of God, of Goddess, of the Beloved. I had cleared the mirror of my heart, and I finally understood: *Each of us is a reflection of the Divine. And that divinity comes into the world, through us, when we love.*

The intercom buzzer summoned me. I pressed the *Listen* button.

"You cah is heya. Da driva say to tell you his name's Harvey."

I smiled as I pressed the *Talk* button. Hollywood's favorite pookah and my old friend had arrived to take me to the airport. "Thanks, I'll be right there." My heart began to sprint.

"*Look at all the swans!*" I stopped in my tracks. Nonna and I had spent the afternoon at the beach and had walked home arm in arm to find a lake full of beauty. She'd invited me for the weekend and I had taken the earliest possible bus. I had missed her.

"Every season is beautiful, but it's truly a place meant for the indulgences of summer." Nonna sighed happily. "Okay, let's count." She put on her glasses.

"Thirteen, and two over there."

"Yes, the two that live here all year round. Since they haven't had any babies this year, I imagine the rest'll be allowed to remain."

"So beautiful!"

Nonna pulled open the porch's screen door. "Let's make some iced tea. And I must have some cookies around here. Put those things away." She pointed to our aluminum beach chairs. "And get out of that wet bathing suit, and put some music on, and then you can entertain me."

Nonna had already poured our tea and settled into her favorite chair on the porch when I returned from my chores. "Nice, that's the public radio station, isn't it? So, come and sit. Earn your supper. How was Cannes?"

"A lot of fun, a lot of champagne, but not very productive. Being partnered with someone from film royalty gets you red carpet treatment all the way, but people didn't believe that we actually needed money to make films. They kept approaching us for funding. Actually, the whole thing would make a very funny movie. Oh—remember Cutter? He was there! He had a nice role in a film that was screened—*It's a Guy Thing*." We laughed at the title. "He was really terrific, and it was so great to see him; he looked so happy."

"And have you heard from Dale?"

"He's doing great, but he's kicked me out of the nest. Time for me to fly—or crash on my own."

"So, are you in love?"

I looked up from lusting after a cookie, startled. "In love? No. Well, yes. But not the way I want. I mean, I want what I'm feeling. I just want more." Nonna was laughing. "Was that flustered enough?"

She nodded. "Very entertaining. Could you do it again if I asked for another take?"

"I'd rather not." I laughed with her. "Why did you ask me if I was in love?"

"Because ever since you got here you've been radiant. Try the chocolate chip cookies. I made them when you said you'd come."

"Mmm, good. You're a culinary Goddess."

"Don't talk with your mouth full. So, who's making you so happy?" she asked mid-cookie, disregarding her own orders.

"I am. Ever since the marriage ritual, it seems as if there are endless things that make me happy. The kind of happy you feel when you're in love. It's small things. You know, the little thoughtfulnesses we always complain about losing when the romance is gone." I laughed. "Those things. I mean, I forget, get distracted by bills, or stress, or responsibilities. But then there's a moment—I hear a piece of music or eat a perfect strawberry. I notice, I feel the pleasure, I remember where I am, why I'm here.

There are endless ecstasies all day long, and they bring me back to the truth. Am I making sense?"

Nonna nodded. "Go on."

"Small things, like those swans. Like seeing you sitting on the beach. I wake up in love. And all day long there are things making me feel . . . blissful. I love every day, every moment of sunlight or rain, the hunger in my stomach and the food on the table, even the music from a neighbor's apartment and their baby crying. It's all good. I drink wine that longs for my lips . . ."

Nonna smiled as we shared a memory.

"I smell flowers that offer their perfume to me, hear music that's played to be heard by my heart, danced to by my body. But it works the other way; I exist for the wine, for the flowers, for the music. We need each other. We love each other."

"Anything else?"

"That's the ecstasy, not just huge, wild, frenzied altered states, but perfect daily blessings. Experiencing that, *feeling* it, is feeling love. So, I'm in love—with life."

"And your practices?"

"When I got back from France, I decided to create an altar that honored the union of earth and spirit. But then, as I was standing there, I caught a glimpse of myself in the hall mirror and it hit me—*we're* the altars; we're the magic of heaven and earth conjoined. We're heaven and earth walking, talking, making love, creating. And the force of that union, that's desire. It's love."

Nonna nodded. "And you feel it?"

"Yes." I could hear the excitement in my voice. "All the little things thrill me because they're an expression of the Sacred. The love I experience, that I feel, is that divinity." I paused and stared out at the sun on the water, the two swans gliding together through the light. "But, Nonna, I want to love again the way a woman loves a man, I want to experience *that* love. I want love embodied."

"And you should have it."

"I'm worried that I'll just summon another mirror of my longing and neediness."

"When you were younger, your relationships were a mirror of what was missing. Now the mirror will reflect what is fulfilled. Loving, when you are fulfilled, is like breathing. Exhale you give, inhale you receive. It's an instinct of life. You know how to love now."

"The thing is, after all of this, I still want *him*. He haunts me." I sighed and smiled. "I feel as if I've been in love with him my entire life."

"Of course." Nonna smiled at me reassuringly. "You've been traveling towards each other for years."

"But is that real? Or is it just a fairy tale? Sometimes I wonder if I've created an image of a man so unique, so special that he can't be real. And sometimes I think I did that so I'll never fall in love—so I'll never get hurt." I sighed, not wanting to believe myself. "Is happily ever after just in movies?"

"You can have happily ever after—all it requires is the right person to create it with. He exists—you're not creating him, you're *sensing* him. You have your soul; you'll find your soul mate. That's the journey of love."

"His hands—there's always been something about his hands, about working with them. And he does something more, the talent. He's a . . . stand-up guy, I know he is—strong and reliable, with integrity and principles." The description poured out of me. "A man who's sought out challenge, who didn't compromise. The heroism, although he wouldn't think of himself as a hero. And a capacity to *feel*, to really love, to love *me*." I caught myself and hesitated. "Is it just a projection of my daemon?"

"There are some important parts of you in that description. But they're not projections of what's missing in yourself, they're all ways in which you've fulfilled yourself. And because you have, you'll find them, and more, in your soul mate. When the time is right, when you're ready."

"Sometimes I get so scared we won't find each other. I can't bear the thought of his being lonely, of the sadness he must feel." Sadness struck me. "I want him to have love, joy. But it's like he's just beyond reach. Or we're too far apart and he can't see me."

"The connection of soul mates is real. It's the most powerful reality in life. You're connected in your hearts, your souls, your minds, your lives. You've felt it, seen it in visions, dreams. You're moving towards each other—every action one takes influences the other, draws you closer to each other."

I gave a small laugh. "Quantum physics—what happens to half a par-

ticle at one end of the Universe affects its other half at the opposite end of
the Universe."

"A romantic theory of physics?" Nonna smiled.

"Why not? History should be told as a love story, why not the story of
the Universe? Especially if love is the energy holding it all together. Holding us together." A sweet peacefulness was settling over me. "I've never
given up. I've always had faith."

"Knowing, trusting that he's also longing for you, dreaming of you, is
a very profound magic. When you first opened your heart and called out
for love, and your daemon came to you, you cast your first love spell—for
your soul mate."

A pulse of excitement raced through me. "That spell's still working,
isn't it?"

Nonna smiled. "You had a lot of preparation to do before it could be
fulfilled. We all do. There's nothing more powerful than love. When
you're ready to open your heart again, the spell will manifest. Probably
when you least expect it! So, what will you do until you meet?"

"Until?" My hope glowed brighter with her words.

She nodded and smiled and pushed the plate of cookies at me.

"I'll prepare, I'll love, I'll have faith. I'll live a life that honors my love
for him. My life is my magic, I know that now."

"You can't experience it if you can't envision it."

"Back to basics. Thoughts *are* like things, and they do have energy. We
empower them with our emotions and manifest them with our actions. Air,
fire, water, earth and Spirit."

"Just like dreams." Nonna patted my hand.

"But, Nonna, I don't want to dream anymore. I want the reality."

"So, you're ready for your dream to come true?" Nonna stared at me
over the top of her glasses.

I nodded. "He doesn't have to be perfect, just perfect for me."

The flock of swans exploded from the water and my heart went with
them.

I walked down the gravel driveway, surprised by the
abundant flower borders. My mother was never much for gardening. But

these days she was full of surprises, and it made me smile to think of the one she'd sprung on me a few weeks ago. I'd gone out to visit her, and within moments of my arrival, after offering me a glass of juice, a cup of tea, a cookie, a piece of fruit, she sat me down at the dining room table, saying in very serious tones that she needed to talk to me.

She adjusted her new favorite sweater, a nautical pattern of red, white and blue. She'd been spending a lot of time on a forty-two-foot sailboat lately. She folded her hands on the table and looked at me intently. "You know how much I love you, and that will never change, no matter what. I could never love anyone more than you."

I nodded, wondering where she was headed with such odd words.

"You know I've been spending time with Harold."

I nodded. Harold owned the sailboat.

"A lot of time. In fact, well, I just wanted to ask you how you would feel about my . . . Well, we've gotten very . . . serious about each other. I just want to know how you feel about it . . ." My always-in-charge mother actually seemed nervous.

I smiled. "I think it's great. As long as I don't have to talk to you about safe sex."

Her eyes opened and she slapped my hand and then started to laugh. My father had been dead for several years and I knew that she'd been spending a lot of time with Harold, a widower. He'd been our family's accountant, the husband of one of my mother's closest friends, a chess companion of my father's, and my mother's high school boyfriend.

"As long as you're happy, Mom. That's all that matters. Have fun. You deserve it." Smiling, I reached across the table and squeezed her folded hands. She was happy and she was having fun, more fun than she'd had in a long time, and that made me happy.

I came around the curve in the driveway thinking about that conversation, and stopped. There was a petite young woman, a teenager, with her back to me, sitting on a swing that hung from an Empress of China tree. She was holding onto the ropes, humming and gaily swinging her legs as the seat swayed slowly back and forth.

I wondered who it was, who was joining us this afternoon. And then she turned. Stunned, I recognized my mother. Her youthful, relaxed face lit up with a huge, quick smile as she waved and slid off the swing to come greet me. My vision blurred with a rush of tears. At the age of seventy-two my mother had fallen in love. She was radiant and she was sixteen years old again.

Love is the way light feels. I nourished the light within myself, and every day was filled with sunlight, every night with the moon; even when the clouds came and the rain fell, it fell to sustain the earth and my soul. But there were times that I wept for my loneliness and his. And one night I fell to my knees in a sorrow so great that it felt as if my chest was tearing open—the thought of living the rest of my life without him was unbearable. I begged, I railed, I demanded, I cried, I prayed, and somehow, perhaps, I opened my heart and I made magic.

I also made a home for him in my heart, and sent my love to him, certain that somehow he would feel it, and that it would protect and sustain him. And I opened myself to receive his. I loved as love flowed through me. I *was* love, I lived it in all the endless small and infinite joys of my life, and I was grateful and strong and filled with hope. And that hope was a light, a magic that I was certain would bring us together.

The merry-go-round whirled, spinning calliope music that overflowed from the fairgrounds into the surrounding town. It was August and the heat melted the world into a dizzy mirage. I walked slowly, with a fan of Spanish lace to stir a breeze and to enjoy the pleasures of being female. My father would have said it was hot enough to fry an egg on the sidewalk. To me, it felt hot enough to bubble the contents of a cauldron.

Walking slowly, immersed in everyday magic, I felt Nature's alembic transforming my dreams and desires, prayers and chores into what I did not know, but had begun to sense. Strolling past a church, I tossed in the ring of gold that had never encircled my finger; listening to the music of a passing car, I added the secrets that once hid beneath the surface of understanding. I sat in the shade of a willow tree, read one of my old journals, and decided to add the vows I had made to myself, and to him. I seasoned the mixture as I had been seasoned, with strength and faith and love and a ceaseless longing for his touch.

I would let fate stir the potion, let it bring me what it would—joy or sorrow, his eyes or the dream of them. And while it brewed, I decided I would learn to dance and to cook, to grow flowers and sew a summer dress that swayed when I walked. I would study Italian.

As the summer came to an end, I had wanted time away from the city, to be alone in a strange town, with people I didn't know, faces I wouldn't recognize. Perhaps in a sea of strangers, I would see his. I rented a cottage by the ocean for a few weeks. It was small and yellow with pink petunias and white impatiens planted in the blue window boxes. The bed sagged and the bathroom was too small, but it was clean and snug and filled with sunny air that blew through the windows all day long.

I planted purple morning glory to grow upon the fence, for it stirs the passions, and pink roses by the door to bring my love home soon, rosemary for faithfulness and lavender for luck. I swam in the cold salt water, lay reading on the white beach, and every day I swept the sand out of my little home. I rode an old red bicycle with a wicker basket that I filled at the farm stands, and at night I drove a little too fast in my old car with its top down and the wind whipping my hair into a tangle of rapture. I dreamt, I watched and I waited. And I was happy.

The town was crowded with other summer folks who ate at the expensive restaurants and browsed through the little shops. Three months to pump the blood that would sustain the locals once the season turned lonely. Families and couples surrounded me, but I was content. *The peaches are sweet, the sky is blue, I am in love and my love is true.* Childish poems and gentle thoughts, water poured for my flowers, floating in the ocean, walking between rows of corn in bare feet with the dust between my toes, dancing when the music played, flashes of beauty and rushes of gratitude, and every night wishing on the first star were my spells and prayers. I lifted my life to the love that flowed through me, to the love I waited to feel, and I was filled with joy and patience.

And I was never alone, not anymore. He knew I was waiting; he was on his way; he was with me; I could feel him. I lit a candle in the window every night and kept a light in my eyes so he could find me. I looked for him wherever I went, wondering when he'd arrive, certain that he would. There were times when I turned a corner, pulled away in the car, when I looked over my shoulder feeling as if he had just crossed my path. And

The Love Spell

when the moonlight spilled in through open windows I could feel him

close enough to make me shiver as if his hands were on my skin, his mouth
on mine, his breath, his body entering my body.

I was no longer drawn by a wound, but neither was I afraid, for there were times when I sensed the sharp whisper of pain, the sorrow of being one without the other, a lifetime of waiting and wondering if we would ever find each other. And if that was the wound that I sensed, that drew me to itself, it was a wound that would heal. Love was the power that healed all wounds, the power that lifted us from darkness when we were finally able to give it, and truly ready to receive it. I was able; I was ready.

The town had stretched a banner across Main Street announcing the county fair and the red-and-yellow posters tacked to all the lampposts promised rides and end-of-summer fireworks. Boys rode their bikes and girls clustered at the edge of the long green field, watching as the lights were stretched and the booths set up. The painted rides and games of chance were trucked in by the carnies, the last of the gypsies, the wanderers and road warriors with eyes that seemed too sad for all the noise and color and commotion, or maybe because of it.

"Ten tickets, please." I handed over my money and took the ream of red paper. I turned toward the revolving Ferris wheel of fortune and was knocked backward with a slamming shock.

"I'm so sorry," he said immediately. "Are you okay?" It was a momentary tangle, as if we couldn't untwine ourselves although we were standing apart, staring at each other. His dark eyes were bright and calm as he reached out to steady me. I nodded, stunned. "Well then, there now, I guess you can tell folks we ran into each other at the county fair." He gave me a wide and easy grin.

My heart began to sprint and I couldn't catch my breath. *He looks like a dark-haired Gary Cooper.* He was handsome in an old-world sort of way. His hair was dark and wavy, ruffled by the wind; his hand reached up and dragged quickly through it. It was a large hand. His face was weathered, with an aquiline nose and a square jaw marked by a cleft; he needed a shave. Deep lines ran from the corners of his eyes, but it was the steadiness of their gaze, the way they held me fast, that made my heart stumble.

I smiled. "Funny, I thought we'd met somewhere else."

His grin went lopsided with a short snort of a laugh. "In my dreams maybe." His eyes stayed locked on mine, but I could feel them sliding over me. My pulse responded.

"So they do come true."

"I sure hope so," he said, his grin widening.

I blushed. I was light-headed and it wasn't the heat. I blinked a few times and shook my head. "Sorry, I guess the wind got knocked out of me."

"Why don't we find you a place to sit down." He reached out for my elbow. His fingertips were callused and his touch on my bare skin was like a strike of lighting.

"Hey, Uncle Roark, wait'll you see the cool skateboard court they've got." A sweet-faced boy in baggy jeans and a backward baseball cap came racing up. He grabbed his arm and started tugging.

"Hey, Sport, don't be rude. This is my nephew, Caleb."

"Hi," Caleb said, quickly turning to his uncle. "You gotta come see it. Come on, please, before it gets too crowded."

"Duty calls. You sure you're okay?" His voice was warm, his eyes a little sad as they squinted at me.

"I'll be fine. Go ahead." I smiled and felt the world slide away as he was pulled into the crowd. I got on the Ferris wheel, looked down into the carnival below and tried to find him from somewhere just a mile over heaven. He was gone.

I looked in the foggy, paint-splattered mirror screwed into the back of the bedroom door, turned and examined myself from one angle, then another. I smiled, spun and felt the pale blue silk dress billow away from my body. It was like wearing nothing but a whisper. I touched a single drop of Nonna's potion between my breasts, brushed my hair back into a long ponytail and decided not to wear any jewelry.

This is ridiculous. He's not going to be there. And if he is he'll be with his family. What if he's married? But there was no wedding ring. I'm going; it'll be fun whether he's there or not. I took a last look in the mirror, flipped off the light and stepped into the night. A cool breeze raced over from the ocean and sent a chill skittering over my skin. I tossed the sweater over my shoulders. I could hear the surf pounding a few blocks to my right, the pipe organ to my left. I turned toward the music.

The fairgrounds had captured the daylight with floodlights and ropes of Crayola-colored spots, but capped by a distant black sky it was surreal. It was also smaller, louder and more crowded, with extras filling every inch as if it were a movie set. Waiting for the screen-burning love scene between a good girl and a dangerous roustabout, I jostled and wove my way to the ticket booth. I bought an evening spinning high above the crowd, beneath the rising red moon and the scattering of stars. Clutching the tickets, I turned slowly, wondering if lightning would strike twice, knowing it wouldn't, disappointed when it didn't.

I threaded my way through teenagers in pairs bound by magnetic fields of hormones and lust; older couples holding hands. Kids darted and disappeared, and parents yelled, wild with worry. A stream of people caught me in their swell. We moved toward the north end of the field, where a local band was playing. People danced on the grass in front of the small plywood stage. I watched a father with his little daughter standing on his shoes, a couple in their sixties putting everyone to shame. When the band started playing Roy Orbison, I sighed and turned to leave.

"It's more fun if you dance to it." My stomach clutched as I looked into his smiling eyes, that easy grin. He still needed a shave. He reached out his hand. "Whatdayasay? Wanna make my dream come true?"

I nodded, smiling, unable to speak, my mouth suddenly dry. His hand on my bare skin shocked me. *Let it happen. Trust.* He drew me toward him, and the little clutch in my stomach seized again, stronger and deeper as it plunged. He pulled both hands, tugging my left hand up and behind his neck as his arm came down around me. He took my right hand firmly in his left and drew me in close.

"Quite a move!" I laughed.

"I've been waitin' to use it." His voice, the warmth where my body pressed against his—chest, stomach, legs, palms—made my breath quicken, my hands shake. He pulled back and stared at me and I blushed. He smiled and he pulled me a little closer, his cheek against my hair, my chin on his shoulder. His grip was sure and strong, his steps steady and smooth. He knew how to dance; he knew how to lead. I felt myself yield to the spell of the night, and his arms.

The Ferris wheel lurched to a stop and the metal seat pitched back and forth wildly. My stomach jolted and I clutched the handrail and the small, stuffed dog he'd won throwing baseballs at milk bottles. The rocking eased to a gentle back and forth; we sat poised at the very top, the moon close enough to grab, the breeze flirting with the hem of my dress. I shivered and he stretched his arm around my shoulders.

Suspended between heaven and earth, we talked quietly. He was a carpenter and had all the deeply masculine mannerisms of a working life. But he was also a writer, brilliant and self-educated, who had challenged himself, refusing the siren's call of comfort and conformity, instead discovering his true nature, integrity and worth. I knew it was him. *Did he know?*

There was a thunderous explosion and a flare of light. We turned to see fireworks, flaring carnival colors thrown up against the black sky. I could smell the sulfur mixed with the ocean, feel the chill sliding over my bare legs, the warmth of his body pressed against me, and the constant tug of pleasure that held me to his side. It was perfect.

"I don't believe in fairy tales. But I may have to change my mind," he said with a short, quiet laugh.

"Magic." I smiled.

"Destiny." He studied me thoughtfully. "Well, you may think it's just the magic talking, or the fireworks, but I'm going to tell you straight-out. The minute you slammed into me—"

"I slammed into you?" I stared at him and we laughed. "Oh!" The wheel jerked forward and the seat swung erratically. His arm tightened around my shoulders and he pulled me closer.

"Yeah, when you almost knocked me down today, it was like . . . ," he paused, studying me, "like I was hit by a bolt of lightning. It's been a long time since I've felt anything like that." He paused again. "Maybe never."

I stopped breathing. "Yes."

"I'm being straight with you." His face grew serious and somehow his dark eyes darkened. "I'm not trying to put the moves on you."

"I know."

"Good, 'cause now I'm gonna make my move." I laughed as he leaned into me, his lips pausing a breath away from mine. We remained like that, time stretching, breathing the same air, the charge gathering. And then he pulled me to him, his mouth against mine, warm and sure.

Light exploded inside me, bright and clear. My hand rested over his heart and I could feel it beating against my palm. His kiss was slow and easy, like his smile, gradually pressing deeper inward. The wheel turned and my heart went flying. He took his time and the spark of response caught fire; I exhaled a small sigh of dizzy pleasure as he pulled slowly back and stared at me.

The wheel stopped, the bar lifted and a voice thanked us for riding. He took my hand and we stepped back into the world.

"Will you have dinner with me tomorrow?"

I nodded. He lifted my hand, turned it over and kissed my palm. An arrow of heat flew from his lips into my heart.

"I'll meet you here, at the wheel, tomorrow at seven."

"Yes, wonderful." My breath was a little jagged as I replied. Reluctantly, I tugged my hand from his and suddenly felt like Cinderella. "I . . . Good night." I rushed through the crowd, afraid to look back, afraid that perhaps it was all just a dream. I pushed open the door of my little yellow cottage, closed it quickly and leaned against it in the cool darkness. I could still feel his eyes, his lips. And I could feel the spinning of the wheel, the joy and the fire spreading inside.

The air was just the right amount of cold as we drove the back roads with the windows down, the bright moon above and the music on. He pulled into a dark field, taking the bumpy farm road between rows of high corn. At the field's far edge, he stopped the car and turned off the engine. Darkness and the night's own music—cicadas, crickets, an owl—surrounded us.

"Oh, look," I murmured. "It's so beautiful!" The field was filled with thousands of flashing fireflies, pulsing with incandescent hope as each searched for its perfect other. He got out and opened my door. I took his hand and he eased me around so that my back was pressed against the warm hood of the car.

"Beautiful," he said softly.

The night was soft and close, moist with the smell of earth and wild-flowers. "Yes, it's a gorgeous night." I leaned back, looking from the shimmering fires floating in the field to the star-sprinkled sky.

"That too," he said with a soft half laugh.

I blushed in the dark. He moved closer, laying his palms on either side of me on the car's hood. A flare surged through me and I could feel every nerve sizzling to life. I inhaled his scent of soap and maleness, incense summoning the God, felt the blaze of heat rising as he edged closer— explicit, unadulterated, animal attraction. It was more.

He pressed against me, his lips brushing the side of my neck, whispering softly in my ear. "I want to do things . . ."

The shell that had held me together in his absence shattered. His arms wrapped around me and his eyes held mine, stripping me bare. His mouth met mine, urging and devouring; it was the first time he'd kissed me like that, with fire and greed, as if he couldn't get enough. Touching me until it wasn't enough.

More. I wanted more of his recklessness, his fever; I wanted the way he made me respond. I softened and let go, falling backward into feeling, wanting. I wrapped my arms around his neck, kissing him back with moans of pleasure as I drew him into me. Hopes and hungers, synapses and senses dormant for so long, stirred and then awakened. Dizzy, overwhelmed and overloaded with sensation, I drew back. But as I tried to pull away, he followed, pressing forward, pursuing and holding me close.

"Oh!" I gasped in surprise as he suddenly gripped my waist, lifting me off my feet and sitting me on the car's hood. He leaned into me, spreading my legs as he stood between them. Heat radiated from his body; I rested my hands on his chest, feeling its hardness, his strength. His hands cradled my face and this time the kiss was soft and slow, but just as ruthless and persuasive.

Rough fingertips ran up and down my bare arms, sending shivers along my flesh. His hands slid beneath my blouse, spread wide over my back, and he pulled me tight to him. He bit my neck softly, kissed, lingering, nuzzling, his breath hot; I trembled and felt it all. He pulled back, kissing me again as he cupped my breasts and I moaned. He groaned when I tugged his shirt from his jeans and my hands skimmed over his bared skin.

We kissed and clutched wildly, stoking the fires that rushed through us and bound us together. He pulled my blouse and tugged the bra from my breasts. Need plunged through me as he rubbed and stroked and squeezed. My hands fisted in his hair, my head fell back and I shivered as his tongue and teeth and lips grazed down my neck and found my nipples. He drew on one then the other, soft then suddenly hard, releasing a dart of pain that was wantonly pleasurable. He slid his hand along the edge of my hoisted skirt, dipping down to the inside of my thigh.

"Let me . . ."

I gasped, shuddered. I leaned my head against his chest, breathless, pushing against him. "Wait, please, it's so much, too much." My heart, my body felt as if they would explode into a million burning stars. "I've never felt . . ." I pushed a little harder.

He lifted my chin. "Look at me." His eyes were dark and clouded with need. "Can't you feel how much I want you?" He guided my hand to the proof between his legs and mine.

"And I want you." Desperately. I couldn't think clearly. I could only feel. "But I need to go slower," I said, my breathing quick and shallow. His hands were burning my cool skin. I could feel him struggling with himself, and I relented when he kissed me again. My womb tightened with heat and anticipation as he reached for me.

"I don't think I can go any slower," he rasped, his lips pressed against my temple, his fingers finding the moist evidence of my need. With one hand he summoned ecstasy and peril, but with the other he made me feel safe. "I've wanted you from the first minute I saw you."

My heart wouldn't slow and his words kept it racing. "Please," I whispered. "Wait."

"I'm not going to hurt you. I would never . . ." His breathing was ragged; he didn't move, just wrapped an arm around me and drew me closer. I leaned back, trembling, gently pushing against his chest, and he stepped back.

"When you're ready." He tugged a strand of my hair and stared at me. "I swear I didn't intend to tear your clothes off in the middle of this field. Although it's certainly a good idea." He laughed and I smiled. I slid off the car, down the length of his body, wondering if I was mad to stop him.

He pulled me tight and we stood together quietly, holding each other, breathing heavily, letting the hunger ease. I nestled against him, held fast and secure, while some locked and secret door began to open within me. He pulled back so he could look at me. His eyes were somber.

"My life's good. But there's a part of me's been . . . missing. For a long time." His voice was low, reaching from behind a wall that had kept him safe. And I could feel the hidden, accepted suffering. I recognized it; I felt it. "And now . . . this." He hung his head, staring at the ground, then resting his forehead against mine.

"Yes." I ran my fingers through his hair as I heard the words that reassured my abducted heart. "We're not kids anymore."

He lifted his head and chuckled. "Sure make me feel like one."

"It's just been such a short time."

"It's been a lifetime." He took my hand and, as he had before, kissed my palm. "An odyssey."

I nodded, letting the pleasure flow through me. "I've known you all my life."

"That's how long I've imagined getting my hands on you. And now you make me wait." We laughed. His voice grew quiet and low again. "I knew you were out there. There were nights when I'd swear I could hear you calling me, I could almost feel you." His fingers traced the edge of my cheek, my chin, and I kissed their rough tips. He smiled, ran his thumb over my lips. "I even dreamt about you. I kept looking. I told myself I wasn't suited to a regular relationship. Finally, I gave up. I lived, I was happy enough." He stared at me, touching my face as if convincing himself I was really there. "But it wasn't enough. You were missing."

I nodded. "I hung onto knowing you were out there, somewhere. That you were happy. But there were times it hurt so . . ." I could feel the tears rise. I touched his cheek. "But it taught me faith. I never stopped believing. And now . . ."

"I thought happily ever after had come and gone, but I guess I was wrong."

I leaned into him. "Kiss me."

He did, very slowly.

I stirred, shifted against his shoulder, blinking and yawning. We were in the car; he was staring at the sun rising from the scarlet streak at the ocean's edge.

"Hey, Sleeping Beauty."

"What time is it?" I yawned again.

"Dawn." He smiled, and kissed the top of my nose. I snuggled against him, burrowing into his warmth, his smell, into all that I wanted, until I woke again to find him carrying me into my bedroom.

"Is this a fairy tale?" I asked sleepily as he deposited me on my bed. "Or a dream?"

"Both. Neither. Real life." He pulled off my shoes and covered me with the cotton blanket, staring down at me. "Sleep."

My heart tilted when he turned to leave. "Wait . . . Don't go." I reached out and caught his hand, pulling him back. "Please."

He leaned down and I wrapped my arms around his neck, sighing a soft kiss as he lifted me, rescuing me from my deserted island. A circle of stars spun overhead, flying toward heaven as he sank into the kiss, into my arms, like a dream. "Make love with me."

His eyes darkened, then narrowed intensely. "Everything will change."

"It's supposed to."

He dropped onto the bed beside me, buried his head against my neck, wrapped his arms around me strong and tight as if he'd never let go. I clung to him, my heart opening, my body following. In the early morning silence, I could hear every jagged breath, every unspoken fear and longing. And then he held my gaze with his, with the same certain recognition of our first glance.

"Kiss me," I murmured softly.

His mouth came to mine, gentle but firm, giving and taking with devastating, irresistible patience. A small licking flame of urgency began to spread from the center of my belly. My defenses melted as my body melded to his. He stared down at me, smiling, his eyes full of light and certainty.

"You taste so good." He dipped his tongue into the small hollow of my throat. "And you smell good." I was drunk on his kisses, intoxicated by his touch. He was holy wine, dark and wild, flowing through me.

"I want to see you." His voice was quiet, matter-of-fact, arousing. "Lift your arms."

Gazing at him, my pulse racing, I knew I was strong enough to let go and let him. And to give him everything he wanted. It was what I wanted, and I wanted him. He pulled the dress over my head, slipping the straps of my bra down around my arms. I shivered and reached for him as he ran his fingers along the top of my breasts. He reached behind me and unhooked the bra, looking into my eyes as he pulled it away.

My breath came quick and shallow as his eyes dropped, as he stared, running rough fingers over the soft skin of my breasts. He lowered his mouth to a nipple and drew on it, pulling a moan from my lips and desire from between my legs. He sucked harder and bit gently. Eagerness flared and plummeted downward, the fire spreading in a sinuous, pulling tug of irresistible need, his mouth making my nerves ignite and my body blaze to life.

My fingers curled in his hair, the rough stubble of his chin raked across my breasts, leaving a trail of chafed, awakened skin. I kissed his brow, his cheeks, his neck. My hands shook as I fumbled with the buttons of his old work shirt. I pulled it from him, running my hands over his chest, hardened from work, his arms tightly corded with muscle; he made me feel soft.

A momentary breeze lifted the curtains and I could hear the morning birdsongs. His eyes wandered over me as his hands roamed my body, doing as they pleased, pleasing me, stroking softly, slow and tender. I vibrated beneath his touch, dug my fingers into his shoulders, trailed them down his sides, grasping him as he kept the fire stoked.

The sound of his belt being pulled from his jeans made me shiver, the sound of the zipper made me tremble. He returned to me as the morning sun cast long, golden shadows across the bed, across our bodies, the length of him pressed against me. His kisses were unhurried, possessive and penetrating. I arched beneath him, my body rising to his, taking his mouth, taking his heart within mine, offering everything.

"Yes," I whispered again and again.

Inhaling, he drew me back into himself, seizing my heart and carrying it back into his own. He intertwined his fingers with mine, pulling my hands above my head, deepening his kiss and sending flashes of urgency coursing through me, making me ache to be filled. I stretched beneath him, felt his desire erect and insistent, felt his leg, heavy and sure, wedge between mine, spreading me for him. I curled my leg around his, wrapping us closer, tighter.

He released my hands; my arms were limp and weak with wanting. I curled into him, and his hands dove behind me, along my back and down to squeeze, again, and again, pulling me against him.

"Does that feel good? It feels good to me." He grinned as he watched me buck and squirm, his mouth claiming my nipple again.

My mind blurred, my senses sharpened. I gasped, moaning, and slipped my hand down, curling my fingers around the heavy weight of him. He groaned as I stroked the velvet skin, the swollen hardness. I rose against him as his mouth took mine, his tongue filling, plundering, forewarning me. I hungered and ached and his hands slid between my legs to find the slick softening he had caused.

I shuddered at the scrape of his fingertips against my hidden, biddable flesh. Need swelled, racing through me as he touched me, rubbing me in tender, certain circles. Again and again he brought me to the sharp edge of ecstasy, fondling me, murmuring, "Is that good baby? Do you like that?"

And I moaned, gasped, begged in reply. I shuddered helplessly as the blood raged and my soul blazed. Thickening sensation cocooned around me, around us, and the world began to spin, but his weight pressing against me and his hand gripping mine held me to the earth. He smiled, he kissed, he stroked, questioned and commanded until he had summoned my full abandonment. The earth slipped away and I clung to him, cresting on a long wave of sobbing, shattering pleasure.

"I want you so." Still spinning, I gasped for breath, for him. "Please."

"Open your eyes. Look at me." My eyes fluttered open. His gaze held mine. "Open yourself to me."

His words were like magic unlocking my heart, unlocking the tower where my body's deepest desires had been hidden away. Already softened, I softened further, reaching for him to enter me. His eyes holding mine, he raised himself over me. His hands gripped my hips, lifted them. Carefully, slowly he slid into the pulsing wetness meant for him. He groaned and slid deeper.

I cried out as he plunged further, burying himself within me, filling me. Love coursed through me and tightened around him, drawing him in as deeply as it could. Our kisses were ravenous, his soul entering mine with each breath, each thrust. His fingers twined in my hair and tugged my head back so that my neck arched to his insatiable mouth, his kisses and bites. I could feel him, his power, his consciousness moving through me. His love followed, finding me, ravishing, and penetrating me completely with unrelenting presence. I yielded all, surrendering utterly to love, to him.

"Yes," I whispered.

"Yes, what?" he asked.

"Yes, I love you," I gasped, almost shouted it. Tears shimmered and my heart filled with feelings I couldn't control, words I had longed to say. "I love you," I said quietly, curling my fingers into his.

"Say it again."

"I love you." And all I could do was love.

"I love you." His eyes, dark with ardor, watched me. The need was raw and visible in him. He took my hands again, sliding his fingers between mine, gripping tightly. "Come with me."

I wrapped myself around him, moved with him, my body rocking with his, feeling my need pound wildly through me, feeling his as he took me with long, deep thrusts. I arched to him, giving all that was now his, receiving what had always been mine. Our eyes held as we entwined and merged, ecstasy streaming between us. I pulled him into me as he drove deeper, pushed me higher, moaning as I felt myself rising again, the light growing blindingly brighter as we ascended together.

He clasped me tightly, and we rolled until I sat astride him riding our desire, finding the rhythm of fulfillment, his hands gripping my hips, his eyes held by mine. The air shimmered, filled with radiance, the light flashing like lightning. He cried out, and my heart opened fully in reply. I let go, he took hold and together we found what we'd always longed for, what we were meant to be.

I drifted with him in the morning light that had turned to molten gold, my head resting over his heart, his arms holding me close. It was so natural, so strong and true, as if it were the first time. It *was* the first time. My heart overflowed with gratitude. It was a miracle; it was magic. It was love.

Our love spell had begun.

I wrote the final words of my love spell and smiled. Looking down at the page, I felt wave upon wave of certainty and joy rippling through me. And then my heart opened. He *had* been with me from the beginning, from the very first spell cast by wishing upon that star so long ago. Tonight I did consciously what I had once done unconsciously, and that was all the difference in the world. Now I cast from the fullness of who I had become and all that I could give and all that I was prepared to receive. I cast from the fullness of my heart and my soul.

I closed my journal and put the cap on my pen. I stood in front of the mirror, looking at the light in my eyes. I pushed the screen door open and stepped out onto the porch. The night was gentle and the moon was full. I spread my arms and spun.

You must envision it to experience it. Summon it with every dancing molecule of your body, with every vesper, every wish and prayer, every uttered breath. Feel it! Do not believe—know! Open your heart and love!

The details of how, when, or where we would meet, what he looked like, or how we would make love, might be very different, but I knew someday we would find each other. Already, I could feel him drawing closer. I walked down into the wet grass and to the water in front of Nonna's cottage and I sat, watching the silver moon above float in the black mirror below. And in that mirror I saw what I needed to know. *We are each a love spell cast by the Universe.*

"*Phyllis.*"

Mesmerized by the golden perfection of magic hour, it took a moment to realize that Nonna was calling me. She waved to me from the porch as I turned back to the house. One lunar cycle had passed since the completion of the love spell. The summer was ending.

"It's Gillian. She has an invitation for us." Nonna nodded toward the phone. "And where are your shoes?"

I gave her a quick peck on the cheek and took the phone from her. "Hi!"

"Well, there you are. How was the conference?" Gillian asked.

"Great, inspiring, productive. But I'm going to suggest that the next time we have an international interfaith peace conference we hold it in Jerusalem. *That* would be inspiring."

"And dangerous."

"Nothing's more powerful than love," I replied. "But I am tired."

"Are you getting a rest?" I could hear Gillian's concern.

"Yup, Nonna's going to have to charge me rent if I keep this up."

"Well, it's good you have each other. But I've been worried about you. What did the doctor say?"

I sighed and sat down at the kitchen table. "Good news: She said it wasn't cancer. It's adenomyosis; it's a kind of endometriosis. I can live with it." I paused, exhaling slowly. "Bad news: She said that I probably wouldn't be able to carry to term if I got pregnant." Saying it aloud was part of the process of accepting, but it was hard to say it, and harder to accept.

"Oh jeez, I'm so sorry. You must be heartbroken. I wish I could give you a hug."

"Thanks, Gillybean. Yeah, well, I cried, a lot. But you don't get everything in life, and I've been blessed with so much, I'm truly grateful for that." I sighed, meaning it but still feeling the sadness; I took a deep breath. "I have an amazing life. And there are wonderful things other than babies that I can create."

"Listen, why don't you two come down here to the South Fork this weekend? We've got the house to ourselves and Chris promises to grill that sea bass you love." I could hear how much Gillian wanted to cheer me up. "Nonna said she thought it was a great idea. And there's a big old county fair this weekend—rides, fireworks, the whole deal. It'll be good for you to have a little fun. And you can have the guest cottage. We just painted it this wonderful yellow."

I began to smile and a soft glow began to diffuse from my heart through my body. Gillian didn't know about the love spell. I could feel my heart flutter and quicken—it had grown larger around its holes, and suddenly I knew it was large enough for the love that I had always longed to give and receive.

"Thanks, Gillian. It sounds perfect!"

I went to stand with Nonna on the front porch, watching the first star appear.

"So what did you decide?" Nonna asked, pointing toward the heavens.

I slipped my arm through hers. "That magic is very real." I stared up at the vesper and made my wish. "And love is the greatest magic there is."

Appendix

A Brief Collection of Love Spells, As Well As Elements and Ingredients to Create Your Own

Caveat: A love spell is *never* cast to make a specific person fall in love with you! A love spell is cast to draw the person who is right for you, who is your true love, your soul mate, to you.

A Spell to Remove All Obstacles to Love

First things first! Begin with a spell asking to remove all obstacles that stand between you and true love. Open your heart to the Universe, and on a piece of white paper simply write: *I wish all obstacles that stand between me and true love to be removed, with harm to none.* Then burn it, knowing that the obstacles will disappear as the paper turns to smoke.

The Love Letter Love Spell

To cast a love spell that will work, you have to know what—or whom—you're casting the spell for! Use the element of air—the element of the mind, imagination, and communication—to craft this spell to visualize and conjure your love. Begin by creating one of these powerful incenses:

ATTRACTING LOVE INCENSES

All-Purpose
2 tbs. each of sandalwood, red rose petals, ground orris root
2 drops each of musk and rose oils

Incense to Attract a Man
2 tbs. each of sandalwood powder, ground orris root, High John the Conqueror
1 tbs. pine, valerian
1 pinch each of cinnamon, red pepper
2 drops each of ambergris, musk and civit oils

Incense to Attract a Woman's Love
One tsp. each of cinnamon, anise, ground orris root, clove, and sassafras. Burn the incense on an incense charcoal (Be careful; the charcoal gets very hot!), and as it burns, write a love letter to your soul mate. Open your heart and tell him or her everything that's there, everything you feel, what it is about him/her that you love, *and* what he/she will love about you. Write about the life you will lead together. Since music is magic, you can also play your favorite romantic piece while you're writing. When you have finished your letter, read it aloud. You may also wish to raise energy by dancing your spell of love to the music. Put the letter someplace safe—someday you may wish to share it with your lover.

Ring of Fire Spell

Fire is the element of passion and desire. But fire can be dangerous, just like passion, so you must always be careful when working with it. Put your candles someplace safe when they are burning, far away from anything that might catch fire, and never wear long clothes or long sleeves when working with fire.

Carve thirteen red candles with your name and *True Love* or *Passion*, meditating on the qualities you want in your true love, or your night of passion, as you carve.

Create a circle with the candles and, standing in the center, beginning in the south, light the candles. Sit in the center of the circle and chant the charm for true love's desire, repeating the charm and visualizing, feeling yourself loved and giving love:

In my heart I feel the fire
That will light true love's desire
As I shine you'll come to me
And as I will, so mote it be.

When you feel that you have manifested your intent—when your heart is open and full—ask the Universe to bless your love, ask for permission, and then send your love like an arrow to the heart of your beloved. Release the spell with the words: *As I do will, so mote it be!*

Then blow out all but one of the candles, making your wish as you blow. Put the one burning candle someplace safe, and let it burn until it is gone. You can keep and reuse the remaining candles for an evening of romantic passion, once you have met your love.

Bath of Aphrodite Erotic Love Potion

Water is the element of the emotions, of love and dreams. It is also the element associated with many Goddesses of Love, such as Aphrodite, Venus,

Yemaya, Ezulie, and Lakshmi. Bathing in a love potion is one of my favorite ways of making magic. And what a wonderful place to make love, with the water connecting not only your bodies, but your souls.

Boil, for 20 minutes, in 2 cups of water:

2 tbs. red rose petals
2 tbs. patchouli
3 tbs. damiana
A cinnamon stick or a pinch of ground cinnamon

While the potion boils you should stir it, clockwise, visualizing your true love coming to you, or making love with you.

Strain the herbs from the water, and pour the potion into a tub of warm water.

Add 3 drops each of musk and almond oils to the bathwater. You may also light a single red candle carved with your name and TRUE LOVE. Get in the tub, and as you do, recite the spell, invoking Aphrodite, the Goddess of Love:

Aphrodite from the sea,
Hear my call and come to me!
Bless me with your radiant power
And open me as passion's flower!

Remain in the bath, dreaming of your lover's touch, until you feel his/her presence approaching.

Then rise from the bath and feel the Goddess of Love rising with you. See her in your eyes and feel her in your body.

Dry yourself off and dab your pulse points with Venus oil.

You can also invite your lover to join you in the bath.

Venus Attraction Oil

Women have known for years how enticing perfumes can be. This potion is made from essential oils, so you will only need a small amount to catch a lover's attention.

Mix equal parts of almond, musk, and patchouli oils and add several drops of vanilla extract.

Shake gently, then apply to your pulse points. Inhale deeply and smile.

A Charm for Love

Earth is the element of the body, and so it is the element that helps us to manifest and experience our love and desires in the world. Working with plants, gems, minerals, and stones can all enhance your love spells. Earth is associated with many Goddesses, but especially with Gods of Love and Fertility, like Dionysus, Herne, Cernunnos, Osiris, and Pan.

On the night of the new moon, drink a small glass of red wine or grape juice and ask the God Dionysus to bless you with love.

Then gather together the following items in a pink or red pouch:

One pair of Adam-and-Eve roots
A magnet
Red rose petals
A rose quartz
A pinch of red pepper

From the new moon until the full moon, carry this charm with you, as close to your body as possible.

In the morning after the full moon, release the contents of the bag into flowing water or bury it, giving thanks for the earth's energies and blessings.

Spells for Purification and Banishing Broken Hearts

It happens to all of us, so when it does, a little magic can help you heal.

TO BANISH BAD MEMORIES OR LINGERING
NEGATIVE ENERGIES:
Pack up his/her stuff and get rid of it!

Take a photo of the two of you and cut him/her out of the picture.

Using a white or blue candle, burn his/her half of the photo, or something else that belonged to him/her and as it burns, say the following, or use your own words:

"With no ill will toward (name), with nothing but good intentions for us both, let us release each other in peace and without animosity, let us part honoring the love that we once shared. And let us heal and be able to trust and love again. I accept the loss of love between us. I embrace the lessons I must learn. I release the ties that bind us to each other. I release the ties that bind us. I embrace my freedom. I honor his/hers."

Next, make this wonderful banishing and cleansing incense.

Banishing and Cleansing Incense
1 tbs. each of bay leaves, cinnamon, white rose petals, myrrh, and sage
A pinch of sea salt
You can also just use a bundle of sage and salt water

Open all the windows and doors and, moving counterclockwise, carry the incense or burning sage bundle all around the inside perimeter of your home. Next sprinkle the salt water, counterclockwise, all around the edges of your home. Then take a broom and, sweeping the floors and ceilings, sweep out any and all lingering negative energies. Close the door and the windows.

Now, make this delicious blessing incense.

Blessing Incense
1 tbs. each of lavender, basil, chamomile, and hyssop
3 drops of bergamot oil

As it burns, carry it clockwise around your home. And buy yourself some flowers.

PURIFICATION AND HEALING BATH POTION TO HEAL A BROKEN HEART:
Boil in 3 cups of water, for 10 minutes:

2 tbs. each of lavender, sage, peppermint, chamomile
1 tbs. each of bay leaves, ground myrrh

Strain the herbs and pour the water in a tub of warm water.

Light a white or blue candle on which you've carved your name and HEALTHY, HAPPY, AND WISER.

Get in the tub and feel yourself releasing the toxins of sorrow and disappointment.

Reflect on what you've learned about yourself and who and what will make you happy in love.

As the water drains from the tub, feel the last of your sadness flowing away from you.

Repeat as needed.

And remember: every ending is followed by a beginning!

Timing

Spells to manifest love are best performed during the waxing moon or full moon.

Spells to banish a broken heart or the lingering influences of a bad relationship are best performed during the waning or dark moon.

Spring and summer are wonderful seasons for spells to manifest love.

Fall and winter are good times for spells to banish heartache.

Cast spells on Monday for romance, love, fulfillment.

Tuesday for sex, passion, eroticism.

Friday for love, relationships, fertility.

Perform spells when the moon is in Virgo for marriage, Taurus for earthy and sensual love, Cancer for home and family, Scorpio for hot and passionate love.

Venus is the planet of love.

Goddesses and Gods of Love

GODDESSES
Aphrodite—Greek (passion, love, joy, beauty)
Ariadne—Greek (marriage, devotion, searching for love)
Branwen—Irish (fertility)
Ezulie (love, passion)

Freya—Germanic (love and beauty)

Hathor—Egyptian (fertility)

Ishtar—Babylonian (love, sex) and—Egyptian (love and beauty)

Isis—Egyptian (eternal love)

Melusine—pre–Celtic Europe (love, promises kept between lovers)

Oshun—Yoruban (love, passion, sensuality)

Psyche—Greek (searching for love, fidelity, courage)

Venus—Roman (passion, love, joy, beauty)

Yemaya—Yoruban (fertility, sensuality, love)

GODS:

Angus Og—Irish

Baal—Syrian/Canaanite (lust, fertility)

Cernunnos—Celtic (fertility)

Cupid—Roman (initiating romance)

Dionysus—Greek (marriage, ecstasy)

Eros—Greek (passion, sex)

Hymen—Greek (marriage, first love)

Osiris—Egyptian (eternal love)

Pan—Greek (sex, lust)

Colors

Red—passion, erotic love

Pink—self-love, feminine attraction, Goddess energy

Green—fertility, male attraction, God energy

Purple—agape or spiritual love

Yellow—friendship

Blue—peace, healing

White—purity

Brown—banishing, justice

Black—banishing

Herbs and Oils

Ambergris—to awaken love and emotion
Basil—harmony in love
Rosemary—for remembrance
Cinnamon—to speed up results
Clove
Damiana—aphrodisiacal
Sandalwood
Hibiscus
Patchouli
Orris root
Mistletoe
Vanilla
Ylang-Ylang
Almond—Venus
John the Conqueror—fertility and potency
Musk—sex, desire

Aphrodisiacal Foods

Almonds, hazelnuts, and other nuts
Figs
Dates
Peaches
Pomegranates
Grapes
Apples
Strawberries
Mango
Avocado
Carrots
Asparagus
Oysters

Mussels and other shellfish
Truffles
Chocolates
Wine

Flowers

Roses
    Red—desire, love
    Pink—romance, self-love
    Yellow—friendship
    White—purity
Carnations
    Red—desire, love
    Pink—boldness in love
Tulips—passion
Daisies—innocent love, joy
Lilies—truth and honor
Ivy—loyalty
Lily of the Valley—happiness
Jasmine—sex and the exotic
Stephanotis—marital happiness
Yarrow—marital fidelity
Peony—bashfulness
Lilac—intoxication of first love
White mums—7 of them for the Goddess Yemaya

Stones

Rose quartz—romance, self-love, and self-esteem
Ruby—confidence
Rhodochrosite
Lapis lazuli—fidelity

Pink tourmaline—increases the will to fall in love and to sacrifice
Diamond—lasting love
Garnet—loyalty, attracts profound love
Magnets or lodestones—to bring a lover to you
Carnelian—lust

Books of Interest

Due to space constraints it is impossible to list all the marvelous material available. So this is a very personal selection of diverse and excellent books that I hope you will find both useful and engaging.

Allardice, Pamela. *Aphrodisiacs and Love Magic*, Prism Press, 1989.

Anand, Margo. *The Art of Sexual Magic*, Jeremy P. Tarcher/Putnam, 1995.

Barbach, Lonnie, Ph.D. *For Each Other: Sharing Sexual Intimacy*, Signet/New American Library, 1982, 1984.

Bonheim, Jalaja. *Aphrodite's Daughters: Women's Sexual Stories and the Journey to the Soul*, Fireside/Simon & Schuster, 1997.

Breathnach, Sarah Ban. *Romancing the Ordinary*, The Simple Abundance Press/Scribner, 2002.

Bright, Susie, Ed. *The Best American Erotica 2003*, Touchstone/Simon & Schuster, 2003.

Brockway, Rev. Laurie Sue. *A Goddess Is a Girl's Best Friend: A Divine Guide to Finding Love, Success, and Happiness*, Perigee Books, 2002.

Buckland, Raymond. *Buckland's Complete Book of Witchcraft*, Llewellyn, 1986.

Burkert, Walter. *Ancient Mystery Cults*, Harvard University Press, 1987.

Curry, Helen. *The Way of the Labyrinth: A Powerful Meditation for Everyday Life*, Penguin Compass, 2000.

Curott, Phyllis. *Book of Shadows: A Modern Woman's Journey into the Wisdom of Witchcraft and the Magic of the Goddess*, Broadway Books, 1998.

———. *Witch Crafting: A Spiritual Guide to Making Magic*, Broadway Books, 2001.

Dalton, David. *James Dean, the Mutant King*, Straight Arrow Books, 1974.

Deida, David. *Finding God Through Sex: A Spiritual Guide to Ecstatic Loving and Deep Passion for Men and Women*, Plexus, 2002.

Eason, Cassandra. *A Magical Guide to Love and Sex*, The Crossing Press, 2000.

Ellis, Normandi. *Awakening Osiris: The Egyptian Book of the Dead*, Phanes Press, 1988.

Evans, Arthur. *The God of Ecstasy: Sex Roles and the Madness of Dionysus*, St. Martin's Press, 1988.

Fierz-David, Linda. *Women's Dionysian Initiation: The Villa of Mysteries in Pompeii.*

Frater U. D. *Secrets of Western Sex Magic*, Llewellyn, 2001.

Goddard, Jamie and Kurt Brungardt. *Lesbian Sex Secrets for Men*, Plume/Penguin, 2000.

Henderson, Julie. *The Lover Within: Opening to Energy in Sexual Practice*, Station Hill Openings/Barrytown, Ltd. 1999.

Hendrix, Harville, Ph.D. *Getting the Love You Want: A Guide for Couples*, Harper Perennial, 1988.

Horne, Fiona. *Magickal Sex: A Witches Guide to Beds, Knobs, and Broomsticks*, Thorsons, 2002.

Hunter, Jennifer. *Rites of Pleasure: Sexuality in Wicca and Neo-Paganism*, Citadel Press, 2004.

Johnson, Robert A. *Ecstasy: Understanding the Psychology of Joy*, Harper & Row 1987.

Knight, Sirona. *Love, Sex, and Magick*, Citadel Press, 1999.

Kraig, Donald Michael. *Modern Sex Magick: Secrets of Erotic Spirituality*, Llewellyn, 1999.

Love, Pat, Ed. D. *The Truth About Love*, Fireside, 2001.

Marcuse, Herbert. *Eros and Civilization: A Philosophical Inquiry into Freud*, Vintage/Beacon Press, 1955.

Matthews, Caitlin. *In Search of Women's Passionate Soul: Revealing the Daimon Lover Within*, Element Books, 1997.

May, Rollo, Ph.D. *Love and Will*, Delta/Dell, 1969.

Moore, Thomas. *The Soul of Sex*, HarperCollins, 1998.

Murnighan, Jack, ed. *The Naughty Bits*, Three Rivers Press, 2001.

Nin, Anaïs. *Delta of Venus*, Harvest Books, 2004.

Odier, Daniel. *Desire: The Tantric Path to Awakening*, Inner Traditions, 2001.

Ramsdale, David Alan and Ellen Jo Dorfman. *Sexual Energy Ecstasy*, Peak Skill Publishing, 1985.

Slater, Herman, ed. *The Magical Formulary*, Magickal Childe, 1981.

Swami Muktananda, *Kundalini: The Secret of Life*, SYDA Foundation, 1994.

Watts, Alan. *Nature, Man and Woman*, Vintage/Pantheon Books, 1970.

Woodman, Marion. *The Ravaged Bridegroom: Masculinity in Women*, Inner City Books, 1990.

For information on seminars, lectures, and other programs by H.Ps.
Phyllis Curott, please contact her at:

P.O. Box 311
Prince Street Station
New York, NY 10012
or
www.phylliscurott.com